BLACK CROWN

PAUL CLAMMER

Black Crown

*Henry Christophe, the Haitian Revolution
and the Caribbean's Forgotten Kingdom*

HURST & COMPANY, LONDON

First published in the United Kingdom in 2023 by
C. Hurst & Co. (Publishers) Ltd.,
New Wing, Somerset House, Strand, London, WC2R 1LA
© Paul Clammer, 2023
All rights reserved.

Distributed in the United States, Canada and Latin America by
Oxford University Press, 198 Madison Avenue, New York, NY 10016,
United States of America.

The right of Paul Clammer to be identified as the author of
this publication is asserted by him in accordance with the
Copyright, Designs and Patents Act, 1988.

A Cataloguing-in-Publication data record for this book
is available from the British Library.

ISBN: 9781787387799

This book is printed using paper from registered sustainable
and managed sources.

www.hurstpublishers.com

Printed in Great Britain by Bell and Bain Ltd, Glasgow

CONTENTS

Acknowledgements   vii
List of Illustrations   xi

Introduction   1

  1. Beginnings   11
  2. From Savannah to Saint-Domingue   23
  3. The Colony Ablaze   39
  4. Defending the Revolution   57
  5. Toussaint Louverture Supreme   73
  6. Invasion   91
  7. War of Independence   109
  8. Citadel of Freedom   125
  9. The Empire of Haiti   143
10. Civil War   159
11. Birth of a Kingdom   177
12. Sans Souci   191
13. French Plots   209
14. The Price of Sugar   227
15. Your Majesty's Friends   243
16. The Kingdom Reformed?   261
17. The Fatal Stroke   277
18. Aftermath and Exile   295

Notes   311
Bibliography   349
Index   363

ACKNOWLEDGEMENTS

Writing is a solitary pursuit, but one that is impossible without a larger support network. This book would never have been anything more than an idle daydream if it hadn't been for the many people who helped me will it into being, and it is a pleasure to give my thanks to them here.

My biggest thanks go to guide extraordinaire Maurice Etienne, who first introduced me to Henry Christophe when he took me to Sans Souci and the Citadelle in 2007. Maurice has regularly welcomed me into his home in Milot ever since, and it's no exaggeration to say that *Black Crown* would not exist without him.

I first made the trip to Haiti while working for Lonely Planet, which ultimately led to a year living in Port-au-Prince researching and writing for Bradt Travel Guides. Being able to travel to every corner of this extraordinary country shaped my understanding of the Haitian Revolution and its aftermath in ways that a hundred books couldn't convey. When I started researching Christophe's life in earnest, repeated guidebook commissions for the region allowed me to route flights through the USA to go to archives that would otherwise have been too expensive to visit. Thanks to my editors at both companies for unwittingly enabling me.

In 2015 Raphael Hoermann invited me to present a paper about historic travel guides to Haiti at the Institute for Black Atlantic Research's conference After Revolution: Versions and Re-visions of Haiti. I could not have found a better or more collegiate group of people than those working in Haitian Studies, who have happily welcomed this non-academic into their ranks and encouraged my work. I want to thank Alyssa Sepinwall in particular for her early friendship and support. For reaching behind the academic paywall for me, for sharing unpublished papers or for answering my questions, thank you to Tabitha McIntosh, Grégory Pierrot, Chelsea

ACKNOWLEDGEMENTS

Stieber, Jeremy D. Popkin, Hank Gonzalez, Julia Gaffield, Ada Ferrer, Doris L. Garraway, Matthew J. Smith, Stewart R. King, John D. Garrigus, David Geggus, Sudhir Hazareesingh, LeGrace Benson, Laurent Dubois, Crystal Eddins, Karen Racine, M. Stephanie Chancy, Stephanie Curcy, Roxane Ledan, Rachel Douglas, Jacqueline Reiter and Carrie Gibson. Marlene L. Daut has been a constant inspiration thanks to her work on early Haitian print culture, not least the works of the great Baron de Vastey. J. Cameron Monroe and Gauvin Alexander Bailey were both very generous with their insights on Sans Souci. Nathan H. Dize was always ready with an encouraging word and an answer to a knotty translation problem. My Lonely Planet colleague Tom Masters tracked down an obscure reference for me in Berlin regarding the German vet Otto Braun, and Barnaby Wauters sent me material relating to his late father's ownership of one of the Numa Desroches paintings of Sans Souci. Michael Becker alerted me to the NYC auction of the painting of Prince Victor-Henry and the Princesses Améthyste and Athénaïre, which set in motion a series of events that led to the painting finally being returned to Haiti (Monique Rocourt, former Haitian minister of culture, was a key interlocutor).

My particular thanks to Nicole Willson, who has been a great friend, sounding board and collaborator. It is because of Nicole's passion that Marie-Louise Christophe and her daughters are now remembered through a blue plaque on their London house.

In Haiti, thank you to Patrick Delatour, former minister of tourism and surveyor of Sans Souci, for sharing his knowledge and his library with me. Camille Louis, Valèry Smith and Marie Thérèse Chenet welcomed me behind the scenes at the Musée du Panthéon National Haïtien (MUPANAH). Jean-Patrick Durandis kindly opened the archives at the Institut de Sauvegarde du Patrimoine National (ISPAN) in Port-au-Prince for me, and Daniel Elie of Moun Studio shared his experiences restoring the Palais de la Belle-Rivière. Frantz Duval showed me Bois-Caïman and a variety of other revolutionary sites across the north. Gaetan Mentor generously shared Marie-Louise Christophe's 1821 testament with me. Claire Payton kindly took me to the Archives Nationales d'Haïti for the first time and shared a great day on the road at the Palais de la Belle-Rivière and Crête-à-Pierrot along with Anne Eller. Rodrigo

ACKNOWLEDGEMENTS

Bulamah was likewise an excellent companion exploring the Citadelle and Ramiers. The late Franck Louissaint allowed me to visit his atelier at Université Quisqueya to see his newly finished restoration of Numa Desroches' painting of Sans Souci. Brian Oakes was great company and always ready with a GPS coordinate and a cold Prestige. Finally, thanks always to Jacqui Labrom in Port-au-Prince, who invited me to dinner on my first night in Haiti and has been a valued friend ever since.

I am indebted to the archivists and librarians who made my research a pleasure. Thanks to the staff at the British Library, UK National Archives, Schomburg Center for Research in Black Culture, Boston Public Library, Cambridge University Library, King's College London, the Bodleian Library, Houghton Library at Harvard and the National Library of Jamaica. My particular gratitude goes to the staff of the Archives Nationales d'Haïti, Bibliothèque de Saint-Louis de Gonzague and Bibliothèque Nationale d'Haïti who do such tremendous work on such tiny budgets. I also thank the Digital Library of the Caribbean, and those researchers who kindly shared their own material with me, not least when Covid-19 meant it was impossible to do archive work in France.

In the UK, thanks to Alex von Tunzelmann who suggested over coffee at the British Library that there might be a book to be written. Philip Hatfield (then Caribbean curator at the British Library) provided the clinching argument, while a commission to write about Henry Christophe from *History Today* was an important first proof of principle. Alan Booth gave crucial early encouragement, and Jenny Savill offered valuable feedback when my first chapters weren't really ready for a book proposal. Miranda Kaufmann introduced me to my wonderful agent Charlie Viney. Enormous thanks to Charlie and to Michael Dwyer at Hurst Publishers for seeing the potential in bringing Henry Christophe's story back into the light.

Finally, I can't properly express my love and gratitude to Robyn, who has been my constant companion throughout this project as she is in everything in my life. Thank you for not falling off the roof of the Citadelle that time.

Paul Clammer
May 2022

LIST OF ILLUSTRATIONS

1. King Henry I of Haiti, painted in 1816 by Richard Evans. GRANGER—Historical Picture Archive / Alamy Stock Photo.
2. Memorial to the Chasseurs Volontaires who fought in the siege of Savannah in 1779, showing Henry Christophe as a drummer boy. Rosemarie Mosteller / Alamy Stock Photo.
3. The slave ship *Marie-Séraphique* at anchor in the bay of Cap Français. Pictures Now / Alamy Stock Photo.
4. ean-Baptiste Belley. Niday Picture Library / Alamy Stock Photo.
5. The burning of Cap Français in June 1793, when Christophe fought in defence of the city. Archives Charmet / Bridgeman Images.
6. Léger-Félicité Sonthonax holding the 1793 emancipation proclamation while pointing to a torn-up copy of the Code Noir. Danvis Collection / Alamy Stock Photo.
7. Engraving of Toussaint Louverture, thought to be taken from a portrait he gave to the French agent Roume. *Prints, Drawings and Watercolors from the Anne S.K. Brown Military Collection*. Brown Digital Repository. Brown University Library. https://repository.library.brown.edu/studio/item/bdr:231347/
8. Haitian revolutionary battle. © Aunaies / Bridgeman Images.
9. The trial of Captain Marcus Rainsford in 1798. Christophe presides at the centre, with Moyse at his left. Courtesy of the John Carter Brown Library (Box 1894, Brown University, Providence, R.I. 02912).
10. A French general and officer, painted in Cap Français in April 1802 by Jan Anthonie Langendyk, shortly after Christophe's return to the French side. Royal Collection Trust / © His Majesty Charles III 2022. RCIN 915306.
11. Imagined engraving of Jean-Jacques Dessalines from 1805, shortly after he was crowned Emperor of Haiti. Courtesy of the

John Carter Brown Library (Box 1894, Brown University, Providence, R.I. 02912).

12. Christophe overseeing the construction of the Citadelle in the first years of Haitian independence. Author's own photo.

13. A French propagandist image from 1806 of Christophe burning Spanish towns during the Santo Domingo campaign. Courtesy of John Carter Brown Library (Box 1894, Brown University, Providence, R.I. 02912).

14. Alexandre Pétion, first President of the Republic of Haiti. *Prints, Drawings and Watercolors from the Anne S.K. Brown Military Collection.* Brown Digital Repository. Brown University Library. https://repository.library.brown.edu/studio/item/bdr:231273/

15. Coats of arms of the Kingdom of Haiti: King Henry I, Baron de Vastey, Baron de Béliard, Duc de Marmelade. College of Arms MS J.P. 177, fol. 1r (arms of le Roi), fol. 18r (arms of le Duc de Marmelade), fol. 67r (arms of le Baron de Béliard), fol. 76r (arms of le Baron de Vastey). Reproduced by permission of the Kings, Heralds and Pursuivants of Arms.

16. The Prince Royal Victor-Henry aged 12 painted in 1816 by Richard Evans. Zuri Swimmer / Alamy Stock Photo.

17. William Wilberforce, one of Christophe's most eager correspondents. Bridgeman Images.

18. Prince Saunders, who introduced smallpox vaccination to the Kingdom of Haiti. Courtesy of the John Carter Brown Library (Box 1894, Brown University, Providence, R.I. 02912).

19. Jean-Pierre Boyer, Pétion's successor as Haitian president. *Prints, Drawings and Watercolors from the Anne S.K. Brown Military Collection.* Brown Digital Repository. Brown University Library. https://repository.library.brown.edu/studio/item/bdr:231277/

20. Thomas Clarkson, whose advice and support was actively courted by Christophe. © Wilberforce House Museum / Bridgeman Images.

21. Ira Aldridge, painted a year after he portrayed Christophe on the London stage in 1825. Art Collection 2 / Alamy Stock Photo.

22. 49 Weymouth Street, Marie-Louise Christophe's final residence in London. Author's own photo.
23. The Citadelle Henry today. Author's own photo.
24. The ruins of Sans Souci Palace today. Photo by Cameron
Monroe.

INTRODUCTION

On a Monday evening in mid-November 1825, Londoners were dressing to go to the theatre. It was a sharp night in what would be a cold winter, and the weather no doubt influenced how far theatre-goers were willing to go for their entertainment. Those close to the West End could choose the Theatre Royal on Drury Lane, where a performance of *Romeo and Juliet* was followed by *De La Perouse*, a dramatisation of the mysterious disappearance of the French explorer in the South Pacific in 1788. The nautical theme continued a short walk away on the Strand, where the Adelphi Theatre was presenting an adaptation of *The Pilot*, James Fenimore Cooper's tale of a sailor in the American Revolution. However, on this chilly autumn night those prepared to brave the winds across Waterloo Bridge could head south to Lambeth, where the Royal Coburg Theatre was featuring a playbill that was revolutionary in both subject matter and presentation. The play was called *The Death of Christophe—King of Hayti*, and the lead role was played by an African American actor called Ira Aldridge, starring in his first season on the London stage.[1]

When the Royal Coburg had first opened its doors seven years earlier, such was the splendour of its decoration that *The Times* called it the handsomest theatre of its size in London.[i] It had an extravagant and much admired mirrored curtain that reflected the audience back on itself, and despite the complaints of the essayist William Hazlitt that the audience put him more in the company of 'pickpockets, prostitutes, and mountebanks' than the theatrical muses, the Royal Coburg was generally regarded as a place where respectable gentlemen could take their wives and daughters. The theatre lacked the licence that would have allowed it to put on Shakespeare or other

---

[i] The Royal Coburg Theatre still operates today as the Old Vic.

1

dramatists, so its programme relied instead on farces, melodramas and comic operas. It was also known for the speed at which it could put on productions dealing with topical affairs, getting around its licensing restrictions by interlacing straight dramatic scenes in its plays with musical interludes.[2]

The Death of Christophe was the last in a series of four plays at the Coburg featuring Aldridge in the lead. He had made his debut in early October in Aphra Behn's *Oroonoko*, the story of an African prince who leads a failed slave revolt in Surinam. The play leant heavily on a theatrical trope of the period in its depiction of the enslaved lead as a noble but tragic figure whose story must end in heroic sacrifice. What made this particular production so radical was that for the first time the title role was played by an actor of African descent.

Prior to Aldridge's appearance at the Royal Coburg, African stage roles were played by white actors in blackface. That a black actor could even play such a role was considered ludicrous by many, and on the day of Aldridge's London debut one newspaper cruelly compared him to a novelty animal act.[3] Aldridge had already experienced such prejudice in his native New York, where he had performed for the short-lived African Theatre at a time when slavery was still legal in the city. When the theatre put on a production about a slave uprising in the Caribbean, a mob burned the venue to the ground. It was this incident that prompted Aldridge to leave America for good to try his luck on the British stage.[4]

In an attempt to counter low public expectations for his performances, the Royal Coburg grandly billed Aldridge as a 'Tragedian of Colour, fresh from New York', but his imposing presence and natural stagecraft quickly won over the sceptics. Critics who had sharpened their quills in anticipation of deriding the apparent burlesque of a black actor on the stage were quickly forced to revise their opinions. One reviewer openly admitted his advance distaste, noting that he had anticipated a 'sooty child of ignorance', but ended up praising Aldridge's graceful step and dignified attitude, noting that 'his acting will gratify many and astonish all'. Newspapers instantly dubbed him a valuable addition to the theatre, with one even noting that his colour was rather less problematic than his American accent. Even when one racist review was widely reprinted in the London newspapers, Aldridge was able to turn it to his advantage. Its writer had mockingly described him as the 'African Roscius', in reference to the Roman actor who had instructed Cicero, but Aldridge reclaimed the title as his own, and would proudly reproduce it on playbills throughout his long and celebrated career.[5]

Aldridge's *Oroonoko* proved such a success that its producers immediately followed it up with three more plays featuring him in the lead, each running for a week. The first two, *The Libertine* and *The Negro's Curse*, were also slavery related. The third required Aldridge to play a different sort of character altogether. For his final role, the Royal Coburg revived a tragedy called *The Death of Christophe—King of Hayti* that it had previously put on five years earlier, proclaiming it on their playbills as a commentary on 'those terrible commotions which attended [Haiti's] first organization as an Independent Nation', and the 'struggle made by a negro Population for a municipal Freedom'.[6]

The background to the play would have been very familiar to a London audience. Before 1804 Haiti had been known as the colony of Saint-Domingue, the Caribbean pearl of the French empire. It was a fabulously wealthy colony that fully produced half of the world's sugar and coffee and was responsible for a third of all France's maritime trade. Saint-Domingue was also a place of irredeemable brutality, as its riches were the product of the violence used to enforce the labour of some half a million enslaved Africans. Yet over the course of a bloody revolution that had lasted more than a dozen years, the slaves of Saint-Domingue had not only emancipated themselves by force of arms, but had also defeated a massive army sent by Napoleon Bonaparte to subdue them. In 1804 the sovereign nation of Haiti was declared, which became, after the USA, only the second nation in the Americas to free itself from colonial rule. Much to its new rulers' chagrin, Haiti's success on the battlefield had brought with it diplomatic isolation. Nations whose wealth depended on colonial slavery were reluctant to have official relations with a people who had so violently freed themselves from bondage and expelled their colonial masters. Indeed, when Aldridge took to the stage in November 1825, Haitian independence had only finally been recognised by France just a few months earlier—and even then only after Haiti's president Jean-Pierre Boyer agreed to pay an indemnity of 150 million francs to its old colonial master for the diplomatic privilege,[ii] a sum demanded to compensate the French planters of Saint-Domingue for the loss of their human 'property'.[7]

The Haitian Revolution had been led by the mercurial figure of Toussaint Louverture. He had led his people to the brink of independence only to be captured by his enemies and shipped to France to die in an icy mountain dungeon—a shameful act commemorated shortly afterwards in a sonnet by William Wordsworth. Henry Christophe, the hero of the Royal Coburg play, was in some regards a much more familiar figure to the theatregoers. Though far less known today, Christophe had been one of Louverture's most trusted lieutenants. The audience would have quickly recalled the broad outlines of his story—how Haiti had been split by civil war soon after independence and how Christophe had created a kingdom for himself in the north of the country. For a decade, he had been a staple of the English newspapers. His agents spent freely across London, commissioning extravagant pieces of jewellery, fine courtly dresses for the royal family and fleets of state coaches that were put on display to an approving public. Stories of his wealth were legion, and readers in coffee houses and across the breakfast table were regularly enlivened by newspaper accounts of the court cases involving the scandal-ridden British admiral of his navy and Christophe's other representatives in London.

Christophe was even a well enough recognised figure to appear in a London waxwork show. He was displayed next to a Jacobite rebel and the traitorous Captain Blood, who had attempted to steal the crown jewels during the reign of Charles II. This placing suggests a certain ambivalence towards the Haitian king. While the audience at the Royal Coburg may have remembered amazing stories of Christophe's grandiosity, they would have also recalled the reports that his rule had been a harsh one, and that he had died by his own hand after a popular uprising against him, surrounded by the great wealth he had extracted from his country. This was the story that *The Death of Christophe* would recount, with Aldridge playing the part of the doomed monarch.

[ii] The sum was later reduced to 60 million francs, but when fully repaid it represented around $21 billion paid by Haiti to France at modern exchange rates.

INTRODUCTION

The fall of the Kingdom of Haiti was an ideal dramatic subject for a theatre like the Royal Coburg that prided itself at putting on topical material. The play was first performed there in early 1821, just seven weeks after the news of Christophe's death had arrived in London. Because of the rush to get it into production, the script remained necessarily sketchy about the details of the king's downfall. The cast of characters was largely invented. Christophe took centre stage alongside his patient queen, who was christened Alraida for want of knowledge of her real name, Marie-Louise. Opposing the king was his rival General Boyer, president of the Republic of Haiti, leading an army against him. The dynamic of the play was fleshed out by stock characters from the company's repertoire, whose familiarity to the audience would have helped fill in the blanks in the story. Fan Fireproof, a semi-comic widow with a trail of twenty-seven dead husbands behind her, took centre stage in her role as a brave heroine of liberty. Alongside her were her two grandsons, Jem and Jerry Heartmouse, written as weak-kneed conscripts in Boyer's regiments, forever dreaming of the quiet life until the abuses of Christophe's soldiers rouse them into taking a stand against the tyrant's rule.

A single copy of *The Death of Christophe* has survived in manuscript form, now held at the Harvard Theatre Collection. Almost certainly the Royal Coburg's own prompt copy, it contains detailed stage directions and musical cues as well as notes on the costumes and sets. Christophe's royal palace is imagined as a magnificent lakeside oriental pavilion, its tropical setting further highlighted by richly plumaged birds flying overhead. Slaves fan the air with large leaves to underscore the stifling decadence of the court. Drums and trumpets announce the arrival of the king, which are quickly silenced by a pistol shot offstage as a petitioner is executed by the hand of the king himself. The audience is thus introduced to a paranoid and suspicious ruler who is quick to do violence to anyone he does not trust. 'It is my last and full reply to those rebellious subjects who would abuse their monarch with perpetual petitioning', Christophe proclaims. The audience is left in no doubt as to why his subjects have risen up against his rule.[8]

Aldridge's king is a hard and capricious man, but also one cruelly used by courtiers like the villainous Duke of Marmelade, who encourages the regal excesses in the hopes of overthrowing Christophe to claim the crown for himself. The patient and saintly queen pleads to her husband's conscience, asking him to rule lightly to win the love of his subjects rather than cowing them with an iron fist. But Christophe is deaf to her entreaties, and in rejecting her, sets himself on the path to self-destruction. The plotting at court is set against a series of pantomime set pieces, as the Royal Coburg regulars infiltrate the kingdom and rescue the condemned from the royal dungeons. As Boyer's troops mobilise, Christophe tries to rally his own army while dealing with the plot against him at court.

The play's last act opens on the eve of the final battle for the kingdom. Christophe paces inside a tent with a growing awareness that power is slipping through his fingers. 'Save me, save me, mighty powers of justice!' he mourns, filled for the first time with doubts: 'What is this I see? What spectres rise before my shocked and aching sight? Horror? They still are there! Accursed be the hour, the madness of ambition, seized upon my heart!' But this brief flicker of doubt is quickly snuffed out by the self-confidence that first brought him to the throne. Aldridge summoned all the fury he could muster to carry Christophe towards his fate: 'Angels and demons all array themselves against me. Be it so, my strength may fail me, but my unawed [sic] spirit to the last share dares defiance in all shapes, whether of earthly or unearthly potency!'[9]

The audience may have recalled the newspaper reports stating that when Christophe was faced with a real mutiny of his own, he chose to commit suicide rather than submit to the indignity of defeat. Legend recounts that he loaded the pistol himself with a silver bullet. In this early staging, however, Aldridge (who would build his career playing the great Shakespearian tragedies) was denied a famous death scene. The Royal Coburg's producers chose a more dynamic ending instead, with General Boyer's troops storming the Citadelle Henry, the mountaintop fortress at the heart of the kingdom. In a heavily choreographed musical scene, its walls are breached amid heavy fighting, before a simple black banner is raised above the walls announcing that 'the King has destroyed himself'. As a flag of truce proclaims that peace is restored to Haiti, the players staged a last musical tableau before their final curtain call.

The revival of *The Death of Christophe* was a great success, and its run was extended by an extra week. The positive reviews helped set Ira Aldridge up for a career on the British stage that would last for forty years. The Haitian government was so pleased with the production and the heroic role it gave to President Boyer, that its consul in London made Aldridge an honorary captain in the Haitian army.[10] The story the play presented of Christophe's downfall was true only in the broadest of brush strokes, but it seemed agreed upon by all that justice had been served to a man who had been little more than a tyrant. The Haitian republic was finally starting to be recognised on the world stage, and the story of the short-lived black kingdom began to be reduced to a footnote, a failed experiment on the road to nationhood.

Yet there was another side to Henry Christophe that was missing from the brutality portrayed on the London stage. Until his death he had also been a talisman to Britain's abolitionist movement. Its members regularly lauded his kingdom as an example of what could be imagined in the colonies if slavery was ended. Sir Joseph Banks, the ageing president of the Royal Society, corresponded directly with Christophe and lamented that were it not for his advanced years he would not lose a day in setting out for the kingdom.[11] William Wilberforce and Thomas Clarkson, the great architects of Britain's abolition of the slave trade, regularly advised the Haitian king. Clarkson was even given diplomatic credentials to treat with the French government on Haiti's behalf. For them, Christophe was the model of an Enlightenment monarch; Wilberforce's pro-slavery detractors even claimed that he was quicker to cheer the king of Haiti at dinner than he was the king of England. The same newspapers that printed the salacious details of the bankruptcies, fistfights and divorces of Christophe's British representatives also regularly reproduced sober proclamations from the king that demonstrated the progress made under his rule. These ranged from the creation of a mass education system along British lines to the successful introduction of the smallpox vaccination to Haiti. Christophe may have been mocked at the London waxworks, but his portrait by Richard Evans was hung at the Royal Academy to favourable reviews. The artist had been a student of Sir Thomas Lawrence, the favourite portraitist of Regency England, and had travelled to Haiti at the height of Christophe's rule along with a host of teachers, farmers, doctors and missionaries, who all saw great potential in the young kingdom. Royal Navy ships were regular visitors, and admirals of the West India squadron were hosted to great cheer at the Haitian court. While Christophe's representatives in London lobbied the British government for diplomatic recognition, so too did plenty of British merchants, as well as their American counterparts in Washington, eager to take advantage of the trading opportunities the new nation offered.

Christophe's life had followed the most incredible of trajectories. He had been born into slavery during the brutal heyday of the Caribbean plantation systems. Through more than a decade of revolutionary turmoil he lifted himself from obscure beginnings to become one of the richest and most powerful military leaders in Saint-Domingue. He helped Toussaint Louverture eliminate his rivals and consolidate black rule in the colony, and when Napoleon Bonaparte sent an invasion force to wrest back French control in 1802, it was Christophe who burned his own city to the ground rather than let the fleet land unhindered, and then helped lead the guerrilla war to defend the freedom of his newly emancipated people. His ambition was boundless. He had been one of the key signatories of Haitian independence, but after a murky conspiracy resulted in the murder of the country's first leader, Christophe's personal ambition helped cleave the country in two in a bitter civil war. When Haiti's split became permanent, he sought to consolidate his rule by founding a dynasty that would help bring his people the benefits of civilisation as he saw it and cause them to be welcomed into the commonwealth of nations. As king, Christophe had chosen the phoenix as his heraldic device to symbolise his country's fiery rebirth. His new country was a beacon of what could be built from the ashes of slavery. He may once have been enslaved, but as sovereign he toasted George III as a brother and was flattered to receive approving comments from no less a figure than Czar Nicholas I of Russia.

The revolution that had been midwife to the Kingdom of Haiti had been an earthquake for the imperial powers. The creation of an independent black nation at the epicentre of New World slavery was an almost unthinkable act. Nation-building in this context was an extraordinary challenge and there was no rule book to follow. Christophe sought to defend his people's new-found freedom by constructing the strongest and proudest state he could imagine. In doing so he imposed a strict authoritarian rule on the very people who had supported the revolution and given him the opportunity to rule. To build up strong defences against the jealous eyes of the French, who plotted to retake their lost plantation wealth, Christophe used the colonial master's tools to micromanage the lives of his people, taking land from would-be farmers seeking their own independence through self-sufficiency in order to put them back to work growing the very crops they had once burned in revolutionary defiance. This tension at the heart of his rule was a familiar one faced by leaders who rose to power in periods of great turmoil that was only resolved when, laid low by illness and faced with rebellion from the ranks of his own army, Christophe turned his gun on himself. The cruel tyrant that Aldridge played on the stage of the Royal Coburg may have been a caricature, but it would not have struck home had it not borne at least a kernel of truth.

For all the Royal Coburg's invention of the details of Christophe's downfall, they at least did well in their choice of having the battle at the Citadelle Henry, the most potent symbol of Christophe's rule, as the play's climax. Christophe personally directed the construction of this fortress, which sits atop the sheer slopes of a mountain looking out to sea across the plains of northern Haiti. First built as a last line of defence against a possible French invasion, it subsequently morphed into the most visible symbol of Haitian independence. It was so imposing that even in its day it was known as the Gibraltar of the Caribbean. Today the fortress—together with the ruins of the royal palace at its base—is Haiti's only UNESCO World Heritage site and is visited by tourists who take horses to its lofty perch to marvel at what still remains of the largest fortress in the Americas. It remains a colossal achievement of vision and perseverance, though local guides are also quick to sigh that it was built by forced labour under Christophe's orders, and that its many dozens of cannons—all captured from the French, Spanish and British armies during the Haitian Revolution—had never fired a shot in the kingdom's defence. It is an equivocal place, both a symbol of national freedom and of personal ego. In this it is the perfect monument to its builder.

For a long time following its final success in 1804, the Haitian Revolution and its legacy were largely ignored by the outside world. In recent decades more scholarly and public attention has rightly been paid to it, and it is increasingly recognised as one of the three great revolutions that shook the Atlantic world at the end of the eighteenth century. Unlike those in the USA and France, the Haitian Revolution was the only one that promised full equality to all its citizens. But the story of what happened next has remained even less known outside the country. As one of the major figures who helped pull Haiti from the ashes of revolution to proud statehood, Henry Christophe was one of the most remarkable figures from the Age of Revolutions. *Black Crown* is my attempt to shed light on the path he took to build a proud and free Haiti.

1

BEGINNINGS

In the closing months of 1818, Baron de Vastey was sitting at his writing desk in Milot in northern Haiti, working hard on his new book, *An Essay on the Causes of the Revolution and Civil Wars of Hayti*. In it he would tell for the first time not just the story of the slave revolution that had expelled the French from the world's richest colony, but also the central role played by his master, Henry Christophe, who was now in the seventh year of his reign as King Henry I of Haiti. The instructions from his patron were clear. 'My desire,' advised the king, 'is, that it may, in what regards my life, be a plain and clear statement of facts, and that those who knew me in early life, when they see those facts in the book, may vouch for their truth.'[1]

Vastey (pronounced *Va-tay*) worked in the immense palace of Sans Souci, a three-storey slice of neoclassical grandeur that was the pride of the Haitian kingdom. There was no finer building in the whole of the Caribbean. From his offices, Vastey could walk through mirrored halls into grand reception rooms painted with scenes from classical mythology where the gods had been reimagined as African heroes, or salons hung with portraits of the royal family by an English painter who had been engaged to teach at the king's academy of arts by William Wilberforce. The palace was kept fresh in the tropical climate by means of an elaborate system of pipes laid under the mahogany floors that brought in cool water from the surrounding mountains before feeding it into a large fountain flanked by two bronze lions at the foot of the palace's grand staircase. Through tall French windows Vastey could look out over the neatly kept royal gardens to the spreading star apple tree under which the king received petitions from his subjects every Thursday. Past this were the separate palaces for the queen and prince, the stables and coach house for Christophe's gilded state carriages imported from London, and the barracks and stables of the household regiments, from where the royal dragoons in their sky-blue uniforms trotted out on parade. Sans Souci was commissioned by Christophe to be the symbol of a confident new political power. It was a place where British admirals could be entertained, a centre of learning to educate the sons of a new nobility, and a counting house for the coffee and sugar that provided the kingdom's wealth—all harvested by free farmers who had once toiled as slaves but were now paid fairly for their labours. A royal mint stamped coins with the king's likeness, and his arms was displayed on the masthead of the *Gazette Royale d'Hayti*, a newspaper printed at the palace's own press and distributed to the foreign merchants who traded in the kingdom's ports. Beyond all this, Vastey would be able to see the narrow road that wound up the dark green of the surrounding mountains to the great fortress of the Citadelle, hidden high in the clouds above. This masterpiece of modern military engineering was built under Christophe's direct supervision and was defended with dozens of cannons that had been captured from the French, British and Spanish armies that had fought unsuccessfully to control Haiti. Although foreigners were banned from visiting the Citadelle, it was said by observers to be able to garrison 3,000 troops.

Vastey was ideally placed to write the story of the kingdom's spectacular rise. His father, Jean, was a white colonist from Normandy who had married Elisabeth 'Mimi' Dumas, born of a wealthy mixed-race planter family from the town of Marmelade, near Milot. In keeping with the metropolitan aspirations of Saint-Domingue's free coloured population of the time, he was likely educated in France. Returning to the colony aged fifteen, he had joined Toussaint Louverture's army to become a participant in the Haitian Revolution.[2]

Ennobled as a baron by Henry Christophe, Vastey had been given a crossed quill and sword as his coat of arms. The heraldic choice was a good one—he had helped draft the kingdom's book of laws known as the Code Henry, served as secretary to the king and tutor to the Prince Royal, and was soon to become keeper of the royal family's archives. As a writer, Vastey was vociferous in his defence of Christophe's reign. He had published a series of fierce broadsides aimed at the French government and its supporters who had had once owned plantations in the country and still hoped to return Haiti to bondage. In 1814 he published *The Colonial System Unveiled*, a book that catalogued in raw detail the sadistic violence that had been the motor of Saint-Domingue's slave economy, and in doing so he produced one of the earliest systematic attacks on western colonialism by a writer of African descent.

In his new work he was turning his attention to the revolution that had given birth to Haiti, and that culminated—in his eyes— with the crowning of Henry I. A proper accounting of the king's judicious rule and civilising influence would strengthen the arguments against those who saw the very fact of Haiti's existence as an existential threat to its slave-holding neighbours. 'Having established our rights by the sword,' Vastey had written in an earlier work, 'we acquire a new lustre in the eyes of the world, when we defend them by the pen. Our reputation becomes greater and more glorious, and we include ourselves, in reality, in the number of civilised states.'[3]

By the time Vastey was putting his quill to paper, Christophe had been a figure on the international stage for more than a decade, and stories of his origins and rise to power had been published in newspapers in Britain, the USA and France. In seeking to explain him, these reports had frequently taken unknown sources and added detail upon contradictory detail until any original truth was hard to discern. That Christophe had not been born in the country he ended up ruling was universally agreed, but the rest was a tangle of conjecture. The idea of him coming from St Kitts (formerly St Christopher) and thus of having adopted the name of the island of his birth held obvious appeal, and this rapidly became the dominant narrative after it first appeared in English newspapers in 1805.[4] But hard facts eluded the commentators. Some said that he was born a slave, others that he was the child of free parents. Wildly differing anecdotes suggested that he had been a cook, a tailor, or a mason. Others reported that he had fought and even been wounded while fighting in the American Revolutionary War, or that he had never been anything grander than a waiter in a colonial hotel. He had been all of these things, or perhaps none of them at all.

13

The truth, wrote Vastey, was that Christophe had been born on the tiny island of Grenada at the opposite end of the Caribbean to Haiti, a great distance in every way from the future riches of Sans Souci. The royal almanacs that the kingdom printed every year officially recorded that he was born on 6 October 1767. The fact that Grenada was a British possession was important, and was regularly brought up when Christophe was lobbying the British government for recognition of Haiti's independence. Jean-Gabriel Peltier, a journalist who had served as Christophe's political agent in London, would frequently pepper his correspondence to ministers at Whitehall with comments that Christophe was 'English by birth' and thus would make a loyal and intelligent ally to the British government against the French.[5]

For all Vastey's certainty about Christophe's place of birth, he showed frustratingly little interest in recounting the early years of his subject's life. He would like, he tells us, 'to dwell more at length upon the more remarkable traits of the heroic life of Henry', but alas he had too little space in which to tell them.[6] It was far better, perhaps, to focus on Christophe's achievements as monarch than to tarnish them by asking too many questions about his potentially humble beginnings. Christophe himself only once publicly alluded to his origins, in an account that was published long after his death. Declining the invitation from a Royal Navy captain to dine on board his frigate, he gave his reasons for never trusting to put his foot on board a ship: 'My father was brought across the sea from Africa, and never returned ... the sea is treacherous.'[7]

Fortunately, two unpublished letters by British observers help add detail to Vastey's brief account. In 1799, Hugh Cathcart, a merchant who provided occasional intelligence reports to the British authorities in Jamaica, spent time with Christophe when he was on campaign in the south of Saint-Domingue. Over the following years, Cathcart and Christophe exchanged regular letters about future business relationships and were close enough to exchange intimacies about each other's families. During this early campaign, Cathcart reported back to his superiors that Christophe was 'a native of Grenada, and has been upwards of twenty years in this country. He was formerly Maître d'Hotel, at the Courone [sic] of the Cape and a slave. He is now supposed to have amassed a fortune of two millions of livres of this colony, very near two hundred and fifty thousand dollars.'[8]

A second account comes from Edward Corbet, who was the British commercial agent in Port-au-Prince during the later years of the Haitian Revolution. In early 1803 he sent an extensive report back to his superiors on the state of the war against the French, including short biographies of some of its leading lights, writing 'The negro chief Christophe is a creole of Grenada, and of some little education.' As if in anticipation of later debates over Christophe's origins, he drily concluded that 'it is not perfectly known what led him to his present situation in St Domingo'.[9] The use of 'creole' in this context meant a person born in the Americas. But if Christophe had been in Saint-Domingue for twenty years when he met Cathcart and Corbet, he would still have been a child when he left Grenada. What circumstances could have brought a boy born into obscurity halfway across the Caribbean to his new home?

Grenada is part of the Windward Islands chain, sitting at the far southern rim of the Caribbean, just a day's sail from the Venezuelan coast. A mountainous almond-shaped island, just 34 kilometres long, for centuries it was home to the Kalinago people, whose ocean-going war canoes discouraged repeated attempts at European colonisation ever since it was visited by Columbus on his third voyage to the Americas. This changed in the 1600s, when the prosperous tobacco and sugar plantations of nearby British Barbados inspired the French to take full control of Grenada. A treaty was brokered with the Kalinago to allow limited French settlement but was quickly broken by the newcomers in a series of bloody massacres. The native population plummeted and the few remaining Kalinago fled the island or took refuge in the densely forested slopes and ravines of the interior. Grenada's low-lying areas were divided into plots for sugar and tobacco plantations and the island was turned into a farm-factory complex to make colonial goods to send to France. With no substantial native population left to press into a labour force, the colonists imported enslaved Africans to work on the plantations, profiting from the trade winds that made the transatlantic crossing from the west coast of Africa to the Windward Islands faster than to the rest of the Caribbean.[10]

Tiny Grenada produced modest profits throughout the eighteenth century, but it was overshadowed by the booming French colonies of Saint-Domingue and Martinique. Nevertheless, Grenada was subject to the same strict mercantilist trade rules laid down in Paris, which meant high import taxes and a strictly curtailed ability to trade with its British Caribbean neighbours. Grenada resented the strictures laid down by its distant metropole, and when a Royal Navy squadron appeared on the horizon during the Seven Years War the colonists saw little benefit in defending French rule and surrendered without firing a single shot. At the war's conclusion in 1763 Grenada was formally ceded to Britain.

At the time of the British takeover Grenada's population was less than 14,000. As elsewhere in the Caribbean, the enslaved massively outnumbered the free. For every Grenadian citizen, there were nine more people in bondage. The free were not entirely white European as might be supposed. Around a quarter—some 455 souls—were either African or of mixed African-European descent. This free community was concentrated mainly in the capital, St George, and other towns where they mostly worked as merchants and tradesmen, but some were prosperous enough to own plantations of their own and the slaves that came with them. When the British surveyed their new island possession, they recorded 'Jeanette, a free Negro woman' who was wealthy enough to be the owner of eighty-two slaves on the 160-acre estate at Tyrell Bay, which was one of Grenada's largest plantations. Piero, a free black woman, was noted as holding 38 acres and three slaves, while in 1808, Louis la Grenada, a free coloured man, bequeathed freedom to thirteen slaves on his death, including his 'favourite child Peggy'.[11]

'The early years of a slave are not likely to furnish many incidents for the historian or biographer; nor have any particulars been preserved of the life of Christophe, during the period of his bondage': so wrote the Methodist missionary William Harvey dismissively in *Sketches of Hayti*, his account of a visit to the Haitian kingdom in the final year of Christophe's rule.[12] But while the paper trail is scanty, it is still possible to recreate the world into which he was born, thanks to a vivid account of slavery in Grenada left by to us by Ottobah Cugoano. Born ten years before Christophe near Assinie in modern-day Ghana, Cugoano was the son of a prominent figure at the court of the local ruler, but at the age of thirteen he was kidnapped by slavers, sold to an intermediary and shipped to

Grenada. Later freed in England by his owner, Cugoano became a prominent abolitionist campaigner in London. His 1787 *Narrative of the Enslavement of Ottobah Cugoano, a Native of Africa* was one of the earliest accounts in English of the slave trade written by a formerly enslaved African.

Cugoano recounted for his readers the terrible moment of realisation when he and his fellow captives were transferred to the ship that would transport them to the Caribbean: 'There was nothing to be heard but the rattling of chains, smacking of whips, and the groans and cries of our fellow-men. Some would not stir from the ground, when they were lashed and beat in the most horrible manner.' The loading continued until the ship's hold was crammed with chained and sweating bodies. Dysentery and fever spread quickly in the squalor of the tightly packed holds; during the voyage captives were only allowed on deck briefly each day to exercise. Slave ships were slung with netting around the decks to prevent suicide by jumping overboard. The crew lived in permanent fear of their captives rising up against them, and this seems to have been the case during Cugoano's passage. With death 'more preferable than life', he wrote, 'a plan was concerted amongst us, that we might burn and blow up the ship, and to perish all together in the flames'. The plot was discovered, but although Cugoano spares his readers a description of the bloody reprisals, accounts from other ships suggest these would have ranged from torture to beheading, with the dead thrown to the sharks that always followed the slave ships on their grim voyage west.[13]

After landing, Cugoano spent nine months in Grenada labouring on a sugar plantation amid conditions of 'brutish baseness and barbarity'.[14] Meagre rations were complemented with casual violence. A common misdemeanour was to be caught chewing on a piece of sugar cane for sustenance while working, for which the guilty person would be lashed or have their teeth pulled out. From land clearing and hoeing to weeding to cutting, the work was endless. Even the tough, razor-like leaves of the sugar cane seemed to fight against the slaves. At harvest time they worked from before sunrise until after sunset, carrying the canes to mills that ran through the night to stop the precious sugar from fermenting and spoiling.

Acts of resistance were common. Grenada's mountainous interior was refuge to populations of runaways who attempted to form

17

their own free communities. They were dubbed 'maroons', derived from the Spanish word *cimarrón*, meaning wild, a term first applied to escaped livestock brought by early settlers. The maroons regularly raided plantations to steal cattle and supplies, causing alarm among the colonists and the launch of retaliatory expeditions by local militias.

The combined effects of hurricanes, unrest and deterioration under a tropical climate mean that few records from Grenada exist from before 1785, and detailed searches in the archives there have yielded no clues to Christophe's precise origins. It is possible that his parents may originally have come from the Senegambia region or Sierra Leone in West Africa. In an unpublished memoir, William Wilson, an Englishman who spent time at Christophe's court as tutor to the Prince Royal, wrote that Christophe's features 'shewed [sic] his Mandingo parentage', a generic term for the primarily Muslim Mandinka people of those regions. In keeping with the pseudoscientific racial classification common at the time, Wilson observed that they were notably tall, handsome and natural aristocrats: 'The men do not find a ready sale for the same reason perhaps that an Englishman would rank low in a market of white slaves—he would be turbulent and impatient of forced labour, and more ready to fight his owner than to serve him.'[15] This was the perfect material, Wilson seems to suggest, for a future revolutionary and monarch. While this could simply be read as confirmation of bias on Wilson's part, it is interesting to note that in *The Colonial System Unveiled*, Vastey lists the Mandinka as the first of all African races with a propensity for civilisation, possibly paying a subtle tribute to his king's ancestors by describing them as 'civil, hospitable, hardworking cultivators with a talent for the sciences'.[16]

Although precise records for the arrivals of French slave ships in Grenada no longer exist, they shipped relatively few captives from Senegambia or Sierra Leone to this part of the Caribbean during the eighteenth century. If Christophe's roots did lie there, his parents were more likely to have been brought to the island by English slave traders soon after the island changed hands in 1763. That we are reduced to such conjecture is the result of the yawning hole in the stories of those sold into slavery. 'Consumed with grief, their hearts filled with bitterness and despair, never more would they see the land that gave them birth', wrote Vastey of those carried across the water in chains, and whose ancestry remains forever lost. 'Every bond that could attach them to their former lives was broken, destroyed forever', he continued.[17] A Haitian Vodou song puts it even more simply: 'In the belly of the slave ship, we are all one.'

Born of recent arrivals rather than into the relative prosperity of Grenada's free coloured class, the child Christophe entered the world in a state of bondage. A baby born into slavery in Grenada did well even to survive its infancy. One plantation manager on the island noted that pregnant women and infants were deliberately neglected, in the hope that suckling children should die: 'for they lost a great deal of the mother's work during the infancy of the child'.[18] Planters considered it cheaper instead to keep importing fresh blood directly from Africa, rather than care for the welfare of those they had already enslaved. Slaves were at the bottom of the pile at a time when even the land itself seemed to rage against its inhabitants. Christophe was born at the peak of the Caribbean hurricane season, when the simple thatched huts that made up the majority of slave quarters would have offered meagre shelter to a nursing mother and infant. In 1770 when Christophe was three and still too young to be put to work, sugar ants ravaged agriculture across the island. 'I have seen the roads coloured by them for miles together,' wrote one witness to the plague, 'so crowded were they in many places that the print of the horse's feet would appear for a moment or two, until filled up by the surrounding multitude.'[19] The insects would return annually for almost a decade until they were finally wiped out by a hurricane that also laid waste to much of the island. In the same period the main port of St George's was twice destroyed by fire, while remote coastal communities feared the raiding parties of pirates who landed on moonlit nights to kidnap slaves to sell elsewhere.

While the Africans laboured on the plantations and in the houses and workshops of the free, the colonists themselves were split by sectarian division. Incoming Protestant settlers from England and Scotland repeatedly clashed with the French Catholics who had preceded them. The outbreak of the American Revolution in 1775 saw a brief declaration of unity when the island assembly voiced open support for the rebel North American colonists, in whom they saw

19

reflected their own familiar grievances about colonial tariffs and restrictions on free trade. But when France joined the war against the British, Grenada's governor feared that half the white population would turn against him.

Grenada was left dangerously exposed to invasion when the Royal Navy's formidable Caribbean fleet sailed from the region in mid-1779 to protect merchant ships en route to Britain. A local militia had been raised to supplement the small garrison of regular soldiers at St George, but in reality only the loyalty of the British colonists could be depended on. In the event, such small numbers proved inconsequential. When a French fleet of twenty-five ships of the line and ten frigates was sighted on the horizon on 2 July, the days of British rule in Grenada were numbered.

The commander of the French forces was Admiral Jean-Baptiste Charles Henri, the Comte d'Estaing. Now in his fiftieth year, d'Estaing was a veteran of the Seven Years War, where he was captured during the French siege of Madras, paroled and then taken prisoner again after leading a fleet against the British in Sumatra. Despite this poor luck, he still managed to rise through the ranks, and at the war's conclusion he was rewarded by being made the governor of Saint-Domingue. He served there for two years before becoming the naval inspector at Brest, the French navy's most important port, where he was working when war was declared against the British. He quickly set sail to take his battle back to the old enemy.

Despite the modest size of the British forces, the battle for Grenada was a bloody one. The British refused the French articles of surrender, so d'Estaing ordered the sacking of St George. When the Royal Navy eventually returned and attempted to retake the island, they lost two ships in a disastrous fight with the French fleet, and the British governor was sent to Paris as a prisoner of war. The governor's high status ensured him a relatively comfortable captivity, but other prisoners were less fortunate. Any free coloured members of the population found to be carrying arms were taken into slavery as possessions of the French crown. The island's enslaved population simply swapped one set of masters for another.

D'Estaing stayed less than a fortnight on the island. Returning Grenada to French rule was a prize in itself, but it was only one piece in the larger war against the British. His fleet was due to sail to North America to lend support to the rebel colonists. To do this he had to pick up fresh troops and supplies from Saint-Domingue. Flush from their victory over the British, the French prepared to leave Grenada. D'Estaing's officers counted the governor's silver plate as one of the spoils of war. Others reputedly took human prizes, leaving with members of Grenada's enslaved population to serve them in the coming campaign.

That Christophe was taken off Grenada by this method has become part of the foundational myth of his life, with the first accounts appearing in the last years of Christophe's reign as king. The Haitian historian Joseph Saint-Rémy, writing in the middle of the nineteenth century, has given us the most detailed version, albeit without citing his sources. According to Saint-Rémy, the eleven-year-old Christophe was on an errand for his master, travelling from Sauteurs in the north of Grenada to St George, when he was met by an unnamed French officer. This officer asked if Christophe would join his service. Christophe was apparently so charmed by the officer's appearance and eager to escape his current situation that he happily accepted the offer. In reality, a young enslaved boy would have been rather less likely to experience the encounter in quite the fairy-tale manner that Saint-Rémy suggests, though in later life Christophe certainly proved adept at grabbing whatever opportunities came his way.[20]

The fate of Christophe's mother and father, along with their identities, remains unknown. But as the French fleet set sail, whatever childhood he had managed to eke out in Grenada slipped over the horizon forever. Born to captives brought from Africa, he now faced his own uncertain passage by ship. Henry Christophe was heading to war.

2

FROM SAVANNAH TO SAINT-DOMINGUE

On Franklin Square in Savannah, Georgia, five uniformed figures pose in bronze atop a giant granite plinth. They are French soldiers from Saint-Domingue, raising their muskets against an unseen army of British redcoats who had captured the city during the American Revolutionary War. One of their number sits slumped and wounded, showing the price the unit had paid during the subsequent siege. To their right, a boy not yet in his teens but in the same uniform as the others looks across in alarm at his fallen comrade and attempts to beat out a report on the drum that weighs him down. But something unusual marks this monument out from all the others that commemorate the war. The soldiers are black, and the drummer boy is the young Henry Christophe.

The part played in the 1779 siege of Savannah by the Chasseurs Volontaires—the free black soldiers from Saint-Domingue depicted in the statue—is a celebrated one in Haiti. When the French threw their military weight behind the nascent American republic against the hated British, nearly 550 free black soldiers sailed from the French Caribbean colony to join in the fight. By their actions in the cause of liberty they are seen as the precursors of those who would fight in the Haitian Revolution, and the list of those who are said to have served is a who's who of that later struggle. That Henry Christophe was among their number is a key part of this piece of national mythology. In his 1819 history of the Haitian Revolution, Baron de Vastey was quite clear: 'The king served in the wars of the United States of America and was wounded at the siege of Savannah.'[1] But as with many details of Christophe's birth and early years, a child soldier who was possibly enslaved or possibly free slips easily through the gaps in the archive, and sorting fact from fiction is a slippery affair.

Christophe would have had two weeks to adapt to life on board the d'Estaing fleet as it sailed from Grenada to the port of Cap Français in Saint-Domingue to pick up more troops for the American campaign. He would not have been the only child on board. Every ship had its complement of cabin boys, known as *mousses*, and boys even younger than him were common, learning the ropes and serving officers until they were old enough to work as sailors. Free black sailors were common across the Caribbean, and slave ships working the Middle Passage were known to put African boys to work and to train them up as sailors to enhance their market value.

Cap Français was one of the most prosperous cities in the Americas, far overshadowing the colony's capital, Port-au-Prince, to the south.[i] It had been established on the island of Hispaniola in 1670 by French colonists, less than 32 kilometres from the spot where Columbus had attempted to establish the first European settlement in the Americas on Christmas Day 1492. The land was home to the Taíno people, and under their chief Guacanacaric they had initially aided Columbus. But as more ships arrived from the east, each driven by Spain's insatiable appetite for the riches of what they had thought was the gateway to China, the Taíno were ravaged by European arms and imported diseases. Those who survived were forced to labour in the Spanish hunt for gold. By the middle of the sixteenth century, the genocide was almost complete—just as Spain started to lose interest in Hispaniola altogether, in favour of the far greater wealth flowing from its new conquests over the Aztec and Inca empires. The promise of Spain's first American colony was reduced to it becoming a transit point for the bullion-rich convoys of galleons returning to the mother country, and much of the island was abandoned to the ghosts of its original inhabitants. Freebooters filled the vacuum, and Hispaniola soon became a haven for buccaneers during the golden age of Caribbean piracy, with its most notorious port on the island of Tortuga off the northwest coast.[ii] As

---

[i] Cap Français was first known as Cap François. Today Cap-Haïtien is Haiti's second largest city.

[ii] The term buccaneer is derived from *boucan*, the Taíno word for smoked meat. Before turning

France expanded its imperial ambitions in the region, it slowly took control of the western portion of Hispaniola and suppressed the wilder excesses of the pirates, gradually turning them into tobacco cultivators. When Cap Français was established, it quickly became the most important port in their new colony of Saint-Domingue, created when Spain formally ceded ownership of the western third of the island in 1697.

It was the introduction of sugar to Saint-Domingue that allowed France to do what Spain never managed, and turn the colony into a going concern. When the Comte d'Estaing's fleet arrived in Cap Français, the port was undergoing its boom years and was the heart of France's Caribbean empire, with its dockside warehouses piled high with hogsheads of sugar to feed the metropole's sweet tooth along with coffee, cotton, indigo and other agricultural produce. Of this, Christophe would initially have seen little. Having joined the fleet as the spoils of war it is unlikely that he would have been allowed on shore during the two weeks that d'Estaing would spend in port, for fear that he would abscond. For him Cap Français remained on the horizon, a line of gleaming stone buildings in the bright Caribbean light with their neatly tiled roofs and church tow-ers pushed up against the green peak of the Morne du Cap. But even seen from the deck, the buildings clearly demonstrated the colony's importance, as did the guns of the heavily fortified batteries that the fleet had to pass under as it steered through the narrow passage in the reefs that guarded the harbour entrance. And while his ship was moored among a forest of masts, and small boats flitted back and forth from the wharves, Christophe would also have understood the ultimate source of the city's wealth. Amid the frigates and ships of the line, and the merchant sloops being loaded with barrels of sugar and bales of cotton, the slave ships carried a far grimmer cargo. Saint-Domingue was the largest slave society in the Caribbean.

Cap Français had no formal slave market, and when a new slave ship arrived from Africa buyers would be rowed into the bay to view those to be sold on board. A detailed painting of the slave ship

---

to piracy, European settlers on the island hunted the wild cattle and pigs left by the Spanish and sold the meat to passing ships.

Marie-Séraphique of Nantes shows the vessel in the harbour in 1773 following its third transatlantic slaving voyage. Dozens of naked Africans from Angola are brought up from the hold by the crew to be paraded before prospective customers. A rich feast has been laid for the wealthy citizens of Cap Français, with the artist mockingly including several African children clustered around the coat tails and raised glasses of the diners. The gentility of the meal takes place on the half-deck firmly behind the safety of the *barricado*, the tall wooden wall erected on all slave ships to protect the crew quarters and to provide a firing position from which to quell potential on-board rebellions. A landing boat brings new buyers alongside the ship, while another rows back to shore carrying the enslaved to their fate. Two of the buyers are women and are attended by black maids. One is white, the other mixed race. Like Grenada, Saint-Domingue had a free coloured population, many of whom owned slaves them-selves. The painting records that the *Marie-Séraphique* spent a month at Cap Français following its voyage from Angola, and that in that time Captain Gauguy sold 333 Africans into slavery: 187 men, 73 women and 73 children.[2] The *Marie-Séraphique* was far from unusual. Cap Français was the destination for one third of all French transat-lantic slaving voyages, and at the colony's height it was consuming nearly 20,000 slaves a year.

Christophe may well have witnessed such a scene from the deck of his ship while the fleet was taking on the colonial soldiers that Saint-Domingue was providing for the war effort against the British. The sale of slaves would have been no shock to someone born into bondage, but even if he had not previously seen the haggling for flesh over brandy and bone china, the new troops who came on board would have been a shock to him. In their dark blue coats with green cuffs, white breeches and yellow-plumed hats, they were every bit as impressive as any of the finely dressed colonists. But crucially, they looked exactly like Christophe. In Grenada, he had just witnessed white Europeans fighting each other while the island's enslaved and free coloured populations looked on from the side-lines. But in Saint-Domingue, free black men were setting sail to fight the British.

The soldiers, known as the Chasseurs Volontaires, had been raised specifically as part of France's support for the American revo-lutionaries. Like all colonies, Saint-Domingue had a militia for local defence. But the white population often resented military service, which extended to helping settle civil disputes and catching runaway slaves. Conversely, the free coloured population often saw joining the militia as a way of gaining social status. When he served as governor of the colony, d'Estaing had recognised the abilities of the free coloured militia and sought to expand their military role, to the dismay of the majority of colonists. Though increasingly unwilling to serve at arms themselves, they were even more reluctant to have large numbers of non-white soldiers in the garrisons. As a result, all militia units had to be commanded by a white officer, and no man of colour was allowed to rise above the rank of sergeant.

The prospect of fighting in a war against Britain offered more excitement than regular militia service. Patriotic fervour was fanned by *Affiches Américaines*, Cap Français' main newspaper, which encouraged men to enlist by asking: 'What Frenchman does not experience a reawakening of his courage and ardour to fight against the enemies of the State?'[3] Recruitment was further encouraged by the active support of Captain Vincent Olivier, the city's most celebrated free black officer and a friend of d'Estaing. Vincent was reportedly 119 years old and had been given his freedom from slavery following a French raid on Cartagena in 1697. Yet few white colonists heeded the call. As a result, when the fleet finally sailed from Cap Français, more than three quarters of the 700 newly raised militia were from the free coloured community.[4]

Some of the new recruits were perhaps motivated less by patriotism or the excitement of going to war than by a need to resolve their legal status. Several of the recruits passed themselves off as free when entering the service while still remaining technically enslaved. A government dispensation waived the costs of slave manumission to those in uniform during a time of war.[5] Is it possible that it was this mechanism that allowed the young Christophe to attain his freedom?

Baron de Vastey omits any suggestion of enslavement from his comment that the king had served in Savannah, but Hérard Dumesle, a Haitian writer who toured northern Haiti soon after Christophe's death and who was a fierce critic of his rule, says that he was freed by right following the Savannah campaign.[6] The advertisements for runaway slaves published in *Affiches Américaines* in the following years contain several mentions of those claiming that they had received their liberty as a result of their service under d'Estaing. One of them, the smallpox-scarred Jean-Pierre, had been sixteen at the time of the Savannah campaign. So had Jean Lefevre, a mixed-race wigmaker from Port-au-Prince, who said he had signed up with his mason brother Jean-Baptiste.[7] Service as a drummer was also customarily accepted as a justification for manumission, as its prominent battlefield role attracted plenty of enemy fire.[8] It was this role that Christophe played in the Savannah campaign, according to popular Haitian tradition.

Whether in such a short period of time Christophe could have learned the complicated drum rolls needed during manoeuvres is a moot point. The muster rolls from the Chasseurs Volontaires have not survived, and the names of only relatively few enlisted men are known; Christophe's is not among them.[9] For Vastey, it was important that his king had served at Savannah, or at least appeared to have served. Dumesle, the arch-critic, concurred. But whatever role they thought he might have played, the reality of the militia's experience during the campaign was somewhat less heroic than the memorial statue at Savannah portrays.

D'Estaing's fleet arrived off the Georgia coast at the start of September and prepared to help its American ally laying siege to the British. To get here from Grenada, Christophe had travelled from the far south of the Caribbean to its northernmost limits. Although Georgia was at one with the other colonies in rebellion against the British crown, Savannah was in many ways tied far more closely to the Caribbean basin than it was to its neighbours further up the Atlantic seaboard. From its river port it sent rice, lumber and horses directly to the Caribbean colonies, the value of which far outweighed its trade with New England. All the produce was worked by slaves landed at Tybee Island in the mouth of the Savannah River, and it was here that Christophe disembarked with the rest of the colonial troops. Biting winds and heavy rain hampered the landing of the ships' guns needed for the siege, and were a cold shock to those born in the tropics.

While the French ships blockaded British attempts to relieve the siege by river, the Chasseurs Volontaires were put to work digging trenches. Savannah sat on a bluff above the southern bank of its river surrounded by marshy woodland and rice plantations, against which the British had raised protective earthworks. The Saint-Domingue contingent were to dig trenches to allow the French and American soldiers to creep close enough for an attack. It was necessary siege work, but a far cry from the excitement promised to Christophe when they had first come aboard in Cap Français. Even when they were on campaign, the Chasseurs Volontaires were unable to escape the rigid racial hierarchies of their home. D'Estaing meanwhile attempted to negotiate the British surrender, only to be confounded by delaying tactics and light skirmishes that allowed the British to secretly bring in reinforcements through hidden channels in the marshes around the city, while continuing to improve their own defences.

After nearly two weeks of hard labour, the industry of the Chasseurs Volontaires had brought the trenches to within 300 metres of the defensive lines around Savannah. The British commander was so alarmed by this progress that he ordered a sortie against the works. On the morning of 24 September, three companies of British light troops launched a surprise attack. It was the first substantial ground fighting between the British and French in the war, and the Chasseurs Volontaires suddenly found themselves at the heart of it. The French officers were caught entirely off guard and their troops barely had time to fix bayonets before their positions were almost entirely overrun. There was a confused melee until reinforcements could be brought up, at which point the British—satisfied with their incursion—fell back. Together, the French soldiers and the Chasseurs Volontaires then enthusiastically chased the retreating British back to their lines. It was during this messy counter-attack that the Saint-Domingue contingent 'covered themselves in glory', in the words of one early Haitian historian.[10] For all their valour and composure under fire, however, the soldiers' charge against the defences was bombarded with grapeshot from the British guns, resulting in the loss of more than 100 troops killed or wounded. It was this shellfire that perhaps caused Christophe's alleged wound, described by Vastey.[11]

Following this action, the siege continued inconclusively until d'Estaing took charge of both the French and American forces and decided to directly assault the city's defences. After a heavy artillery bombardment he led two columns through the swampy lines in an attack on the town on 9 October. The action came three days after Christophe had celebrated his twelfth birthday in the mud of the trenches. The French high command had criticised the Chasseurs Volontaires' officers over the bloody price of their charge nearly three weeks earlier, and this time they were not to take part in the fighting. Their role was to feint a pre-dawn attack to help draw out the British troops, after which they were kept strictly in reserve. The battle was a bloody failure for the French and the Americans. D'Estaing and his second-in-command Fontanges, also from Saint-Domingue, were at loggerheads about tactics. In the event both were wounded in the fighting, while a Polish general also fighting for the Americans was killed in a cavalry charge. The assault was quickly turned back by a British counter-attack, and such was the scale of losses that the French were shamed into requesting a truce. The French and Americans had lost over 200 killed and 560 wounded.[12]

The black soldiers were only finally called into action a week later when d'Estaing decided to cut his losses and pull his men entirely from the theatre, and needed troops to cover the evacuation. The manoeuvres were carried out against a storm of blame between the French and American generals as to who was responsible for the fiasco. Feeling personally affronted, d'Estaing immediately set sail for France; he would never command a unit in combat again. As the rest of the French departed, the Chasseurs Volontaires were dealt with almost as an afterthought. Some were mistakenly put on a troop ship bound for France, where they were forced to spend an icy winter waiting for transport to take them back to Saint-Domingue. Others were redeployed to Grenada, where Christophe might almost have returned home, concluding his adventures with nothing more than a uniform and stories of a distant war. But his future lay in Cap Français, and it was there that he landed at the close of 1779, finally stepping off the ship and into one of the richest cities in the Americas.

Cap Français far outshone both Savannah and Grenada's St George in both population and wealth. It was the size of colonial Boston and laid out in a neat grid lined with fine buildings made of imported French stone and topped with slate and terracotta tiles. A quarter of its buildings had two storeys, many with large shady verandas to catch the breeze. Behind their facades there were leafy courtyard gardens, which their owners proudly stocked with aviaries of exotic birds from West Africa, South America and the Mississippi, and ponds full of goldfish from China. The main roads were paved, with raised pavements to protect pedestrians from dust and traffic. At the centre of the city, one of the largest churches in the French empire faced the main square. Elsewhere the imposing government building, barracks and even a Masonic temple spoke to the powers invested in the colony. There were several hospitals, and public fountains provided fresh water piped in from the nearby hills. For entertainment, theatres put on the newest French plays and there were debating societies and even a waxwork museum. Earthier tastes were catered for by the many billiard halls and gambling rooms, as well as bathhouses with mixed private bathing which were frequented by the city's prostitutes. Those scandalised by such goings-on could hopefully find spiritual reassurance in the presence of a convent on the outskirts of the city. In essence, Cap Français was a slice of France transplanted to the Caribbean, dubbed by many visitors the 'Paris of the Antilles'.[13]

Yet for all its obvious wealth there was one fact that could not be ignored by Christophe as he explored his new home. Its lime-washed buildings gleamed so brightly that one commentator said they could be unbearable to look at under the tropical sun. Their whiteness seemed almost overcompensation, since they were a front for the bloodiest of imperial endeavours. Cap Français may have been architecturally French, but demographically it was African. Less than a quarter of its population was white. The rest were black or of Afro-European descent, and more than two thirds of these were enslaved. Cap Français was the busiest port in Saint-Domingue, and it sat on the edge of the wide and well-watered Plaine du Nord, home to over 200 sugar estates interspersed with hundreds of smaller plantations growing cotton and indigo. Where the edges of the plains began to fold up into the mountains of northern Saint-Domingue, planters had found fertile ground to cultivate nearly 2,000 coffee plantations. The produce of all these estates was funnelled through the city's warehouses and wharves, and behind it all was the forced labour of some 200,000 enslaved workers.[14] The income this generated for France was extraordinary. In the late eighteenth century Saint-Domingue produced fully two thirds of the world's sugar and half of its coffee.

While Britain fought its own subjects in North America, the produce of Saint-Domingue was worth more than that of the thirteen rebellious colonies combined.

Christophe would have experienced this at its starkest during the market at Place Clugny, known locally as the 'Black's Market'. Every weekend up to 15,000 enslaved people would travel from their plantations to the market. They brought with them the excess produce of the kitchen gardens they used to supplement the meagre rations doled out to them on the plantations, and in doing so helped feed the city itself. This weekly influx doubled the city's population and gave the enslaved the opportunity to briefly carve out their own autonomous space. The jurist and chronicler of Saint-Domingue, Moreau de Saint-Méry, who complained that Cap's tiny police force was inadequate at the best of times, wrote that the enslaved would go 'armed with big clubs' and rent rooms for gambling and noisy parties. During these brief moments the urban enslaved could openly flaunt the city's regulations in what white colonists judged to be a disorderly fashion, with the police merely 'quiet onlookers at their misconduct'. However, the noise and press of the market at Place Clugny could also be used as a stage for the colonists to remind those from the plantations of what awaited them on their return should they step out of line. Even the city's free coloured population did not escape such punishment, including one man who was publicly clapped in irons amid the produce, with a sign telling all that he had been condemned to three years of hard labour for striking a white man.[15]

What were the chances for a boy of twelve like Christophe, newly arrived in a city like this? The only help he would have received would potentially come from those Chasseurs Volontaires in Savannah who may have taken pity on him—or seen opportunity in a boy with no family or means of support. Raised in Grenada, Christophe spoke English, but from his time on the Savannah campaign would have had to quickly pick up French or, just as likely, Kreyòl, the lingua franca of Saint-Domingue born out of the babel of French and a dozen African tongues brought on the slave ships.[16]

In 1824 when Hérard Dumesle gave an account of his tour of the ruins of Christophe's kingdom in his *Voyage dans le nord d'Hayti*, he attempted to understand the origins of a man he saw as a tyrant.

Dumesle sought out differing accounts of Christophe's early years and synthesised them into a single narrative. According to Dumesle, Christophe arrived in the city from Savannah under the wing of a Chasseur Volontaire named Petigny, who encouraged the boy to find work as a mason. Once settled, however, Christophe attached himself to a Frenchman named Badeche, a retired officer from the Cap Français garrison who ran a distillery and was an inveterate gambler.[17] Christophe then moved on to an inn called the Couronne, where he would work until the storm clouds of the Haitian Revolution eventually broke over Cap Français. In naming both Badeche and the Couronne, Dumesle tied together the two names most closely linked to Christophe's youth which had already been cited individually in second-hand reports while he was still alive and would wind like strands of DNA through all subsequent accounts of his life.

The first mention of Badeche was in a French biographical dictionary published in 1806 that named him as Christophe's owner in Cap Français. This account describes him as a merchant in the city and was translated and cited in multiple narratives throughout the nineteenth century until it became an accepted part of Christophe's biography. The same process occurred for the Couronne, first mentioned in connection with Christophe in 1819, the name of which ('The Crown') seemed a particularly irresistible piece of foreshadowing for a man who made himself king of his own country.[18]

Of the two names, Badeche has left the lightest trace in the record. He does not appear in any of the surviving cadastral surveys of Cap Français residents or in any of the listings for merchants' houses printed in *Affiches Américaines*. However, that newspaper does offer a tantalising glimpse of a possible connection to Christophe through an advertisement for a runaway slave published there in April 1789:

> Henry, mulatto, mason by profession, aged about 22 years, height 5 feet 2 inches, quite nice figure, strong feet & legs, always open-mouthed, ran away about four months ago; he was seen in the neighbourhoods of Acul, Périgourdins & Grande-Ravine du Limbe. It is in this last area where he learned his trade as a mason, with the free black Pierre-Paul; it is believed that he calls himself

free, and uses the name Badeche: those who have knowledge are requested to arrest him, and to give notice to Monsieur Paquot, former receiver of wrecks in Cap Français, rue Bourbon. There will be two portugaises reward.[19]

The districts listed in the advertisement lie 16 kilometres west of Cap Français, where the road to Port-au-Prince leaves the sugar plantations of the Plaine du Nord to climb into the Massif du Nord mountains: ideal territory for a runaway to hide themself. The age listed matches Christophe's official date of birth as recorded in the Kingdom of Haiti's royal almanacs, while the description of working as a mason ties in with the account produced by Dumesle. Unfortunately, these encouraging signs are undermined by the advertisement's physical description of the fugitive. Contemporary accounts of Christophe by those who had met him all mention him as being considerably taller than the short figure sought in 1789 by Monsieur Paquot. These descriptions also depict Christophe as being dark-skinned rather than having the lighter skin of mixed ancestry, a fact also borne out by the royal portraits that Christophe himself would later commission.[20] Although the advertisement must refer to a different person, it is possible that it could have been a source for a case of mistaken identity, where details became misremembered through Haiti's turbulent years of revolution and early independence to add to a narrative that can never be fully confirmed or disproved.

Contemporary accounts linking Christophe to the Couronne inn appeared nearly ten years after the first public mention of Badeche. In 1814 the essay *Observations of a Frenchman on the Slave Trade and the State of Saint-Domingue* was the first to suggest that Christophe had worked as a waiter, snidely remarking how eagerly he had served at table for the Marquis de Rouvray, copying his patron's manners. Rouvray had been the commanding officer for the Chasseurs Volontaires at Savannah during their fateful charge against the British lines. The anonymous writer was possibly Dauxion Lavaysse, who had led a French diplomatic mission to Christophe's kingdom in the same year, and the essay contains many attacks on the alleged pomposity of the Haitian royalty.[21] A French history of the Haitian Revolution published four years later is the first to name his place of work as the Couronne.[22] But two earlier unpublished accounts by acquaintances of Christophe also lend support to Christophe having worked at the inn.

As we have seen, the British agent Hugh Cathcart who knew Christophe wrote in a private letter that he was 'formerly Maître d'Hotel, at the Courone [sic] of the Cape and a slave'.[23] A second account was collected around 1814 in Paris by Moreau de Saint-Méry. He interviewed a woman from Saint-Domingue named Praxelles who claimed to be godmother to one of Christophe's daughters. While repeating the story that Christophe had been born in St Kitts, Praxelles recounted that his master 'was the long-time owner of the Café de la Couronne on Rue Espagnole where Christophe worked'.[24]

The Couronne inn, also known as La Couronne de France, did indeed stand on Rue Espagnole, the city's busiest thoroughfare. While most inns in Cap Français were small ventures tucked along the quayside catering to merchants, sailors and others fresh off the ship, the Couronne was a much grander affair, occupying a large city block that allowed it to offer a locked yard for carriages and stabling for animals, along with twenty master beds for guests.[iii] At the time of Christophe's arrival in Cap Français it was owned by the widow Husard and her business partner Monsieur Briot. It changed hands several times during the 1780s, but aware of its good reputation for food, the new owner Monsieur Gaye advertised in 1788 that the inn still kept 'the same white chef'. Under Gaye, the Couronne prospered. In 1790 he announced that he had increased the number of servants at the inn and added improvements to the rooms in his continued desire to earn the esteem of his patrons.[25]

As with Lavaysse's early account of Christophe working as a waiter, many nineteenth-century foreign accounts of his alleged time at the Couronne carry a derisory tone, mocking the presumption of his rule when his due place was really in the scullery. 'His hands are less fit to wield the sceptre, than the frying pan at the inn of the Cape', blustered one commentator in 1819.[26] In contrast, popular Haitian retellings of this period in his life are far more cel-

---

[iii] The site of the Couronne inn in modern-day Cap-Haïtien is currently occupied by a soft drink depot. Pleasingly, it sells Champagne Cola Couronne, one of the most popular soft drinks in Haiti.

ebratory. There was no place for misguided snobbery when the motor of the Haitian Revolution had been the mass of enslaved Africans from the fields. Here the Couronne is posited as a social and intellectual centre for debates where Christophe could eavesdrop and learn from the French patrons, gaining insights into the colonial mindset that would serve him well during the struggle for freedom. His skill in the kitchen wasn't overlooked either—in one account he was a celebrated master 'of turtle vol-au-vent and wood pigeon' and the fragrance of his puff pastry would carry all the way down the street.[27] Although this sounds fanciful, it is not entirely without precedent. Louis Desrouleaux, an enslaved chef born in Kongo, had been a notably successful pastry cook in Cap Français. He earned enough money through his baking to purchase his freedom and open a boarding house. Desrouleaux eventually owned several properties in the city, and even bailed out his former master when he ran into financial straits. His heirs formed one of the more prosperous free black families in Cap Français by the time Christophe settled there. His son, also named Louis, served with the Chasseurs Volontaires in Savannah, and it is likely that he and Christophe knew each other.[28] A modern mural of Christophe's life on display at the Citadelle Henry combines these disparate elements of his early life by showing him bayoneting British soldiers at Savannah while wearing a white chef's hat.

Depending on his free status, Christophe may have lived at the Couronne or sought accommodation in the district of Petite Guinée ('Little Africa') on the slopes above Rue Espagnole. This was home to most of Cap Français' free black population and unlike the grand buildings that made up much of the city, consisted mainly of tightly packed wooden houses, many of them thatched. Before becoming the city's majority black quarter, the area had originally been known as the Saint-Christophe quarter, named for the French émigrés who had settled here after the British captured the island of St Kitts early in the eighteenth century.[29] Given this, it is easy to see how Christophe, born far from Saint-Domingue on an island that had also changed hands from French to British control and on his own in a new city, could have been taken as a native of St Kitts, possibly even acquiring his surname in the process.

The densely populated streets of Petite Guinée also provided opportunities for those like Christophe who were living in the limbo between free and enslaved. Most urban slaves lived with their masters, but a report written in 1785 noted that as many as 2,000 slaves in the city paid their masters a regular sum, after which 'they do not see their masters for two or three months ... They rent rooms where they please, where they can commit the worst excesses'. Others simply ran away from their masters. A sweep of Petite Guinée by the city authorities during this period caught 200 slaves living as free in the district.[30] Passing as free in this way was the best option for someone like Christophe, brought to Cap Français via an unorthodox route and for whom no records exist to indicate either that any colonist in Saint-Domingue ever claimed ownership of him or of his formal manumission. It was a precarious existence, but he had already experienced much in his short life. Carving out a life in Petite Guinée and at the Couronne would be the first big test of the initiative and self-belief that would see him forge a path through revolution and civil war to one day crown himself king in this very city.

From his experience at Savannah with the Chasseurs Volontaires Christophe had received an early indication that life even as a free black person in Saint-Domingue fell far short of legal and social equality with the white French. Now, as he matured into his teenage years and listened to patrons of both colours at the inn, the reality of life in his new city became ever clearer to him. The size and wealth of Cap Français surely offered him greater opportunities than his old home in Grenada, but those opportunities were severely constrained by the colony's politics. Christophe found himself in a minority twice over. He was free but black in a city run by white colonists, and he was black but free in a society where the over-whelming majority of the population were enslaved Africans. The wealth being created in Saint-Domingue could be seen every day passing the Couronne inn on its way to the docks to sweeten the salons of Paris and Bordeaux, but the system that produced it was built on the most unjust and unstable of foundations. At the end of every harvesting season, the slaves outside Cap Français would burn off the remains of the old sugar crop to encourage new growth. One stray spark was all that was needed to set the entire colony alight.

3

THE COLONY ABLAZE

After the siege of Savannah veterans of the Chasseurs Volontaires would have found themselves welcomed into a larger network of free coloured officers, militia and rural police in northern Saint-Domingue. Military service was seen as one area where those of African descent could advance socially within a network that offered status and support to its members, especially for those without kinship ties or other connections to white colonists.[1] The young Christophe would certainly have taken advantage of these connections. One figure at the centre of this network was the Senegalese-born Jean-Baptiste Belley, who had served at Savannah and was a lieutenant in the city's militia by 1781. He was a popular and well-connected figure: between 1777 and 1788 he appeared as a legal witness to sixty baptisms, marriages and funerals in Cap Français for the city's free black community.[2] Christophe and Belley would later serve together when revolutionary fires swept across the city, and they likely met for the first time when Christophe was working at the Couronne, with Christophe perhaps even serving him a drink in January 1784 after Belley had been named godfather at the baptism of Noël Coidavid, a child who would one day become Christophe's brother-in-law.[3]

A support network was essential in order to thrive in a deeply segregated city like Cap Français. For a person with black skin, freedom still meant anything but equality with the white colonists. Throughout the eighteenth century the colonial authorities found themselves increasingly afraid of Saint-Domingue's growing and increasingly prosperous free coloured community. Nearly a quarter of the colony's slaves were owned by those who had some African

39

ancestry, and many poor whites who had come to the colony to make their fortunes had only done so by marrying entrepreneurial free black women for their wealth—women who were subsequently vilified in racist screeds for their allegedly insatiable sexual appetites. Their mixed-race offspring horrified white observers; in his history of Saint-Domingue, Moreau de Saint-Méry embraced Enlightenment racial theory by classifying the colony's people according to their ratio of white and non-white blood, from mulattoes and quadroons to those who appeared phenotypically white, yet whose race was kept in legal doubt by having a mother who was one eighth black.[4] To keep Saint-Domingue's free coloured population further in check a series of laws forbade them from practising law or medicine, or giving their children French names. A law passed in 1779 forbade them from affecting 'the dress, hairstyles, [or] style of whites'. The colony's census even clearly demarcated those who had some European ancestry and were likely to have been born free (labelled *gens de couleur*) from those whose free status was somehow stained by their former enslaved status (*nègres libres*).[5]

Racial discrimination seeped into every facet of life. When he became king, Christophe regularly enjoyed the opera—a love that he would have developed in colonial Cap Français. Such was the wealth and prestige of the city that *The Marriage of Figaro* was performed here only months after making its debut in Paris. But if Christophe had attended this performance, he would have had to sit at the rear of the theatre in segregated seating that reinforced the colony's racial and social hierarchy, while still allowing for the 'improving' effects of high culture. In the words of one official in the similarly run sugar colony of Martinique, exposure to French theatre caused those of African descent to lose some of the 'barbarity of their origin', allowing them to 'become civilized in their manners and custom'.[6]

Christophe's Catholic faith was also likely forged during this time. Attending services at the grand parish church on Place d'Armes, he may even have gained further insight into what a free and prosperous life for a black man might look like in Saint-Domingue. A free coachman named Toussaint Breda, twenty-five years Christophe's senior, was a regular attendee and had his own bench in the church for his family.[7] He had formerly been enslaved on the Breda plantation that gave him his name, and was still working for his former master, after a brief attempt to make his way as a coffee planter. Like the infant Noël Coidavid, Christophe would soon know this coachman well, serving as one of his most trusted lieutenants after he rechristened himself Toussaint Louverture. But for the present the two could only listen to the bells and contemplate their meaning: when they tolled for a funeral, the local black population would say 'One good white is dead, the wicked ones remain.'[8]

Working at the busy Couronne, Christophe would have caught many important events in the life of the city. In July 1781 he would have rushed outside at the sound of an enormous explosion that sank the powder ship of Admiral de Grasse, who was on his way to fight the British in their American colonies.[i] In April 1784 patrons would have shared news of the hot-air balloon that had flown over the Gallifet plantation (the first such ascent in the Americas), while later that year he would have taken cover as a series of earthquakes shook the city, one of which was strong enough to destroy a dozen houses. And throughout this period there would have been the constant passage of buyers making their way down to the wharf when a new slave ship moored in the harbour carrying its sad cargo from Africa. The hunger for captives was insatiable. In 1790 alone, 66 ships arrived in the port carrying nearly 17,500 captives: some 336 people fed every week into the slave machine.[9]

The modest freedoms that some slaves enjoyed in Cap Français at the Sunday markets were in stark contrast to the lives their compatriots endured on the plantations. On the northern plain and beyond they were woken before dawn and laboured until sunset. The strongest among them planted and harvested sugar cane while children weeded around the plants. What free time they had was dedicated to their garden plots, as proprietors often ignored their obligations to provide food in order to increase their own profit margins. During harvest time the slaves were worked even harder. Mills and boiling plants ran around the clock so that the freshly cut

---

[i] Had the ship been anchored closer to the rest of the fleet when it exploded, Admiral de Grasse might not have had the forces to prevail at the Battle of the Chesapeake, possibly altering the outcome of the American Revolutionary War.

cane would not spoil before it could be processed. Skilled artisans such as those overseeing the refining process were treated with relative privilege, as were those working in the master's house, but all were subjected to the empire of the whip. The 1672 Code Noir that set out laws for the treatment of slaves was honoured largely in the breach. The vast numbers of slaves brought to Saint-Domingue were testament to the planters' cold economic calculation that their bottom line was better served by working their slaves to death than by investing in their welfare. Mortality rates among the enslaved were so high that numbers could only be sustained by importing more and more people into the colony. Birth rates were so low that some masters offered financial rewards to women who successfully weaned their infants, many of whom were only born as a result of rape. Women who had abortions were often targeted for special punishment for depriving a planter of their future 'property'.[10]

'And so it was that on each plantation there existed a white despot, who had the barbaric right of life and death over the unfortunate blacks in his keep,' wrote Baron de Vastey in *The Colonial System Unveiled*, published in Haiti in 1814, 'Death hovered over our heads as over those of the lowliest animals; and when they wanted to deal it out to us, the only thing that gave them any pause was the question of which form of punishment to choose.' Vastey laid out an unflinching catalogue of the horrors perpetrated, naming individual masters and overseers. On the Gallifet plantation where the hot-air balloon had been raised, the owner was notorious for having his slaves hamstrung, rubbing hot peppers into whipping wounds and submerging incalcitrant workers in a dark water-filled dungeon. Among colonists, this plantation was considered one of the best run in the region: a popular planters' saying was to be 'happy as a Gallifet slave'. Vastey demurred: 'The slaves of Saint-Domingue were civilly dead: they inhabited this earth as if they did not really inhabit it; they lived as if they were not really living.'[11] In 1788, when slaves attempted to hold one plantation owner to account for staking two women accused of poisoning to the ground and burning their legs, he defended himself by saying that only violence could keep the enslaved in their place. Officials found in his favour.[12]

This brutality was technically illegal under the Code Noir, but planters who were outnumbered nearly ten to one in Saint-

Domingue by the enslaved saw it as the only way to maintain order. Colonists lived in perpetual fear of a slave uprising. When Christophe first arrived in Cap Français, stories were still told of François Macandal, a slave burned at the stake in the city's main square for trying to incite such a revolt. Macandal had gone maroon from his plantation halfway between the city and the town of Limbe, and in January 1758 was arrested and accused of waging a campaign of poisonings that had spread terror across the north. When one of Macandal's alleged co-conspirators was interrogated, he spoke to the colonists' deepest fears by claiming that 'if he identified all the slave poisoners and malefactors he would never finish, since they were found on all the plantations'. The ultimate aim was to weaken the white population so that the enslaved could reclaim their freedom. The poisoning paranoia mixed with a fear of 'heathen' African religions, and Macandal was convicted of making magic amulets and sentenced to death.[ii] During his execution he managed to briefly escape from his bonds, and although he was recaptured and forced back into the flames, he quickly became a legendary figure among both the enslaved and the colonists for his claim that the whites could never kill him, and that he would transform himself into a fly before the moment of death instead.[13]

Listening to the patrons at the Couronne inn, Christophe would have been one of the first to hear of other events that might threaten to shake the colony. In 1789 Louis XVI summoned the French legislative assembly, called the Estates General, for its first sitting in 175 years. Only delegates from the metropole were invited, but a party from Saint-Domingue travelled to Versailles to demand representation. A pointed discussion unfolded as to how many delegates might be allowed to be seated. When colonists asked that their numbers reflect the population of Saint-Domingue, one assembly member commented:

> the free blacks are proprietors and taxpayers, and yet they have not been allowed to vote [in the Saint-Domingue Colonial

---

[ii] Macandal's birthplace in Africa is unknown, but his name is likely derived from *makunda*, the word for amulet in the Mayombe language of the lower Congo basin. French accounts typically rendered his name as Makandal.

Assembly]. And as for the slaves, either they are men or they are
not; if the colonists consider them men, let them free them and
make them eligible for seats; if the contrary is the case, have we,
in apportioning deputies according to the population of France,
taken into consideration the number of our horses and mules?[14]

There would be several attempts to answer these questions in both
France and Saint-Domingue over the coming years, until the colo-
ny's enslaved population forcefully volunteered its own solution.
For now, any debate over colonial representation was dominated by
the Club Massiac, the powerful planter's lobby that was ever quick
to remind delegates of the centrality of the colonial trade to the
French economy. Ranged against them (and massively outnumbered
in terms of their support) was the abolitionist Société des Amis des
Noirs, founded in 1788. On 22 October 1789 the Marquis de
Lafayette hosted a dinner for the society in Paris, attended by the
celebrated British abolitionist campaigner Thomas Clarkson and two
of the wealthiest members of Saint-Domingue's free coloured community, Julien Raimond and Vincent Ogé. Both Raimond and Ogé
appeared white, but as each had one grandparent of African ancestry, they were denied any political rights in Saint-Domingue. Both
were rich from owning coffee plantations (Raimond's in Aquin in
the south of the colony, Ogé's in Dondon, 26 kilometres south of
Cap Français) and owned large numbers of slaves. In keeping with
the abolitionist campaigns in Britain at the time, the society was
gradualist, seeking only a ban on the slave trade followed by ame-
lioration of colonial slavery leading eventually to its abolition.
Raimond and Ogé argued that giving political representation to
Saint-Domingue's free coloured community was the only way to
guarantee the colony's future stability, and that they were the only
ones capable of restraining the colony's slaves—an argument they
had earlier tried presenting to the Club Massiac. In hoping to outlaw
the racial prejudice against themselves they sought to align their
interests fully with the white planter class, though Ogé did allow
that promises of a gradual abolition of slavery were the best way to
forestall fears of a slave revolt.[15]

Despite their similar wealth and status, the two men chose different approaches to claiming their rights. While Raimond decided to

remain in Paris to lobby the National Assembly alongside influential figures like the Abbé Grégoire, Ogé saw that the main struggle was to be found in Saint-Domingue. When he returned in October 1790, he discovered that the revolutionary atmosphere had already been carried there from France. Colonial assemblies had been set up in the major cities as white colonists grabbed eagerly at the promise of more political autonomy and freer trade; but they had no desire to share power. The granting of political rights to the free coloured population was explicitly rejected. The Declaration of the Rights of Man and of the Citizen that Ogé had seen so celebrated in Paris was a document to be treated with fear and suspicion in Cap Français, as its calls for the recognition of universal rights was deemed inadmissible in the toxic racial system that underpinned the colony. It was no accident that members of the Club Massiac had even tried to prevent him returning to the colony and he had had to return via the USA, a journey part-funded by Clarkson. Dismayed at what he found on his arrival, Ogé gathered his supporters and decided that if his rights would not be granted willingly they would have to be taken by force.

Ogé joined with Jean-Baptiste Chavanne, a Chasseur Volontaire veteran of the Savannah campaign who had seen his own petition to join the provincial assembly rejected on the grounds of race. Together they gathered around 300 men and captured Chavanne's hometown of Grand Rivière, a short distance from Dondon. After repelling one attempt by the Cap Français militia to recapture the town, they fled across the border into Spanish Santo Domingo in the hope of launching a guerrilla campaign. The two men were captured in February 1791 and extradited back to Cap Français to be sentenced to death. Their very public executions were held on Place d'Armes on 25 February and were almost certainly witnessed by Christophe, who would have recognised the ruined figure of Chavannes as he and Ogé were led into the square with ropes around their necks. After being made to repent their crimes, they were slowly broken on the wheel. 'I was so shocked that I turned my head so as not to see, but I heard their horrible cries', recalled one French member of the National Guard unit tasked with keeping order.[16] After their torture the two men were beheaded. Two days later a further twenty-two people were condemned to death for their part in the uprising and their heads placed on spikes along major roads as a warning to others.[17]

Christophe had understood that membership of the free coloured militia was a way of raising one's status in the colony, so to see another member of the Savannah campaign killed so cruelly was a salutary lesson about the lengths to which the colonists would go when their power and status came under threat. In the eyes of the whites, however, their reaction to Ogé and Chavanne's attempted uprising was entirely proportionate. They had only to be thankful that the men did not attempt to raise the enslaved population in their support. By early 1791 white fears that the new ideas of liberty arriving from France would spread beyond the free coloured population to the people who laboured on their plantations, who cooked their food and waited on them at table, were palpable. When their worst fears regarding a slave revolt were finally made a reality six months later, many whites laid the blame directly at the door of the revolutionaries in France, never once bringing themselves to understand that those they had torn from Africa in the belief that they were subhuman could nurture dreams of freedom of their own.

On the morning of 23 August 1791 the inhabitants of Cap Français woke to find a fine cloud of ash floating towards the city. The northern plains were on fire. One by one, and then by the dozen, the rich sugar plantations that stretched from the city to the mountains were set ablaze, as those who laboured there rose en masse to destroy the crops and machinery that were the source of the colonists' wealth and their own suffering. Within a week more than 180 sugar plantations in 7 parishes had been completely destroyed; within a month all of the north's 27 parishes were in ruins and more than 200 sugar plantations and 1,200 coffee plantations had been destroyed. Among those who had risen up against the system were the 808 enslaved people on the Gallifet plantation, which was now turned into an armed camp. By the end of November perhaps as many as 80,000 former slaves were in revolt—more than half of the total enslaved population of northern Saint-Domingue.[18] Cap Français had been attacked three times by this new rebel army, which had seemingly appeared out of nowhere, and its citizens— including Christophe—were now under siege.

The plan for the mass uprising had been set at a secret meeting on the night of 14 August. While the streets of Cap Français thronged with thousands of slaves bringing produce to the Sunday market, a group of conspirators began to gather in the woods at Bois-Caïman on the Normand-le-Mézy plantation just off the road between Cap Français and the hill town of Limbe. It was perhaps no accident that this was the plantation from which Macandal had fled before plotting his poisoning campaign. The attendees were all high-status slaves from around 100 plantations—coachmen and plantation drivers who were natural leaders, afforded positions of trust by their masters. The leader of the plot was Boukman Dutty, a coachman and priest, along with Jean-François Papillon and George Biassou. A fourth leader was almost certainly the free coachman from Breda who kept his own bench in the Cap Français church, and whose status allowed him to move freely about the north, hiding in plain sight. He would soon adopt the name by which he would become one of the most famed figures of the Age of Revolutions: Toussaint Louverture.[19] The mass uprising was set to begin just over a week later when the Colonial Assembly was due to meet in Cap Français, providing an opportunity to target Saint-Domingue's political leadership in a single attack.

On the night of 22 August the leadership gathered at Bois-Caïman for a second time to finalise the details of the plot and to hold a religious ceremony to dedicate themselves to its success. With Boukman presiding alongside a priestess named Cécile Fatiman, a black pig was sacrificed in a ceremony that took elements of West African and Kongolese religious traditions and blended them together to create something new and unique. Colonial commentators like Moreau de Saint-Méry had written with deep suspicion of 'vaudoux' dances that many slaves liked to attend, not realising that by forcing together those from disparate parts of Africa they might forge new syncretic religious identities of their own, even going so far as to steal whatever elements of French Catholicism they found useful. In this way, Saint-Domingue's slave system gave birth to Haitian Vodou, and the ceremony at Bois-Caïman would prove its founding myth.[iii] As the participants

---

[iii] Today a Ministry of Tourism sign proudly points the way to Bois-Caïman, a small farming community lying off the highway beyond the southern outskirts of Cap-Haïtien. A bright mural next to a Vodou temple commemorates the ceremony, while a short hike in the hills above

tasted the blood of the pig, Boukman gave the oath through which the slaves would regain their freedom:

> The Good Lord who created the sun which gives us light from above, who rouses the sea and makes the thunder roar—listen well, all of you—this god, hidden in the clouds, watches us. He sees all that the white man does. The god of the white man calls him to commit crimes; our god asks only good works of us. But this god who is so good orders revenge! He will direct our hands; he will aid us. Throw away the image of the god of the whites who thirsts for our tears and listen to the voice of liberty which speaks in the hearts of all of us.[20]

White refugees flooded into Cap Français. The insurgents had killed dozens in revenge attacks as the enslaved paid back their masters for the years they had suffered at their hands. 'Their savage barbarity has spared neither age nor sex', wrote the American slave trader Nathaniel Cutting without irony to the US secretary of state and fellow slave owner Thomas Jefferson, telling him that the violence 'would make Nero blush'.[21] In fact, while many colonists died in reprisal killings, there were almost as many instances of individuals being saved from death by those they had enslaved. Toussaint Louverture notably saved the wife of his former master by escorting her to safety when the Breda plantation was about to be overrun, while figures like doctors and priests who could help the insurgent cause were taken hostage and protected.

Where was Christophe in these earliest days of the northern revolt? As with much of his early life the archive is frustratingly silent. In his epic five-volume biography of one of Christophe's great

---

takes you past the ruins of colonial aqueducts to a cave painted red and blue—the colours not just of the Haitian flag but of the warlike Vodou spirit Ogue Feray, who is often associated with the revolution. Candle stubs and empty rum bottles are witnesses to regular offerings here. The day after visiting I was taken by a local guide to a sacred mapou tree near the old Breda plantation, which I was told was the real Bois-Caïman site. Later yet I learned of a third and even more secret location where the ceremony was allegedly held, but which only Vodou initiates were allowed to visit. I was left feeling that there was no such thing as the 'real' site of Bois-Caïman: it had simultaneously taken place nowhere and everywhere, in the hearts of all those who had risen up against the French.

rivals, the revolutionary leader and later president of Haiti, Alexandre Pétion, published in 1857, the historian Joseph Saint-Rémy suggests that in 1791 Christophe was serving in the maréchaussée or rural police. No supporting evidence is provided, but it is possible that William Wilson, the English tutor to Christophe's son after he crowned himself king, was referring to the same when he noted in his unpublished memoir that 'in the earliest days of the revolution, when both sides armed the negroes, Christophe led a small body of men known in the French army as Guides or guides [sic], in which employment he became distinguished by his capacity and courage'.[22] The maréchaussée were almost exclusively recruited from the free black and mixed-race communities, many of whom had previously served in the militia, including veterans of the Savannah campaign. It was a role that brought a good salary; at 800 livres per year, a trooper earned roughly double that of a journeyman carpenter. This was further topped up by a share of reward money, since one of the main roles of the maréchaussée was to capture and return slaves who had absconded from plantations: 30 livres for a slave captured outside their parish, and double that for capturing a maroon pursuing freedom on the border with Santo Domingo.[23] Amid the brutal racial politics of the colony, membership of a group such as the maréchaussée would have reinforced his social status in his community, as well as redefining his own precarious position as someone with no formally free status and no family network to rely on. Throughout his life, Christophe would strongly identify with the interests of the urban classes over those who worked in the fields, alongside a firm belief in the necessity of maintaining the plantation economy irrespective of whether the labourers were enslaved or free. Membership of the maréchaussée may be an early indication of how these views would evolve over time.

In the first weeks of the uprising, the Marquis de Rouvray, Christophe's commanding officer of the Chasseurs Volontaires at Savannah, was put in charge of leading military efforts against the former slaves on the northern plain east of Cap Français. Rouvray had attended the meeting of the Estates General in France and was a firm supporter of equal political rights for the colony's free coloured population, and now led their militia out into the field.

'The free mulattoes and negroes, chiefly mounted', were some of the first troops to enter the burned remnants of the Gallifet plantation, but their eagerness to fight still meant little to the short-sighted members of the Colonial Assembly.[24] Rouvray criticised their refusal to cede any ground on political rights and was quickly proved right as to the potential consequences. By the end of the year the colony's second city, Port-au-Prince, erupted into fighting—not between the free and the enslaved, but between the white colonists and the free coloured community, as the two populations divided themselves into armed camps. But for all his prescience on this issue, Rouvray (who owned slaves himself) failed to understand the larger earthquake that was happening around him. He thought that slaves were incapable of independent action and found it easier to believe that their revolt was sparked by the arrival of revolutionary ideas from France, stirred up by provocateurs from the Société des Amis des Noirs, than that the belief in liberty could have arrived on the slave ships from Africa in the heart of every captive and was only waiting for the right moment to spark into action. It took time for this idea to sink in, but his wife Madame de Rouvray came to a conclusion that many colonists would soon follow: the only way to ensure the safety and stability of the colony would be to wage a war of total extermination, not just of their former slaves but also of the free coloured population, who would be branded and deported, or be sterilised while children to prevent any future where the races might mix.[25]

Hopes in the colony that France might send a military expedition to assist the colonial authorities in restoring order were dashed in early 1792 when news arrived that the country had declared war on Britain, Spain and Holland. By this time, the south of the colony had also become a battleground, with many plantations in open revolt. In the north, the rebel leader Boukman had been killed, but attempts to negotiate a peace deal with the other slave army leaders had faltered. At this stage their demands were an amnesty for those who had taken up arms and a general improvement in working conditions on the plantations. Complete abolition was not yet part of the plan. After the outbreak of war in Europe, Spanish authorities on Saint-Domingue's eastern border began to actively arm the rebel armies. Cap Français held firm but continued to be attacked.

Christophe may well have taken part in its active defence when the army of Biassou led a raid on the hospital at Haut-du-Cap on the city outskirts, where he had once been enslaved. For Nathaniel Cutting there was no rescuing the colony as things stood:

> While the Insurgents can obtain ammunition from the Spaniards it will be almost impossible to quell them, and I begin to be of the opinion that it will be most prudent for Government to enter into a Treaty with them similar to that which the Government of Jamaica formerly made with the Maroon Negroes in that Island;[iv] otherways the expence [sic] of protecting the plantations will exceed their Revenue.[26]

Cutting's belief never came to pass, but on 28 May 1792 a ship arrived in Cap Français carrying news that would have horrified Madame de Rouvray. Seven weeks earlier the French National Assembly had declared the political equality of the races. The colony's free coloured and black communities were granted full rights as citizens, including the ability to vote and stand for election. The decision to abolish racial discrimination was presented as the best way to maintain the political and economic foundations of the colonial system. From this moment the French empire would only recognise two categories of people: free and enslaved.[27] For someone like Christophe this was a transformative moment, a legal guarantee of his status in the new French state that was being built. In September a new set of revolutionary commissioners arrived from Paris to help implement the reforms. They were led by a Brissotin lawyer named Léger-Félicité Sonthonax and Etienne Polverel, both of whom carried abolitionist sympathies and were viewed with deep suspicion by many white planters.

In a little over a year the political and economic order of Saint-Domingue had been turned upside down. A few plantations still operated with their enslaved workforces, but exports had crashed. Most of the countryside was in a state of insurrection, and although none of the major towns and cities had fallen, many of them were

---

iv The First Maroon War in Jamaica (1728–39) concluded with a treaty whereby the colonial authorities recognised the independence of the maroon communities and their right to self-governance.

wracked by unrest and disorder, either between the colonists and the free coloured class, or between the colonists themselves as the white French divided into royalist and republican factions. For republicans like Sonthonax and Polverel, the revolution in France was an opportunity to trim the wings of the colony's largely royalist rich white planter class, as much as it was to enforce the new laws on racial equality. In the spring of 1793 they left Cap Français to restore order to a fractious Port-au-Prince and cities further south, disarming white militias as they went and conferring their blessing on the free coloured military leadership in the region, which was led by a mixed-race planter named André Rigaud who they promoted to general. Rigaud had been an early supporter of Ogé and Chavannes, and like the latter (and Christophe) may have served with the Chasseurs Volontaires in Savannah in 1779.[28]

While they were in the south, a new threat to the revolutionary order arrived in Cap Français in the shape of General François-Thomas Galbaud, the colony's newly appointed military governor and a former planter from Port-au-Prince. From the outset Galbaud was dismissive of Sonthonax and Polverel as naive newcomers who did not understand the true nature of Saint-Domingue, insisting that as he held a military command he would not take orders from any civil commissioners. He saw himself firmly on the side of the white planters, who began to lobby him for support from the moment he landed in the city. The commissioners, they told him, wanted to destroy Saint-Domingue by arming the slave armies and setting them against the white population. Sonthonax had insisted that every regiment in Cap Français have at least one officer of colour. White troops had attempted to mutiny against the ruling, which only prompted Sonthonax to form new units entirely made up of members of the black and free coloured communities. They took heart from Galbaud's pronouncement on France's new race laws: 'I adopt equality; I even want it. But here it is pushed too far.'[29] The stage was set for a clash that would tear the city apart, with Christophe as both witness and participant.

The two commissioners rushed back to Cap Français knowing that the city was being turned against them, but also that they could rely on the free coloured population for support. Their first meeting with the new governor was a disaster; Galbaud was particularly shocked at Sonthonax's declaration in response to the planters' charges that he was against his own race: 'Understand, citizen, that the only thing white about me is my skin.' After they refused his invitation to dinner, Galbaud abused them publicly and fights broke out on the dock between white sailors and the commissioner's free coloured supporters. Knowing that it was likely to provoke a show-down, but confident in their ability to prevail, Sonthonax and Polverel had Galbaud arrested on charges of sedition and placed on a ship in the city's harbour.[30]

It was a risky move. There were dozens of ships moored off Cap Français, many of which had been stranded for months with no cargo to carry and a mass of disaffected sailors on board. Galbaud managed to galvanise the crew of one ship and then another, prom-ising them that he would lead them in an attack on the city to depose the commissioners and restore white control once and for all. Roused to action, this impromptu marine force of several thousand men swarmed onto the wharfs of Cap Français on the afternoon of 20 June. There was desperate hand-to-hand fighting between these white counter-revolutionaries and the supporters of the commis-sioners, who were almost entirely made up of the city's free black militia. One of the combatants was Jean-Baptiste Belley, now hold-ing the rank of captain. Another was Henry Christophe. According to Saint-Rémy, by 1793 Christophe had transferred from the maréchaussée to an artillery militia unit led by an officer named Séraphin, created by Sonthonax for the city's defence.[31] This is the moment when Christophe finally makes his first proper appearance in the written archive, defending his adopted city in the name of racial equality. As the sailors looked to be gaining the upper hand, Sonthonax sent an urgent order to the commander at Haut-du-Cap 'to place at the disposal of Henry Christophe two pieces of eight-pounder cannon for the service of the civil commission'.[32] Christophe was in the thick of the fighting and by sunset the attack on the city had been repulsed; Galbaud's brother Cézar, who had been one of the first to urge him to take up arms against the com-missioner, had been killed.

A second attack was launched the following morning with such vigour that the commissioners and the units that included Christophe and Belley were forced to flee to Haut-du-Cap on the southern outskirts of the city. The arsenal was captured and the doors of the jail were flung open. Cap Français was given over to looting and anarchy. Whether deliberately or by accident, fires were started. Strong breezes carried the flames from roof to roof, and within moments the entire city was an inferno. White residents fled in panic onto small boats and took shelter on the ships; in the aftermath many would simply sail for Philadelphia or New Orleans as refugees, never to return. The commissioners' supporters blamed the fire on Galbaud's men, while the white colonists put the blame on the town's slaves. Others yet claimed that Sonthonax and Polverel had set the fires as part of a radical conspiracy to destroy the colony.[33]

In truth, the commissioners were horrified. Hundreds had been left dead and barely a fifth of the city was left unscarred by the fire. A map produced several months later to survey the damage showed block after block destroyed, including the plot where Christophe's inn, the Couronne, had stood. Only the immediate area around the government house and barracks and a short stretch of the quayside were left unscathed.[34] Galbaud's attempt to preserve the white-dominated system has ended up destroying its most beautiful city. His men had retreated rather than try to take control of what remained, but Sonthonax and Polverel barely had the manpower to claim control of what would remain when the fires were extinguished. Only one group had the power to take and hold Cap Français, and they had been camped within striking distance of the city since they rose against the planters in August 1791. If they could be won to the commissioners' side, Sonthonax and Polverel could truly save the colony for France. Delegates were sent out to the 10,000-strong army of former slaves camped on the northern plain to invite them into the city to defend it against the white counter-revolutionaries with a striking offer:

> We declare that the will of the French Republic and of its delegates is to give freedom to all the Negro warriors who will fight for the Republic ... All the slaves declared free by the delegates will be equal to all free men [and] will enjoy all the rights belonging to French citizens.[35]

Their daring plan worked. Several thousand insurgents flooded into the city and put themselves under the commissioners' command.

Three weeks later, Sonthonax extended the offer of freedom to the families of those who joined the republic, while Polverel proposed reforms to the plantation system, suggesting that when the revolution's armies had been defeated, fighters would be given land, and plantation labourers offered a share of the profits. On 24 August a public meeting of 15,000 people was held in the ruins of Cap Français which ended with a vote overwhelmingly in favour of general emancipation. Christophe would have attended, and as the celebratory cries went up in the crowd, he perhaps reflected on the journey that had brought him here, from childhood slavery in Grenada through a shadowy self-emancipation, to helping win, with his own hands, his permanent freedom as a citizen of the French republic. But the question remained: with slavery abolished, what sort of Saint-Domingue would rise from its ashes?

4

DEFENDING THE REVOLUTION

On 14 July 1793, six weeks before the general emancipation proclamation, Léger-Félicité Sonthonax oversaw an elaborate ceremony amid the charred ruins of Cap Français to mark the fourth anniversary of the storming of the Bastille in Paris. A crowd of nearly 7,000, the majority of them black and newly emancipated, heard him speak in front of a newly planted liberty tree topped with a red Phrygian cap, as he sought to tie together the white, free coloured and the formerly enslaved under the same republican banner. Henry Christophe would have attended as a member of the city's militia and joined in the singing of the Marseillaise and the public oath of loyalty to the Republic. It was less than two years since the start of the slave uprising, and a new and radical future for Saint-Domingue was being born. For Christophe the future was also being reshaped in a more practical way. The day after the celebrations, on the feast of his patron saint Henry, he got married.

Christophe's bride was fifteen-year-old Marie-Louise Coidavid, who was another member of the Cap Français free black community.[i] The Kingdom of Haiti's royal almanacs list her date of birth as 2 May 1778.[1] One Haitian tradition holds that she was born in Ouanaminthe near the border with Santo Domingo, but her family name appears nowhere in the parish's baptismal records, and in her will Marie-Louise herself states that she was born in Cap Français.[2] Her mother may have been a free black woman named Marie-Jeanne, whose daughter, Marie-Louise, was baptised on 19 July 1778, with the

---

[i] The alternate spelling of Coidavy (and occasionally Codary) is also used in some accounts.
[ii] Port-au-Prince was renamed Port Républicain in 1793.

57

free black Joseph Pevrette and free 'mulatress' Marie-Louise recorded as godparents.[3] The child was born outside wedlock so the father's name was not noted, but on 30 October 1783, when Marie-Louise was aged five, a Marie-Jeanne from Petite Anse just outside the city married Jacques Coidavid, a 44-year-old free black non-commissioned militia officer in Cap Français.[4] Two months later, Marie-Jeanne gave birth to Marie-Louise's brother, Noël Coidavid, whose godfather was Christophe's comrade Jean-Baptiste Belley. Two years later their sister Genevieve was born.[5]

Jacques Coidavid likely knew Christophe through the militia, and he would have taken part in the defence of the city alongside his future son-in-law and his son's godfather. Before the revolution he may have worked as an innkeeper (there is no evidence of any connection to Christophe's Couronne) and was wealthy enough to have owned more than one slave. In 1786 he pawned an enslaved twelve-year-old girl named Marie Therese Celine to a white merchant for 330 livres in forgiveness for a debt and 660 livres in cash.[6] An account of Christophe and Marie-Louise's marriage was recorded in the 1814 memoir by Praxelles, godmother to one of their daughters, which suggests that Christophe and his future father-in-law did not always enjoy good relations, although Praxelles mistakenly suggests that Jacques Coidavid died before the wedding:

> After the burning of the Cap, Christophe, now free, wanted to marry the woman who is today his wife. She is the daughter of a rich and highly esteemed free black who lived in the Cap in Petite Guinée in the neighbourhood of the Café de la Couronne. This father, named Codary, turned down Christophe, who only was able to take his wife after her father's death.[7]

In September, Christophe got his first taste of the political rights conferred by French citizenship by exercising his new-found right to vote. Three delegates from the colony were chosen to deliver the news of slavery's abolition to the National Convention in Paris. The group's composition was highly symbolic: a white Frenchman named Louis Dufay, the mixed-race Jean-Baptiste Mills born in Saint-Domingue and Jean-Baptiste Belley, the survivor of the Middle Passage from Senegal. The men were welcomed into the National Convention to generous applause. Dufay recounted the failed white counter-revolution and how the armies of the enslaved had rescued the colony at its darkest moment. Belley followed with an even more rousing speech:

> I was a slave during my childhood. Thirty-six years have passed since I became free through my own labour, and purchased myself. Since then, in the course of my life, I have felt worthy of being French ... it is the tricolor flag that has called us to our liberty.[8]

When a deputy proposed a vote on the abolition of slavery across France and all its territories, it was immediately agreed on. As the French Revolution entered its most radical phase, the power of the colonial lobbyists of the Club Massiac appeared on the wane. Sonthonax had been an early supporter of abolition, but his emancipation proclamation had been as much an act of expediency as principle. He came to understand that the insurgent armies were the only force capable of defeating his white rivals, made up of slaves who had emancipated themselves by taking up arms. Through their actions, on 4 February 1794 (16 Pluviôse, Year 2, in the recently adopted republican calendar) they had forced France to abandon slavery throughout its entire empire.

In Saint-Domingue the formal recognition of this new reality was not initially playing out as Sonthonax had hoped. Most in the rebel armies had little reason to trust his declaration: they had not waited for liberty to be granted, and were supplied arms by the Spanish who had already promised to confirm their freedom. On the same August day of Sonthonax's first declaration another equally persuasive appeal was made by one of the rebel leaders, proclaiming that he was the sole guarantor of liberty:

> I am Toussaint Louverture, you have perhaps heard my name. You are aware, brothers, that I have undertaken vengeance, and that I want freedom and equality to reign in Saint-Domingue. I have been working since the beginning to bring it into existence so as to establish the happiness of us all.

It was an audacious pronouncement from the former coachman from Breda. He matched his refusal to treat with the French by launching a lightning military campaign, and quickly captured a series of key towns including Plaisance, guarding the mountain road between Cap Français and Port-au-Prince, and Petite Rivière in the heart of the fertile Artibonite Valley.[ii] In December he took the strategic port of Gonaïves. It was a measure of Louverture's charisma and tactical wit that many of these fell with barely a shot fired: the Gonaïves garrison simply invited him into the town and pledged him their arms.[9] As Louverture's star rose he began to separate himself from the other leading rebel leaders, Jean-François and Biassou, both of whom outranked him in the Spanish command. His forces clashed violently with Jean-François' troops and he accused Biassou of trying to sell women and children into slavery in the areas he controlled. The Spanish tried to broker a reconciliation conference between the three men, but the split proved irreparable.

The French republicans were put further on the back foot by the arrival of a new player bent on taking advantage of the colony's turmoil: the British army. The week after Belley was elected as a delegate to Paris, British troops landed in Môle Saint-Nicholas and Jérémie, the two ports that sat at the very tips of Saint-Domingue's northern and southern peninsulas. Saint-Domingue lay so close to Jamaica that it was too tempting for the British to ignore, in the belief that it would be an easy prize to pluck. The initial response to their arrival suggested this would be the case, and like Louverture they took the towns peacefully. The white planters of Jérémie and Môle Saint-Nicholas quickly switched their loyalties to the British crown, believing that British rule would mean the return of slavery. In this they had the full-throated support of Pierre Victor Malouet, an influential French baron and staunch supporter of the slave system, who had exiled himself in London after the fall of the French monarchy. Across the Caribbean, the British swiftly captured Martinique, Guadeloupe and St Lucia,[iii] and in February 1794 Malouet signed an accord with the British government on behalf of the colonies allowing a continuation of slavery in the occupied French Caribbean. Saint-Marc, the Artibonite Valley's port, fell to the British in the same month that Louverture captured Gonaïves, and in June 1794 the British captured Port-au-Prince. The colony was being carved up. In the north, no more than the immediate

---

[iii] Grenada, Christophe's island of birth, had been restored to Britain in 1783 as part of the Treaty of Paris that ended the American Revolutionary War.

areas around Cap Français, Fort Liberté and Port-de-Paix were securely under French republican control. Only in the south did the republic continue to hold large chunks of territory under the military leadership of André Rigaud in Les Cayes, who had won some success in wooing the rebel armies of the southern mountains over to the French side.

With the republic so firmly on the backfoot, troops in Cap Français were put to work helping to clear the wreckage of the burned-out city. The wooden houses of the Petite Guinée district were particularly badly damaged in the conflagration, and for Christophe, finding new accommodation for himself and the now-pregnant Marie-Louise would have been a priority. He did at least have the comfort of an improved status. After his service in the defence of the city he was promoted to captain and transferred to the 2nd Regiment of Grenadiers.[10] His commanding officer was Pierre-Michel, one of the leaders of the slave armies who had answered Sonthonax's desperate call, and who had been raised to the rank of lieutenant-colonel as a result.[11] Pierre-Michel's command was at Fort Belair near the city gates. Jacques Coidavid was also promoted to lieutenant-colonel of the artillery battalion and stationed at Fort Belair, raising the possibility that he, Christophe and Marie-Louise may have lodged together here for a period.[12] These promotions of black officers were common examples of the new colony that Sonthonax wanted to build. Supporting him was Saint-Domingue's new governor Etienne Laveaux, who had been quickly installed after Galbaud's fall. The former free coloured ranks were equally rewarded for their loyalty, and Laveaux and Sonthonax together put the city's entire military under the command of Jean-Louis Villatte, another Chasseur Volontaire veteran of Savannah.[13]

On 15 May 1794 Marie-Louise gave birth to a son whom they named François-Ferdinand. Christophe had been enslaved at birth, but his first child was born free with all the rights of French citizenship—rights that his father was taking up arms to defend.[14] That defence became much easier later that week when Toussaint Louverture took the decision to abandon Spain and join the republican side. Suggestions were beginning to circulate in the colony that France would make Sonthonax's freedom proclamations permanent. Louverture now accused Spain of wanting black people to continually fight each other until they could be reduced back to slavery. 'Let us unite together forever,' he wrote to Laveaux, 'And, forgetting the past, work from now on to crush our enemies and take vengeance against our perfidious neighbours.'[15] As Louverture pledged himself to the tricolour the towns he had held for his Spanish paymasters swiftly came back under French control. The following month Louverture was appointed as the military commander of the entire western province and ordered to mop up the last of the Spanish forces and then take the fight to the British.

When Louverture switched sides, he brought with him some 4,000 battle-hardened soldiers along with a new officer corps that would help reshape the future of Saint-Domingue. His two leading officers were Jean-Jacques Dessalines and Moyse. Both had once been enslaved and had close personal ties to Louverture. Moyse was his adopted nephew and was born on the same plantation in Breda. Dessalines' origins remain more clouded, but he was most likely born around 1758 on the Petit-Cormier plantation in Grande Rivière.[iv] This plantation was rented for a short period in 1779 by Louverture himself, during an unsuccessful attempt to become a coffee planter. The plantation lease came with eight slaves, one of whom was Dessalines.[16] Whatever personal history had passed between them, Dessalines joined Louverture's forces around October 1792 and had risen quickly in the leader's eyes through his military acumen.

Prior to the revolution Christophe had viewed his best chance of improving his position to be through membership of the Cap Français northern military officer class dominated by the mixed-race community. But now there was a different model for advancement. Louverture, Moyse and Dessalines had all been enslaved. Like Christophe, Louverture's father was born in Africa and transported to the Caribbean, and his son had freed himself through his own endeavours and was now on the cusp of becoming one of the most powerful men in the colony. Christophe remembered Ogé and

---

[iv] Dessalines had facial scars which some French observers suggested pejoratively were evidence of the 'savagery' of his birth on the African continent. Moyse was marked in a different way: he had lost an eye to a white planter.

Chavannes being broken on the wheel in 1791: Ogé had refused to countenance the thought of freeing his slaves to support his attempted uprising, preferring to put the interests of class above race. In comparison, Chavannes had argued that allying with the enslaved was the only way to win true political freedom. In this new free black officer class, and with the growing political career of Belley, Christophe could perhaps see how a new future might unfold. He was quick to tie his fortune to theirs.

Throughout the summer of 1794 republican forces were finally on the move. In the south, Rigaud pushed the British out of Leogane, a town guarding the approach to Port-au-Prince, and harried the redcoats almost back to the gates of Jérémie. Louverture took the campaign to Jean-François and Biassou and continued to capture towns along the northern mountain chain. In Europe, Spain suffered a series of battlefield defeats against France and sued for peace. In the resulting Treaty of Basel signed in June 1795, Spanish Santo Domingo was formally ceded to France. Cut off from their patrons, Jean-François and Biassou fled from Saint-Domingue. Biassou settled in Spanish Florida and Jean-François moved to Spain. Jean-François had tried to base himself in Havana, but again fell victim to colonial racial politics: the authorities refused to give the loyal Spanish general permission to stay, as they feared his presence would inspire Cuba's own enslaved population to rise up against their masters.

Christophe's unit under Pierre-Michel in Cap Français was now regularly serving under Louverture's command and carrying out operations across the north. He almost certainly took part in the October action that routed the Spanish from the towns of Saint-Michel and Saint-Raphaël, as well as the December campaign against Jean-François in which two columns led by Dessalines and Moyse routed him from his stronghold in Grande Rivière. The fighting was particularly heavy at Saint-Raphaël, where the defenders had dug themselves into a fortified position defended by artillery and a moat. Two cavalry charges were repulsed before a third finally overran the position. Both Louverture and Christophe were noted horsemen, but still their victory came at the loss of 200 men. On 4 November Laveaux visited Louverture in Dondon to commend him on a new round of army promotions. Christophe was promoted to major and mentioned alongside Dessalines and Moyse as an officer of note. Also promoted at the same time was Louis Desrouleaux, the Savannah veteran and son of the Kongo-born pastry chef, as well as the mixed-race officer Augustin Clerveaux from Marmelade, who was proving to be another highly capable leader.[17] In January 1795 Christophe was back in the field with Louverture in the Artibonite Valley fighting against the British. The preferred tactic was the hit-and-run ambush. After his troops had waited patiently for four days, a lightly defended supply column heading out from Saint-Marc presented a golden opportunity to strike. The republican forces captured seven heavily laden wagons and successfully repulsed a counter-attack, leaving more than sixty British troops dead at the scene. In a letter to Laveaux, Louverture singled out Christophe for his leadership in the fight.[18]

After their sweeping successes in 1793, the British positions in Saint-Domingue were now overextended and undersupplied of both food and men. The Artibonite Valley had been ravaged by fighting and drought, and actions like Christophe's ambush led to a severe food shortage among the British in Saint-Marc. Disease was also to be an important line of defence for the defenders of the revolution. Around a quarter of the 1,300 troops in the city were permanently hospitalised. The British were fighting to restore slavery in Saint-Domingue, but their ranks were constantly thinned by yellow fever and malaria, which were first brought to the colony in the bellies of the slave ships. Their position in Port-au-Prince was even worse. The city was regarded by many colonists as having an unhealthy atmosphere and had been captured when the tropical rains provided plenty of stagnant pools for disease-carrying mosquitoes to breed in. By the end of 1794 1,000 British soldiers had been buried in the city and barely a third were fit for active duty.[19] The longer the occupation went on, the higher the casualty list climbed. By the time the war was over, Britain's losses would range somewhere between 50,000 and 70,000 men, the overwhelming number of them to disease. The British politician Edmund Burke acidly noted that the army had been fighting to conquer a cemetery.[20]

For all its enemy's woes, the republican side was also perpetually short of materiel. Louverture's soldiers were accomplished, he told Laveaux, but were 'naked like earthworms', surviving on basic rations of plantains and saltfish. When he tried to arrange a raid on Saint-

Marc, Louverture complained that 'I am entirely short of ammunition, having spent it all on the various attacks against the enemy.' When a large shipment of gunpowder was finally sent to the field for another action, he wrote to Laveaux that 'it is as though I had been ill, and you are sending me the right cure for my disease'.[21]

Yet one of Louverture's greatest skills was the speed with which he could adapt to changing circumstances. In the early days of the revolution, he had learned guerrilla tactics from fighters who had been veterans of African wars before being captured and transported to the colony. They were masters of exploiting their familiarity with the terrain, using feints, ambushes and the unnerving sound of drums to unbalance an enemy who could rarely see them. Now Louverture demanded military training manuals to instil discipline into his troops and hone their musketry skills. This blend of African and European approaches created a motivated and highly flexible fighting force, able to travel rapidly over long distances in loose order and then quickly come together to carry out precise military actions. Late in 1797 a British officer travelling incognito in Cap Français watched Christophe and Moyse drill their troops, and was almost incredulous at the precision with which the manoeuvres were performed:

> At a whistle a whole brigade ran three or four hundred yards, then separating, threw themselves flat on the ground, changing to their backs or sides, keeping up a strong fire the whole of the time, till they were recalled; they then formed again, in an instant, into their wonted regularity. This single manoeuvre was executed with such facility and precision, as totally to prevent cavalry from charging them in bushy and hilly countries. Such complete subordination, such promptitude and dexterity, prevailed the whole time, as would have astonished any European soldier who had the smallest idea of their previous situation.[22]

The cohesion of the soldiers was further encouraged by a corps of officers who were promoted on merit as well as on their dedication to the revolution, and although the majority of Louverture's officers were black, he was keen to promote mixed-race and white officers under his command in the hope of creating a unified class that would provide future leadership for the colony.

However, not all those who had rebelled with Louverture were so trusting of his leadership. Just as he was able to exploit the experience that many of his troops had from fighting in African wars, others who had been subjected to the Middle Passage saw little reason to throw their lot in with the French just because their leading officers shared their skin colour. They wanted nothing more than to be able to live their own lives free from a colonial system that had stolen them from their homes. Maroon bands still hid themselves in the mountains, carrying out raids on towns and encouraging plantation workers to run away. Louverture worked hard to woo these fighters and had one notable success, persuading the influential maroon leader Sans Souci to come over to his side along with his lieutenant Petit Noël Prière. Sans Souci subsequently became one of Louverture's most loyal officers, but other maroon leaders refused to have any dealings with his army. Of these the most powerful was Macaya, who had fought with Louverture when he was allied with Spain. He had rejected earlier republican entreaties to join with them, declaring that he was the subject of three masters: 'The king of Congo, master of all the blacks; the King of France, who represents my father; and the king of Spain, who represents my mother.'[23] In truth, Macaya and the other maroons wished only to be subjects to themselves. They had been among the first to rise up in 1791, and their refusal to treat with the authorities even when slavery had been abolished raised questions that would continually trouble the revolutionary leadership long after Haiti had declared its independence from France.

Similar questions were being asked on the plantations. When Sonthonax abolished slavery he did not mean to completely destroy the economy that had built Saint-Domingue. Indeed, funds were even more desperately needed to rebuild after the destruction of the previous years. The newly free were required to remain on their plantations and work to grow the same sugar, coffee, cotton and indigo to send back to France that they had done when they were enslaved. The difference was that they were now to be paid, with one third of the produce given over to the workers and their share divided up according to their role and sex (women were to be paid two thirds of a man's wage, despite making up a higher proportion of the fieldworkers). After a year on their plantation they were allowed to apply to move to another location, but continued agricultural labour was all their new liberty offered them. Some workers were granted title to the gardens they had tended while enslaved, but there was no offer to redistribute land to the workers to turn them into self-sufficient smallholders.[24] It was small wonder that many workers continued to go maroon and to slip quietly away into the mountains.

Louverture used a mix of persuasion and threats to get workers to return to the fields, often deploying his soldiers to ensure that production would resume. He abhorred the 'laziness' of those who preferred to till privately for themselves rather than contribute to the colony's reconstruction, and regularly wrote to Laveaux that he was busy 'gathering the cultivators, the drivers, and the managers, exhorting them to love work, which is inseparable from liberty'.[25] This moralising was not always welcomed by the cultivators, who also noticed that while he was forcing them back to work he was also wooing white planters who had fled the colony to return and play their part in its reconstruction. Farmers often ended up working for the same people who had run the plantations when they had been enslaved. It was hardly surprising that from 1795 rumours started to spread that Louverture was planning a restoration of slavery. Local strikes became common as farmers pushed back against managers eager to reclaim their positions of superiority.

One of the most serious disturbances took place in February 1796 around Port-de-Paix in the northwest. Several whites were killed when farmers rose up in protest at the dismissal of their leader, a former militia commander named Etienne Datty, and the abuse they faced from white planters when they tried to sell their produce in town. Louverture sought out the rebels for a parley. During the meeting Datty pledged his support for Louverture, who he described as 'the father of all the blacks' who worked on their behalf, but told him straight that the promise of liberty had been betrayed and that the whites wanted to make them slaves again. Louverture's reply was equivocal: he sympathised with their situation and persuaded the men and women to return to their fields by reconfirming Datty as their local leader. But he also condemned them for their actions, saying that liberty brought its own responsibilities and the farmers had their part to play in showing how a colony freed from slavery could prosper. His pleas were only successful for a time. Once the spotlight of Louverture's charisma had moved on, the farmers were left in much the same position as before. Three months later, Datty's band rose up again and began to destroy their plantations. This time Louverture's sympathies with the farmers' plight only went so far, and he sent Dessalines and a body of 500 troops to force them back to work.

Louverture was a self-made man who believed in discipline and the nobility of labour. In a speech two years later he drew on the industriousness of bees to illustrate his idea of how the colony should be run: 'Assembled in a hive they constitute a republic: they all work, and each individual creature through its endeavours participates in the happiness of the collectivity, and they even chase away those members who withhold their labour, refusing to tolerate any idleness in their midst.'[26] Christophe would find much to admire in this model. He had also raised himself by his own wits, and quickly came to agree with his general that individual liberty must be subservient to the need to defend the freedoms of the new Saint-Domingue they were trying to build. The colony was still at war and Datty's mutiny had taken place not far from the front lines with the British army near Môle Saint-Nicholas: internal dissent could not be allowed.

A month after the attempted uprising in Port-de-Paix, the revolutionary order was faced with another internal threat, this time from a fellow officer. The free coloured community in Cap Français had begun to chafe under the new system, seeing themselves as being passed over for opportunities under Laveaux, who preferred to promote and reward the 'nouveaux libre' men who had recently been enslaved rather than those who had been free before the revolution and who enjoyed more status and wealth. Their leader was Jean-Louis Villatte, who for some time had been trying to enlarge his own power base. On more than one occasion he had successfully encouraged Louverture's troops to defect to his command, promising better pay and conditions than those offered by his rival, who kept his soldiers perpetually on campaign. On 20 March the discontent broke into violent action when Villatte's supporters stormed into the governor's house and arrested Laveaux. The coup leaders released a statement announcing that Laveaux had lost the support of the people and had been replaced by Villatte. Just one of Villatte's officers dissented and managed to get a message to Pierre-Michel at Fort Belair before he too was arrested. Pierre-Michel rushed a letter over the mountains to Louverture in Gonaïves, asking for military support. In the meantime, he ordered Christophe to lead a body of troops into the city to demand the release of Laveaux. Villatte had perhaps expected more time in which to consolidate his position, but Pierre-Michel's swift actions quickly blunted the coup. There was no direct fighting between Christophe's men and Villatte's, but the threat of his troops and the news that Louverture's army would soon be marching on the city clearly shook Villatte. After a day and a half in custody the governor was released into Christophe's care and taken under protection to Fort Belair.[27] When Louverture finally arrived in Cap Français several days later, Villatte had fled along with 600 of his men and Laveaux was restored to his office.

At a public ceremony to celebrate the defeat of the short-lived coup, Laveaux feted Louverture as the saviour of the colony from its enemies within and without. For the governor, his general was 'the black Spartacus, the leader announced by the philosopher Raynal to avenge the crimes perpetrated against his race'.[28] Louverture was equally flattering of Laveaux, whom he frequently addressed as his father in his letters, but the statement was still an astonishing one. Less than five years since the Bois-Caïman uprising, the former slave was being described by France's highest official in Saint-Domingue as the ultimate guarantor of the colony's survival. In one pamphlet written by a white supporter of Laveaux soon after the coup attempt, a contrast was drawn between the former slaves who had broken their shackles and now defended the republic and the people of colour who had behaved treacherously against France.[29] In truth, Villatte had many supporters among the recently enslaved and Louverture had several mixed-race officers serving under him, but the introduction of this racial element immediately muddied the complicated politics of revolutionary Saint-Domingue. Once expressed it was hard to put back in the box, and it quickly became an easy proxy to describe the battles yet to come over control of the revolution. Some twenty-three years after the event, Baron de Vastey attempted to rewrite history in his *Essay on the Causes of the Revolution and Civil Wars of Hayti* by lumping together the white republican supporters of Louverture and the 'coloured' party as enemies of the revolution, who showed the general 'the basest flattery' while plotting 'fresh contrivances for his destruction'.[30] In Vastey's eyes, only the black officers were capable of being truly loyal. Christophe was one of those whose loyalty was rewarded. For his actions in defending Laveaux he was promoted to the rank of colonel and given command of his own troops at Petite Anse, guarding the eastern flank of Cap Français and the surrounding northern plain.[31]

It was a very different Saint-Domingue that Sonthonax returned to in May 1796. He and Polverel had been recalled to Paris to account for their actions after general emancipation had been declared. For nearly two years, the European war meant that France had paid scant attention to the colony, but now he came back as part of a new civil commission to put affairs more firmly under the direction of the metropole. When Sonthonax had departed Saint-Domingue in 1794, Louverture had only just abandoned Spain in favour of the French and the two men had never met. It was immediately clear that there would be a struggle between them for political power. Despite the pledges of brotherly love and a belief in racial equality, the highly educated Sonthonax could not stop himself from patronising Louverture. He was suspicious of Louverture's commitment to republicanism, partly on the basis of his strong Catholic faith and partly on an innate belief that Africans could only imagine being ruled by a king (in 1793 he had written that a crown 'can be understood by the most stupid of Africans; even the most sophisticated of them cannot conceive of the idea of a republic').[32] Where Laveaux had been happy to trust Louverture's well-proven military acumen, Sonthonax now insisted on interfering in military affairs despite having no army experience. In the north he saw conspiracies where none existed and even attempted to order the arrest of Pierre-Michel who had held the line against Villatte, while in the south he alienated General Rigaud who he suspected of encouraging the very same coup.[33]

The opportunity for Louverture to restore what he deemed to be a more appropriate balance of power came a few months later when elections were organised to send new representatives to France. Both Laveaux and Sonthonax were persuaded to stand. Louverture believed that Laveaux would be a passionate defender of Saint-

Domingue, while Sonthonax likely decided that he would better serve the revolutionary gains he had helped give birth to from Paris. Despite the tension between him and Louverture, he was happy to accept the general's help in getting himself elected.

The assistance that Louverture lent was not subtle. The elections were held in Cap Français, where Pierre-Michel broke local ordonnances by riding through the city with a large body of armed horsemen to ensure that its citizens knew who held the balance of power. Christophe nominated himself as chief elector of Petite Anse, attending the electoral meeting with so many soldiers in tow that they outnumbered those citizens who had a right to vote. His intimidating tactics went as far as instructing voters who they should cast their ballot for. A subsequent complaint to the electoral commission was ignored. At another meeting it was alleged that former slaves who were ineligible to vote were given ballots with the names of 'their fathers', Sonthonax and Laveaux, already written in.[34]

After helping Louverture ensure the election of his preferred candidates, Christophe was back in the field to mop up the last resistance being offered by the general's former comrades. The region of Grande Rivière in the mountains south of Cap Français was still home to maroons who had pledged loyalty to Jean-François, who had spent the last year raiding the northern plain. It was rumoured that they had opened relations with the British, who were supplying them with arms. In February 1797 four columns marched against them in a plan drawn up by Colonel Charles Vincent, a sharp-minded French military engineer who Louverture had put in charge of the rebuilding of Cap Français, and who had quickly become close to the black military leadership. After a short campaign, the last of Jean-François' men were beaten at Vallière. Christophe was commended for his leadership in the action.[35] For the first time since 1791 it could be reported back to Paris that the north enjoyed 'the most perfect and established tranquillity'.[36] Two months later British-controlled Mirebalais finally fell to the republicans. Louverture was rewarded by being made commander-in-chief of the entire Saint-Domingue army. Sonthonax was finally encouraged to leave the colony after lingering for nearly a year after his election. On the cusp of Christophe's thirtieth birthday, Saint-Domingue was almost entirely under free black French control, with only the last British outposts left to deal with.

5

TOUSSAINT LOUVERTURE SUPREME

The first known image of Henry Christophe was published by Captain Marcus Rainsford in his 1805 book *An Historical Account of the Black Empire of Hayti*. Rainsford met Christophe in unfortunate circumstances in early 1798 when his ship was forced to shelter from a storm at Fort Liberté. The Anglo-Irish Rainsford was absent without leave from his regiment and had been in Cap Français masquerading as an American while surreptitiously sketching the city's defences. He was searched on disembarking and arrested as a spy. Christophe was summoned to oversee his trial, which was pictured in one of the book's engravings. Rainsford appears in chains, flanked by two black soldiers, while being questioned: 'General Christophe, a relative of Toussaint, being in a neighbouring district, presided, and Muro [Moyse] sat on his right-hand. They interrogated [me] with the utmost discrimination and acuteness, appearing perfectly conversant with the nature of the business.' Christophe's sharp mind was noted: 'Not a look nor an attitude escaped him—and he darted his eye, in which both seemed to have centered [sic] an uncommon degree of fire, over every part of the prisoner, the form of whose very head-dress, he insisted, was not an Americain [sic]!' In the engraving, Christophe points accusingly at Rainsford's papers on the table while Moyse raises a finger in question and a secretary transcribes Rainsford's answers. Not knowing better, the engraver dressed Christophe and Moyse in the uniforms of the British West Indian regiments with Christophe in a round hat topped with a cockade and showing the white facings of his unbuttoned lapels.[1]

While their likenesses are clearly imagined, both Christophe and Moyse are portrayed in a commanding and respectful manner. This seems surprising given that Christophe ordered Rainsford to be put to death for his crimes, only for the sentence to be reduced to deportation after the judgement was sent to Toussaint Louverture for approval. In fact, after returning to England Rainsford became a vocal supporter of the revolutionaries. His book (which also included a handsome full-length portrait of Louverture) was published as a show of support for Haiti's newly proclaimed independence. Any resentment against Christophe was outweighed by respect for his abilities: ten years later Rainsford was acting as a lobbyist for the Kingdom of Haiti and was awarded an honorary rank in its army.[2]

That Louverture could offer clemency to an enemy officer reflected his increasing superiority on the battlefield. Rainsford arrived in Saint-Domingue with the last British reinforcements. The army was perpetually short of manpower and supplies, and by 1798 the British held little more than the towns they had captured during their first flush of success five years earlier. In March that year Christophe was on campaign against them around Arcahaie, north of Port-au-Prince. Although he sustained heavy losses against the British cavalry after engaging them on the flat, he successfully encouraged 300 of their black soldiers to defect to his side. All of them had been enslaved.[3] By the end of April the British commander General Maitland approached Louverture to sue for peace. On 8 May Port-au-Prince was handed over to the republicans and in August Maitland signed a formal treaty of withdrawal with Louverture. At a meeting between the two in Môle Saint-Nicholas, days before the last active British soldiers left Saint-Domingue for good, Louverture was toasted at a feast held in his honour and gifted the silver tableware that had graced the banquet. The new French agent Gabriel Hédouville, who had arrived in the colony five months earlier, was not invited: the British knew who held the real power. A secret treaty signed the following year between Maitland and Louverture formalised trade between British Jamaica and Saint-Domingue, even allowing for the import of arms.[4] Although trade policy was strictly a matter for London and Paris, Louverture's victories had persuaded him that building an independent power base was the surest way to defend the gains of the revolution.

More British gifts were sent in January during a final exchange of prisoners. In Cap Français Christophe was gifted porter, rum and ham in recognition of his own standing in the city. Still officially command-ing at Petite Anse, he was now living in a comfortable townhouse in the centre of the city on Rue Dauphine just off the Place d'Armes, on a plot that had been rebuilt after the fire of June 1793.[5] It was five blocks from the old site of the Couronne inn and large enough to accommodate his growing family. On 9 May 1798 the five-year-old Ferdinand Christophe was joined by a sister who was christened Françoise-Améthyste.[i] The Christophe family was prospering.[6]

Despite the speed with which Christophe had helped Louverture bundle Sonthonax out of the colony, he owed much of his new prosperity to the man he once cheered in Cap Français after the proclamation of emancipation. Years of war had left many planta-tions abandoned. Despite Louverture's attempts to woo back absen-tee white planters, more than 210 sugar plantations were left untended in the north alone. To restore them to production Sonthonax had offered their leases for sale. Many were snapped up by the new black officer class, who under Louverture's tutelage were already experienced in encouraging farm workers back to the land. The new tenants began to amass the wealth that once had been the preserve of the white colonists, even allowing for the share of profits paid to their labourers. As rents flowed back into the colo-ny's treasury, the senior officers benefitted further from the money that could now be spent on the army.[7] Few records have survived, but by 1800 Louverture was known to have leased twenty-three plantations and owned a further eight.[8] One French officer who knew Dessalines personally claimed that he had taken thirty-two plantations for himself, while Moyse was estimated to have an annual income of 1.2 million livres.[9] As commanding officer at Cap Français, Christophe was also well placed to ensure that every pos-sible profit was squeezed from the export trade. In February 1799, Louverture wrote to him to approve of the way he ensured that foreign merchants were made to buy their coffee in specie while imports were paid for in sugar, ensuring that gold and silver remained in the colony.[10] Hugh Cathcart, sent to Saint-Domingue

---

[i] In naming her, the Christophes were perhaps paying unwitting tribute to the figure of Princess Améthyste, a former pupil at the Cap Français convent who in the earliest months of the 1791 uprising had led Vodou rituals to encourage resistance against the colonists.

by Maitland as trade representative, got to know Christophe well and wrote that 'he is now supposed to have amassed a fortune of two millions of livres of this colony, very near two hundred and fifty thousand dollars'.[11]

Even accounting for exaggeration, the sums are considerable and many white colonists were open in their resentment towards this new prosperous black class. For Jacques Périès, a white clerk working in the Cap Français treasury, the worst of all the officers was Christophe, whose new-found wealth allowed him to live 'like a sybarite ... no black man ever carried sensuality so far'.[12] The French naturalist Michel Etienne Descourtilz, seemingly unaware of the old sumptuary laws that forbade free blacks to dress in the same manner as whites, was horrified to see black officers powdering their hair and wearing garish cravats and gold jewellery—sights made worse for him against the backdrop of the war-ravaged city which was still 'buried under the debris of looting and of devastation'. After being 'badly received' by Christophe when attempting to present his official business, Descourtilz huffed that this gaudy officer was the 'enemy of my colour'.[13]

One of the most resentful figures was the new French agent. Hédouville did everything he could to undermine Louverture and those who surrounded him. He blocked army promotions and attempted to ban officers from directly leasing plantations. He spoke of his desire to reduce the number of enlisted men as well as their rations, claiming that the soldiers sold their bread and preferred cheaper cassava instead.[14] On a more fundamental level, Hédouville was deeply suspicious of Louverture's rapprochement with the British. He believed that the revolution should be exported to Jamaica instead of trade being increased between the two colonies and was dismayed by Louverture's policy of giving amnesties to white planters who once had supported the British.

On arriving in the colony, Hédouville had been told by one French officer that 'with [Louverture], you can do everything; without him, nothing'.[15] In October 1798, after just six months in the colony, Hédouville was to discover just how sage that advice had been. In a bold attempt to clip the army's wings, he ordered the removal of Moyse from his command at Fort Liberté. While Moyse was absent from the city he sent a force of nearly 3,000 mostly

European soldiers to disarm his 5th Regiment. Moyse's men refused to stand down, even after being threatened with cannons loaded with grapeshot. In the bloody fight that followed, over 200 black soldiers were killed. When news spread of the killings, local cultivators rose as one and began to set fire to their plantations, fearful that the French were intent on returning them to slavery.[16]

Hédouville had severely overreached himself. He ordered Louverture to suppress the revolt but the general demurred, and after taking control of Fort Liberté he told the cultivators to march on Cap Français instead. Ten thousand of them were soon camped outside the city gates, waiting for Louverture to arrive to 'restore' order, which he did by ordering his men to take control of the city's key military posts. Dessalines took control of Haut-du-Cap, and as commander at Petite Anse, Christophe would have ensured that Hédouville was pinned down from the east. Anxious to avoid confrontation the citizens of Cap Français hastily demanded that Hédouville and his supporters should leave the colony immediately for having encouraged the anarchy around Fort Liberté. The agent and nearly 2,000 white soldiers and officials soon sailed for France. By mobilising the army and the people, Louverture had strengthened his grip on power. He quickly chose as his own agent the loyal and pliable Philippe-Rose Roume, a white creole who like Christophe originally hailed from Grenada.[17] For his part in the affair, Christophe was named Chef de brigade in charge of the Cap Français district, with a supervisory role over the area around Fort Liberté.[18]

Although Hédouville had been forced to flee in shame, his attempt to reduce Louverture's power had found one key supporter: General André Rigaud. Like Louverture, Rigaud had successfully fought the British and deflected attempts to place himself under direct French political control when Sonthonax was agent. He answered to Louverture as commander-in-chief, but since the middle of the 1790s had effectively turned Saint-Domingue's southern peninsula into his own personal fiefdom, centred on his home city of Les Cayes. The two of them had an uneasy relationship. Louverture suspected that Rigaud had played a part in encouraging Villatte's coup in 1796, while Rigaud feared that the rise of Louverture's officer class threatened the interests of the mixed-race merchants who had been free before the revolution and saw themselves as the natural inheritors of white political power. Hédouville exploited the fears of both men. Before departing the colony, he launched a public broadside against Louverture, claiming that his true goal was either independence or to sell the colony to the British. He further threw 'the apple of discord between these two chieftains' by writing privately to Rigaud to release him from Louverture's chain of command, encouraging him to take full administrative control of the south.[19]

Tensions between the rivals grew throughout 1799. On 18 June, just four days after Louverture had signed his secret treaty with the British at Arcahaie, Rigaud sent 4,000 men into the southern town of Petit-Goâve to depose its Louverture loyalist commander. Two days later Grand-Goâve fell under his control. In response, Louverture replaced the commander of Port-au-Prince with his brother-in-law Paul, while Roume ordered southern cultivators to rise up against Rigaud. The War of Knives had begun. 'The tri-colour standard was seen to wave in both armies; each fought for and in the name of the French Republic. What then was the source of this civil war? What its necessity? Who its author?' wrote Baron de Vastey in his *Essay on the Causes of the Revolution and Civil Wars of Hayti*.[20] The after-effects of this conflict were still playing out when Vastey took up his quill some twenty years after its conclusion. The complicated divisions of the time were explained away as a simple racial conflict, with Vastey blaming the 'generals of colour' who were easily manipulated by the whites. He neglected to mention that within a month of Rigaud's seizure of Petit-Goâve war had erupted all over the colony and many black officers like Pierre-Michel chose to take up arms against Louverture.[ii]

One of the first places to rise up in the north was Môle Saint-Nicholas. Louverture wrote to Christophe on 15 July from Port-au-Prince, ordering him to take action against the 'apostles' of Rigaud who he feared might be operating in Cap Français:

> The Eastern district [around Fort Liberté] must also be the object
> of your attention in such critical times; you know how restless the

---

[ii] Likewise, Colonel Paul Romain, the mixed-race officer who had been entrusted by Hédouville with relieving Moyse of his command at Fort Liberté, sided with Louverture and later became a key supporter of Christophe after Haitian independence.

inhabitants of this part of the colony are; form camps to protect the area ... and bring down armed cultivators from the mountains if you believe you will need them.

He urged Christophe to show his opponents no mercy, ordering him to put to death those suspected of encouraging the uprising: 'I am counting more than ever on your unflappable severity; let nothing escape your vigilance.'[21]

In a letter written the following week about unrest at Héricourt, southwest of Cap Français, Louverture showed the closeness of the two men by advising Christophe simply to do as he would himself.[22] Dessalines was even more vehement in his assessment of Rigaud's partisans in a letter to Christophe. To him they were existential enemies, 'unworthy of pardon; national vengeance must be brought to bear upon them, and all good citizens must unite to stop them carrying out their destructive schemes'.[23]

After Moyse and Clerveaux had pacified Môle Saint-Nicholas, preparations were made for a full-scale invasion of the south. Edward Stevens, the American trade representative in Cap Français, estimated that the force Louverture assembled was 55,000 strong. It was comprised of two columns: one led by Dessalines (newly promoted by Roume to commander of the army of the West) and the other by Christophe. Moyse, who had been named commander of the army of the North, remained in Cap Français to defend the north. Stevens regretted the decision, as Christophe had become a respected administrator in the city:

I could rather have wished that this change had not taken place. 'Tho' [Moyse] is a man of energy and decision, and I have always been upon the best terms with him; yet I think he wants the coolness and good sense of [Christophe], from whom I have been long accustomed to obtain everything I wished.[24]

Louverture's decision to send Christophe on campaign was recognition that while Moyse was the fiercer battlefield commander, Christophe's mind was more keenly attuned to logistics—a result perhaps of taking his education through the patrons of the Couronne inn rather than in the fields. Hugh Cathcart was in accordance with this view: '[He] appears to possess fully as much influence and power, as either Dessalines or Moyse ... he is equally as ambitious, and far superior to either of them in abilities, knowledge of the world (if I may be allowed to use the expression) and in his resources.' Cathcart gave some indication of these resources when he reported back to Maitland:

> He brought with him from the Cape, one hundred and fifty caval-rymen, fifty of whom were dressed as hussars, and 2000 infantry, by far the best dressed of Toussaint's troops (they went by the name of Colonel Christophe's Army). He also brought with him provisions and ammunition, sufficient for three months, and 1,800 doubloons (in gold) to pay them, in a brig named the *Rebecca*, that he has freighted from Doctor Stevens. The cargo consisted of five hundred barrels of flour and one hundred barrels of pork, besides clothing, one brass 12 pounder and one brass 16 pounder, and two hundred balls for each, with ammunitions. He told me that he has not troubled Toussaint for any of the above articles, but has fur-nished them at his own expense.[25]

Christophe also commandeered three English ships docked at Port-au-Prince to bring further supplies from Gonaïves. When one of the captains objected, Christophe had him beaten, prompting Cathcart to complain to Louverture. Christophe was unrepentant. It was a trifling matter he said, and the captain should count himself lucky: 'Had the master been a Frenchman and had conducted himself in such a manner, he would have ordered him shot. He seemed much surprised that I should have viewed the business in such a serious light, as to have complained to Toussaint of his conduct.'[26]

The northern army mustered in Leogane at the end of September. Its first objective was the southeastern coffee port of Jacmel, where the commander Louis Jacques Bauvais had attempted to declare neutrality. For Louverture, controlling the town was essential to avoid being outflanked as he moved on Les Cayes. When Christophe and Dessalines were ordered to lay siege to the town, Bauvais fled on a ship bound for the Danish island of Saint Thomas, leaving the garrison in charge of a 23-year-old Rigaud loyalist named Birot.[27]

Jacmel sat on a wide bay surrounded by a grand amphitheatre of hills. Birot energetically put the town's population to work digging trenches around a series of fortified blockhouses guarding the main approaches. Christophe set up camp at the Ogé plantation 3 kilometres north of the city, with Dessalines' troops on the town's western edge. By November, Jacmel was invested by almost 20,000 men, but Birot rejected Dessalines' offer of amnesty to all who surrendered.[28] The defenders' morale received an early boost when an attempt by Christophe to clear out nearby Marigot ended in a rout. Birot had left just 200 men in Marigot, which was squeezed into a narrow strip between the sea and steep wooded hills. With no easy approach, the troops of Christophe's 1st and 2nd demi-brigades were repeatedly beaten back, and then caught by a counter-attack that allowed Marigot's defenders to punch through the northern line and reach safety in Jacmel. The town's defenders claimed that Christophe lost 400 men in the action.[29]

This early setback put a hold on future offensive actions until more cannons and mortars could be brought down from Port-au-Prince. Knowing that no siege could be successful unless Jacmel's supply lines from the sea were cut, Louverture planned a naval blockade of the port. To do this he turned to the US trade representative Stevens. The two men had a good rapport, and Stevens had been a legal witness to Louverture's secret treaty with the British. The request could not have been better timed: the USA was in the middle of a 'quasi-war' with France and direct trade with Paris had been banned. Trade with Saint-Domingue was a handy workaround for US President John Adams, and the USA quietly followed Britain in recognising Louverture's power as being discrete from France. As US policy was invested in Louverture personally, the general had no hesitation in asking US ships to help blockade Jacmel. If Stevens initially hesitated, his support for Louverture was confirmed when his own ship was attacked near Port-au-Prince by a frigate flying Rigaud's colours. Soon enough, three US navy ships were cruising off Jacmel, with one even joining in the bombardment of the town—probably the first instance of the USA intervening militarily in a foreign territory.[30]

The blockade could not have come soon enough for the northern army. A full-frontal night assault led by Louverture himself was beaten back by Birot's troops. In the bloody melee, Christophe narrowly avoided being slashed with a bayonet, and such was the defenders' vigour that even Dessalines proclaimed, 'what wonders

81

wouldn't I do, if I had these brave men in my ranks!'[31] The battle of 5 January 1800 would be the last direct attack on Jacmel. As Christophe and Dessalines regrouped they knew they could afford to be patient. The same could not be said for those they were facing. While the siege guns slowly worked on Jacmel's defences, the blockade meant that its people were further reduced by food shortages. By the end of January every dog, cat and rat that could be caught was eaten. In recognition of the desperate situation Birot proposed an honourable surrender, but his garrison shouted him down. In response Birot stole out of the city in the dead of night, becoming Jacmel's second commander to abandon his post. Rigaud tried twice to relieve the town. When a column of 500 men proved woefully inadequate, he sent one of his most trusted officers, Alexandre Pétion, with just two companies of soldiers in rowing boats to slip past the naval blockade and reinvigorate the defence. The new troops were welcomed but the city residents were horrified to learn that Pétion had only brought with him a few barrels of manioc flour. By the time he arrived people were reduced to eating grass and boiled leather to stave off famine.[32]

Pétion quickly realised that his mission was an impossible one. After six weeks in which Dessalines and Christophe only became bolder in testing the impoverished garrison, he took the drastic measure of expelling part of the civilian population to relieve the pressure on his supplies. An unrecorded number of women 'consumed by hunger, with children given life at their exhausted breasts' were sent towards Christophe's lines. In the only detailed account of the siege left to us, by the historian Thomas Madiou, they walked straight into a barrage of gunfire. Those who survived were rounded up and marched to Christophe's tent, where he reportedly threw bread and biscuits at their feet and laughed as they scrambled pitifully for crumbs. His cruelty satisfied, the women and children were thrown into a well and a fire set at its mouth to suffocate them.[33] It remains impossible to know exactly what took place. Madiou wrote his history in the middle of the 1840s in full knowledge of the rivalry that would subsequently unfold between Christophe and Pétion, and found himself firmly on the latter's side. But while both men were still living, Pétion's supporters frequently used the siege of Jacmel to defame Christophe. The newspaper editor and former secretary to Pétion, Jules Solime Milscent, wrote a pamphlet accusing Christophe ('a tiger with the face of a man') of not just killing 500 people in the well but personally running a sword through a pregnant woman.[34] The events were raw enough that a century later the celebrated Jacmelliene poet Alcibiade Pommayrac made the killings of the women and children a central part of his poem remembering the siege.[35]

The killings were the final straw for the Jacmel garrison. On the night of 12 March Pétion led out the town's remaining inhabitants in a desperate bid to flee. Two cannons opened fire on Christophe's lines to create a diversionary attack while the column picked its way along the banks of the Jacmel River. When Christophe realised what was happening his troops were quick in pursuit. Pétion's column lost all its order as it climbed into the cover of the mountains, and his men were picked off one by one until they were beyond the range of the muskets. In the official report that followed it was claimed that Pétion only escaped by abandoning his men, while the civilians were left wandering dazed in the woods to be found days later with nothing but wild sour oranges for food.[36] When Dessalines marched into Jacmel the following morning it had been reduced to a ghostly shell. Christophe refused to join the final scene of triumph. He was angry that Pétion had escaped and proclaimed that the city should be razed to the ground for all it had cost them after months of siege.[37]

When Pétion straggled into Grand-Goâve he had just 800 men with him—fewer than half of those who had broken out of Jacmel. He found only temporary respite. After securing the southeast, Dessalines marched across the mountains to attack the town. Again Christophe's 1st demi-brigade was in the vanguard, and this time the northern army prevailed swiftly. Pétion abandoned Grand-Goâve and ordered the town to be put to the torch, leaving his enemies to conquer its ashes. Pétit-Goâve fell soon after, followed by Miragoâne, whose bridge guarded the road to Les Cayes. As the northern army rolled forward, Rigaud's supporters melted away. Rigaud appeared to believe until the last moment that Hédouville would send French troops to support him, but in June a new proclamation arrived from France reconfirming Louverture's position as the head of Saint-Domingue's army. It was signed by Napoleon Bonaparte, who had seized power in Paris in the 18 Brumaire coup the previous November. Louverture immediately announced a general amnesty for all those who had opposed him, and the last of Rigaud's power collapsed. Louverture marched into Les Cayes on 14 July unopposed. Rigaud, Pétion and the senior southern command made their way clandestinely to Tiburon on the farthest western tip of the southern peninsula and boarded ships to Saint Thomas and Curaçao, from where they sailed to France to nurse their resentments.[38]

Christophe was not present for the entry into Les Cayes. When Rigaud's forces collapsed soon after the capture of Grand-Goâve, his troops were ordered back to the north. He arrived in Cap Français to find a very heavily pregnant Marie-Louise. Their second daughter, Anne-Athénaïre, was born in the house on Rue Dauphine on 7 July. With Belley in France and unable to stand as godfather, they chose a mixed-race friend from Petite Anse named Vilton, whose sister was married to one of Christophe's aides-de-camp.[39] There were also changes on the city's political front. While Christophe had been on campaign, Louverture had decided that the French agent Roume was behaving in too independent a manner. Moyse was charged with organising northern cultivators to again camp outside the gates of Cap Français to demand that only Louverture could truly represent them. Inside the city, Joseph Bunel, who served as Louverture's treasurer and envoy to the USA, went door to door with his wife Marie to get signatures on a petition demanding Roume's removal. The Bunels were close friends of the Christophes, and whether or not Marie-Louise joined the protests herself, she was likely one of the women who supported them by embroidering Louverture's name in gold thread on banners that were paraded through the streets.[40] At one stage, Moyse went as far as imprisoning Roume. It was dramatic political theatre, and when Louverture duly arrived in the city to be welcomed as its saviour, he magnanimously pardoned Roume for any perceived misdemeanours. Suitably chastened by this demonstration of power (and placed under effective house arrest in case the lesson be forgotten), Roume was ready to endorse whatever policies Louverture put before him.

The first of these was to lend political cover for Louverture's plans to unify the island of Hispaniola under his rule. Spanish Santo Domingo had been ceded to France in 1795, but there had been few practical moves to integrate the colony. Slavery still existed across the border and Spanish troops occasionally mounted cross-border raids to kidnap people to work on their plantations. In January 1801 Louverture led Moyse's troops to bring the colony under republican rule and finally abolish slavery across the entire island. It is possible that Christophe may have originally been involved in the planning of the campaign: the previous May, Louverture wrote to him to say that he was going to send him on an important mission to Santo Domingo and that he would discuss it with him in person. Unfortunately, no further paper trail has survived, and in the end the only known support that Christophe gave to the campaign was to provide a number of artillery pieces from Cap Français to Louverture's army.[41]

With Rigaud vanquished, Roume tamed and Santo Domingo under his rule, plus his excellent personal relations with the British and Americans, Louverture's rule was undisputed. Born on a sugar plantation to enslaved parents, he had risen to become one of the most powerful and capable leaders in the entire French empire. This final consolidation of power was celebrated with the new ranks he awarded his key officers: on 12 February Dessalines and Moyse were given the ceremonial ranks of Divisional Generals of the west and north, while Christophe was promoted to Brigadier General, retaining his special role in command of Cap Français and the surrounding districts. According to the account of one sympathetic French general who knew Christophe, he was 'so modest that his friends had to beg him to apply for the rank', but Louverture was more confident in his officer and commended him for his particular role in defending the city against the internal threats carried by Rigaud's partisans. The events of Jacmel went unmentioned.[42]

Even before the conquest of Santo Domingo Louverture had begun to plan for Saint-Domingue's future. As always, the plantation was at the heart of his plans. In October 1800 he issued a strict decree that would govern the way that the plantations were to be run under his rule, effectively putting them under martial law. Workers were banned from leaving their plantations and ordered to obey their managers as if they were under military command. Vagrancy was to be severely punished and the army made responsible not just for administering discipline but also for the productivity of the plantations. Along with their new military promotions, Dessalines and Moyse were also made Inspectors of Agriculture—military enforcers of plantation labour.[43] In a later decree, Louverture banned the sale of small plots of land for private cultivation lest they draw labour away from the sugar and coffee plantations, and attempted to bring in an internal identity card that reminded many of the pass once issued by masters that was used to allow their slaves to travel to markets.[44] 'If I made my people work it was for them to understand the price of liberty without license, it was to prevent the corruption of morals,' Louverture would record later, 'It was for the general happiness of the island, and in the interest of the republic.'[45] It was an outlook that greatly appealed to Christophe, and in later years when drawing up his own set of laws to govern Haiti he was profoundly influenced by the disciplined morality of Louverture's agricultural programme. As part of the officer class who had become substantial landowners thanks to Louverture, he was of course also heavily invested personally in its success.

In February 1801 Louverture announced plans to consolidate his power further with a proposal for a new constitution for the colony. The move was in response to Bonaparte's seizure of power as French consul. Bonaparte's letter to Louverture confirming his rank included promises that the liberty and equality of all citizens in Saint-Domingue were to be inviolate, but he also produced a new constitution that had potentially serious consequences for the colony. It stated that the colonies had different 'habits and customs' compared to France and so should be governed by ill-defined 'particular laws'. The announcement was recognition that the political winds in France were blowing in a new and troublesome direction. The First Consul was no radical: his wife Josephine came from a wealthy planter's family in Martinique and Bonaparte himself was sympathetic to the exiles who stalked Paris complaining about the loss of their slaves. That Louverture chose 4 February to announce the formation of his own constitutional assembly was no accident: it was the anniversary of France's official abolition of slavery: a policy that he had helped to win on the battlefield. But the assembly also reflected Louverture's economic programme for the colony. Most of the members were white planters who were supporters of his strict agricultural policies. The veteran campaigner Julien Raimond was one of three mixed-race members. Only one black representative was chosen, Louverture's own nephew Moyse, but he refused to take his seat in protest at the prominence given to white representatives of what he saw as the pre-revolutionary order.[46]

Saint-Domingue's new constitution was unveiled at a public ceremony in Cap Français in July. Christophe, Moyse and the rest of the black officer class watched their commander preside over a ceremony where the white planter from Port-au-Prince (and father of an imprisoned Rigaud loyalist), Bernard Borgella, read the entire constitution to the gathered crowd, after which it was blessed by Corneille Brelle, a Breton priest who had become Louverture's personal confessor. 'There can be no slaves in this territory; servitude is permanently abolished. All men are born, live and die free and French', Borgella announced. All men were equal before the law irrespective of their colour and were free to pursue any form of employment according to their virtue and talent.[47] As a declaration of racial egalitarianism it was unmatched by any existing comparable constitution of the time. There was to be a strict class hierarchy however, as the constitution entrenched the plantation workers' place in the colony's 'family', labouring in the fields. At the very top sat Louverture, who was proclaimed Saint-Domingue's governor-for-life, with the power to nominate his successor. He had taken Bonaparte's declaration that the colonies should be subject to special laws and subverted it to his own interest, confirming Saint-Domingue as an inalienable part of the French empire but granting himself the right to pass laws without any reference to Paris.[48]

One of Christophe's confidantes, the military engineer Charles Vincent, was entrusted to carry the new constitution to Paris for approval. Vincent was highly sceptical of the document and told Louverture that he feared the constitution would be seen as a manifesto against France. Before he sailed from Cap Français he left Christophe an unsealed letter further outlining his objections, and urged his friend to use his 'usual sagacity' to suggest to Louverture that he moderate his principles. In reply, Christophe reportedly told Vincent that he was 'the only European who really loves the people of Saint-Domingue. You have always told us the truth. The draft constitution was written by our most dangerous enemies.'[49] If Christophe truly shared Vincent's concerns it is unclear whether he ever passed them on to Louverture, but in September of that year, Roume, now banished to Philadelphia, attempted to stir the pot by writing to the French government suggesting that Christophe might prove himself a leader more loyal to France than the new governor-for-life.[50] In his *Essay on the Causes of the Revolution and Civil Wars of Hayti*, Baron de Vastey clearly articulated Christophe's position in hindsight by distancing himself from any French sympathies he may have once held and pinning the blame firmly on Louverture's white counsellors:

> They suggested to him the formation of a Constitution which should render Hayti nearly independent of France; which he should have done completely or not at all; for such a measure admitted of no medium: it was necessary to be either *dependent* or *independent*, the one or the other; and Gen. Toussaint, by rendering himself partially independent of France, exposed himself to her vengeance, without giving himself the means of resisting her.[51]
> [italics in original]

While Louverture was waiting for Bonaparte's reply he had to face down one final challenge to his authority. In October he was in Saint-Marc to attend Dessalines' wedding to Marie-Claire Heureuse when he received news that the north had erupted in revolt. Cultivators in Marmelade, Dondon, L'Acul and Grande Rivière had risen up against the harsh agricultural system, and in Limbe chains had been displayed as apparent evidence that Louverture intended to bring back slavery. On 21 October alarms were sounded across Cap Français. The American consul Tobias Lear wrote that its citizens were 'tremblingly alive to every symptom of insurrection'. Lear was reassured by Christophe, who told him that the sound of shooting was due to 'the want of discipline in some of the Corps' after rounding up idle labourers who were hiding in the city from their plantation managers. 'There is no serious cause to apprehend any disturbance', he reassured the consul.[52] In fact, Christophe had just uncovered a conspiracy to overthrow his command. A group of men and women, 'tumultously assembled', had gathered near the wharf and fought back against efforts to disperse them. Christophe seized the leader, a man called Trois Balles, who revealed the plot and gave up the names of his co-conspirators. Throughout the night Christophe's men arrested seventy further plotters. 'The whole of this was performed with so little noise and confusion,' wrote Louverture in his report on the affair, that thanks to 'the prudence and activity of General Christophe ... calm was quickly restored to Cap Français.'[53]

The following day was indeed calm, but on the morning of 23 October Lear was again with Christophe when 'an alarm took place in the City which spread dismay over every countenance. A cry of *shut your doors* ran like electricity through the streets—and terror spread in every quarter [italics in original].' Christophe reacted with 'utmost coolness' and left to investigate.[54] Riding out with his dragoons he realised the plantations were again in revolt. People were streaming towards the city speaking of attacks against whites just as they had in August 1791. This time, however, the cultivators were badly organised and fled before the disciplined charges of Christophe's troops. At Port Margot and Limbe he successfully ordered them back to the fields; when he returned to Limbe later to find them attempting to take up arms again he had the town commander arrested for sedition. From here he wrote to Louverture to inform him of events. Louverture was already rushing north to Marmelade and sent Dessalines, fresh from his wedding, to help quell the trouble. Christophe continued his work on the northern plain, where his men rapidly restored order. The violence of the attempted revolt was quickly suppressed, but only after more than 350 people—mostly white men, women and children—had been killed. Most shocking for Louverture, however, was the discovery that the figure behind the uprising had been none other than his own nephew Moyse.[55]

Moyse had been appalled by the direction of Louverture's plans for the colony. As agricultural inspector, he was known to be particularly lenient towards workers and had been a supporter of granting small plots of land to soldiers as smallholdings. For him, Louverture's interests were increasingly aligned with those who had reigned over the plantations before the revolution. 'It is always in the name of the interests of the metropole that [Louverture] scolds me', he said, underlining where his sympathies lay by stating 'I will love the whites only when they have given me back the eye they took from me in battle.'[56] For Moyse the only way to defend black freedom was to expel them from the colony altogether, abolish the plantations and proclaim complete independence from France. He laid his blame equally at the feet of Christophe and Dessalines for helping to uphold Louverture's system of penal agriculture.[57]

When Moyse was summoned to meet with his uncle and commanding officer he found him in no mood for leniency. He was arrested and taken to Port-de-Paix where he was tried and sentenced to death. As a final sign of defiance, when the firing squad was lined up before him Moyse refused a blindfold and personally ordered the men to open fire. In Cap Français, Louverture's fury at this personal betrayal was made public. Several officers, including the Limbe commander arrested by Christophe, were blown from the cannons in front of the entire city garrison to show the fate of those who dared to question his system. In an angry speech he expanded the list of would-be traitors to vagrants, cultivators who sought to escape the plantations, idlers and libertines who sapped the moral fibre of the colony. Army officers who tolerated such behaviour would be punished; any that encouraged treason were to be summarily executed.[58]

Dessalines was put to work rooting out those who had taken part in the failed uprising. Several hundred soldiers and farmers were killed in these reprisals, which were deliberately bloody to drive home the message that dissent would not be tolerated. Christophe's role in this operation has not been recorded, but he most likely remained in Cap Français to ensure the smooth running and security of the city. He had performed well in the crucial hour, and for his role in quashing the rebellion he was given Moyse's old position as the highest ranking general in the north.[59] Whatever doubts he may have privately entertained about Louverture's new constitution, he had proved his loyalty to his commanding officer and his political system. That system allowed Louverture to nominate his successor as governor-for-life, and with the execution of Moyse there were now only two possible men who could stand as candidates: Jean-Jacques Dessalines and Henry Christophe.

6

INVASION

Charles Vincent reached Paris in October 1801, just as the last of the Moyse uprising was being put down. Christophe and Louverture would be celebrated in the French newspapers for their actions, but Napoleon Bonaparte was in no mood to learn of Saint-Domingue's new constitution. For six months he had been debating what to do with the colony. His initial lauding of Louverture was replaced with deep suspicion after the unauthorised conquest of Santo Domingo. As the words of the colonial lobby dripped into his ears, he decided that the black general needed to be put in his place. Plans for a military expedition were prepared and then given new impetus in the summer of 1801 when London offered a peace deal to end the long war between Britain and France. With the British blockade of French ports ended, it was finally possible for a fleet to sail for Saint-Domingue.

An army of 21,000 soldiers was assembled to embark from the Atlantic port of Brest, many of them veterans of the wars that France had fought almost continually since 1793. To lead the largest military expedition of his career Bonaparte chose his own brother-in-law, General Charles Victoire Emmanuel Leclerc, who had served with him in his Italian campaigns and was married to his sister Pauline. She was to accompany the expedition too. As stories of Saint-Domingue's wealth were still common currency, many French officers signed up with the hope that they might claim a plantation as spoils of war and return home as 'rich as a creole'.

Vincent warned Bonaparte that Saint-Domingue could not be conquered militarily, reminding him that its climate was 'destructive' to European soldiers and that Louverture had already seen off

the British and Spanish.[1] To counter this Bonaparte hoped to use
stratagem as well as force. Leclerc was to make assurances that
France would 'never place irons on those she has recognised as free'
and offer Louverture and his command retirement with full military
honours—provided they leave the colony.[2] Louverture's Paris-
educated sons, Isaac and Placide, accompanied the expedition to
offer their father assurances of France's peaceful intentions, which
they received during a private audience with Bonaparte himself.
Only if Louverture offered resistance would the military fist then be
unleashed. After what Bonaparte still hoped would be a swift victory, all black officers above the rank of captain were then to be
deported, allowing for a new start for the colony. Keen to be part
of this project were André Rigaud and Alexandre Pétion, who
eagerly signed up for the expedition.[3]

Other orders were left unwritten. Bonaparte almost certainly
planned a return to slavery in the colony. As well as dispatching his
armada to Saint-Domingue, forces were also sent to Martinique and
Guadeloupe, where slavery was to be restored. Only a year earlier
Bonaparte appeared reconciled to black freedom. 'They will produce less sugar, maybe, than they did as slaves,' he said, 'but they
will produce it for us and will serve us, if we need them, as soldiers.
We will have one less sugar mill; but we will have one more citadel
filled with soldiers.'[4] Now, threatened by Louverture's ambition,
he set his face in the opposite direction.

Rumours of a French fleet began to circulate in Saint-Domingue
the moment news arrived of the peace between Britain and France.
Louverture was forced to call for calm. It was inconceivable, he
said, that France could attack a colony that he had led back to prosperity. Yet he too nursed his own suspicions and reminded his followers that France 'does not have the right to enslave us, our freedom does not belong to her. It is our right, and we will know how
to defend it, or else perish.'[5] Orders were issued not to allow any
French ships to land without his express permission.

The French armada was spotted off the eastern tip of Santo
Domingo at the end of January 1802. On spying the size of the fleet,
Louverture's worst fears were confirmed. 'We must perish,' he is
reported to have said, 'all of France has come to Saint-Domingue.'[6]
The number of ships was even greater than he realised, as Leclerc

had already split his forces to send squadrons to simultaneously seize all the major ports. As Cap Français was the biggest prize of all, it was here that Leclerc directed his own ships.

Christophe had been busy preparing the city for their arrival. As his troops drilled, he ordered the streets swept clean and lamps lit to show how life was prospering under his rule. Theatres were packed for nightly performances, and every Sunday Christophe hosted dinners for the city's most distinguished citizens at the governor's palace.[7] When he learned that the fleet had been spotted and would arrive the following day, he declared that nothing would give him more pleasure than to receive the French 'in their own home'.[8]

To set the terms of that welcome Christophe had ordered the removal of the buoys marking the safe passage through the reefs that guarded the harbour. When the French fleet arrived, it was met with two warning cannon shots from Fort Picolet, the main fort of Cap Français. To Leclerc's dismay he was reduced to anchoring at distance and sending an envoy to Christophe demanding his ships be allowed to land, along with a copy of Bonaparte's message to Saint-Domingue.

The proclamation began with the assurance that the colony's inhabitants, 'whatever your origin or colour', were all French and free, and that now peace reigned in Europe the mother country was finally able to send troops to protect its colonies. 'Should any one whisper in your ear, "These forces are destined to despoil you of your liberty;" answer, "it is the Republic that has given us liberty; the Republic will never suffer it to be ravished from us"', it continued. Leclerc brought peace and security, but there was a sting in Bonaparte's words. Anyone who defied him would be 'a traitor to his country, and the wrath of the Republic shall devour him as fire devours your parched sugar canes'.[9]

Leclerc's accompanying letter to Christophe was no less emphatic:

> I learn with indignation, Citizen General, that you refuse to receive the French squadron, and the French army that I command, under the pretext that you have received no orders from the Governor-General [Louverture]. France has concluded a peace with England, and its government sends to Saint-Domingue forces capable of subduing the rebels; at least if any are to be found. As to you, General, I confess it will grieve me to account you among them.

Leclerc ordered Christophe to immediately surrender his command and held him responsible for the consequences should be refuse.[10]

Christophe snorted at the suggestion:

> You say that the French Government has sent to Saint-Domingue forces capable of subduing the rebels, if any such be found; it is your coming, and the hostile intentions you manifest, that alone could create them among a peaceable people, in perfect submission to France. The very mention of rebellion is an argument for our resistance.

He reiterated that he could only act on Louverture's orders, and referred to Leclerc's troops as 'so many pieces of cards which the least breath of wind will dissipate'.[11] To stall for time, Christophe rushed an urgent letter to Louverture, asking him to come to Cap Français as soon as possible.[12]

Christophe's rebuff dismayed the city's ruling council. A delegation led by the black mayor César Télémaque petitioned him to change his mind. Knowing the risk that Christophe had been ordered to burn the city rather than hand it over, they reminded him of the conflagration of 1793 when Christophe himself had fought so hard to defend the city against the flames. 'You speak like a planter,' he told Télémaque, 'I can place no confidence in you.'[13] A delegation of American merchants led by the US consul Tobias Lear was simply told to board up their houses for safety.[14]

Leclerc's reluctance to force a landing bought Christophe an extra day, but with Louverture absent and news arriving that the French had captured Fort Liberté under fire, Christophe realised that action was needed.[15] The city police were replaced by soldiers under his command. Women, children and the infirm were ordered to leave the city for their safety. Marie-Louise joined the procession with Ferdinand, Améthyste and Athénaïre, who was still a toddler. Christophe saw that the family's prize possessions were loaded onto carts. The treasury and other strategic buildings were emptied, and Christophe's officer Barrada oversaw the distribution of torches and inflammable material.

As the city held its breath, Leclerc seized his moment. He ordered a landing at L'Acul to surprise Christophe from the rear, but the only local pilot he could find deliberately misdirected the fleet, delaying its landing by several hours. This was all that Christophe needed. When the city had been razed after white counter-revolutionaries had tried to seize it, it had helped usher in the emancipation proclamation. Now the stakes were even higher, the fire would be a deliberate act of sabotage. Louverture had cautioned that destruction and fire were the best weapons against invasion. As the sun began to dip, Christophe gathered his men in front of the warehouses along the waterfront and ordered a torch. Within minutes orange flames were licking up into the darkening sky. Soldiers across the city followed their commander's lead. Government offices were fired, as were the barracks and the now empty arsenal. The church was not spared, nor was Christophe's own house.[i] As the inferno spread, some citizens tried to protect the hospital, but were beaten back by the flames. Others who had ignored the order to leave now scrambled up the mountain overlooking the city. A few people, including Tobias Lear, managed to slip into boats and row towards the French ships. The men who received them could only watch as the dark waters of the bay reflected back the growing inferno and the explosions from the forts as their magazines exploded one by one.

As the French troops that had landed at L'Acul approached Cap Français the following day, the city was still ablaze. It would take three days to extinguish the last of the fires. For now, control of the city was still contested. It was into this scene that Louverture finally arrived, meeting Christophe by the shell of the main hospital. Christophe was forthright in defending his actions in reducing the city to smoke and ashes: 'What do you expect, General? My duty, necessity, circumstances, and the repeated threats made by the general commanding the squadron forced me to do so.' Of course, Louverture was relieved that Christophe had followed his orders to the letter, but in a memoir he wrote to Bonaparte the following year he sought to exonerate himself and reflect the blame back onto his subordinate for his 'rigorous method' of defending the city.[16]

The imminent arrival of the French left little time for a conference. Louverture ordered Christophe to retreat with his soldiers to

---

[i] A popular Haitian tradition (albeit one unmentioned by the official report into the destruction) holds that the signal to burn the city was given by Christophe setting fire to his own house.

Bonnet-à-l'Evêque, an easily defensible spot folded into the mountains 16 kilometres south of Cap Français. The heavily wooded slopes here were pocked with limestone caves that were now pressed into use as bases for guerrilla war. Marie-Louise and the children were sent to safety at Grand Rivière while the Cap Français treasury was stashed in the deep caves of Dondon, guarded not just by their inaccessibility but also by the symbolic petroglyphs carved into the cave walls by the region's original Taíno inhabitants.[17] Getting there was a close-run thing: soon after Christophe took his leave from Louverture, his troops had their first encounter with French troops. There was a scrappy melee and Christophe's horse took a musket ball, forcing him to dismount and swim the river at Haut-du-Cap in order to escape.[18]

It took time for Leclerc to fully land all his troops in the ruins of Cap Français, by which time Louverture had issued orders to adopt a scorched earth policy. All of Saint-Domingue's towns must burn to slow the French and buy time until 'the rainy season that will rid us of our enemies'.[19] He also hoped to raise the cultivators on the plantations to bolster his forces, but in many places was surprised when the farmers reacted with cynicism. 'When we took up arms with Moyse against the whites, didn't the governor exterminate us?' they asked, 'Why doesn't he resuscitate Moyse, if he wants to fight the whites!'[20] Christophe, despite having played a key role in suppressing that uprising had more luck, perhaps through having shown his commitment to rebellion by his act of arson. For a week he criss-crossed the plantations to raise the cultivators, urging them to ignore the amnesty that Leclerc was now offering and to join his 2,000-strong core of well-trained soldiers.

It took a week for Leclerc to fully organise his forces. Although Port-de-Paix in the northwest had also been burned rather than surrendering, Leclerc's generals had successfully taken the rest of Saint-Domingue's port towns and he now plotted his moves to enact Bonaparte's orders as quickly as he could. Three divisions would set out from Cap Français, Fort Liberté and Port-de-Paix to create a cordon across the north, hoping to flush the enemy out of the mountains. At the same time, a fourth division would march up from Port-au-Prince to trap the rebels in a pincer movement. On 17 February Louverture and Christophe were formally declared outlaws from the laws of the colony and the French forces finally began to move into the field.

The central prong of the northern attack was led by General Jean Hardy, who was charged with bringing Christophe to heel. Some of Hardy's troops had surprised Louverture on the outskirts of Cap Français the day after landing and almost shot him before he managed to flee, an event that filled the general with confidence that this would be a short-lived campaign. Within a day he was able to test this proposition when he engaged Christophe in his first action. Christophe was entrenched with his troops at Bois-le-Pin, a peak that guarded the eastern approaches to the town of Marmelade. 'They had a red flag flying and sent back the words "War to the Death!" when we offered to treat with them', wrote one French officer. But it appears that Christophe allowed himself to be surprised by the attack, and after offering 'serious resistance' he decided to protect his forces by withdrawing, leaving his food stores to be captured.[21]

Christophe moved west towards Ennery, where Louverture kept his plantation, but again he was chased from his positions by the French and lost men and supplies.[22] Louverture was likewise put under pressure. At Ravine-à-Couleuvres, he attempted to fight the first pitched battle against the French on his own terms. With 3,000 troops, he blocked a narrow valley that was an important passage through the mountains and sent decoys to tempt in the French column led by General Rochambeau. The trap worked, and his grenadiers rained fire down on the French before the engagement devolved into desperate hand-to-hand combat. Louverture eventually withdrew and both sides claimed victory in the fight, though his side had taken many casualties. It was clear that a new approach was needed before his forces began to melt away or surrender to Leclerc.[23]

The plan he devised was simple. Dessalines still held his forces at full strength and was ordered to lure the French into battle at an easily defensible site, acting as an anvil to break their main strength. When exhausted, the French would be attacked at their rear by Louverture and Christophe's reconstituted forces. What European troops remained could then be easily pinned back to the coast.

The location that Louverture picked for this battle was Fort Crête-à-Pierrot, built by the British where the Artibonite Valley began to rise into the mountains. It sat on a narrow hilltop, with a steep escarpment looking down on one side to the Artibonite River and the town of Petite Rivière. On the remaining sides, a wide field of fire gave the defenders a strong advantage against troops attacking uphill, while trenches dug outside the walls strengthened the defenders' position even further. With some 1,200 soldiers garrisoned inside the fort, Dessalines waited for the French wave to break upon his position.[24]

He did not have to wait long. Leclerc believed that a victory here would quickly pave the way for complete military control of Saint-Domingue. Several French divisions were soon converging on Crête-à-Pierrot led by General Jean Boudet, who had followed the bait from Saint-Marc which Dessalines had left in ashes like Cap Français. Joining Boudet from Port-au-Prince was Alexandre Pétion, who now commanded the artillery of the 13th demi-brigade. Two years after he fled the disastrous siege of Jacmel, he was no doubt eager to take the fight back to his opponent.

The first assault on the fort was a disaster. The French officer Pamphile de Lacroix, who took part in the siege, recorded how local plantation workers guided the advancing troops through the terrain in order to make a surprise night attack, not suspecting that they were being led into a trap. When they spied a number of their enemy apparently asleep outside the walls of the fort above them, Lacroix's soldiers charged. The dozing soldiers immediately took cover in hidden trenches, and the whole of the fort seemed to burst into a great volley of fire. Exposed on the hill in bright moonlight, the French fell in their dozens. When they had regrouped, a second assault met with the same fate and left one general with two musket wounds. Dessalines then exposed his assailants a third time by ordering his troops to fix their bayonets and feint a counter-attack, luring his enemies back into the field of fire. When the battle was concluded, several hundred French soldiers were dead.[25]

The battle turned into a siege, and Louverture's plan that it would suck in more and more French troops began to bear fruit. Two more French divisions arrived as reinforcements, but Crête-à-Pierrot's superb position made it easy to defend. On such poor terrain, Pétion's artillery proved ineffectual. For three weeks Dessalines stood firm. 'Take courage,' he exhorted his troops, 'The

French cannot hold out against us here in Saint-Domingue. They will fight well at first, but soon they will fall sick and die like flies.' He warned them that the road ahead would not necessarily take a straight path: 'Listen well! If Dessalines surrenders to them a hundred times, he will betray them a hundred times.' Only then would they prevail against the French, who would be forced to take to their ships and flee. 'Then,' declared Dessalines, for the first time making explicit the endpoint that the revolution had been inexorably heading towards, 'I will make you independent. There will be no more whites among us.'[26]

While Crête-à-Pierrot was besieged, Louverture ordered Christophe to regroup at Grand Rivière, where their wives were quartered. When the first rumours of the French armada had begun to circulate, the two generals had turned the area into a sizeable munitions dump. From here, Christophe set out on the offensive again. He ranged across the northern plain, urging cultivators to burn whatever cane fields were still under production. He raided the towns of Terrier Rouge, Trou du Nord and Limonade, while at Sainte-Suzanne the former maroon officer Sans Souci repulsed a French counter-attack, capturing many white soldiers in return. Christophe wrote to Louverture, praising the bravery of his soldiers who had just flushed the French out of Quartier Morin and Petite Anse, both barely outside the city limits of Cap Français itself.[27] A week later he even managed to place an artillery piece on a hill outside the city and put it under fire for the first time since the arrival of Leclerc's fleet, before abandoning the camp in a running battle.[28]

The clash was reported by Tobias Lear, who ended his letter by noting rumours that Dessalines had been forced to abandon Crête-à-Pierrot. His tone suggested that the French had easily carried the day, but it soon became apparent that the victory had been pyrrhic. Christophe, who had been privy to the original strategy, was much clearer about the outcome, writing to Louverture that his soldiers had cheered to learn how 'those who were inspired by the powerful zeal of liberty had so thoroughly humbled their enemies'.[29]

Christophe was further invigorated after an unexpected encounter at Dondon. General Hardy had been one of those sent to Crête-à-Pierrot, and now his column was retiring in a 'hellish' routine of 'fatigue and deprivation' to Cap Français, harassed by ambushes all the way from the Artibonite Valley.[30] His troops were completely unprepared when they chanced by accident on Christophe's base in the heat of the afternoon. The column broke instantly as the rebels came out of the rough woodland to pursue the French at bayonet point. 'With a handful of men in the gorges and defiles of Dondon,' Christophe cheered later, 'we defeated, dispersed and cut to pieces the troops of Hardy's division.' By the time the shattered Hardy reached Cap Français, he had lost almost 400 men.[31]

By the beginning of April, a military stalemate had settled on the colony. The French had been bled white at Crête-à-Pierrot, and it was quickly becoming clear that beyond the towns and cities they could barely control any territory that lay beyond musket range. For Louverture, his forces could roam with increasing freedom in the countryside, but losses on their own side meant that attacks on French positions were becoming harder to sustain. Troop ships continued to arrive at Cap Français and Port-au-Prince, and some of his commanders had already surrendered. Christophe's commander, Paul Romain, summed up the situation: his troops had burned their way across the northern plain but had still failed to make any significant breakthroughs against the French.[32] It was vital that the revolt survive until the rainy season began, when tropical fever would return a vital weapon to their armoury.

At the start of April, Louverture opened a secret correspondence with the French general Boudet, who had been wounded at Crête-à-Pierrot. He proudly defended both the military decisions he had taken since the arrival of the Leclerc expedition and his record as governor-general in restoring order to the colony. Affirming his dedication to France, he suggested that his own retirement from the politics of Saint-Domingue had been long planned once his task of fully restoring agriculture had been completed. While Louverture openly advised Boudet of his mistrust of Leclerc, he made it clear that there was room for a political settlement to the war.[33]

The letter was bait. Louverture had written to the general from Christophe's mountain camp at Dondon, and it is likely that he consulted with his most trusted lieutenant when opening the channel to Boudet. With no clear military solution on the table, negotiations with the French would buy them time to plan for a longer campaign. If so, the lure worked. Less than a week later, Christophe received an approach of his own from the French. It was written by his daughter's godfather, Vilton, at Petite Anse. Within days, Hardy and Leclerc were also writing to Christophe, sparking an extraordinary set of correspondence that gives one of the best insights into the political thinking of the revolutionaries that has survived.[34]

Vilton's first letter of 16 April played on the 'ancient friendship' between the two men and expressed regret that Christophe, who had once shown such 'devotion to the French nation' had pursued a course of action that had plunged him and his family into the most frightful misery. Passing over the bloodshed of the previous months as if it were a modest disagreement over a hand of cards, Vilton felt sure that Christophe's actions were purely the result of 'evil counsels'. He told Christophe that Leclerc held a high opinion of him, and he offered a clean slate to all who came back to the French side. By doing so, Vilton pressed his old friend, 'you will secure for yourself and family every happiness that you can desire; especially if you should desire to quit the colony ... you will be certain of a liberal fortune, and may enjoy it peaceably, under the protection of France, in the country of your choice'.[35]

The letter was followed by a note directly from Leclerc, assuring Christophe everything that Vilton had said was true. 'I will keep the promises which have been made you,' wrote the general, 'but, if it is your intention to submit to the Republic, think on the essential service you could render her by furnishing the means to secure the person of General Toussaint.'[36]

Christophe answered Vilton the following day. There was none of the affable tone of old friends, rather an acknowledgement that their relationship allowed Christophe the luxury of speaking frankly. He described himself as 'a Frenchman, loving and respecting France', who hoped to have his 'confidence in the government of the mother country fostered and confirmed from day to day'. It was Leclerc who had betrayed that confidence:

Saint-Domingue, wholly French, enjoyed, as you know, the profoundest tranquillity; there were no rebels to be found: by what fatal blindness, then, did it happen, that France has come with all the terrors of war and the artillery of destruction? Not to subdue the rebels (for rebels there were none), but to create them amongst a peaceable people, and furnish a pretext to destroy or enslave them.[37]

Slavery was the word that Leclerc dared not yet speak aloud, but Christophe understood that it was at the heart of the enterprise. He had seen the letters written by colonists hoping that France would return Saint-Domingue's people to bondage, and the actions of the French army had only proved their point. His honour—his one true possession—had compelled him to take actions for which he would not apologise:

> What happiness, what fortune, what splendid establishment, of myself and my family, could ever have offered me consolation for the grief of seeing my fellows reduced to the last degree of misfortune beneath the burthen of slavery? ... My sentiments have never varied; I have always been the same man. But, placed as I was, by my fellow citizens, as a sentinel at the post where it was my duty to watch over the preservation of liberty, more dear to them than their existence, how could I do otherwise than alarm them at the approach of the blow aimed at its annihilation?

For all his defiance, Christophe was careful to leave a door open to the French. He suggested to Vilton that there was 'no sacrifice that I will not make for the peace and happiness of my fellow citizens, if I am but convinced that they shall all be free and happy'. If these assurances could be given, he would gladly return to the fold and help restore tranquillity to the colony.

General Hardy now took up the correspondence. Their recent clashes had taught him to respect his opponent, and he addressed Christophe with the 'frankness of a soldier, unacquainted with shifts and evasions'. The two of them were equals rather than rivals, both fighting to defend the liberty proclaimed by France. He urged Christophe to abandon the 'crafty men' who had poisoned his thinking, and hoped they would soon 'embrace as brothers'. With this in mind he offered Christophe a parley, assuring him that should negotiations fail he would be free to return to his camp unhindered.[38]

'The candour with which you address me is worthy, in all respects, of a soldier like yourself', Christophe replied. If only Leclerc had spoken to him in such a manner 'instead of proposing to me an act of treason and infamy, which would degrade me in my own eyes', he would happily have taken up Hardy's offer. In response to Hardy's defence of revolutionary liberty, Christophe countered that Saint-Domingue's freedoms had been 'bought at the price of our blood' and forced France to act. Invoking the French constitution of 1799 and the accompanying declaration that the liberty and equality of the newly freed would always be preserved, he urged Hardy to read up on his law. Only these guarantees could convince him that France's intentions were benign. Furnish these proofs to the people of the colony who 'water and fertilize it with their sweat', Christophe proposed, 'and our interview will be crowned with the happiest success'.[39] He would return to the French camp and Louverture would gladly do the same.

In a separate letter to Leclerc, Christophe said that it would be perfidy to help the general arrange Louverture's surrender: 'He is my commander, and my friend. Is friendship, Citizen General, compatible with such monstrous baseness?' But everything would change if Leclerc could show him the printed laws that still guaranteed freedom: 'In the name of my country, in the name of the mother country, I call for these salutary laws. Produce them, and Saint-Domingue is saved.' He and Louverture would lay down their arms and come in as equals rather than supplicants.[40]

Leclerc grabbed at the opportunity. 'The uneasiness you testify to me is of a nature easy to be removed', he replied. He gave his oath that those who had been slaves would remain forever free, but asked Christophe to wait a little longer for the written proof: 'That code is not completed: I am engaged upon it at this moment.' But he invited Christophe to a parley, offering the same assurances as Hardy that should they fail to come to an agreement, Christophe would be at liberty to return to his troops: 'If you come, and we understand each other, the war will have lasted so much shorter time in the colony. If not, calculate my means and your chances of successful resistance.'[41]

Christophe remained in contact with Louverture throughout this correspondence and sent copies to his commander along with his replies. On the day he received Leclerc's offer he wrote to Louverture for his opinion. Due to the highly sensitive nature of their plans, he sent his dispatch via one of his most trusted officers to receive Louverture's response verbally. He was accompanied by an armourer named Roy to help with the manufacture of bullets: even while negotiations were ongoing, maintaining their fighting capability remained of vital importance. In the same letter Christophe also confirmed receipt of a package that he would send on to Paul Louverture, the general's captured brother-in-law who had been the commander in charge of Santo Domingo when Leclerc's fleet had arrived, and who was now under house arrest in Cap Français. That Louverture had remained in contact with him through this period suggests further layers to his plotting. 'On this matter, I will fulfil your intentions and recommendations precisely', Christophe coolly noted.[42]

The exact nature of Louverture's response remains unrecorded, but the next day Christophe delivered Leclerc the reply he had hoped to hear. He wrote that he was reassured by the general's words, which '[revived] in my mind the hope of seeing tranquillity, peace, and prosperity, returned to this too-long agitated colony, under the auspices of liberty and equality'. The following day he would meet with Leclerc at Haut-du-Cap. If all went well, not only would he lay down his arms, but Louverture would also happily 'throw himself into the arms of the Republic'.[43]

For Leclerc, the news could not have been more welcome. Although he had threatened Christophe with the consequences of continued rebellion, he knew his army was in poor shape. The same day he had drafted a letter to the governor of Cuba about the terrible conditions in Saint-Domingue, urgently requesting that he send hundreds of mules and horses for the French army. Now he could instead write a proclamation announcing that the war was over, and reiterate that all citizens were equal in the eyes of the law regardless of their skin colour.[44]

At 11 o'clock on 26 April Christophe came down from his mountain camp to Haut-du-Cap to conclude the peace deal. The bridge here was the symbolic frontier post between the French-held city and a countryside under de facto rebel control. At a brisk ceremony, Christophe formally submitted to Leclerc and had his rank in the French army reconfirmed. With him were 1,200 soldiers who were allowed to remain under his command, and a further 2,000 armed cultivators who were ordered to return to their plantations.[45]

Two days after Christophe surrendered, he received his first orders from the French command. Leclerc sent him to Limbe on the road to Port-au-Prince. Here he was instructed to take the surrender of a commander named Lafleur who had refused to come over to the French without receiving personal reassurances from Christophe. Leclerc was so pleased at the leadership that Christophe showed in the mission that he ordered Limbe to be reoccupied not by French soldiers but troops reporting directly to Christophe.[46]

Leclerc was sufficiently encouraged by Christophe's compliance that he quietly absolved him of all responsibility for burning Cap Français. The officer Barrada, who had helped Christophe prepare the torches, was formally scapegoated for setting the city ablaze, along with a black member of the colony's ruling council called Annecy. Both were deported in irons to the Mediterranean island of Elba.[47] Christophe's outlaw status was formally rescinded, along with Louverture's to encourage him to surrender. Leclerc also cancelled a planned appropriation of Christophe's plantations. As his house in Cap Français was reduced to charred bricks and beams, Christophe appears to have brought Marie-Louise and their children down from the hills to settle back in Petite Anse.[48]

Louverture chose to wait a few days before making his theatrical submission. Christophe's aide-de-camp, Colonel Robillard, continually ferried messages between the two of them, keeping Louverture apprised of developments in the French camp. On the same day that Lafleur laid down his arms, Louverture wrote to Christophe to underscore the need to stick to their common strategy. For the first time on paper he went as far as alluding to a major offensive against the French that would come when they had recovered their strength.[49]

Louverture arrived on the outskirts of Cap Français on 6 May, accompanied by a heavily armed honour guard. His meeting with Leclerc was testy; Louverture's men never once let their hands drop from their weapons. But he was appeased by Leclerc's attempts to make peace and offered his own olive branch to the French. Claiming ill health from months in the field he begged leave to retire to his plantation at Ennery and withdraw from political life.[50]

The peace was concluded at a dinner the following night. Louverture was guest of honour alongside Christophe and Dessalines, who had also surrendered. Amid a fraught atmosphere, Louverture refused all Leclerc's hospitality except for a piece of cheese from which he carefully shaved the sides with a knife, all but accusing his host of trying to poison him. On the opposite side of the table was Alexandre Pétion, now an unlikely comrade under French orders, along with one of Pétion's officers, Jean-Pierre Boyer. Unwittingly, Leclerc had gathered alongside Louverture the four men who would collectively rule Haiti for its first four decades of independence. If there was a moment to carry out Bonaparte's orders to immediately deport the most senior rebel officers from the colony, this was it. Instead, the evening passed in a sombre mood, and it was some relief to the French general when Louverture departed the following morning for Ennery.[51]

Christophe and Dessalines were still required for active service. Not all the rebels had decided to surrender, including Sans Souci. Leclerc was confident that his new officers would take the lead in bringing them to his side so that he could finally enact Bonaparte's orders for the colony. He wrote to the First Consul, advising him that he was relying on them as it was becoming increasingly difficult to field his European troops, and confidently reassured Bonaparte that not only was Christophe thoroughly loyal, but he had now thoroughly 'mastered' the spirit of Dessalines as well.[52]

This might have been bravado on Leclerc's part, but it was necessary for him to believe it. The rainy season had arrived and the half-burned ruins of Cap Français offered even more potential breeding sites for mosquitoes than normal. On the day that Christophe surrendered, the city hospital recorded its first death from yellow fever.[ii] In no time it was completely overwhelmed. Leclerc wrote to Paris that 6,000 of his men were sick with fever and as many as 50 were dying every day.[53] Hardy had written to his wife to celebrate the end of the fighting, and expressed a hope that now the hot season was arriving he would have more time in the shade of his new garden outside Cap Français. Within weeks he too had succumbed to yellow fever.[54]

[ii] The fact that mosquitoes were vectors for yellow fever would not be known for another century. The American merchant Unity Dodge blamed the severity of the outbreak on the French themselves, noting that the disease originated 'not so much from the impurity of the air as from the imprudent & negligent manner which [the] strangers are accustomed to treat themselves before & after the first symptoms appear'. See Dodge to James Madison, 23 May 1802, Founders Online, https://founders.archives.gov/documents/Madison/02-03-02-0311 (accessed 22 April 2022).

For all this, Leclerc was not entirely naive. He may have trusted Christophe and Dessalines to help settle the military situation, but he recognised the threat still posed by Louverture, despite his professed retirement from public life. It was inconceivable that he should be allowed to remain at liberty. Only by sending him to France could Leclerc make the colony safe. In the month after Louverture's surrender, Leclerc's correspondence became increasingly full of suspicions that the general was indeed playing a double game and continuing to plot against French rule. His fears appeared to be confirmed by Dessalines, who fed the general stories that Louverture was allowing the rebel Sylla to continue to operate against the French near his plantation at Ennery. Leclerc trusted Dessalines, without suspecting that he may have been plotting to assume Louverture's leadership role himself.[55]

On 7 June Louverture was invited to a meeting with the French general Brunet, which he uncharacteristically attended with only a small entourage. It was an ambush. Louverture's guards were quickly overpowered and Louverture placed under arrest. Within the day, he was on board a frigate moored off Gonaïves. His wife Suzanne and his two sons and niece would soon join him as prisoners. Leclerc wasted no time in ordering the ship (ironically named *The Hero*) to immediately set sail for France. As it pulled away from the harbour, Louverture is said to have declared: 'In overthrowing me, you have cut down in Saint-Domingue the tree of black liberty, but it will grow back for its roots are deep and numerous.'[56]

Louverture and his family would never see Saint-Domingue again, nor would he know if those roots would ever grow back. But the rains that brought disease to the French could also return the tree of black liberty to life. It was now the job of Christophe—and a possibly duplicitous Dessalines—to help it flower.

7

WAR OF INDEPENDENCE

As Saint-Domingue's governor-general, Toussaint Louverture had written to Napoleon Bonaparte as an equal, and although he was borne across the Atlantic to France as a prisoner, he still expected an audience with the First Consul to explain his actions. But Bonaparte refused to even receive his letters. Instead, Louverture was imprisoned at Fort Joux, a medieval castle high in the Jura Mountains. He was stripped of his rank and uniform and treated to a deliberately punitive regime, placed on near starvation rations and denied enough firewood to heat his freezing alpine cell. When he fell sick, he was denied a doctor. After eight months of cruel treatment, he was found dead in his cell on 7 April 1803, felled by pneumonia and a stroke. French newspapers were silent on his death. The news would not reach Saint-Domingue until the middle of the summer, by which time the Haitian Revolution had entered its final and bloodiest act.

The success of that revolution was harder to divine in June 1802. When news reached Paris of the new settlement in Saint-Domingue, it was widely believed that not just Dessalines but also Christophe had been the first to move against Louverture. 'The Captain-General [Leclerc] himself praises the conduct of these two black generals. They are the authors of many evils, but if they continue to behave as they have done recently, the clemency of the French people is boundless, and the Government can forget their past', wrote one commentator.[1] Within two weeks of Louverture's deportation Leclerc wrote happily to Bonaparte that 'the south is disarmed. Dessalines is disarming the west. Within 15 days, Maurepas, Christophe and Clerveaux will have disarmed the north', concluding that France would soon fully control the whole colony.[2]

What explains the motivations of Dessalines and Christophe? Dessalines' move against Louverture was common knowledge among the French command, and Christophe must surely have known of it. Dessalines had been the first to raise the prospect of independence when besieged at Crête-à-Pierrot, and may have suspected that Louverture wanted Saint-Domingue to remain tied to France. He may also have worried that he was unlikely to be picked by Louverture as his successor. A short-term show of loyalty to France would allow disease to thin the ranks of the European troops until they could be ejected, with Dessalines emerging to consolidate power with Christophe as his deputy. The lessons of the Moyse revolt had been absorbed: potential rivals must be eliminated and the cultivators pressed back to work to produce the sugar, coffee and other products that would help rebuild the shattered colony. Leclerc had even gone so far as to reconfirm the positions that Dessalines and Christophe had held under Louverture, as Inspector General of cultivation and commander of the north respectively. He may have thought this a clever move to consolidate his own power, but in fact he was offering them impunity to act for their own interests rather than those of France.

The first week of July brought an opportunity to put this plan into action, when Christophe's troops took to the field against Sans Souci, the great maroon survivor and Louverturian loyalist. Before the defection to France, Sans Souci had been under Christophe's command, but he deeply disliked his superior officer. The exact reasons have not been preserved, but he surely saw the violent suppression of Moyse's supporters as the polar opposite of everything he had stood for since he first took up arms. He surrendered to the French along with the rest of Louverture's high command with the express intention of betraying Christophe as a traitor, as Dessalines would do to Louverture. But disgusted by Christophe's apparent new-found cosiness with Leclerc, Sans Souci soon picked up his arms and took his rebellion back to the mountains around Grand Rivière, to fight against both the French and their black confederates.[3]

Sans Souci was a nimbler fighter than Christophe and was highly adept at turning the terrain to his advantage. In their first battle Christophe had to be satisfied with rounding up little more than a few armed cultivators and a cache of arms when his rival slipped out of his grasp.⁴ 'If Sans Souci was a soldier,' Christophe complained to the French general Pamphile Lacroix, 'I flatter myself that I could catch him, but he is a cowardly and cruel brigand, who has no qualms about killing those he suspects; he knows when to flee, and covers his retreat by leaving only desolation behind him.' Yet even when discussing the figure who was becoming his most implacable opponent, Christophe couldn't help but give credit to Sans Souci's military acumen: 'He is [fighting] better than we did at the time of your disembarkation ... the new insurgents seem to want to follow Toussaint's method of war; if they persist, we will have difficulty reducing them.'⁵

As July progressed there were more uprisings on the plantations. Christophe blamed the white colonists, some of whom had begun to speak hopefully of a return to slavery. 'In the name of the Blacks, I say no liberty, no colony!' he told Leclerc: 'They now have the audacity to proclaim their freedom-killing doctrines under a republican government. Take care, Citizen General—instead of preserving peace, these gentlemen are rekindling the fires of civil war.' Christophe singled out one figure as a particular threat—General Donatien Marie Joseph de Rochambeau, who had captured Fort Liberté in February while Leclerc was fruitlessly negotiating his landing at Cap Français: 'He is the implacable enemy of the men of colour and consequently of the Blacks, and his behaviour will infallibly lead to their taking up arms against the Government.'⁶

Those outside French circles saw more clearly that the black officers were playing both sides. When Dessalines was sent to crush an insurrection on the plantations around Port-de-Paix in August, one English merchant in Cap Français drily noted that he 'contrived to let his stores and ammunition fall into the hands of the enemy'. Christophe was apparently no better: when rebels started burning plantations close to the city and Christophe marched against them, 'he let them get possession of his camp and stores as Dessalines had done before'.⁷

One white colonist complained in a letter that now Christophe and Dessalines were in command, 'the black colonels with their epaulettes pave the streets and are preparing for combat', adding with a shudder, 'they are even our masters'.⁸ This swagger is on display in a striking watercolour sketch done by the artist Jan

Anthonie Langendyk, who arrived in Cap Français on a Dutch troop ship at the beginning of April. On the left of the scene stands a splendidly uniformed general, whose dark blue coat with red facings is set off by copious amounts of gold trim. A French tricolour tied in a dandyish knot around his waist complements the matching colours of the ostrich feathers in his bicorn. His sabre at his hip, he has removed a glove to receive a theatrical bow from his lieutenant. The junior officer, more modestly attired, doffs his hat and meets his commander's gaze with a knowing look.

The general's identity is not given. Langendyk arrived in Saint-Domingue just as Christophe was opening negotiations for his surrender to the French, and only stayed for a few months before leaving the colony. Surviving officer lists from the Leclerc expedition make it unlikely that the general was one of the few black officers who sailed from France, suggesting that Langendyk pictured one of the leaders who had just submitted to Leclerc and retained their rank—possibly even Christophe himself, whose love of a good dress uniform was well documented.[9]

If Leclerc suspected the double game the generals were playing, he had little choice but to stick with them. Yellow fever was tearing through his army with abandon, leaving the black troops as his only reliable auxiliaries. Fresh European reinforcements were said to step off their ships and straight into the cemetery. The city's ruined hospital was a series of shelters thatched with sugar cane, with its patients exposed to the mouldering effects of the rain and burning sun alike. As despair set in, 'the sick were avoided from the fear of contagion, and for the same reason the dead were left without burial'.[10] Those on active duty responded to their frustrations with increased violence. 'The paths and the forests were covered in blood', wrote one officer of his progress through the mountains. Frustrated by constant ambushes from an enemy that refused to fight them in the open, Leclerc gave orders that all black combatants be shot on sight rather than taken prisoner. Those accused of giving support to the rebels were summarily hanged, and mass drownings were performed in Cap Français' harbour to dissuade others from picking up arms.[11]

In September news arrived that the French had restored slavery in Guadeloupe. At a dinner hosted by Pauline Leclerc, Augustin

Clerveaux laid out an ultimatum. He had himself been free before the revolution's outset, he told the general's wife, but 'if I fancied that the restoration of slavery would ever be thought of here, I would become a brigand in an instant'.[12] Despite this, Leclerc remained convinced that he could bend the black officers to his will. Christophe could soon be sent to France, he wrote to Bonaparte, 'without the slightest fear that his departure will trigger an insurrection', while Dessalines 'begged me not to leave him in Saint-Domingue'.[13] Dessalines had just further proved his apparent loyalty by capturing and executing Charles Bélair, a senior officer and nephew of Louverture, and his wife Sanite, who together had led 200 soldiers in mutiny against the French. That Bélair was a potential rival to Dessalines once the French had been defeated apparently escaped Leclerc's notice.

Leclerc was further encouraged to learn that Christophe had agreed to send his son Ferdinand to Paris for his education. The idea was not new (it had first been suggested in 1801), but it was a gamble on Christophe's part, if not the result of active French coercion. Louverture's sons, Isaac and Placide, had both attended school in France, and perhaps Isaac at least had reassuring words to offer; he had been sent away when he was just a year older than Ferdinand. Christophe appears to have trusted his contact in Paris who helped with arrangements. His one letter to Christophe on the subject was unsigned, but the correspondent was intimate enough to send his 'sincere compliments to your wife, a thousand hugs to your little children'. The reaction of Marie-Louise to her son's departure into an uncertain future can only be imagined, but perhaps she was reassured slightly when it was decided that her sister Marie would accompany the child to France.[14]

As Ferdinand was preparing to sail, his father was clear with the French command that trust went both ways. At dinner with General Boudet, who was also to accompany his son to France, Christophe again warned that fears were growing that slavery might return to Saint-Domingue as it had in Guadeloupe, and such rumours could only embolden those thinking of revolt: 'If you had the same colour skin as us, you might not be as confident as I am, entrusting my only son [to France].'[15]

Leclerc knew that Ferdinand's passage would be one-way and believed that Christophe would soon follow his son into French exile along with every other black officer. This would then allow the restoration of the colony to its former glory in the only way he now believed was possible: by reducing the population once more to slavery. Every black person who had fled to the mountains should be killed, and half of those still on the plantations on the plains, he wrote to Bonaparte, allowing that 'children under twelve years' would be spared.[16] Although he had overseen the increasing violence of the French troops during the summer of 1802, Leclerc would not live to see this project to its conclusion: exactly five weeks after proposing it he was dead from yellow fever. But before he died, any illusions he had maintained about his control over events were violently stripped from him when the entirety of the black command mutinied against the French.

Clerveaux and Pétion, stationed at Haut-du-Cap, were the first to cross over. When rumours began to spread on 13 October that the French were about to disarm the colonial troops, they spiked their artillery and marched their units out to join the rebel encampments on the plains. Fearful of the contagion spreading, Leclerc quietly sent his head of artillery, General Allix, to meet Christophe at his headquarters at Petite Anse before news of the mutiny could reach him. Allix was known to have good relations with the black officers, and his memoirs warmly recall the fine lunch that Marie-Louise served while he and Christophe discussed the fragile military situation. Christophe insisted that he was loyal to France but refused to meet directly with Leclerc to prove it. Explaining the delicate balancing act that he was being asked to perform, Christophe compared himself to a bear who had its claws strapped to sieves to help it walk on a frozen pond. When the bear finally managed to stand up on the slippery ice it was shot. 'I don't want to be that bear', Christophe told Allix bluntly.[17]

Allix was unaware that Christophe had received advance notice of the mutiny and was stalling for time. When the sun set that evening, the plains around Cap Français were once more set ablaze by the rebels. The sugar cane went up like a match, causing a conflagration that would burn on and off for the next two weeks. The following morning Clerveaux and Pétion led their soldiers in an attack on Haut-du-Cap, supported by troops loyal to the maroon leader Petit Noël Prière. Leclerc's troops managed to repel the attack, but when he signalled urgently to Christophe for reinforcements, Christophe refused to even let his messenger leave Petite Anse. In response, Leclerc ordered the last remaining colonial troops in the city to be disarmed and held on ships in the harbour.[18]

For two days Christophe kept his own counsel while the sounds of skirmishes blew into his camp. Pétion had warned him of the risks of sending his son to France, and it was perhaps regret over this decision that caused Christophe to waver at the crucial hour. But at dawn on 18 October, Christophe finally sent Leclerc word that he would march against Clerveaux, Pétion and Petit Noël Prière, telling him that the rebellion in the north would soon be crushed. Drawing up his 600 troops under a fluttering tricolour, he then marched straight to the bridge at Haut-du-Cap and calmly led his men into the rebel encampment.[19]

Petit Noël Prière was outraged by the apparently casual nature of this volte-face. His cavalry mobbed Christophe, pulling up their reins at the last moment to brandish their arms and spit obscenities at him. Christophe, backed by his own soldiers and with a cocked pistol in his hand, reacted coolly when Petit Noël Prière screamed that he would kill the French traitor. Only the intervention of Clerveaux and Pétion, likely forewarned of Christophe's arrival, stopped the scene ending in bloodshed. Christophe and Pétion made unlikely allies, but now Pétion placed himself bodily between Christophe and Petit Noël Prière, calling for unity against their common enemy. The situation was defused, but as the maroon leader stalked off, he coughed bitterly that the account was still to be settled.[20]

Perhaps eager to ease tensions himself, Christophe decided that his first action against the French should be elsewhere. He rushed instead with a small detachment of troops to Port-de-Paix, hoping to win more defectors to the rebel side by stratagem. Arriving at a post manned by Polish troops, Christophe ordered them to immediately withdraw, citing the danger of enemy fighters in the area. The unwitting Poles complied, only to be marched into town where they were greeted by the cheers of black troops who immediately made their true loyalties known, including one man who was completely naked but for a pair of epaulettes hanging around his neck, who cheered 'Vive le général Christophe!' The crowd threatened the thirty Poles just as violently as the maroons had threatened Christophe at Haut-de-Cap, but he had won valuable hostages that he hoped he could use for a prisoner swap. He told their officer, 'I will exchange you for the band of black musicians that were kept in Cap Français, so send one Polish soldier with my letter to [General Leclerc].'[21]

The prisoner swap was refused without consideration. Instead, Leclerc ordered the black colonial troops held in the Cap Français harbour to be summarily drowned. More than 1,000 men were killed in total, and their bodies were left to rot in the sun as they washed up east of the city.[i] Before leaving Port-de-Paix, Christophe ordered the Poles to be executed in retaliation. Within a week, the last remaining French forces abandoned the city.

Christophe next led a raid against Limbe, which was still commanded for the French by his trusted lieutenant Paul Romain, who duly handed the town over to his superior officer. Rebel morale was boosted shortly after by the news from Gonaïves that Dessalines had also finally defected and was now waging war against the French in the Artibonite Valley.

On 28 October, with rumours arriving that Leclerc was seriously ill and the city's command in disarray, Christophe led his troops against Cap Français for the first time, hoping to squeeze the city by taking the blockhouses that guarded its approaches. In a three-pronged blitz, Christophe and Clerveaux's brigades attempted a pincer movement against one of the positions, while Petit Noël Prière's maroons were given the unenviable task of charging the hilltop gun position at Charrier. They suffered the highest casualty rates as a result.[22] The French barely managed to hold their positions, and over subsequent nights the insurgents launched raid after raid, depriving their opponents of sleep. On 2 November, his fever heightened by the sense of siege, Leclerc finally succumbed to yellow fever.

Christophe kept the city under fire for another week before withdrawing to reorganise his forces. Although he was now the rebel

---

[i] When the British consul to Haiti, Charles Mackenzie, visited Petite Anse in 1828, his guide took care to show him the high-water mark where 'the bodies that escaped the voracity of the sharks were cast on shore'. See Charles Mackenzie, *Notes on Haiti: Made During a Residence in that Republic*, 2 vols. (London, 1830), vol. 1, p. 168.

army's most senior officer in the north of the colony, enforcing the chain of command was no easy feat. Sans Souci still refused to accept Christophe's authority, contemptuously demanding instead that Christophe place his own troops under the command of those who had never surrendered to the French.[23] When Christophe chose to make his new headquarters back in Dondon, the maroons and local cultivators harassed his troops to such an extent that he was forced to relocate to Marmelade, where Clerveaux commanded. As skirmishing between the factions continued into January 1803, Dessalines had to be summoned to help broker a peace.[24]

Dessalines gave his wholehearted support to Christophe as the head of the army in the north and urged unity between the factions. He made a conciliatory gesture to the maroons by ordering Christophe to move his base to nearby Milot, and placed Dondon under the command of Petit Noël Prière, who he promoted to colonel under the command of General Paul Louverture. In Grand Rivière he paid tribute to Sans Souci's fighters and their dedication to liberty, honeying his words by just enough to win the maroons over to join with him against their common enemy.[25]

The peace did not last long, if it was truly meant to. When Dessalines had returned to the Artibonite Valley, Christophe invited Sans Souci and fourteen of his senior officers to a meeting at the Choiseul plantation on the edge of Milot. The plan was ostensibly to discuss strategy, but instead the maroons were seized by Christophe's men and bayoneted to death. In one brutal action, almost the entire maroon leadership in the north was wiped out. Christophe may not have been able to best them at guerrilla war, but as in his strategic surrender to the French, he knew when deception could help consolidate his position.[26]

The timing of the killings, straight after Dessalines had theatrically ordered his most senior officer to move his headquarters to placate the maroons, suggests that Christophe was acting in concert with his commander. Three years later, when Dessalines was collating papers relating to the struggle against the French, he asked Christophe for any records relating to the killing of Sans Souci, only to be met with Christophe's apology that his memory of the 'Choiseul Affair' was hazy and his papers from that time had been lost during the war.[27]

The French were undergoing their own adjustments in command. After Leclerc's death, General Rochambeau in Port-au-Prince assumed command of the army, but he was forced to travel by sea to Cap Français to take up the position, as the overland route was now too dangerous for his soldiers. When he learned of Sans Souci's fate he immediately reached out to the remaining maroon commanders, including Petit Noël Prière, encouraging them to take vengeance against the man who had killed their leader and offering a large reward to whoever delivered Christophe's head to him in Cap Français.[28] At the same time, newly arrived battalions from France allowed him to order a lightning assault on the rebel-held towns of Ouanaminthe and Laxavon in the northeast, in the hope of drawing Christophe into the open.

The plan worked. Both towns were captured quickly, and when Christophe rushed to Laxavon to attempt to recapture it he was immediately hit by a combined infantry and cavalry counter-attack that left his brigade reeling. Christophe was wounded in the head and left some 300 men dead on the battlefield, as well as his regimental colours.[29] It was France's biggest victory in the north for months. Worse was yet to come for Christophe. Petit Noël Prière's maroons were waiting for him as he retired to Milot, and launched a ferocious attack of their own. Christophe's retreat quickly turned into a rout. He fled first to Marmelade to join his forces with Clerveaux's, but such was the relentlessness of the maroons and their command of the terrain that Marmelade was also abandoned, and Christophe and Clerveaux were forced out of the mountains entirely to take refuge in Gonaïves. When Paul Louverture went to try to negotiate a ceasefire with Petit Noël Prière, he was taken captive and beheaded.[30]

When Dessalines learned of the maroon's victory he was incandescent. His plan to remove their leadership had backfired, and he now reverted to direct military action. Hastily assembling three columns of his most battle-hardened soldiers, he marched on Dondon from three sides, smashing into the maroon town without mercy. In one bloody battle he crushed the maroons as a military force for good. Petit Noël Prière fled into the mountains and took no further part in the war.[31]

The French victory at Laxavon was to be a high-water mark. Just as Leclerc had complained constantly to Bonaparte of his overstretched supply lines, now Rochambeau took up the chorus, adding his own demand that he be allowed to formally bring back slavery to the colony. In the meantime, what violence he could inflict on black rebels and civilians alike became increasingly unhinged. This 'monstrous agent of Bonaparte', wrote Christophe's secretary Julien Prévost in 1814, 'spared neither sex, children or the elderly'. Imported Cuban hunting dogs were trained to attack anyone with black skin, practising on straw men stuffed with animal entrails, while in the cities prisoners were drowned, burned alive or even piled in the holds of ships to be gassed with sulphur.[32]

After recovering in Gonaïves from his head injury, Christophe returned to the fray in the north. In the first week of February his fighting capacity was bolstered by a shipment of muskets and gunpowder from an unknown British ship.[33] Christophe and Romain led their most successful raid on Cap Français yet, briefly overrunning his old garrison at Fort Belair, along with the hospital, before staging a tactical withdrawal. The French lost 410 killed in the attack. They were forced to reduce the garrison even further when they had to send reinforcements to the island of Tortue, near Port-de-Paix, which was under a fresh attack. The French had set up a network of hospitals here, believing its climate to be healthier than the mainland, but were now under siege on the island. Three weeks of bloody fighting ensued, again with the loss of several hundred soldiers. In a further act of humiliation, when the Cuban hunting dogs were finally deployed they either refused to attack or turned on their masters.[34]

By now the insurgency seemed to be everywhere. Dessalines had taken the war to the south, and from Saint-Marc to Jacmel the French were increasingly being pinned back to the coastal towns. In March, Rochambeau temporarily moved his headquarters to Port-au-Prince to deal with the new theatre of war, horrifying the citizens of Cap Français who felt they were being abandoned to face Christophe's raids alone.

In May 1803 Dessalines called a conference of senior officers from across the colony to plan the final stage of the war. It was held at Pétion's headquarters at Arcahaie, midway between Port-au-Prince and Saint-Marc. Here, in a moment as legendary as the Bois-Caïman ceremony that launched the revolution, Dessalines is said to have taken a French tricolour and symbolically torn out its white strip. The remaining red and blue were given to his goddaughter, a seamstress called Catherine Flon, to create the flag of the new country that would arise when the French had finally been expelled from Saint-Domingue.[35] In a further nod to the rebels' now explicitly anti-colonial agenda, Dessalines' secretary Boisrond-Tonnerre suggested that the insurgent forces be renamed the Indigenous Army.

With victory in sight, Dessalines began to put out diplomatic feelers to help shape the peace that would follow. He wrote to US President Thomas Jefferson to assure him of the 'loyalty and good faith' that American merchants would continue to receive in their ports and the abundant harvests they would have access to. Jefferson, who believed the revolutionaries were 'cannibals' who were threatening the USA's own slave system, declined to open a correspondence with him.[36] George Nugent, the British governor of Jamaica, proved more receptive. On 18 May, the same day that Catherine Flon was stitching together the red and blue of the new flag, Britain had declared war on France.[ii] Sensing the strategic advantage to be gained over the French in the Caribbean, Nugent ordered the Royal Navy in July to begin a blockade of Cap Français and Port-au-Prince. Rochambeau's hopes of any more reinforcements from France were finally extinguished.

On 28 August a Royal Navy ship landed in Gonaïves with two envoys charged with exploring Britain's future relationship with Saint-Domingue under Dessalines. One of them was Christophe's friend Hugh Cathcart, the former British agent to the colony. Cathcart advised Dessalines and Christophe that Britain was keen to have good trading relations, but sought assurances that Saint-Domingue's white planters would be welcome to return as they had under Louverture. He also requested that the Royal Navy be allowed to take possession of the ports of Môle Saint-Nicholas and Tiburon for the duration of the war with France. Dessalines rejected both points out of hand. British merchants would be welcomed across the colony, he said, but the lesson of their freedom struggle was that whites could no longer be permitted to own land on the island. On the matter of the ports, Christophe suggested that while

---

[ii] This date, known as Flag Day, remains a national holiday in Haiti today.

handing over control was out of the question, the navy would always be welcome there to take on supplies and could stay 'even six months if they chose'.

Dessalines told the British that he would be overthrown by his troops if he dared to concede more. Instead, he urged the British to supply him with more arms to help defeat their common enemy. The discussions stalled after three days. The prospect of a commercial treaty was no closer, but Dessalines and Christophe were gratified that the British had at least treated them as an equal power.[37] This tentative new relationship was bolstered a fortnight later when HMS *Vanguard* was anchored off Saint-Marc to monitor Dessalines' siege of the town. The French garrison had been reduced to eating its horses and was on the verge of surrender when the ship's captain persuaded Dessalines to let them be taken into British captivity.[38] The same day, the French abandoned Fort Liberté after their positions were shelled by Royal Navy ships, although in this instance the French were ferried directly to Cap Français. In theory this allowed them to continue to fight, but in practice it put an even greater strain on the resources of a city now under siege from land and sea.[39]

For months, the pages of the *Gazette Officielle de Saint-Domingue* in Cap Français had tried to maintain the illusion of normality. Weddings were announced and readers could enjoy news from France, perhaps imagining themselves in Paris where a pair of kangaroos had recently been exhibited, and allowing themselves to remember a time when Cap Français had been a pearl of French culture. But the war was impossible to ignore even for the newspaper's editors. Listings were included for properties confiscated from mutinied colonial officers that were put up for sale, including the plot where Christophe's own house had stood on Rue Dauphine.[40] But as Christophe tightened the screw with a relentless series of raids and the naval blockade bit hard, the city's confidence began to fray. Now the newspaper printed lists of warehouses full of coffee that could not be exported, and passenger lists of those citizens lucky enough to arrange departure on a rare American schooner. By the middle of October there was barely a sack of flour left in the city. Christophe stationed roving cavalry squadrons across the northern plain to prevent the French from foraging for supplies.

When one company of sixty men was dispatched to find food, only thirteen made it back to the city.[41]

On 8 October Port-au-Prince finally fell to Dessalines. Victory was in the air. He barely let his troops rest before marching them north, with Cap Français firmly in his sights. In heavy rains at the start of November, some 15,000 troops gathered in Limbe and waited for the weather to clear.[iii] When the clouds finally broke on 17 November, Dessalines and Christophe laid out their plans for the final assault. Their meeting was held on the Normand-le-Mézy plantation where the Bois-Caïman ceremony had launched the revolution thirteen years before. Whereas that ceremony had been held in the deepest secrecy, Christophe now proudly paraded 2,400 of his own infantry plus a detachment of cavalry and three artillery pieces before his commanding officer.[42]

Christophe's months of raids had worn the city down but also taught him the dangers of a direct assault. The French forces were reduced to 3,200 men, but the city's defences remained formidable, not least the blockhouses guarding the road from Haut-du-Cap. To circumvent them Christophe led his troops in a wide loop northwest to the hamlet of Port de France, from where they could seize the mountain heights above the city.[iv] It was torturously slow progress. The muddy trails were so steep in places that the cavalry was forced to abandon its horses, and the artillery had to be exhaustingly hauled up by hand. But the few French sentries the troops encountered scattered before them, and by sunset on 17 November, Christophe had the entire city within his field of fire.

The assault began at dawn the following morning. As Christophe's men began to rain shells into the city, Dessalines sent his main body of troops into battle. Three times they smashed against the blockhouses at Breda and Vertières. Generals Capoix and Vernet both had their horses shot from under them, while Clerveaux narrowly escaped death after having his epaulettes blown off. The battle raged all day. It was only when a third blockhouse at Charrier was captured and its guns turned on the French that the outcome became

---

[iii] The main square in Limbe is still called Nan Canno to commemorate the place where Dessalines drew up his artillery.

[iv] Now the village of Labadie—also known as Labadee, Haiti's only private cruise ship resort.

inevitable. At the close of day when the rains returned to wash the blood into the soil, Dessalines had lost over 1,200 men dead and 3,000 wounded, but the approach to Cap Français was finally open. The Battle of Vertières was the last pitched battle that the French would fight in Saint-Domingue. At midnight Dessalines received a message from Rochambeau offering his complete surrender and the immediate departure of all French forces.[43]

It took ten days to finalise the evacuation. Dessalines issued a proclamation to the city's residents assuring them of their safety when his forces took control of the city, while also corresponding with Admiral Loring of the Royal Navy, whose flagship was moored off Cap Français ready to take the French into custody in Jamaica. The slow pace was a frustration to Christophe, who wrote to Rochambeau to say that he would fire on the French ships with red-hot shot if the departure plans were not speeded up. The evacuation began the next day.[44] As the last troops sailed from the harbour, Dessalines finally marched his troops into the city, and just as the white strip had been torn from the tricolour at Arcahaie, so did he strip the French name from the city, rechristening it Cap-Haïtien.

One last French garrison remained in Saint-Domingue at Môle Saint-Nicholas. On 5 December its troops finally abandoned their posts and sailed into captivity in Jamaica. On the same day in 1492 Christopher Columbus had made his first landfall on the island just a few kilometres along the coast. Saint-Domingue's colonial experiment had lasted exactly 311 years. Now it was time for a new free nation to be born.

8

CITADEL OF FREEDOM

Dessalines, Christophe and Clerveaux made a provisional declaration of independence at Fort Liberté on 29 November 1803, the day before taking possession of Cap Français, vowing that having 'asserted our rights, we swear never to yield them to any power on earth'.[1] This statement had still referred to Saint-Domingue, but a different name for the country had to be chosen to demonstrate a clear break from its colonial roots. The founders reached back three centuries to tie their freedom struggle to the traditions of the island's original inhabitants and resurrected the name the Taíno had first given their land: Ayiti, or Haiti.[2] On the first day of January 1804 in Gonaïves, Dessalines led his generals in the signing of the official declaration of independence. Christophe's signature was the second to be added to the document.

An early draft of the Haitian declaration of independence, modelled on that of the United States, was passed over by Dessalines for inadequately reflecting the sacrifices needed to overthrow the colonial system—not just those of Haiti's soldiers, but also the generations of the enslaved whose bones lay beneath the ground. His secretary Louis Félix Boisrond-Tonnerre commented bitterly that to take a true accounting of the cost they would need 'the skin of a white to serve as a parchment, his skull as an inkwell, his blood for ink, and a bayonet for a pen'.[3] In Boisrond-Tonnerre's history of the revolution, the first written from the perspective of the victors, he further expanded on the mental anguish of being forced to write in French, having had the language of his African ancestors stolen from him.[4] It was a theme that Dessalines expanded on at Gonaïves. Vowing that Haitians must 'live independent or die', he repeatedly stated that the dead would hold the living to account as the new nation was built: 'Remember that you had wanted your remains to rest next to those of your fathers, after you defeated tyranny; will you descend into their tombs without having avenged them? No! Their bones would reject yours.' The price for Haiti's liberty was eternal vigilance against anyone who sought to return the country to chains. Dessalines vowed that Haiti would not seek to export its revolution or trouble 'the peace of neighbouring islands'. But pledging to defend Haitian independence he declared 'Anathema to the French name! Eternal hatred of France!'[5]

There was no delay in setting the tone for how Haiti would be governed. Dessalines adopted Louverture's old title of governor-general and, like his former commander, gave himself the power to appoint his successor. He likewise believed that the road to reconstruction ran through the plantations and made agriculture a central plank of his policy. On 2 January he issued an order cancelling the leases on all plantations, setting the stage for their nationalisation. Two days later Félix Ferrier, the head of the new administration in Cap-Haïtien, wrote to Christophe for advice on the leases for the city's warehouses. Christophe replied that they too would become public property.[6] In time, leases would be doled out again to army officers, but the interests of the plantation workers themselves remained an afterthought. They were allowed to keep a quarter share of plantation profits as sharecroppers, but given no choice as to whether they wanted to remain on the land working for the state.[7] Years of war had left Haiti severely depopulated, and Dessalines knew the plantations were chronically short of labour. He issued orders to stop plantation workers running away to the cities by posing as market vendors, and even went as far as offering American merchants $40 a head to bring back those former citizens of Haiti who were 'suffering in the United States for want of means of returning', to help with reconstruction.[8]

When the Royal Navy ship HMS La Pique called at Cap-Haïtien in the middle of January, it delivered a letter to Christophe from Hugh Cathcart, reminding him of his promise made in Gonaïves to welcome British vessels. He told Christophe that Rochambeau had been sent to England as a prisoner, and in a tacit if unofficial early acceptance of Haitian independence, requested 'an almanack for the present year, commencing with your new Constitution'. Although Christophe was unable to oblige Cathcart at this point, he said he would generously host any passing Royal Navy ships, stressing his pleasure in being able to assist a close friend, and adding that 'Madame Dessalines, my wife, and [Madame Dessalines' niece] Miss Juliette are very grateful for your good memories. They say the most obliging things about you to me.'[9]

Christophe was also keen to keep an eye on new arrivals in Cap-Haïtien. All ships landing in the harbour were inspected by the city commandant Jean-Pierre Richard. Richard had been born in Kongo and gained a gruff reputation among foreign merchants for treating them with disdain, upending the old racial power hierarchy they represented. Richard sent one Philadelphia trader, Condy Raguet, for questioning by Christophe, who received him 'as if disturbed from sleep ... with a Madras handkerchief around his head'. The general closely questioned the merchant 'with all the dignity and importance of a great man addressing his inferiors', asking him of news from France and America before finally allowing him to go about his business.[10]

Raguet wrote home that though the city's buildings still showed the scars of war, its markets were thriving with every kind of fresh produce on offer. These bounties were particularly on display in mid-February, when Christophe and Madame Dessalines hosted a banquet at the governor's house. Attendees were dazzled by the enormous marquee in the gardens, decorated with flowers, mirrors, chandeliers and marble statuary. A table set for 250 guests groaned with 'beef, mutton, turkies [sic], ducks, chickens, wild fowl, turtle [and] oysters', along with fruit, jellies and cake and endless bottles of claret, Madeira and champagne.[11]

The banquet was a public coming out for the new regime. According to Raguet, Christophe dressed for the occasion in a scarlet coat, 'embroidered, I may say covered, with gold lace, for the cloth was scarcely visible, with two golden epaulets, a large military hat with gold lace border, boots with gold borders and tassels, an embroidered vest, and pantaloons of yellow nankeen, beautifully worked in front'. His officers were all similarly attired. The dresses of his wife and the other female dignitaries were modest by comparison but set off by their hair that was decorated with artificial flowers, beads and combs. Their jewellery drew plenty of admirers, not least Madame Dessalines' gold watch set with diamonds and mounted on a ring. The feast concluded with Christophe toasting Dessalines, the King of England and the President of the United States, before the tables were cleared away and an orchestra played for the guests until sunrise. After breakfasting in the cool of the morning, Raguet reeled back to his lodgings, amazed at the lavish spectacle where 'every distinction of colour appeared to be laid aside, where the black and the white, the yellow and the brown were spontaneously intermingled'. It was a good omen for a country so recently emerged from war.[12]

Numerous similar events were held throughout February, sometimes hosted by Christophe and at other times by leading French citizens who had stayed after Rochambeau's evacuation. At one of these Raguet was scandalised by the mixed-race wife of a French officer serving under Christophe who dressed in men's clothes, while other female attendees arrived on horseback wearing pantaloons under their gowns. At another, hosted by the city's merchants for Madame Dessalines, a hot-air balloon and fireworks were released—though the evening was marred when the bench on which the guest of honour and Christophe's wife were sitting collapsed, sending the women sprawling. The party immediately ceased and smelling salts and a doctor were called for. Raguet dismissed the accompanying gloom as the laughable behaviour of sycophants, but he appears not to have noticed that Marie-Louise was eight months pregnant at the time.[13]

In later years, Marie-Louise would fondly recall how she had accompanied Christophe during every stage of the war 'with her children on her back, often without any other food than wild fruit and berries, and generally exposed to the weather, sometimes half clothed'.[14] The rich banquets could not have provided a greater contrast. There was more good cheer when Victor-Henry Christophe was born on 3 March, one of the first children to be born in free Haiti.[15] But the joy of his safe arrival would have been tempered by fears for their eldest son Ferdinand, now cut off from them in France. Toussaint Louverture's fate must have convinced them that, at best, he was now a hostage of Bonaparte's regime. On his arrival in Paris, Ferdinand had indeed been given an interview with the

First Consul, but instead of being sent to the prestigious National Colonial Institute where he had been promised an education he was dispatched to an orphanage called the Hospice des Orphelins. His trunk containing his clothes, a fur coat for the winter and two sets of silverware engraved with his name was confiscated. Marie-Louise's sister Marie, who had accompanied him, was locked up in the asylum of La Salpêtrière. Ferdinand became ill and dull-eyed at the orphanage, but still retained some of his father's grit. He resisted the orphanage's attempts to teach him shoemaking, insisting that he had been sent to France 'to get a fine education, not to be a cobbler'. In 1805 the French authorities learned of a plot by an American captain to rescue the child and take him to the USA and then back to his family, suggesting that Christophe had arranged for a supporter in France to keep watch over him. But the violence and deprivation of the orphanage's regime proved too much, and after two years Ferdinand died shortly after his twelfth birthday, his body covered with abscesses.[16] His death was not publicly acknowledged by Christophe until 1817, at a memorial service led by Ferdinand's sisters, Améthyste and Athénaïre.[17]

The uncertain fate of Ferdinand was a reminder that despite the public celebrations, Haitian freedom was precarious at best. The French had evacuated Saint-Domingue in abject defeat, but they had maintained a garrison in Santo Domingo in the eastern part of the island and it was feared that this could be used as a bridgehead for another invasion. Dessalines' response was twofold. The first was to address the perceived threat to security posed by those French citizens who had remained in Haiti. The second was to learn the lessons of Leclerc's invasion and draw up a proper plan for national defence.

In the third week of February, Dessalines ordered his commanders to round up any citizens known to have given active support to the French army in the final stages of the war.[18] A week later he was in Jérémie to oversee the confiscation of all French property. Most of the French citizens in the town were summarily executed.[19] A similar pattern followed throughout the southwest, although it appears that local commanders were reluctant to carry out advance orders to kill any French citizens in their towns until prompted by the arrival of Dessalines. In Cap-Haïtien Christophe banned French citizens from leaving the city and had all vessels searched on departure.[20] When a small number of French slipped out of the harbour by disguising themselves as American sailors an order was issued to arrest their neighbours for failing to inform the authorities of the plot.[21]

In early March, HMS *Desirée* docked in Cap-Haïtien carrying several French citizens from Port-au-Prince who had disguised themselves as sailors and carried their children on board in sacks.[22] Hoping to repeat the exercise, its captain quietly sent sailors' uniforms on shore to be distributed among those French wishing to leave. Harbour guards only discovered the plot when some of the French were being rowed to the frigate. The English captain was summoned from the theatre where he was attending a play and, in the resulting stand-off with Christophe, almost came to blows after his sword was briefly confiscated. The English captain demanded satisfaction for the apparent insult and ordered the *Desirée* to display its broadside to the harbour with its cannons fully uncovered. Denied a pilot to make its way out of the harbour, it remained at anchor like this for a day, threatening to fire on the town until it was finally allowed to depart with some thirty French men, women and children on board.[23]

The first killings in Cap-Haïtien did not take place until 13 April, when some sixty French were rounded up and put to death. Two weeks before Dessalines had issued an order to naturalise Haiti's remaining French, and rumours swirled that those killed had been identified through this new system.[24] The action, led by Christophe's officers Joachim and Ferrier, was more likely prompted by the news of Dessalines' imminent arrival in the city. The governor-general had taken a lesson from the reluctance of other commanders to carry out his executions. He came to Cap-Haïtien via Dondon, where he had quietly arranged to take the submission of Christophe's old rival Petit-Noël Prière and his band. These last remaining maroons were eager to prove their new loyalty to Dessalines, and on arrival in Cap-Haïtien gave themselves over to the bloody work of rounding up the French. Christophe refused to play a part in the massacre, but nevertheless was made to give up twenty French that he was sheltering in his house.[25] Over six days the majority of the city's French population was killed, but it was not until the very end that Christophe played an active role, leading a procession of prisoners to the cemetery at La Fossette. While a military band played patriotic music and with Christophe's soldiers looking on, the last French were put to death by Dessalines' 4th Regiment.[26] When the killings were concluded, Dessalines immediately left the city for the northwest. To conclude his display of power he had Petit-Noël Prière and his supporters arrested and sent to his headquarters where they were summarily executed.[27]

At the end of April, Dessalines gave a speech at Cap-Haïtien justifying his actions. With Christophe at his side he invoked the same themes he had used in the declaration of independence, including the need to appease the restless souls of those killed under slavery: 'Yes, we have rendered to these true cannibals war for war, crime for crime, outrage for outrage; yes, I have saved my country; I have avenged America.'[28] Dessalines had little doubt that the killings would appal foreign observers, who would see it as a far greater crime than the deaths of the several hundred thousand black men and women who had died under French rule in Saint-Domingue. But the killings have troubled generations of Haitian historians ever since, who have shuddered with equal horror and admiration at the events. 'Moral standards condemn him, but does not the logic of public salvation cleanse him from blame?' asked Thomas Madiou: 'The very incarnation of the principle of freedom, he was barbaric in the face of colonial barbarism.'[29] Dessalines himself was pre-emptively cynical: 'Hang a white man below one of the pans in the scales of the customs house and put a sack of coffee in the other pan,' he reportedly said, and 'the other whites will buy the coffee without paying any attention to the body of their fellow man.'[30] The British authorities in Jamaica ended treaty talks with Haiti after the killings, but the speed with which many foreign merchants returned to do business a few short months after witnessing the round-up of the French only confirmed Dessalines' suspicions.

Christophe was perhaps more ambivalent. When lobbying the British government in 1807, he had his agent stress the actions he had taken to protect the French under his rule, comparing Christophe to the Bishop of Lizieux, who had saved many lives during the massacres of the Huguenots in sixteenth-century France.[31] Indeed, despite the bloody enthusiasm of the soldiers at La Fossette, many of Cap-Haïtien's French appear to have survived the killings through Christophe's patronage. Some with useful skills allied themselves with the new Haitian state, including a doctor named Justamont, who became surgeon-general to Christophe's army, and the Breton priest Corneille Brelle who had celebrated Louverture's constitution in 1801.[32] A nun called Jeanne Germaine Saint-Martin was also saved, possibly on the intervention of the deeply devout Marie-Louise; some years later Christophe would even order the rebuilding of her convent.[33] But Christophe could not protect others close to him. He had employed Monsieur Arnaud as one of his interpreters, whose sycophancy made him unpopular with the foreign merchants, who accused him of being 'a perfect slave to Christophe ... forever cringing behind his chair with, "General, I hope you are well today"'. Arnaud had been sheltered through the earliest violence before being stabbed on the street and left to die.[34] Cap-Haïtien's French population at independence was probably around 1,700, of which perhaps fewer than 200 survived the killings. The death toll was roughly equal to the number of black soldiers Leclerc had drowned in the city's harbour on a single day when Christophe mutinied against him.[35]

With Haiti's internal enemies defeated, Dessalines now turned his thoughts to his national defence plan. In April 1804 he ordered that the interior be fortified with a chain of nearly thirty mountain-top forts. Should France attempt another invasion, the coastal ports would be immediately fired and the army retreat to the forts to wage guerrilla war.[36] Haiti was divided into six military divisions, with each commanding general responsible for building the strongholds in their area. As commander of the North Division, Christophe was given the largest workload, with a total of eight forts to be built. Forts Rivière and Neuf were ordered for the old maroon stronghold of Grand Rivière. Above Milot would stand Fort La Ferrière. To the east, Forts Sans-Quartier, Brave and Jalousière would guard Marmelade, while the road that led south over the mountains from Limbe was to be protected by Forts Dahomey and Bayonnais. Together they formed a protective chain along the mountains bordering the northern plain, with the southernmost outpost only a short distance from the group of five forts that Dessalines ordered to protect his new capital at Marchand in the heart of the Artibonite Valley.[37]

Even before the order was issued Christophe had begun to move Cap-Haïtien's arsenal to the interior. The city's businesses were shuttered for two days and almost the entire civilian population was pressed into service to carry arms and ammunition 20 kilometres inland. The work was overseen by Colonel Noel Joachim, who Christophe also chose to manage the most ambitious construction project of all: Fort La Ferrière—later to be known as the Citadelle Henry or, more simply, the Citadelle.[38]

While the majority of the forts built during this period were relatively simple affairs, everything about the Citadelle was to be superlative. Its location was the most imperious in the country, atop the long narrow ridge of Pic la Ferrière mountain above Christophe's old stronghold at Milot. At over 900 metres high, the peak was frequently swathed in clouds, but on a clear day it commanded views to Cap-Haïtien and out to sea, and south across the mountains into the interior. When completed, the fort would eventually cover 15,000 square metres, making it the largest fortress in the whole of the Americas. Its multilevel batteries were at the cutting edge of military architecture, providing a murderous field of fire for those sides of the Citadelle not protected by a precipitous mountain drop, while also protecting the slopes on which crops could be grown for supplies against a siege. Water came from a series of massive cisterns and an internal moat that further protected the fort's interior. The walls eventually towered 45 metres high and were never less than 4 metres thick.[39] One kilometre away at the southern end of the mountain ridge was a series of four redoubts collectively called Fort Ramiers, protecting the approach from Dondon.[i]

Christophe's chief of engineers was Henry Barré. The national defence plan kept him in constant demand, and Christophe wrote to him regularly on the building of the forts in Marmelade or, in one instance, ordering him to send a team of carpenters and other workers to Marchand on Dessalines' request.[40] The engineer Faraud was left to oversee the day-to-day construction of the Citadelle alongside Colonel Joachim, with Christophe as project manager ensuring that the works were run with military precision. His letters of the

---

[i] The area containing the Citadelle—known collectively as Haiti's Parc national historique—Citadelle, Sans Souci, Ramiers—was inscribed on the UNESCO World Heritage List in 1982.

time show a constant barrage of instructions: ordering materials and provisions, assigning labourers and blacksmiths, and chiding any officers who failed to meet his strict standards. During the revolution, Christophe had been close to Charles Vincent, the French military engineer charged by Louverture with improving Saint-Domingue's fortifications. Vincent had been aware of plans to build a gigantic defensive fort in the centre of the colony in 1792—plans that he had criticised for their expense and over-ambition.[41] Christophe had perhaps discussed the project with his friend, and seen the Citadelle as the opportunity to make such an ambitious plan a reality at the heart of a defensive network stretching across the north. Work on the site was driven at a ferocious pace, and by the end of 1804 the new *Gazette Politique et Commerciale d'Haïti* newspaper in Cap-Haïtien could already note with satisfaction Haiti's new 'unassailable citadels rising above the clouds' and pay particular tribute to Christophe's achievement in mounting his cannons 'in the most formidable position' at the summit of Pic la Ferrière.[42] When Christophe became king in 1811 he made Faraud a baron and named him Director of Engineers. His coat of arms bore a pair of architect's dividers with the motto 'Citadelle Henry'.

Christophe also gave thought to a home for his own family. Marie-Louise and the children were spending much of their time in Gonaïves with Madame Dessalines, where shortages of essentials made for a rude contrast with the banquets of the first months of independence. 'I beg you to have the laundry-woman hurry with my linen, for the children and I are on the point of being without any and you know that it is difficult to get washing done here,' she wrote, while dealing with a teething Victor-Henry, adding that 'the sugar that you told me to expect has not yet arrived; this delay grieves us very much, since we had awaited it impatiently, and especially Madame Dessalines, who is expecting her mirrors by the same boat.'[43] Their house in Cap-Haïtien was ruined, so Christophe set about building a mansion in Milot, from where he could oversee construction of the Citadelle. Although no description of the residence survives, it is possible that Joachim was influenced by his commanding officer when building a villa of his own in Milot, which one visiting American described as being 'pleasantly situated with a piazza in front and a flower garden in the rear', with a parlour decorated with engravings of military leaders including George Washington.[44]

In August news arrived that Napoleon Bonaparte had declared himself Emperor of France. Boisrond-Tonnerre and another of Dessalines' secretaries, Juste Chanlatte, decided that their governor-general could not be outshone by the man whose armies they had vanquished, and proposed that Haiti should also become an empire. Within a week letters had been sent out to the generals asking them to sign a letter nominating Dessalines to become Emperor Jacques I.[45] The official declaration was then backdated to January to remove any sign of French influence. The coronation was held on 8 October in Port-au-Prince, exactly one year to the day after Dessalines had liberated the city. The celebrations began before dawn with 'a most tremendous roar of cannon and musketry', according to an American supercargo who witnessed the event. In front of the army and almost the entire population of the city Christophe read the act nominating Dessalines as emperor for life, although the noise of the excited crowd made it almost impossible for him to be heard. After the oath of office Dessalines led his troops on foot to the cathedral to attend mass. That night the city thronged with a crowd that 'danced, sung, and leaped through the streets'. The following morning Dessalines and Christophe travelled to Cap-Haïtien, where the celebrations were repeated and a victory arch erected in the emperor's honour.[46]

When the celebrations had subsided, Dessalines wrote to his imperial 'brother and cousin' Bonaparte to inform him of his coronation. In an extraordinary broadside, he professed regret that the lessons taught to him by 'your late brother-in-law' Leclerc and Rochambeau and the fate of Toussaint Louverture meant that he could find no Haitian willing to travel to France as his ambassador, not least while Bonaparte regarded him as a rebel and brigand rather than the leader of a free nation. He urged Bonaparte to forget his desires to conquer an island 'whose shores are forever closed to you', and instead proposed a peace deal in the most provocative manner possible. Dessalines asked Bonaparte to return his sister Pauline, Leclerc's widow, to Haiti, so that the two of them could marry and the Haitian people could see 'the widow of the vanquished in the arms of the victor' and the 'Corsican blood [which] would join with the Black' in their children.[47]

Dessalines' pugnacious tone reflected a frustration that while he had dealt with the French in Haiti, his new empire was still threatened by the presence of a French garrison on the eastern part of the island. Its commander at Santo Domingo, General Jean-Louis Ferrand, remained determined to take the war to the Haitians in whatever way he could. He outfitted privateers to carry out raids along the coast, and on capturing one Haitian vessel had its entire crew killed. In early 1805 he announced plans to capture any 'rebels' found along the border with the French territory and sell them into slavery. For Ferrand, only repentant submission to Bonaparte could bring an end to the hostilities, but for Dessalines only one final victory over France could bring his new empire the peace it deserved.[48]

Plans for an attack on Santo Domingo were finalised in Marchand during the celebrations held to mark the first year of Haiti's independence. Five thousand troops formed up in silent ranks on a freshly prepared parade ground, along with every officer of significance from the revolutionary war, to pay homage to their victory. Christophe led the military salute, drilling the soldiers with such precision that when ordered to kneel after presenting their arms, the entire crowd also fell to the ground. After a massed volley of 200 cannons Boisrond-Tonnerre gave a speech filled with fiery denunciations of the French.[49]

The expectation was that the expedition would be launched at the end of the rainy season. The British heard rumours of it in October but declined to offer the naval blockade that they had provided a year earlier.[50] In Cap-Haïtien Christophe began to ready his soldiers. Always proud of his army's appearance, he wrote to Dessalines that he had ordered 10,000 new uniforms to be made. Tailors were chosen for their skills and their ability to source sufficient quantities of blue cloth, while women were pressed into service sewing new shirts.[51] No detail was too small for Christophe's attention, and for the next three weeks he sent out a constant stream of orders to his officers. Troops were drilled, ammunition was prepared, rations of biscuit and salt fish were issued and border security tightened.[52] On 13 February 1805, Christophe finally received detailed orders from Dessalines for the campaign.[53]

Christophe's force was one of three columns set to converge on Santo Domingo, with Dessalines leading a division from Marchand

and Pétion a third from Port-au-Prince. His route involved capturing several towns along the way, but the start of the campaign suggested that the weather would be an equally tough opponent. While the south of the island was drying out, the north had received heavy rain. Local floods meant that it took two days for Christophe to reach his chosen muster point at Fort Liberté. In some places his soldiers had to follow the coastline, marching chest-deep in the waves, while elsewhere engineers were deployed to break down riverbanks to allow the artillery to proceed.

The settlements in French Santo Domingo nearest the border had been abandoned by the time Christophe arrived, and it was not until a week into the campaign when the column reached Santiago that any military resistance was encountered.[ii] A 'very lively' battle ensued, with Christophe losing as many troops crossing the town's swollen river as in the actual fight. After the French troops fled in disarray, Christophe was left to conquer a series of ghost towns; in Cotuy, only the priest remained to help guide his army to a safe crossing point on the river.[54] To hold the area, he left in charge his Spanish-speaking brigade chief, José Campos Taváres, who had been born and enslaved in Santiago, with strict instructions to take a full census of the local district's people and livestock.[55]

The northern column reached Santo Domingo on 10 March to find the city walls already invested by Dessalines and Pétion. Christophe was instructed to set up camp on the uncultivated left bank of the Ozama River, with the city's harbour and its shipping within range of his guns. A constant barrage from the Haitian cannons quickly forced the ships to take shelter on the open sea, and in a dispatch to Dessalines, Christophe confidently reported that the shells and musket fire were forcing the city's residents to take cover 'on all fours', while the cries of drowning sailors had been heard well into the night.[56]

Ferrand had evacuated much of the city's civilian population to reduce the number of mouths he had to feed, leaving him with garrison of 800 men plus a further 1,500 militia. He felt more than confident in his position: 'The brigands are always under the walls, and I have reason to believe that they are more disgusted than us, at

---

[ii] Haitian sources refer to Santiago by the French name of St Yague.

a siege that they did not foresee to be so hard.'[57] His own cannon could still return fire against Christophe's positions, and he was able to send out two large sorties against the lines manned by Pétion's commander General Magny. At times the fighting was at such close quarters that bayonets were more useful than muskets.[58] Both sides took significant casualties, but it was only when General Geffrard arrived to reinforce the Haitian positions with his army of the south the day after the second sortie, that Ferrand may have started to worry about Santo Domingo's fate.

Over three weeks the siege slipped into a slow and steady rhythm of barrages and counter-skirmishes. 'There is nothing new worthy of reporting,' Christophe wrote to Dessalines, 'except that I have been doing a lot of shooting this morning.'[59] Dessalines ordered mining work to be carried out to weaken the city walls, and at a general staff meeting on 26 March ordered a full assault for the following day. But when the troops were at their reveille the next morning, it suddenly became clear that the attack on Santo Domingo was to be no triumphant rerun of the fall of Cap Français. French sails had been spotted on the horizon. A month earlier, a naval squadron sent to the Caribbean to harass British shipping had recaptured Dominica, and by chance its admiral had chosen this moment to call at Santo Domingo before returning to France.[60]

Fearful that the ships were part of a much larger armada intent on conquering Haiti, Dessalines ordered an immediate withdrawal. The Haitian army quietly abandoned their positions and departed 'in the greatest silence', such that the French did not immediately realise that the siege had been lifted.[61] The retreat at least provided an opportunity to put into action Dessalines' scorched earth plan to deny invaders any advantage. Before the proposed assault on the city, his generals ordered their men to muster all the Spanish inhabitants and their livestock that they could find to take back to Haiti. Christophe had his troops comb the woods for runaways and arrange them into a convoy to be marched back to the northern sugar plantations that were so chronically short of labour. They would also be put to work on the fort-building programme. He wrote ahead to the commander at Ouanaminthe to prepare 'plantains, potato or cassava for around 600 Spanish prisoners' who would be sent to work on the Citadelle. To guard against a French attack, orders were also sent to the fort to prepare its artillery and have any remaining gunpowder at Cap-Haïtien removed to the interior.[62] As Christophe retreated north through Cotuy, Vega and Santiago he had each town systematically razed. When his troops finally arrived back at their barracks they brought with them 1,649 prisoners of both sexes, 748 children under the age of 15, plus a French surgeon, 5 priests and all the livestock they could muster.[63]

The invasion never came, but the fear of attack pushed Christophe to demand ever faster progress on the Citadelle. For much of the next six months he was a constant presence at the site. Every commander in the north was ordered to send him twenty-five workers from each plantation, with a particular call for masons and carpenters. The Spanish prisoners were screened to find wheelwrights or blacksmiths to meet the fort's insatiable demand for skilled labourers. The Citadelle became an enormous mountaintop labour camp, with a spell on site there the punishment for any Haitian soldier guilty of indiscipline. Several of Cap-Haïtien's remaining French citizens who were deemed a security risk were also sent to the work site.[64]

The fort's location posed its own challenges. An endless chain of porters carried building supplies to the mountaintop, from bricks scavenged from ruined French plantation buildings to the sugar cane whose juice was mixed with sand and lime to make mortar, and the barrels of herrings that fed the workforce. Arming the Citadelle was even more of a trial. Christophe ordered the coastal forts stripped of their artillery to be sent to the interior, and he obsessed over the making of gun carriages for their transport and installation, and the sufficient provision of ropes for the mammoth task of hauling them up the mountain.[65] The majority of the artillery pieces weighed over 2.5 tonnes, and many of them double that, but in total 163 cannons and mortars were ultimately sent to the Citadelle, along with an equally epic supply of cannonballs. In amassing such a battery, Christophe created an inadvertent tribute to the convoluted history of the Haitian Revolution. Some cannons bore the French royal coat of arms, while others carried republican mottoes from revolutionary Paris or had been captured from Naples during Bonaparte's war against Italy. Spanish and British artillery were also added: the Citadelle's oldest cannon dated from 1719 and was decorated with the coat of arms of the Duke of Marlborough.[66]

Haiti's new imperial constitution was published in May, along with an accompanying penal code. On the morning of 16 June Christophe held a general levy in Cap-Haïtien, where he was pleased tell Dessalines that the assembled crowd had listened to his reading of the documents 'in the most profound silence', until erupting at its conclusion with a thousand cries of 'Long live his majesty, the Emperor!'[67] The opening section of the constitution summoned up a free and sovereign state that permanently banned slavery: the first country in the modern world to do so. All citizens were to be equal under the law irrespective of their colour, though all would be designated black, and every man was urged to be 'a good father, a good son, a good husband, and above all a good soldier'. As Dessalines had suggested to the British, no foreigner was permitted to own land or manage a plantation.[68]

The celebrations were marred by the death the previous week of General Clerveaux after a short illness. Clerveaux was only a few years older than Christophe, who mourned the loss of this 'friend of liberty'. The French surgeon-general Justamont, who was also close to Clerveaux and attended him in his final hours, later claimed that Christophe had had him poisoned.[69] Haitian historians of the mid-nineteenth century seized upon this story to confirm their prejudices against Christophe, but irrespective of the cause of Clerveaux's death, the passing of one of the main signatories of independence only strengthened Christophe's own position.[70] When Dessalines announced a military reorganisation the following month, Christophe was named as head of the entire army and his most loyal officer, General Paul Romain, was given command of Clerveaux's old division.[71] Christophe was now comfortably the second most powerful figure in Haiti.

Prior to his promotion, Christophe had toured the northwest on a military inspection. He had expected to find the same brisk efficiency with which he ran Milot, but he was soon dismayed. The trip revealed neglected plantations and the regiment at Môle Saint-Nicholas so struck down by desertions and 'in such disorder that I [Christophe] could not review them' for a parade. Work had not even begun at the site chosen for Fort Trois Pavillons in the hills above Port-de-Paix. The officer in command was replaced by a Christophe loyalist and 100 soldiers from the garrison were immediately dispatched to work on the new fort, along with two workers from every plantation in the area.[72] But the malaise was an early sign of a wider dissatisfaction across the north. Within months Christophe was active again across the area, as rumours of Vodou dances and conspiracies against the government swirled around the north and increasing numbers of workers went maroon from the plantations. The empire of Haiti was barely a year old, and its greatest challenge was about to come knocking on Christophe's door.

9

THE EMPIRE OF HAITI

Christophe was with Dessalines in Marchand in January 1806 to mark the second anniversary of Haitian independence. Foreign merchants gossiped afterwards that the centrepiece of their banquet was the sugar skeleton of a white man. The two of them were finally beginning to feel confident that despite France's continuing presence in Santo Domingo, Haiti's foreign enemies were on the back foot. A Royal Navy campaign in the Caribbean was disrupting French shipping, and on 11 January they gleefully learned that Napoleon Bonaparte's navy had been definitively smashed at the Battle of Trafalgar.[1] It was now to the task of state-building that the two of them turned, and it was here that tensions would arise so quickly that the Haitian empire would struggle to survive the year.

The malaise that Christophe had uncovered at Môle Saint-Nicholas was an early indicator of trouble. The problem arose from the question of liberty. What did freedom mean for a new country in a world of colonial slavery? Dessalines and Christophe believed that the military was the only guarantor of the freedom won through the revolution, and the only way to build a strong country was to rebuild the plantations and put trade at the heart of its foreign relations. The more sugar and coffee Haiti could export, the more gunpowder it could buy. The imperial constitution thus put order and duty at the heart of nation-building, with its citizens destined to defend the revolution by becoming either good farmers or good soldiers. Dessalines and Christophe had risen to prominence under Toussaint Louverture, and their project to create a new nation from scratch was a continuation of the ideals he espoused as governor-general of Saint-Domingue. But to the foot soldiers of the revolution, the majority of whom had been born in Africa and undergone the Middle Passage, freedom had a completely different meaning. Freedom for them meant individual liberty, and if they were to labour it would be to cultivate their own plots, left alone in self-sufficiency rather than be forced to labour for someone else. Later dubbed the counter-plantation movement by the Haitian historian Jean Casimir, this was the liberty that sparked Moyse's revolt against Louverture and animated maroon leaders like Sans Souci and Petit Noël Prière. For Christophe, these were figures from the past. He had fought them all and come out triumphant, and believed their ideas had no place in the country that he was helping Dessalines to build. 'Work never dishonours a free man', Christophe advised one of his commanders, but the struggle to convince a people so recently in bondage to follow his maxim would occupy him for years to come—and tear Haiti into two in the process.[2]

Reliable estimates are hard to come by, but the years of war may have reduced Haiti's pre-1791 population of around half a million by a third, and possibly by even more.[3] For leaders like Christophe, who also needed manpower to complete the defensive forts, it was a challenge to find enough people not just to work in the fields but to enforce the labour system. For peasant farmers and soldiers hoping to strike out on their own, this was less a problem than an opportunity. While many chose to go maroon in the sparsely populated interior where they could make new lives for themselves undisturbed by the state, others took refuge on islands off the coast. In November 1805 Christophe directed General Capoix to clear out 'an infinity of soldiers and cultivators' who were hiding in the marshy inlets of Mancenille near Fort Liberté.[4] At other times he sent soldiers to disrupt the informal maroon economy by destroying the canoes of independent coastal traders, or to arrest those ranching wild cattle or depriving the state of tax revenue by illegally logging dyewood.[5]

Cultivators remained tied to the plantations they worked on and forbidden to change their residence. Even marriage between those living on different plantations was forbidden lest movement between the two places undermine agricultural productivity, a fact that Christophe took seriously enough to reprimand one local civil servant for allowing such a wedding, despite his instructions being 'very specific in this respect'.[6] The old practice of petit-marronage from Saint-Domingue, running away from a plantation but staying nearby to be with family, soon returned. The discovery of maroons living near Petite Anse, so close to Cap-Haïtien, illustrates the problems the authorities had trying to control the workforce. Complaining about having to return cultivators who were regularly absconding from one location to another, Christophe sighed that no sooner were they 'chased out the door, they returned through the window'.[7] To crack down on the problem, Dessalines ordered the resurrection of Toussaint Louverture's identity cards, each bearing the individual's name, age, place of residence and profession.[8] The extent to which the passes were issued remained patchy, but anyone caught not carrying one was in theory liable to arrest.[i]

The Spanish prisoners from the Santo Domingo campaign had proved to be poor workers. Those on plantations near the border had to be moved to the interior to stop them trying to escape back to their homes. The remaining French in Cap-Haïtien were largely allowed to go about their business until April 1806, when six of them fled to the Spanish part of the island by canoe. One of the escapees was Norbert Thoret, a tailor who had won the favour of both Christophe and Dessalines by sewing their uniforms, along with his wife. All those who fled had been regarded as trustworthy by Christophe, making their actions seem an act of personal betrayal. He ordered all the French in the city to be rounded up as punishment. 'I have sent all the white men and women of this town to live in the mountains under the responsibility of the military commanders,' he told Dessalines, 'who will distribute the women to the various plantations where they will be under the supervision of the managers and drivers, and the men to the various fortifications, to work.' The crackdown was so severe that Christophe had to reassure Cap-Haïtien's foreign merchants that no action would be taken against them.[9]

The restrictions on labour and movement meant land that should have been growing crops proved fertile ground for disquiet.

---

[i] The identity card was to be issued at a cost of 1 gourdin (a quarter of a gourde), or roughly half the weekly wage of a labourer. By comparison, a regular infantry soldier earned about 1 gourde a week. Christophe's salary as head of the army was around 4,500 gourdes per year.

Vodou's revolutionary potency was deemed so threatening to domestic tranquillity that Christophe ordered the suppression of dances and the arrest of anyone selling magic charms. Even his own generals weren't above suspicion: in December 1805 Christophe scolded Capoix for allegedly holding a midnight mass where a crucifix and saintly images were displayed upside down. 'You are a Catholic, you believe in the Christian religion', he told his general, reminding him that his rank obliged his personal behaviour to be beyond reproof lest it feed unseemly rumours. Although the report proved unfounded, there was clearly power in such stories. When a tale began to spread that Dessalines planned to enslave Haitian children, Christophe quickly ordered the rumourmonger to be shot by a firing squad.[10] Anti-slavery was a cornerstone of Haitian independence, and the militarised nature of state agriculture left the nation's founders acutely sensitive to accusations that their system was in any way analogous to the colonial slave system.

Christophe's accusations against François Capoix had not come out of a vacuum. It was Capoix who was the general overseeing the northwest when Christophe made his inspection there and found the garrisons in disorder. He had been regarded as a potential threat by his general and emperor ever since.[11] A raid by French troops on the border town of Ouanaminthe in October 1806 provided him with the opportunity to deal with him once and for all. Christophe was near Gonaïves when he learned of the raid and rushed to the border, only to find that Capoix had already repelled the skirmishers. In a dispatch to Dessalines, Christophe choose to take full credit for the victory. After helping secure the border Capoix was ordered back to Cap-Haïtien. He never arrived. Before his departure, Christophe summoned his generals Paul Romain and Dartiguenave for a meeting. On 10 October they surprised Capoix on the road at Fosse-Limonade and had their soldiers take him prisoner. 'Your master Christophe is lucky to have caught me in such a trap,' Capoix reportedly cried as he realised his fate was sealed, 'Finish it quickly.' Moments later he was dead. The following day Christophe wrote to Dessalines that they had carried out 'your order' and that Capoix's three aides-de-camp were now in his custody. Romain rushed to Capoix's stronghold of Port-de-Paix to quell any potential trouble from his old regiment, and any threat imagined from the hero of the Battle of Vertières was extinguished for good.[12]

Dessalines' satisfaction at the elimination of a potential rival proved short-lived. On the same day, an even greater threat to his rule was taking shape in the south of Haiti. His plans for state ownership of plantations had been piloted by Christophe in the north, but when he attempted to replicate the system further south it was met with severe resistance. Southern Haiti was a very different place to the north. It remained the power base of the old wealthy free coloured class who had prospered under André Rigaud and then been crushed during the War of Knives—in no small part due to the actions of Dessalines and Christophe. Now they believed that their interests were threatened again. Just as the abandonment of plantations during the revolution had allowed the black officer class to grow rich, so the free coloured officers had acquired more land in the south and west. Their mercantile background created a different vision of Haiti to Dessalines' imperial project, one rooted in private property rights and individual liberty rather than one of national defence through a centralised state. When the emperor toured the region in the summer of 1806, he complained that the registration of land titles, a precursor to nationalisation, had barely begun. He demanded the process be speeded up, and in doing so helped spark the revolt that brought down his entire empire.[13]

Complaints about Dessalines' rule had been festering in the south for several months, but it took his new orders to bring them out into the open. First among the complainants was General Etienne Elie Gérin from Anse-à-Veau. Gérin was the Minster of War and one of the signatories of Haitian independence, but he had originally been a colonel under Rigaud. Dessalines' southern tour crystallised the fears of both Gérin and Alexandre Pétion in Port-au-Prince that the land reforms were a grave threat to their power base. Rumours began to spread that the emperor's real aim was the complete elimination of the old free coloured class altogether.

Shortly after Dessalines began to push forward his southern land reforms, disorder broke out in Les Cayes. An imperial land inspector was beheaded, which was the trigger for the city's military command to declare themselves in revolt. It was the first stage in a carefully planned rebellion. Within days almost the entire southern peninsula rose up. Gérin praised the actions of the mutineers and delivered a broadside against Dessalines' tyranny. The families of planters were being 'stripped of their property [and] thrown in the streets' and troops were left unpaid while the ammunition needed to defend the country was wasted on lavish imperial parades, he said. Haiti was being trampled on by an oriental despot who would make even the French butchers blush. 'Liberty, good God, is a vain word in this country,' wrote Gérin, 'We don't dare utter it openly, though it sits atop the declarations [of independence].' Colonel Wagnac, commanding at Les Cayes, was equally clear: 'The people have risen up en masse; we have drawn the sword, and we shall not put it back in the scabbard until you order it.'[14]

The person to whom Gérin and Wagnac addressed their declarations was Christophe. They despatched their letters by ship to Cap-Haïtien and pleaded with him to intervene in their favour. Flattering him that they had always looked to him as the next in line to the throne, they pledged to recognise Christophe as the new head of the empire if he would only help overthrow Dessalines. Christophe is not thought to have received the letters. The letterbook of his daily correspondence at this time contains no reply, and the only recorded letters he sent in subsequent days are a prosaic round of orders regarding runaway cultivators and the continued construction of the Citadelle. When he did learn about the rebellion on 16 October, he wrote to Dessalines of his hope that he would deploy 'the severity of the law against the authors of this catastrophe'.[15]

On the same day Gérin, Pétion and almost the entire army command in the south and west signed a document in Port-au-Prince entitled *Resistance à l'Oppression*, pronouncing the Dessalines regime dead. It drew heavily on liberal French republican ideals to offer a manifesto of what a Haiti freed from dictatorial rule could look like. Arguing that Dessalines had betrayed the prize of freedom, they promised a 'true liberty' based on the rights and duties of all. Soldiers would be paid, cultivators protected and planters (many of whom 'had been thirty years in possession of their lands, but whose titles had been lost during the late commotions') have their property respected. As authors of the document, they described themselves as merely the vessels of the will of the Haitian masses rather than political conspirators: 'The people, as well as the army, weary of the unbearable yoke imposed upon them ... by spontaneous movement, broke free. Yes, we have thrown off our chains!'[16]

Declaiming any personal ambition, they pledged that the army would not rest until it had placed at the head of the government 'a man whose courage and virtues we have long admired, and who, like us, was the object of the tyrant's humiliations'. At the very moment that Dessalines was heading south to confront them, Gérin and Pétion pronounced Henry Christophe the new head of state.[17]

The manifesto's authors knew that it was just words unless backed up by further decisive action. Dessalines had to be removed. The opportunity came on 17 October, when Dessalines had left Arcahaie on the road towards Port-au-Prince. He was riding ahead of his trusted 4th Regiment with only a light bodyguard, unaware that the city had already risen against him. It was only when he reached the bridge at Pont Rouge, in a wooded area on the outskirts of the city, that he realised he was heading into a trap. Soldiers with fixed bayonets sprang from the trees to surround him, along with Gérin and General Yayou, who had once been a follower of both Sans Souci and Petit Noël Prière. Pétion had chosen to remain in Port-au-Prince. Dessalines was indignant. After a brief stand-off as the troops hesitated to act against their emperor, a volley of musket fire rang out and Dessalines fell from his horse. His lieutenant Charlotin Marcadieu attempted to protect his wounded commander but was himself cut down by a cavalry sabre. As Gérin watched, Yayou administered the fatal blow. It was a cruel poetry: a former maroon from northern Haiti allying with the old southern free coloured class to fell a man who had campaigned against them both. There was no ceremony of recognition, just the brutal stripping of Dessalines' corpse with his fingers cut off for their jewelled rings and the dismembered body left abandoned in the road.[ii] Only later was it recovered by a woman named Défilée, a camp follower devoted to Dessalines, who according to Haitian tradition placed his remains in a sack and buried him in an unmarked grave, weeping in fear for the 'fallen country' that she believed would be left behind in the wake of his murder.[18]

[ii] The site at Pont Rouge today is near Carrefour Aviation on Boulevard Jean-Jacques Dessalines (Grand Rue) in Port-au-Prince. A new memorial to Dessalines designed by the Haitian architect Daniel Elie was erected on the site in 2015, replacing an older version destroyed in the 2010 earthquake.

Gérin was keen to press on to Marchand to seize the imperial treasury, but Pétion's cooler head prevailed. Rather than proceed north, they attended a thanksgiving Mass in Port-au-Prince and then wrote to Christophe to explain their actions and pledge him their loyalty as Haiti's new leader. Gérin blamed the heightened spirits of his men for the mutilation of Dessalines' body, insisting that they were trying to arrest the emperor when he foolishly reached for his pistol in self-defence.[19] Otherwise, the tone was entirely unrepentant. The south had acted to save Haiti from despotism. Pétion wrote:

> We should not have concluded our work, General, if we had not been penetrated with the recollection, that there existed a chief calculated to command the army, with all that latitude of power, of which until now he had only the appearance. It is in the name of the whole of this army, always faithful, obedient, and well disciplined, that we beseech you, General, to assume the reins of government, and enable us to enjoy the plenitude of our rights, and of that liberty for which we have so long fought.[20]

As Gérin and Pétion took up their pens, a different narrative was being crafted just north of Port-au-Prince by Christophe's ally André Vernet, the Minister of Finance. Alongside the scribes Juste Chanlatte and Boisrond-Tonnere, he penned a furious declaration lamenting the 'tyranny of parricide' carried out against the nation's founding father and vowed to 'avenge the emperor or die'. This document was also sent north to Christophe, along with a separate letter from Vernet describing the events around Dessalines' killing.[21] The question was, which account of Dessalines' killing would reach Christophe first, and which side would he ally himself with?

Vernet's dispatches were the first to arrive. Christophe immediately wrote back, describing the great pain he felt on learning the news of this 'fatal accident, so disastrous to this country'.[22] The emperor's death seemed to have taken him by surprise, but given the eagerness with which Gérin and Pétion appeared to place themselves in service to Christophe as the new head of state, the question has always remained as to what he knew about the conspiracy against Dessalines.

In the early 1840s when the Haitian writer Thomas Madiou was compiling his epic history of the country, he interviewed many of the surviving protagonists from the independence era and claimed

THE EMPIRE OF HAITI

that Christophe was fully aware of the plot against Dessalines. Madiou wrote as a republican partisan who was highly critical of Christophe and his later royal pretensions, and in his account Christophe had already conspired against his emperor with Gérin's predecessor in Les Cayes, General Nicholas Geffrard. Only Geffrard's untimely death in May 1806 had prevented an earlier move against the emperor. His source was Dessalines' inspector of agriculture in the south, Joseph Inginac, who reportedly discovered a cache of letters from Christophe to Geffrard complaining about Dessalines' rule. Instead of reporting them to Dessalines, he quietly destroyed the correspondence instead.[iii] Madiou admitted the plot was hearsay, but his need to make sure that Christophe's hands were equally dipped in blood have coloured all subsequent accounts of the events at Pont Rouge.[23]

On the day Dessalines was killed Christophe wrote to Romain, who had overseen the dispatch of Capoix only days earlier, to advise that with Dessalines moving against the southern insurrection he should increase local surveillance to foil the plans of any 'malicious men'. No other northern generals received such orders. Christophe's regular correspondence was only interrupted with the arrival of Vernet's news on 19 October.[24] His shocked reply was dashed off so quickly that the handwriting changes halfway through the letter. The neat copperplate of his usual secretary, Julien Prévost, suddenly disappears, to be replaced by the looser and more urgent hand of another. Christophe sent a further three letters to Vernet that day, urgently asking for more updates and ordering that the capital at Marchand and the imperial family be protected. He sent general orders written with 'tears of blood' to all his divisional generals with the news and ordered their troops to be placed on high alert. Particular attention was paid to the garrison at Saint-Marc, the closest city to the border with Haiti's western province.[25] Christophe sent a further two officers direct to Port-au-Prince with a letter for Pétion asking for more details about the killing.[iv] He wrote of his

---

[iii] To further muddy any paper trail, Inginac's own papers were destroyed in Port-au-Prince during Haiti's 1843 revolution.

[iv] Christophe initially believed that Dessalines had been killed at Sibert, a plantation slightly further north from Port-au-Prince than Pont Rouge.

dismay on learning of Dessalines' death and expressed his trust that Pétion would do whatever he could to prevent potential disorder in his ranks.[26]

Christophe's letters to Vernet and his officers were passionate, but his tone to Pétion was cool and business-like. Since the siege of Jacmel six years previously there had been no love lost between the two men. When Christophe was made head of the army in 1805, it took Pétion three weeks to write to congratulate him and a further three for Christophe to reply. According to Christophe's letter-book, this was the only correspondence that they had exchanged in the previous eighteen months. The northern and southern halves of Haiti had long operated on parallel tracks, and Dessalines' assassination now threatened to pit the two against each other again. Christophe had not yet received word that Pétion intended to nominate him as head of state, but as an active and enthusiastic supporter of the plantation system, he was unlikely to agree to the wholesale reforms that the southern generals had proposed in their declaration against oppression.

Christophe made no public announcement about the killing of the emperor, but sent cavalry and artillery to secure strategic roads across the north. He wrote to Dessalines' widow to offer his condolences and spoke of the anxiety he felt over her husband's death. Addressing her as his *commère*, or godmother, he told her that despite 'the great project of our enemies' to split the country in two, he would do all he could to avoid any further shedding of blood. 'As soon as I am allowed to be absent [from my command], you will see my flying to you', he wrote, adding his wife Marie-Louise's tears to his own.[27]

Pétion also wrote to the empress, but his letter offered no soft words, just the idealism of his manifesto against tyranny. He explained how Dessalines had profaned his title, so the sacrifice of her husband had been a sadly necessary one. As he praised her personal virtue, Pétion asked her to forget who she had been married to and, in the name of the army, offered her instead the cold comfort of becoming the adopted wife of the entire country, 'which knew no hatred except against one oppressor'.[28]

When Christophe finally received Gérin and Pétion's manifesto and accompanying letters he wrote to Vernet to say how they had

THE EMPIRE OF HAITI

troubled him, and he would need to reflect carefully on their contents. Without giving any indication of his likely course of action, he urged his comrade not to be afraid but to keep confidence in him and his military strength.[29] But his mind was made up: he may not have played a part in Dessalines' demise, but he would not fail to take advantage of it. He summoned his generals to Milot and presented them with the evidence from the south. In response they pledged him their loyalty and urged him to take up the reins of government that he had been offered. 'It will not be a chief that we will have,' they wrote, 'it will be a father surrounded by his children, who will aspire to nothing but their happiness and their prosperity.' The choice of language was carefully measured. In Christophe's private letters, he continued to respectfully refer to Dessalines as 'His Majesty', but in recognition of the changing situation he now allowed the publication of a declaration that referred to the emperor as 'the head of a hydra that was about to devour us'.[30]

On the same day, he made his first replies to Gérin and Pétion to accept the position of head of state. Judging their actions to have been a 'cruel necessity', he was prepared to answer their call to the 'honourable and painful place of government'. He repeatedly underscored his lack of ambition as he undertook to serve the country, but nonetheless showed that he would now not merely react to events but would seek to shape them himself. He called for order from the southern and western armies, subtly mentioning that his own soldiers were freshly paid and provisioned. Christophe also demanded a new constitutional settlement to be agreed by a national assembly. 'I will tell you the time and place where this assembly should be held, and the number of members who should participate', he advised Gérin. Picking the 'notable, enlightened and friendly men' who would make up this body would be crucial to shaping the new political landscape.[31]

Crucially, Christophe refused to travel to Port-au-Prince. Instead he had Pétion send his envoy General Bonnet by ship to the north. In a careful piece of political theatre, Bonnet was summoned to meet him in the imposing mountain fastness of the Citadelle.[v] The

---

[v] Writing to Pétion on 26 October about the imminent arrival of the envoy, Christophe for the first time refers to Dessalines as the 'so-called Emperor'. Regrettably, this is the last surviving

meeting did not go well. Christophe had just learned that two of Dessalines' secretaries, Etienne Mentor and Boisrond-Tonnerre, the man who had put iron into Haiti's declaration of independence, had been executed in Port-au-Prince. Christophe angrily accused Bonnet of trying to hide these crimes and loudly claimed that the insurrection against Dessalines had been driven by southern ambition rather than principle. Bonnet retorted that had that been the case they would have simply driven north and overwhelmed Christophe's troops. The meeting degenerated even further when Christophe discovered that Pétion had subverted Christophe's authority as head of the army by quietly placing one of his own supporters in a key army position. 'Do I not have the right to make promotions, I who have been proclaimed head of the government?' he declaimed, 'Well then! I will also make myself strong, and I will not let my throat be slit like Dessalines!' Any fragile trust that might have existed dissolved into suspicion and accusation. When Bonnet left for Port-au-Prince he refused Christophe's offer of a military escort and later reported to Pétion that northern troops had tried to ambush him at Gonaïves.[32]

The raised temperatures did not bode well, but in public Christophe portrayed himself as the sole figure who could unify the country. In his first proclamation as head of state, made in Cap-Haïtien, he warned that the removal of a bad government was no excuse for anarchy. He praised the army for upholding the honour of the Haitian flag and pledged improved pay and equipment in return for their loyalty in maintaining order. Cultivators on the plantations, 'whose happiness lies in your work,' were urged to keep to their labours, while the patriotism of all citizens was called on to close ranks against any supporters of Haiti's enemies they might find and to inform the authorities of their 'perfidious insinuations'.[33]

Who those enemies might be or why Christophe had replaced Dessalines as the nation's leader was not explained; it took nearly three weeks after the assassination for any sort of official narrative to appear, printed in the pages of Cap-Haïtien's *Gazette Politique et Commerciale d'Haïti*. For some time, explained the newspaper's edi-

---

entry in his letterbook (Foyle Special Collections Library, King's College, University of London, FCDO2: FOL.F 1924 HEN, *Letterbook 1805–1806*).

tor, discontent had been breaking out in several parts of the empire. Injustices and acts against both public and private individuals had excited 'a general disgust of the government which has just been overthrown'. Loyal officers had pledged to fulfil their constitutional duty to replace a bad leader; it was only their fear of violent reprisals that had led to the killing at Pont Rouge. The actions had been carried out in perfect secrecy so as not to disturb commerce and agriculture, and a new constitution was planned to correct the errors of imperial rule, which would allow all Haitians to 'forget our past misfortunes and enable us to enjoy the happiness for which we have long been yearning'. The names of those responsible for Dessalines' death were deliberately omitted, but the newspaper advised that all the documents related to the plot would soon be released. A pamphlet containing all Pétion and Gérin's letters and their manifesto was duly printed in Cap-Haïtien, but to maintain Christophe's image of being above such politics, none of his replies to them were included in the edition.[34]

In truth, the fight for Haiti's future had barely begun. Pétion perhaps imagined that Christophe would be satisfied to accept his new title and let the organisers of the revolt against Dessalines steer the new constitutional settlement in their favour. When Bonnet had visited the Citadelle he reportedly suggested that the lesson of Dessalines' misrule was that any powers of any future head of state should be curtailed in favour of a legislature. It was clear that the road to any political settlement would necessarily be backed up by force of arms. Pétion encouraged his own poorly paid troops to blame the head of the army for their ills. 'My comrades, if you have received only two and a half gourdes [instead of five] it is according to the orders of General Christophe,' he told the men in their barracks, 'But, on the other hand, be convinced that my voice will always be heard whenever it is a question of defending your rights.' When Christophe sent his own envoy, Dartiguenave, to Port-au-Prince to sound out the loyalty of the army, he was refused access on the grounds that the situation was too volatile and he had insufficient authority to continue.[35]

Christophe demanded answers. 'I could not expect, General, that an officer sent by the government could have any difficulty in fulfilling the mission entrusted to him,' he wrote angrily to Pétion,

'I cannot help confessing to you that I am discovering more and more the thread of all the plots and schemes which are taking place in the West and the South.' Speaking of the forthcoming constitutional assembly, he expressed concern that it would be devoted solely 'to favouring intriguers and giving them the means to feed their passions'.[36] Pétion's reply was bullish. He denied blocking Dartiguenave's mission and asked to know the source of Christophe's accusations so that he could answer them. As for the constitution, he wrote that those who acted on 17 October did so 'to destroy tyranny and to change the form of a government which could not suit them at all, and to establish their sovereignty'. When the new document was prepared, he was ready to fully submit to its will: a moment, he noted, when the Haitian people would finally recognise their true friends.[37]

Pétion believed he had good reason to be confident. As well as preventing Dartiguenave from meeting his soldiers, he had learned that General Yayou had rebuffed an attempt by Christophe to woo him to his side. Furthermore, as Christophe was writing to complain about his envoy's reception, envoys for the constitutional assembly were already arriving in Port-au-Prince. Christophe had agreed that it be held in the city to avoid any suspicion of him influencing its outcome. Pétion grabbed the opportunity to shape its composition. When the northern members arrived in Port-au-Prince at the end of December, they were shocked to discover that the number of delegates had unexpectedly increased from fifty-six to seventy-four, with southern and western representatives making up the extra numbers. Christophe's representatives were thoroughly outmanoeuvred, accusing Pétion at one point of refusing even to tell them the location of some of the meetings they were due to attend. The new constitution was presented to them as a fait accompli. It made Haiti a republic with all legislative powers devolved to a new 24-seat Senate dominated by members from the south and west. The presidency was reduced to a largely ceremonial role, and the position nominated by the Senate to serve a four-year term.[38] Christophe was duly pronounced president, but the northern delegates were up in arms at the stitch-up. Only one figure from the north sided with Pétion's faction to add his name to the new constitution—César Télémaque, the former mayor of Cap-Haïtien who had begged Christophe not to burn the city when the French armada arrived in 1802.

In Cap-Haïtien, Christophe was furious but perhaps unsurprised. Since Dessalines' assassination every political move on both sides had been accompanied by the drilling of troops, and now was the time to put them to the test. Christophe's power resided in the iron of his bayonets, not the paper of a rigged constitution. Pétion's mask had slipped, and force could be the only response to his naked grab for power: 'We must march', exhorted Christophe as he issued orders to his army to prepare to march south. 'Your general does not want to compromise with the enemies of liberty; he does not want to prevaricate with them. He expects you, soldiers of all ranks, to do your duty as you have always done', he continued. The plot of 17 October had begun over southern fears for their property, but now Christophe claimed the right to dispossess his foes of everything they owned: '[Having] raised the banner of revolt; it is only right that they should pay for their disastrous plots with their fortune. March on, and victory will crown the justice of our cause!' His divisions poured south from Cap-Haïtien, Gonaïves and Saint-Marc. At Arcahaie he was joined by Vernet, who was eager to avenge the death of his emperor. By the eve of Independence Day 1807 when Haiti was barely three years old, 18,000 northern soldiers approached the gates of Port-au-Prince, waiting for the order to attack their fellow countrymen.[39]

10

CIVIL WAR

'The fatal moment was arrived,' wrote Baron de Vastey in his history of the rise of Henry Christophe's monarchy, 'Haytian blood had been shed by Haytian hands. Civil war was kindled, and brought in its train all those horrors and misfortunes which yet afflict our wretched and unhappy country.'[1]

Alexandre Pétion had anticipated the possibility that his struggle with Christophe would have to be settled on the battlefield, and sent 3,000 infantry and 300 cavalry north towards Arcahaie to meet the likely attack: but he had not anticipated the speed with which his enemy struck. Christophe had divided his forces in two and sent a second column to loop east to encircle any opposing force. With barely a shot having been fired, Pétion was forced to retire his forces to Sibert, one of half a dozen fortified outposts on the Plaine du Cul-de-Sac guarding the approaches of Port-au-Prince, just 9 kilometres from its gates.[2]

At first Christophe's men tried to parlay; many of them knew those they now faced from the revolution. There was only one legitimate head of state, they called out, as they exhorted the opposing ranks to abandon the traitor Pétion: 'Why should we slit each other's throats to satisfy the ambition of a conspirator, an enemy of his country?'[3] When they were met with refusal, the forts were overrun. Christophe preferred to direct the action from a distance, but Pétion threw himself into the thick of the fighting. His distinctive hat was spotted as he led a cavalry charge, and a squadron of dragoons was sent after him. After a bloody pursuit they succeeded in killing Pétion's horse from under him, but when they closed in for the capture they discovered their quarry was a young officer who had seized Pétion's hat during the melee to protect his commander, who had been able to slip back to his lines unnoticed.[4]

The civil war had almost ended as soon as it had begun, but Christophe's impatience in ordering such a rapid attack now began to tell. The speed with which he had marched his men south had meant leaving his artillery behind. His superior numbers meant that he was able to push the republican troops back to Fort St Joseph on very walls of Port-au-Prince, but he was unprepared for a siege.[i] Pétion was able to bring up cannon and sent for urgent reinforcements from the south. Their arrival swung the pendulum in favour of the defenders. Over the coming days Christophe repeatedly sent his men against the city to no effect. The final assault came on the moonless night of 6 January 1807. The defenders at the walls were too strong and jeered the assailants while taking potshots at them. Two days later Christophe bitterly struck camp and marched back north. In an echo of the failed siege of Santo Domingo, he burned the Plaine du Cul-de-Sac as he left, leaving Pétion a field of ashes.[5]

The American trader Simeon Johnson was in Gonaïves when Christophe arrived in the city, and was impressed by what he saw of his army:

> 'Tis surprising with what little baggage large Armies of 8 or 10 [thousand] men march. A knapsack with a few Bananas &c a calabash for water are their equipment, no baggage waggons, no luggage of any kind to follow tardily after the army. Thus equipp'd, bare-footed, they move with a celerity really astonishing. Hunger, fatigue, rain, heat of the sun has no effect upon them; seldom there are any sick. In the field they are brave in the extreme, having excellent officers & well disciplin'd. No European troops in this climate could succeed for one campaign against them: united they are invulnerable.[6]

The fact that the Haitian forces were no longer united suggested that delivering a knock-out blow to the opposition would be a hard task. After rumours that Saint-Marc was to be attacked by Pétion proved

---

[i] The old city walls ran along the path of Rue des Ramparts in modern Port-au-Prince, on the northern edge of the Bel Air district. Fort St Joseph was located where the road is crossed by the north–south Boulevard Jean-Jacques Dessalines (Grand Rue).

unfounded, Christophe retired to Cap-Haïtien to plot his next move. On 17 February a new constitutional council formally pronounced Christophe the President and Generalissimo of the Land and Sea Forces of the State of Haiti. There was to be no senate to limit his powers, just an advisory state council of his most loyal officers.[7] Pétion and Gérin were declared outlaws, and their officers and general ranks offered an amnesty to encourage them to defect.[8] A further raft of proclamations followed as Christophe began to piece together a new state machinery.[9]

The Port-au-Prince authorities took equal advantage of the break in hostilities. The Senate voted in Pétion as the president of the new Republic of Haiti. Within a few months it adjourned its activities completely to hand over full executive power to Pétion to prosecute the war, turning him into the absolute ruler that he had so vocally denounced Christophe for aspiring to.[10] For Vastey, this reflected the characters of the two men. Christophe, 'a frank and energetic character', had moved openly to defend his legitimacy, while Pétion's Machiavellian streak meant that he 'aimed at accomplishing his dark designs by secret intrigue'.[11]

Christophe spent March and April touring the north and formalising new laws, until the gathering of political breath on both sides was punctured by an outbreak of fighting from an unexpected quarter. In the second week of May the 9th Regiment in Port-de-Paix mutinied. The uprising was led by Jean-Louis Rebecca, who had previously been under the command of Capoix. Now his former troops declared themselves for Pétion and the republic. The revolt was squashed by Romain, but the language of liberty the rebels used showed how easily the seeds of dissent sown by the harsh rule enforced by Christophe for Dessalines could blossom into revolt. 'I took up arms against [him],' Rebecca spat, moments before his execution, 'because he is a tyrant who while speaking of liberty, is restoring slavery.'[12]

Rebecca was named a posthumous hero of the republic in Port-au-Prince, and his mutiny encouraged Pétion to bring forward his own plans for a northern campaign. At the end of May a surprise naval landing by General Bazelais briefly saw Gonaïves fall out of northern control, while Pétion's army tore its way up the coast to lay siege to Saint-Marc. Christophe soon relieved the city and pushed Pétion south, but a month later he was forced back to the northwest when another republican naval landing led to the capture of Port-de-Paix. The expedition's leader was an officer called Lamarre, who had led the defence of Fort St Joseph during January's battle for Port-au-Prince. Port-de-Paix and the surrounding area became a key battleground in the civil war. It would take nearly two years for the region to fully submit to Christophe, and even when Port-de-Paix was retaken, Lamarre stubbornly retreated to the heavily fortified port of Môle Saint-Nicholas, where Pétion's naval superiority allowed him to be easily resupplied.[13]

A pattern quickly unfolded of rapid advances and retreats. With the opposing armies so evenly balanced on the battlefield, the war became a struggle for the loyalties of individual army officers. Deception and strategic defection had been a key part of the revolution, and just as Capoix's ghost had reappeared in Port-de-Paix to inspire his former soldiers, so Pétion faced division in his own ranks. In July 1807 he sent troops to Leogane after uncovering an alleged conspiracy against him led by General Yayou, who had dealt Dessalines the killing blow at Pont Rouge. A few months later, Magloire Ambroise, who had provided the artillery that helped save Port-au-Prince, was arrested in Jacmel on similar charges. In Grand Anse in the far southwest, an officer called Goman had raised the flag of rebellion and began raiding the rich coffee port of Jérémie with apparent impunity. In return for shipments of arms from the north, Goman was happy to nominally ally himself with Christophe while setting up his own maroon republic and seceding from the machinery of state altogether.[14]

Propaganda was an equally important factor in the war between the two states. Reports of the war were published in the north's *Gazette Officielle de l'Etat d'Hayti*, which was the mouthpiece for Christophe's fledgling state and provided a platform for its editor, Dessalines' former secretary Juste Chanlatte, who was a talented polemicist and poet in his own right. The newspaper (which bore the Voltaire quote, 'Each people has had its turn to shine', as its strapline) reprinted foreign news articles and shipping lists as well as government proclamations. Its earliest issues carried extensive coverage of the recent British abolition of the slave trade and its champion William Wilberforce, as well as serialising an essay by Chanlatte that raged against the Senate in 'Port-aux-Crimes' as being illegal, immoral, and acting against the wishes of the Haitian people.[15]

Reports from a newspaper called *L'Ambigu* were also reprinted. Its publisher was Jean-Gabriel Peltier, a French monarchist living in self-imposed exile in London. Peltier, who had once been sued for libel by Napoleon Bonaparte, was a keen supporter of Haitian independence and had offered his services as political agent to Dessalines shortly before his assassination. In April, Christophe's secretary Joseph Rouanez wrote to Peltier asking him to lobby the British government to win diplomatic recognition and a commercial treaty between the two countries. 'There is no one better than you who can fulfil this purpose,' he wrote, 'and work effectively to bring the British government to enter into a treaty with the State of Haiti.'[16] Three months later Christophe also sent Thomas Richardson, a black British merchant based in Cap-Haïtien as a second lobbyist, with detailed proposals to put to the British cabinet. Christophe offered himself as a partner in Britain's war against France. Haiti was a sovereign nation, he said, but one that would be happy to find itself under British protection. He painted Pétion's 'revolt' as a result of intrigues by the French, who were eager to use Port-au-Prince as a base against Jamaica, and proposed a Royal Navy blockade of southern Haiti and the French garrison in Santo Domingo, whose liberation he would then achieve with his own army. With Santo Domingo and Port-au-Prince back in loyal Haitian hands, the entire island would then be fully open to British merchants, who would receive favoured status above all other nations.[17]

Together, Peltier and Richardson barraged Lord Castlereagh, the British Secretary of State for War and the Colonies, with their petitions. Peltier had good reason to hope that his requests for a meeting would be granted, as Castlereagh had once been involved with a grant from the civil list to support the publication of *L'Ambigu*.[18] Their letters were sometimes contradictory: in one, Peltier insisted that Christophe was on the cusp of victory over the south, and held back only out of concern for the loss of innocent lives; in another Richardson urgently asked that Castlereagh prevent the sailing of British ships loaded with military supplies bound for Port-au-Prince, 'as it is not only Pethion [sic] who receives the supplys [sic]—but by that means General Ferrand at Santo Domingo ... as being in confederacy with the people of colour in the southern part'.[19] In October they presented him with a 21-clause proposed treaty between the two countries, reminding him that Toussaint Louverture had once signed an accord with the British government. As well as offering full commercial relations with a British diplomat resident in Cap-Haïtien and protection for British merchants, the offer of placing Haiti under British protection was also included, along with the old proposal that Môle Saint-Nicholas and Tiburon become Royal Navy bases for the duration of the war against France. To further assure the British of his pacific intentions, Christophe promised to restrict his vessels to Haitian waters, and assured the British that as soon as his victory over Pétion was complete he would greatly reduce the size of his army and concentrate on the expansion of agriculture, to the financial benefit of both sides.

Castlereagh was also sent a three-part memoir explaining the Haitian perspective on their nation-building efforts. It likened their situation to that of the USA, which had equally won its independence through insurrection. Conscious of how the British abolition of the slave trade was now leading into a debate about slavery itself, he was told that Haiti could act as a model for the entire British Caribbean, showing how a formerly enslaved nation could be free under the guiding hand of British rule. With a leader such as Christophe ('English by birth', Peltier reminded Castlereagh), London would have the perfect partner to stand together with against French tyranny.[20]

Castlereagh never responded, even when Richardson, who was due to sail back to Haiti, begged for a reply to take with him. The letters may have been ignored thanks to George Shee, Castlereagh's undersecretary, who had his own direct line to Haiti courtesy of Robert Sutherland, the unofficial head of the British merchants in Port-au-Prince. Sutherland had been an early supporter of Dessalines and in 1806 had made his own private attempts to persuade London of the commercial benefits of recognising Haiti. He provided intelligence on the military and political situation there to Shee, including an estimate of the size of its army, based on an order Dessalines had placed with him for a consignment of buttons for new uniforms.[21] Sutherland believed that the 'Black' party of Haiti intended to wipe out the 'Mulatto' party, and made it his mission to help

Pétion in any way he could. He wrote to London accusing Christophe of being an agent for France, and then gave practical support to Pétion by supplying his forces not just with gunpowder but the beginnings of a navy. In the summer of 1807 a Royal Navy admiral commanding in Jamaica learned that Sutherland had just outfitted an armed ship called the *Lord Duncan*, and asked for instructions on how to proceed should he encounter a British-owned warship flying Haitian colours.[22]

The appearance of the *Lord Duncan* signalled a new phase of the civil war. Following Pétion's military landings at Gonaïves and Port-de-Paix, both sides were rushing to build up their infant fleets. For help, Christophe turned to Thomas Goodall, a roguish naval captain from Bristol. Goodall had run away to sea as a boy and served with the Royal Navy in the Caribbean, and in 1806 had been issued with a letter of marque from the Admiralty for his ship, *Young Roscius*, to act as a privateer against enemy shipping. It appears that Goodall intended to prey on French ships that were carrying out raids along the Haitian coast, but after calling at Cap-Haïtien he became acquainted with Christophe and sympathetic to his cause. It was the *Young Roscius* that carried Richardson to and from London, and while there its captain set about procuring more ships for the State of Haiti.[23]

In December Goodall set off from Portsmouth with four other ships in tow. Alongside *Young Roscius* was the equally well-armed *Hopewell*, commanded by John McCulloch, plus three other merchant ships. All were laden with arms. Christophe was also eager to acquire more of the formal trappings of power, and so the *Hopewell* also carried two state carriages 'of fanciful form, with ten harness' that had been built for him in London and then put on public display.[24] When the ships arrived in Cap-Haïtien, Christophe bought the *Young Roscius* outright and a half-share in *Hopewell*, and proceeded to outfit them with French cannons captured during the revolution.[ii] Goodall was named Admiral of Haiti, with McCulloch as rear-admiral.

The two new ships doubled the size of Christophe's navy. They were soon in action against Pétion's forces invested along the north-

---

[ii] Christophe later had the *Young Roscius* renamed *Foudroyant* ('Thunderbolt').

west coast, and in February 1808 successfully landed 600 troops to capture La Tortue island opposite Port-de-Paix. Further along the coast they encountered two armed schooners flying Pétion's flag before the coastal fort at Jean Rabel. Goodall manoeuvred *Young Roscius* alongside one and crippled it with a shuddering broadside. The second was driven onto the rocky shore where it was set ablaze, and the fort recaptured for the north. 'The loss on the side of Pétion exceeded 500 men', Goodall reported afterwards, and the victory was so complete that Christophe declared that it had dealt 'a fatal blow to those traitors and infamous rebels who still adhere to the odious league of Pétion'. Only four of his crew lost their lives, but one was McCulloch, killed by a musket ball in his first action under Haitian colours.[25] On Christophe's orders McCulloch was buried with full military honours at an open-air service in the cathedral at Cap-Haïtien, whose roof was yet to be rebuilt after the revolution. 'Rule Britannia' and 'God Save the King' were both sung during the funeral Mass.[26]

The naval engagement at Jean Rabel had repercussions beyond Haiti. The British government was refusing to engage with the question of Haiti's sovereignty, but the news that Christophe was now employing a Briton as his admiral was a new issue altogether. As one newspaper commented, 'This affair will probably lead to the discussion of a curious question: Had Captain Goodall a licence from the King to enter into this foreign service? If not, in what light is his conduct to be viewed?'[27] Goodall himself understood that his command was unusual. When he invited two Royal Navy officers for dinner while their ship was in harbour at Cap-Haïtien, one of them noted that 'he sent to know whether he might appear in his uniform, remarking, he believed he had no authority to appear before an English captain in his Haytian uniform'.[28] In this instance his dining companions happily replied in the affirmative, but a more stringent legal test would soon challenge both him and Christophe.

In the summer of 1808 Goodall was back in London in the *Hopewell*. With the proceeds of a cargo of Haitian sugar and coffee he made a donation in Christophe's name of £100 'for the relief of British prisoners of war in France', alongside an annual subscription of 20 guineas to the Humane Society.[29] In the hope of winning favour with the Royal Navy, Goodall also announced that the president had ordered the widespread cultivation of hemp with the aim of supplying rope to the British fleet.[30]

When he returned to Haiti Goodall was soon back patrolling the restive northwest coast in the new flagship he had brought from Britain, the *Lord Mulgrave*. Pétion's ships were blockading Port-de-Paix, and Jean Rabel was back under Lamarre's control. Christophe's ordered were precise:

> Set sail with the squadron and head in the direction of Jean Rabel. If you can burn down that town burn it down, after that you will proceed in the direction of Môle [Saint-Nicholas] to see if the rebels are still there. Should this not be the case you will pursue them to the Bay of Saint-Marc where you are sure to capture some of them. I would have liked you to go as far as the Bay of Saint-Marc. However, if the rebel's ships are at the Môle you will cruise in the vicinity to find out whether they remain in that place for they cannot hold out for long, not having the means or supplies.[31]

After lifting the blockade Goodall sailed in high spirits for Môle Saint-Nicholas. Here he met his stiffest opponent yet: HMS *Daedalus*, under the rigid command of one Captain Charlton.

Charlton put the *Lord Mulgrave* to the chase, bringing her alongside with a threatening broadside of cannon. Goodall was detained and his ship sent back to Port Royal in Jamaica, where Charlton intended to claim it as a prize. A second Royal Navy ship was sent to advise Christophe of the encounter. Christophe was outraged by the actions of an officer of a country he regarded as a potential ally, and just as his admiral was about to deal a hammer blow against the southern navy. In a letter to Admiral Rowley in Jamaica, he accused Charlton of behaving as 'the declared protector of the rebels' and of waging 'a single-handed war against a friendly government which has never ceased giving proofs of its attachment to His Majesty's subjects'. The letter was delivered by General Simon—the highest-ranking Haitian official to travel to Jamaica since independence—and Harmer Gaskell, a representative of the British merchants in Cap-Haïtien, who sent their own petition asking the British authorities to bear their interests in mind when resolving the situation.[32]

In Port Royal, the news of the *Lord Mulgrave*'s capture was unhappily received. Captain Charlton's unauthorised actions put Rowley in the unenviable position of formulating an opinion on the delicate question of Haiti's status. Was Haiti still a French colony, albeit one in revolt? If so, Goodall was a traitor to the crown and his ship had been legally seized. But if Haiti was a sovereign state, Goodall was in service to a power that might be called on to harass British merchants carrying out a legal trade with Port-au-Prince. Goodall himself had carried a letter in which he offered to sail joint patrols with the Royal Navy under Christophe's flag. It suggested that 'your excellency might take into consideration that General Christophe is an Englishman ... devoted to the flag he was born under, and never had a greater gratification than when he could be of service to it'.[33] Rowley sought the opinion of Jamaica's Governor and Advocate-General, who suggested the *Lord Mulgrave* be sent to London for the Admiralty to deal with.[34]

After weeks of deliberation, a compromise was agreed on. The *Lord Mulgrave* would be restored to Christophe, while Goodall was sent under arms to England to be examined over his conduct. Rowley breathed a sigh of relief. In London, Castlereagh was given legal advice suggesting that a successful prosecution against Goodall for being in the service of a foreign power (of whatever flag) was slim. This provided him with the excuse to file the case in the same way that he dealt with Peltier's lobbying—by refusing to acknowledge it. Goodall was quietly released.[35] When he eventually made his way back to Haiti in November 1809 it was at the helm of another ship for Christophe's navy, a 'very beautiful frigate' that was quickly rechristened *L'Haïtienne*. A banquet was thrown in Goodall's honour in Cap-Haïtien as thanks for his loyal service.[36]

The northern fleet now consisted of seven frigates and a small cutter, but a buoyant Christophe demanded ever more ships so that he could begin his blockade of the south. His French merchant friend Joseph Bunel, who now divided his interests between Cap-Haïtien and Philadelphia, was commissioned to outfit a 38-gun corvette in the shipyards of Baltimore. Despite an official trade embargo on Haiti by the USA, Christophe knew well that the illicit trade between the two nations was booming. Some months earlier he had placed notices in the American press criticising the 'unhappy circumstance' of the embargo and taking to task 'the falsity of the infamous impostures my enemies [in southern Haiti] have spread with so much profusion against me'. He urged merchants to avoid the disorder of Port-au-Prince and to sail for the protected harbours of the north instead.[37] Still, Bunel was nervous about leaving port without tangling with the authorities. Christophe told him to sail first for Puerto Rico rather than directly to Haiti, and to 'try as far as you can to avoid meeting any vessel whatsoever'. Bunel successfully delivered the ship in early 1810.[38] Christophe would have regarded the delivery as a particularly sweet win over President Jefferson's blockade.[iii]

Christophe would have hoped that the arrival in Puerto Rico of a ship flying Haitian colours might also bolster his image in the Spanish Caribbean. In June the previous year, the French army had occupied Spain and Napoleon Bonaparte had placed his brother Joseph on the throne in Madrid. On learning this, Christophe immediately wrote to the Spanish governor in Havana pledging that Haiti would recognise only the deposed Fernando VII as Spain's legitimate king. He wrote in solidarity as the leader of a neighbouring country that had laboured under French rule, and proposed a peaceful relationship between Haiti and Spain and trade with Cuba.[39] Governor Someruelos declined to answer, but at the end of 1808 Christophe matched his words with actions by sending military aid to Juan Sánchez Ramírez, the exiled governor of Santo Domingo, who was attempting to liberate the colony from France. The authorities in Puerto Rico reported that Christophe was 'quick and generous' in sending arms, along with his general José Campos Taváres and 300 troops to aid the Spanish. A Royal Navy frigate may even have been involved in the shipping of Haitian men and materiel to the Spanish: a perfect example of the anti-French alliance that Christophe hoped would win him recognition.[40]

When Santo Domingo fell in the last week of 1808, Christophe's assistance helped the Spanish achieve what he and Dessalines had failed to do a few years earlier, expelling France from its final stronghold on Hispaniola. Taváres wrote to Christophe about the

---

[iii] In conversation with the US merchant Simeon Johnson in 1807, Christophe called Jefferson a 'pusillanimous' figure and expressed a preference for vice-president Aaron Burr. Given that he had just declared war on Pétion, it is tempting to believe that Christophe may have been jealous that Burr had been able to kill his long-time rival Alexander Hamilton in a simple duel.

honourable manner in which he had been received by the Spanish and the military counsels he had shared with Ramírez.[41] The aid was well received by the junta in Spain. In February 1809 they wrote to the governor of Havana instructing him to appoint an emissary to 'cultivate relations of friendship with said black chief'.[42] Someruelos had just refused to give an envoy from Pétion permission to land in Havana, and had no intention of opening up diplomatic ties with Christophe or allowing any black leader to parade their independence in the largest Spanish slaving port in the Caribbean. Although he received multiple orders to open official ties with Christophe on behalf of the Spanish crown, he simply refused to comply.[iv]

While diplomatic recognition remained in the hands of unsympathetic actors and his navy continued to raise awkward questions for his neighbours, Christophe still had much to cheer about in 1809. His Independence Day speech that year, delivered in Port-de-Paix, celebrated the expulsion of France from the island and the common cause that had been formed with the 'Haitian Spaniards'. He formally declared construction of the Citadelle, 'the palladium of our liberty', to be complete, with its artillery in position and magazines overflowing with supplies.[43] Despite the drain on manpower caused by the civil war, the fortress had been greatly expanded since the death of Dessalines. Its northern face had been completely remodelled with the addition of a sharp wedged bastion joined to the main fort with a massive rotunda, with walls raised over 40 metres high. Facing out to sea like the prow of an immense stone ship, it shielded the rest of the Citadelle from prevailing storms coming off the coast, making it the impregnable heart of Christophe's government.[44]

The builders had been equally busy at the foot of the mountain in Milot. The mansion that Christophe had built after independence was turned into a palace that he named Sans Souci. The *Gazette Officielle de l'Etat d'Hayti* commended its magnificent setting and the

---

[iv] In April 1812, José Antonio Aponte, a free black carpenter and artist from Havana, was hanged for helping to plan an anti-slavery uprising in the colony. When arrested he was found with a 'book of paintings' containing images of black kings and leaders, which the authorities claimed he used to inspire his fellow conspirators. Among the images that Aponte shared was a portrait of Christophe.

new embellishments to the building that were being added every day. Bunel sent white and slate-grey marble from the USA to decorate the palace, and Christophe had asked Goodall to bring him fine wallpaper from London. The admiral forgot—but later claimed that such was the opulence of Christophe's plan for the palace he nailed gold doubloons to the walls as a substitute instead.[45]

The Citadelle and Sans Souci were material reflections of the confidence Christophe felt that a final victory over Pétion must be imminent. In October 1808 Pétion had personally led another military expedition to Saint-Marc that ended in disaster. When the siege began, a northern counter-attack led by André Vernet cut off the army from its supply lines, while Christophe's navy repelled an attempt to land in the harbour. Within weeks, Pétion's army had completely run out of food. On 18 November a sustained bombardment on his camp caused a reported 300 casualties. Soldiers fled through thickets so dense that their torn uniforms were left hanging on the branches. Pétion tried ordering a counter-attack to cover his retreat, but with his army crumbling he only escaped by disguising himself as a female camp follower—an act of baseness that was 'hardly credible', according to the report delivered to Christophe, but one that the northern printing presses were nevertheless quick to publicise.[46]

In May 1809 Pétion tried again with a new campaign from Mirebalais. It was to be his last major expedition north. After successfully capturing the town of Verrettes, he left General Gérin to consolidate the army's position and retired to Port-au-Prince.[47] A small, fast-moving second column was then ordered to make an audacious dash north across Haiti's central plateau to descend to Grand Rivière, the old maroon stronghold from the revolution and deep in the heart of Christophe's territory. Unfortunately for Pétion, the northern army received advance warning of the incursion and reinforced their positions at Fort Sourde on the banks of the Grand Rivière du Nord. The defending commander repelled a southern cavalry charge by waiting until the horses had almost reached the bayonets of his troops before ordering them to fire. The assault dissolved into a wild retreat. David Troy, one of Pétion's most experienced generals, was killed, and over the following week the army made its disordered way back south. In the northern counter-attack Christophe's troops even captured the strategic republican fort at Boucassin.[48] Gérin's force was now completely cut off. He eventually received word that a ship was being sent to Arcahaie for them if his men could cut their way through, but when rumours began to spread that instead of being returned to their barracks they would be sent to reinforce the garrison at Môle Saint-Nicholas, many of the soldiers chose to desert Gérin instead. He eventually made his way back to Port-au-Prince, utterly humiliated and bitter at having been abandoned by Pétion. In January 1810 he was killed at his home in Anse-à-Veau after being suspected of leading a plot against the president.[49]

Christophe celebrated his successes with a round of promotions for his officers, while Pétion was left with the realisation that he was being permanently outmanoeuvred by his rival.[50] Worse still, the treasury in Port-au-Prince was almost bare. At the end of 1809 Pétion was forced into a series of land reforms to buy his army's loyalty by giving land grants to officers and enlisted men alike. The plots were mostly abandoned coffee plantations or in areas suitable for forestry, and Pétion tried to ban the new owners from taking cultivators from the few remaining sugar plantations to work on them, but this expedient parcelling out of land was another nail in the coffin of the plantation system introduced by the French. Eventually its effects would threaten to undermine the whole basis of Christophe's government.

In April 1810 Pétion appeared to receive a boost in his prospects when André Rigaud landed in Les Cayes. Writing to Pétion on his arrival, Rigaud spoke of the hardships he had undergone to escape his exile in France and pledged his service to the president.[51] Pétion delightedly appointed Rigaud to the command of his southern army and issued him with orders to march against Goman and finally regain control of the rebellious southwest. For Christophe, the news of who would lead the campaign against his most important asset in the region was met with fury. In letters to the British government, he said he saw the hand of Bonaparte in Rigaud's return and urged again the formation of an anti-French alliance that would help bring down Pétion.[52] Royal Navy reports from Jamaica privately punctured this view by advising that Rigaud was 'entirely hostile to the French', but Christophe need not have worried unduly. Rigaud would quickly prove that he was no one's pawn.[53]

Since the start of his insurgency in 1807, Goman had carved out his own quasi-state in the mountains of Grand Anse. His maroons raided Jérémie without a care and every expedition against him soon foundered in the dense forests of the region. Rigaud's army left Les Cayes full of patriotic bluster, but when it arrived in Jérémie Rigaud realised that a different approach was needed. The town was in a parlous condition. The garrison and merchants took advantage of the anarchy to trade with the maroons and undermine the state even further. Rigaud sent envoys to Goman and explained in a letter to Pétion that the terrain was too rugged and the insurrection had gone too far to be beaten by arms alone. His discussions with Goman's officers convinced him that 'gentleness and patience' alone would convince them to put down their arms—but only as part of a wider political settlement. To this end Rigaud proposed that an armistice be negotiated with Christophe, permanently dividing Haiti in two. Peace would return to Grand Anse, and Pétion should give up Môle Saint-Nicholas in exchange for the port at Saint-Marc.[54]

Rigaud did not know that at that moment Môle Saint-Nicholas was on the brink of complete collapse. The failure of Pétion's campaigns in the north had only increased the pressure on Lamarre's garrison. As Christophe added ever more ships to his navy, the blockaded port became starved of supplies. Lamarre pleaded with Pétion for permission to abandon the town, lamenting that the troops who had previously performed such heroism in holding the enemy at bay for so long now shrank from their duty to 'seek, far within the enemy's lines, either inevitable death, or at the best a scanty supply of ground provisions to eke out a miserable existence'. Pétion refused, responding only that 'where the public service is concerned, a heart like you cannot hesitate'.[55] As Rigaud arrived in Jérémie, Lamarre's last outpost on the outskirts of the town had just been captured by northern soldiers. Artillery fire now rained down on its defenders. On 10 July Lamarre was killed while helping to man the ramparts. As the siege entered its closing act, a barge carrying his heart slipped past the blockade to be taken to Port-au-Prince, where funeral orations were performed with full military honours.[56] Lamarre's death meant that the path to complete control of the north was now open. Christophe arrived in Môle Saint-Nicholas to direct the final operations of the siege, and on

26 September the last exhausted remnants of the garrison were taken into captivity.

Cap-Haïtien was illuminated for five nights in celebration. 'Rebellion is extinguished in this quarter,' crowed Christophe at a victory parade in the main square, 'and you have planted on every side the colours of the legitimate authority.' He praised the courage and fidelity of his troops and urged them to show compassion and understanding to those they had fought against, those 'unhappy children of the south' who had shown great bravery despite having been abandoned and betrayed by their officers.ᵛ Casting himself as the father of the entire Haitian people, he announced a general amnesty and urged all Pétion's soldiers to flock to his cause. 'There is more joy in heaven over that one sheep which is found again,' he judged, 'than for the whole flock that hath never strayed.'[57]

The capture of Môle Saint-Nicholas was quickly followed by startling news from the south: Rigaud had drawn his own conclusions from the weakness of Pétion's regime and had declared his own independent state from Les Cayes. The entire southern peninsula had risen to support him, including Gérin's old power base at Anse-à-Veau and two of Pétion's generals in Port-au-Prince.[58] Christophe was quick to try and press home his advantage by sending a peace delegation to Port-au-Prince.[59] They arrived in the city just as Pétion was attempting to broker a peace agreement with Rigaud on the bridge at Miragoâne that formed the boundary between their two territories. News of the delegation caused much disquiet in the republican camp. At this most delicate of moments it was feared that Christophe's envoys were really on an intelligence-gathering mission in advance of an attack on Port-au-Prince. They were immediately dismissed out of hand and told to leave the city. Pétion and Rigaud failed to come to terms, but the northern delegation at least convinced them to come to each other's mutual aid if such an invasion should occur.[60]

Christophe had other plans, however. After his final victory at Môle Saint-Nicholas he now decided to spend his time consolidating

---

ᵛ Even Lamarre could be safely praised now that he was dead. According to Vastey, he was 'worthy of a happier fate' than that of being abandoned by Pétion. See Baron de Vastey, *An Essay on the Causes of the Revolution and Civil Wars of Hayti* (Exeter, 1823), p. 83.

his northern state. To do this required a new political settlement. The title of president was deemed no longer fit for purpose: Christophe now desired a crown.

11

BIRTH OF A KINGDOM

The proclamation of Henry Christophe as King of Haiti was made on 26 March 1811 at Fort Liberté, where seven years earlier he had stood alongside Dessalines and Clerveaux to make their first declaration of independence from France. Fort Liberté was the republican name given to the town during the revolution, but in a nod to how things had changed, the official account of Christophe's ascent to the throne used the town's old name of Fort Dauphin—the French title traditionally given to the king's son. By the time of his coronation, he had the town rechristened as Fort Royal.[1]

The news of the declaration spread 'with the rapidity of the electric flame' and by the time Christophe, Marie-Louise (now the august Queen of Haiti) and Victor-Henry, the Prince Royal, arrived in the capital, they were greeted by 'unbounded transports of affection and joy' and received the congratulations of the civil officers and military ranks well into the evening, as well as that of the city's foreign merchants, who were eager to see how their prospects would fare under this change of rule.[2]

What prompted Christophe's desire to be crowned? His consolidation of rule over the north had involved a gradual remodelling of the state in his image, with the quiet renaming of Cap-Haïtien to Cap Henry the previous summer being the most obvious change noted by outsiders. Another indication of his aspirations could perhaps have been detected in late 1809 with the addition of 'His Gracious' or 'Serene Highness' to his presidential title.[3] He was certainly in a position to capitalise on the most confident political and military position he had enjoyed since the start of the civil war. The return of André Rigaud to the south and his creation of a breakaway state had weakened Pétion, while Goman remained unmolested in Grand Anse. Christophe's navy was increasingly able to blockade some southern ports and had even captured two French privateers in the middle of January. His fleet was further bolstered in the same month by the addition of a new flagship brought by Admiral Goodall from Plymouth. Christophe had it rechristened *Améthyste* for his eldest daughter.[4]

The blockade attracted the disapproving attention of the Royal Navy in Jamaica, but even here Christophe could have been forgiven for feeling his assertive stance would receive little censure. It had taken more than a month of complaints from British merchants in Port-au-Prince for Admiral Rowley to dispatch a sloop from Port Royal to accompany British ships passing through southern Haitian waters. Even then he gave explicit orders not to use force in the event of any confrontation with Christophe's navy.[5]

In the event, no ships were intercepted, but Rowley's cautious approach in dealing with Christophe's regime was underscored even further after HMS *Hyperion* had been accidentally fired on by a Haitian battery off Gonaïves. Its commander, Captain Vashon, subsequently blustered about not receiving adequate satisfaction for the incident after meeting with Christophe, but his short-tempered behaviour prompted Christophe's secretary Rouanez to send his own letter of complaint to the admiral, protesting the disrespect shown by a British officer to 'His Highness', the Haitian president.[6]

Vashon may not have known it, but he had arrived at Christophe's door at a sensitive time. While the officer was kept waiting to be received, Christophe and his council had been notified that Pétion had been re-elected as president in Port-au-Prince. In a bullish inauguration speech to the city's Senate, Pétion had set himself up as the true defender of the revolution. Having weathered the storms of the past four years, his republic promised to continue its firm stance against the 'yoke of tyranny'.[7] This perhaps was the final spur that Christophe needed to make his move. The monarchy was announced barely two weeks after Pétion was sworn in.

The legal act creating the Kingdom of Haiti was signed two days after the pronouncement. It was written by the Council of State led by Paul Romain and André Vernet, and declared that the north's 1807 constitution, written in the chaos of that year, had only ever been unfinished business. Now that the tempests hovering over the infant nation had passed, thanks to 'the genius of the supreme Magistrate who holds the reins of government', it was time for a new settlement to fix the order of things.[8]

In his first speech responding to the announcement, Christophe declared himself mindful of the responsibility of assuming the crown and suggested that his acceptance of the royal title was out of selfless duty rather than personal ambition:

> I have no other happiness than that of the people of Hayti, of whose toils I have partaken; and nothing that interests the welfare of the state can be indifferent to me.

> The nation has judged necessary to its prosperity and safety to elevate me to the throne, and to fix the hereditary succession in my family; I yield to its wish, since it contributes to the public felicity.

> This day, in giving me the measure of all hearts, will never cease to be present to my mind; it will recall to me all that the Haytian people hath done for me and my family, and every moment of my life shall be devoted to recompensing it for its filial tenderness. I will be on the throne, the same as I have been in adversity, and such as becomes a good king to be; and may my descendants inherit successively that pure affection with which my heart throbs for my country![9]

Marie-Louise was equally humble: 'The appellation of Queen, which the nation has just decreed to me, unites me more closely with the fortunes of the Haytian people, to whom I delight in being a tender mother.' She was especially mindful that the fortunes of the nation and her family were now conjoined in her title: 'Seeing my family is destined hereafter to take my place, it will be my pleasing duty to superintend their education with peculiar care, so that my children may be to me my dearest decorations, as on them will one day depend the destiny of my country.'[10]

After the publication of the new royal constitution, the Council of State met in grand assembly in Cap Henry to present it to the public. Military bands struck up in the main square, so that an address from the council could be read to the city's residents to explain the happy reasons why they were no longer citizens of a republic but subjects of a crown:

> Victory, faithful to his arms, has seated itself beneath [Henry Christophe's] colours; tranquillity reappears, order is established; discipline has been permanently restored in the army and in the fleet; conspiracies have been suppressed; the conspirators punished; justice has resumed its course; morals and public instruction have been reformed; cultivation and commerce have been bettered; at length, happiness and prosperity have appeared once more, and promise a lasting duration to the state.[11]

In consequence, the council declared that its heart was at one with the people and the army in deciding that the government of one individual 'is the most natural, the least subject to troubles and reverses, and such as unites, in a supreme degree, the power of maintaining our laws, protecting our rights, defending our liberty, and making us respected abroad'.[12]

The title of Governor-General, as borne by the glorious Toussaint Louverture, was insufficiently grand, they explained, as it implied an officer in the pay of another power. Dessalines was praised as being worthy of his imperial title, but the council conceded that he had been an emperor without an empire. A presidency in the manner of the USA had been examined, but 'though we appear in the same hypothetical situation as the Americans, being a new people, still we possess the wants, the manners, the virtues, and we will add, the vices of the old states'. Furthermore, it was noted that there were plenty of European states smaller than Haiti that were monarchies, all of them recognised by the great powers even though they lacked the resources and wealth of Haiti, to say nothing of its martial valour. Haiti had the same right to self-determination as any of them. The council even approvingly quoted the French philosopher Montesquieu's support for 'paternal monarchial [sic] government' to justify their actions.[13]

It is doubtful that the name Montesquieu would have meant much to the listening crowds, but the address was also written for an international audience. A printed version quickly found itself carried aboard the foreign ships sailing from the city. Christophe's representations in London had so far gone nowhere, but his declaration as king was a new chance to cement his legitimacy as part of a long line of great men, 'sole artizans [sic] of their own fortune', who had founded their own dynasties. A grudging respect was even paid to Napoleon Bonaparte, who had risen from a 'slender reed' to an emperor who had populated the thrones of Europe with his own family.[14]

The idea of a monarchy would equally have been familiar to the Haitians who had been originally brought to Saint-Domingue through the slave trade. 'Are there not in Africa an infinity of empires, kingdoms, and independent states?' wrote Baron de Vastey in an 1814 pamphlet defending Haitian sovereignty. At least one member of the state council, the governor of Cap Henry, Jean-Pierre Richard, was born in the Kingdom of Kongo in central Africa.

It was also known there had previously been what the Haitians might have regarded as kings on the island long before the arrival of Columbus. The Taíno organised themselves under hereditary chiefs called caciques. It was felt particularly auspicious that one of the last caciques had been called Enrique, who fought the Spanish so skilfully that they were forced to sign a peace treaty with him, recognising his autonomy. In the official account of Christophe's coronation, the names of Enrique and Henry bled together so that one acted as the precursor to the other.[15]

While the Council of State gave a sober justification for the creation of the monarchy, they remained keenly aware of their own interests. When Dessalines crowned himself emperor, he failed to bind his officers closely enough to his new regime. Christophe refused to make the same mistake. The creation of a hereditary monarchy was accompanied by the creation of a hereditary nobility. Romain became the Prince du Limbe, while Vernet was named Prince des Gonaïves. Kongo-born Richard became the Duc de Marmelade. The titles brought Christophe the opportunity to reward his supporters with grants of land which allowed them to consolidate their own positions in the new kingdom. Even Goman, fighting his lonely rebellion in Grand Anse, was named Comte de Jérémie. In total, six princes, seven dukes, twenty-two counts, thirty-six barons and fourteen chevaliers were ennobled to populate the new kingdom.[16]

Cap Henry was thrown into a flurry of activity following the proclamation. There were just eight weeks before the coronation, which Christophe planned to be the grandest event ever held in the country. He poured the same energy he had put into building the Citadelle into the creation of his new kingdom. Joseph Rouanez, now Duc de Morin and promoted to secretary of state and foreign affairs, oversaw the raft of paperwork that underpinned the new kingdom. The presidential palace had to be reshaped into a royal household. There was a reorganisation of the military to oversee, incorporating the noble ranks as well as the creation of new royal regiments. Rouanez wrote to Jean-Gabriel Peltier in London to advise him of the creation of the monarchy, so that he could announce it to the British government on the day of the coronation. Peltier in turn wrote on Christophe's behalf to Pope Pius VII in Rome, asking for new orders for the kingdom's clergy.[17]

Christophe's interpreter Alexis Dupuy (now Baron de Dupuy) made sure that the foreign community were kept abreast of developments. A banquet was planned in their honour as part of the celebrations to encourage them to send home positive reports about the kingdom's birth. Dupuy was particularly delighted when, in the final run-up to the coronation, two Royal Navy ships pulled into the harbour at Cap Henry to take on supplies. Their captains were duly accorded pride of place at the festivities as representatives of the British crown. Invitations to the Spanish authorities across the border in Santo Domingo were also sent and accepted. As much as he could, King Henry was coming out onto the international stage—a fact he would ensure was made well known to his rival in Port-au-Prince.

Christophe's other most trusted secretary, the Paris-educated Julien Prévost (ennobled as the Comte de Limonade), was put in charge of the coronation itself, a description of which he wrote up afterwards as *An Account of the Glorious Events Which Brought Their Royal Majesties to the Throne of Haiti*, the first book to be published in the kingdom.[i] The editor of the *Gazette Officielle de l'Etat d'Hayti*, Juste Chanlatte, the Comte des Rosiers, put aside his shipping reports and translations of foreign news to give free reign to his

---

[i] Some foreign commentators later poked fun at the titles of the Comte de Limonade and the Duc de Marmelade, unaware that they were taken from towns in Haiti whose names were bequeathed by French colonists.

poetic music, and composed a series of cantatas to be performed during the coronation's evening entertainments.

Also working hard were the unnamed heralds who were to create the iconography for the kingdom. In total they produced more than ninety detailed coats of arms for the crown and nobility which were gathered together in a remarkable hand-painted volume. This armorial offers one of the most vivid accounts of how Christophe wished his new country to be seen.

The heralds were familiar with European heraldic traditions, but were keen to make their own imaginative leaps in shaping the visual language of the kingdom. To the bulls and stags of traditional western arms, they added animals from Africa and the Caribbean. Elephants, ostriches and hyenas jostled for space with flamingos and manatees. Some coats of arms were literal, such as the crossed quill and sword granted to each of the king's secretaries to promote and defend their monarch. Others took a more delightful direction, such as those of the Baron de Béliard, keeper of the royal gardens, whose shield bore a rake and watering can flanked by two iguanas. The inclusion of mythical elements such as wyverns and gorgons showed that Christophe was laying claim to the long continuity of western monarchs while creating something entirely new, in a world that appeared to begrudge its entire existence. Nothing underscored this more clearly than the arms granted to the capital. On the shield of Cap Henry, a ship tossed by stormy waters finds safe haven in the city's port. The shield's supporters are a pair of black-skinned Hercules figures with clubs and lion-skin cloaks—a hero of classical myth defiantly reclaimed for an African people.

The herald's most important job was to create the arms for the king himself. For a man who had been born enslaved and who had burned his city to the ground rather than cede it to an invading French army, only one creature was deemed appropriate. A crowned phoenix rose from the flames on a royal blue shield dotted with golden stars and announced Christophe's personal motto: 'I am reborn from my ashes'. Two silver ermine lions flanked the shield, and below them the motto of the kingdom: 'God, my cause and my sword'.[18]

Queen Marie-Louise's arms repeated the same motifs, adding a wreath of roses and replacing the gold stars with bees, while the

Prince Royal was given the same arms as his father, with a traditional silver tab on the shield to indicate that he was the heir. Of the
royal family, only Princesses Améthyste and Athénaïre were denied
their own arms, as they awaited those they would eventually acquire
through marriage.

The coronation was set for 2 June, and as the day approached
preparations in Cap Henry reached fever pitch. The city's damaged
colonial cathedral was judged insufficiently grand, so an army of
carpenters erected a new temporary church, more than twice the
size, on the parade ground at Champ de Mars. Roads were fixed and
the palace hung with phoenix-shaped lanterns. On Place d'Armes,
a 25-metre-high column was erected, topped by a transparent globe
with the initials of each member of the royal family and Christophe's
crown. Tailors cut and sewed into the night to perfect the costumes
for the nobility. A royal edict had laid out the strict rules for courtly
attire with as much care as had been given to the coats of arms. The
kingdom's new ruling class were to be dressed in the showiest silks,
with their hats topped with the brightest feathers. Seamstresses ran
through gold thread by the yard to embroider the countless cloaks
and tunics, while shoemakers had to be careful not to confuse the
red morocco leather demanded for the shoes of the princes and
dukes, with the green to be worn by the knights.[19]

At the end of May the city began to fill with civil, judicial and
military representatives from every province. Two days before the
coronation a dress rehearsal was held, during which Christophe
rode on horseback from his palace to the new church for a public
oath of loyalty to the kingdom. The princes and dukes, counts, barons and knights each took it in turn to kneel before the king-appar-
ent to swear obedience to the constitution and faithfulness to the
crown. 'Do you swear on your honour, on what you have most
sacred, to devote yourself to the service of the Kingdom ... to the
defence of the King and of the royal family, the laws and constitutions of the Kingdom, to maintain with all your power freedom,
independence, and to die, if necessary, for the support of the
throne?' Christophe demanded of them. When the oaths were complete, the banners of the army and navy were blessed to a chorus of
artillery fire. Christophe was finally ready to be crowned.[20]

The day of the coronation began before dawn, with the people of
Cap Henry roused by church bells and an artillery salute. As the sun

tipped into the main square the enthronement procession began to take shape.[21] A lone herald, bearing the royal arms with its ermine lions and triumphant phoenix, marched from the gates of the palace. Behind him thirteen more heralds formed up, each representing a different town in the kingdom. As Christophe considered himself king of the entire country, Port-au-Prince, Jacmel and other towns in the south were all represented.

Then came the nobility, more than seventy figures in total. With their rich ornaments they 'could not but astonish the gaping multitude', according to one of the Royal Navy officers present. The knights wore blue coats with white stockings, the more numerous barons dressed in red, while the counts could be picked out by their sky-blue coats and white tunics. 'Embroidered cloaks or mantles gracefully flowed from their shoulders' and their heads were covered from the sun with gold-laced hats and extravagant plumes. To the navy officer they 'exhibited a likeness of the ancient nobility, as they are represented in some of our old paintings'.[22]

As the nobility formed up six abreast, they were followed by the ministers of state. Leading them were André Vernet, minister of finance and the interior, and Paul Romain, minister of war. They wore black coats with red taffeta embroidered in gold, with white tunics and stockings and red morocco leather shoes. The black and red, echoed by the plumes in their hats, matched the colours of the kingdom's new flag. Along with Vernet and Romain marched the secretary of state Rouanez and the minister of justice Jean-Baptiste Juge, the Comte de Terre-Neuve. Behind the ministers strode Christophe's brother-in-law Prince Noël, in his role of royal cupbearer. The cavalry and infantry came next. Squadrons of the new King's Light Horse came first, mounted in ranks of six and wearing sky-blue uniforms with crimson facings and blue plumes in their shakos. They were followed by companies of the King's Royal Guard, marching in their all-white uniforms. Each detachment bore a regimental standard—sky blue for the cavalry, red and black for the infantry—bearing the royal arms and the motto 'God, my cause and my sword'.

An hour after the procession had begun to assemble, the people of Cap Henry finally caught sight of their king. From the gates of the palace trotted six mounted royal aides-de-camp. Close behind them, and to much applause, was the enormous state carriage of Haiti, pulled by eight white horses and flanked by mounted guards. This was the carriage made for Christophe in London and brought to Haiti by Admiral Goodall. The panels of the carriage displayed a sun rising from the sea, surrounded by bees to represent the industry by which Haiti would rebuild itself. In time he would commission an even more spectacular vehicle.[23] Inexplicably, no description of Christophe's coronation dress was recorded in the official account, but the crowds would most likely have seen a figure dressed entirely in white, and perhaps the glint of the morning sun on the gold thread of a tunic. Next to Christophe sat his wife Queen Marie-Louise, and the seven-year-old Prince Royal, Victor-Henry, stretching to see out of the windows to wonder wide-eyed at the spectacle of it all.

The six-horse carriage of Princesses Améthyste and Athénaïre made up the second half of the royal party, accompanied by colonels of the King's and Queen's Light Horse. More troops of cavalry followed, and then the carriage of Madame Dessalines, riding alone as a poignant reminder that the new kingdom had risen from the wreckage of her husband's imperial dreams. Her carriage was at the head of a parade of the duchesses, countesses and other female nobility, all in their court dresses and ordered according to rank. Finally, the red dress uniforms of the 2nd Regiment of cavalry brought the pageant to a close, with Cap Henry's citizens following noisily in their wake, as the procession slowly made its way to the coronation.

It took nearly an hour for the royal carriage to pass the short distance from the palace to the parade ground at the Champ de Mars. By the time it arrived the first ranks of the dragoons and royal guards were already drawn up to receive them. Opposite the new church a splendid royal pavilion had been erected, dressed in green taffeta and carpeted in crimson. As the carriage's mounted escorts peeled off, and equerries stepped forward to help the royal party descend, the top ranks of the nobility busied themselves preparing the symbols of state. 'The two royal crowns are a rare and precious work,' wrote Prévost, 'The richness, the elegance, the finish of the work, and the ingenious manner in which the diamonds were placed; the sceptre, the hand of justice, the jewelled necklaces, the royal cloaks and dresses—everything was worked by Haitians, without having to resort to the use of foreign hands.'[24] The crown was placed on Christophe's head, and he was given the sceptre and hand of justice, an old symbol taken from the French monarchy. The royal cloak, most probably in red silk and embroidered with his crest, was draped around his shoulders. With the final adjustments to his costume complete, Christophe was ready for his coronation. As the royal banner was held proudly ahead of him, and with his son and heir at his side, he marched to the sound of trumpets and drums past his troops and into the church to be anointed as king.

The church erected for the coronation was no less spectacular for its temporary nature. In a little over a month, a dome stretching 25 metres high had been raised over a building that could house hundreds. Inside, nine carpeted arcades held the congregation, with the walls of the nave draped in enormous sky-blue silk drapes embroidered with gold stars. Directly underneath the dome were the royal thrones, shrouded by a crimson canopy fringed with gold and decorated with phoenixes. Around the galleries were the words *Liberty*, *Independence*, *Honour* and *Henry*.

The precisely choreographed coronation ceremony had unexpected French roots. Prévost had taken the entire order of service, from the procession of the royal cortège into the church to the final prayers, from the official account of Napoleon Bonaparte's coronation in 1804.[25] On their entrance to the church, the royal couple were sprinkled with holy water before being shown to the choir. The canopied thrones were to be sat on only at the end of the ceremony; in the meantime they sat in more modest seats to the side of the altar. Waiting for them was the Breton priest Corneille Brelle, who had given the blessing to Toussaint's constitution in 1801 and crowned Dessalines emperor five year later. Now he stood as Archbishop of the Kingdom of Haiti.

After Brelle's opening prayer the king and queen knelt and were ceremonially stripped of the symbols of the kingdom. The chancellor, Baron de Lagroue, stepped forward to take the hand of justice and then quickly retired, taking care not to turn his back on his king. Next, the Duc de l'Artibonite, who had carried the royal banner, took the sceptre. The Grand Chamberlain removed Christophe's crown. Two more nobles removed his cloak, while Rouanez took the jewelled collar and Prévost the ceremonial sword that hung at

Christophe's side. A similar process was repeated for the queen. Now, for the last time as equals before the congregation, they joined the choir in singing the hymn 'Come Creator Spirit' and then laid their hands on the books of the Gospel. After giving a benediction, Brelle then anointed both of them, dabbing their foreheads and hands with holy oil.

Christophe and Marie-Louise now seated themselves for a Mass. When this was over, the symbols of state were brought back to the dais. Each was presented in turn to Brelle, who blessed them before they were returned to Christophe, rebuilding him piece by piece into Haiti's true sovereign. First was the sword, to defend his kingdom. Then the splendour of the royal cloak was protectively hung around his shoulders, that he would enjoy a long and peaceful reign as king. The sceptre and hand of justice were placed in his hands to exemplify the fairness with which he would rule. Finally, Brelle was handed the crown. As he invoked a line of kings stretching back to Solomon, David and Joshua, he solemnly placed it on Christophe's head with the following prayer:

> May God crown you with the crown of glory and justice, with honour and with fortitude, so that by the office of our blessing with righteous faith and the manifold fruit of good deeds you may attain to the crown of the everlasting kingdom, by His bounty whose kingdom and power last for ever and ever. Amen.[26]

Christophe rose for the first time as king. No longer a mere man, he was Henry I and bore other titles besides: Sovereign of La Tortue, Gonâve and other adjacent islands, Destroyer of Tyranny, Regenerator and Benefactor of the Haitian Nation, Creator of her Moral, Political and Martial Institutions, First Crowned Monarch of the New World, Defender of the Faith, Founder of the Royal and Military Order of St Henry.

His first act was to take the queen's diadem and place it on Marie-Louise's head.[ii] As king and queen they took their seats on the grand

---

[ii] Napoleon Bonaparte likewise crowned his wife Josephine as empress. The French emperor's influence apparently persisted beyond Prévost's stealing of his order of service: the Musée de Guahaba in Limbe in northern Haiti contains a large diorama made in the 1970s showing Christophe crowning Marie-Louise in a staged reproduction of Jacques-Louis David's famous painting *The Coronation of Napoleon*.

throne reserved for crowned monarchs. The assembled pages, heralds and nobles—all now their subjects—solemnly processed before the dais. When they were done, the archbishop had one last prayer to offer: 'May God strengthen you on this throne, and may Jesus Christ make you reign with him in his eternal kingdom, he who is the King of Kings and the Lord of Lords, who lives and reigns with the Father and the Holy Spirit, forever and ever.' With that, Brelle bent to kiss his monarch on the cheek, then straightened himself to face the congregation and cried at the top of his voice, 'Long live the King!'

Outside, crowds had gathered under a blazing mid-afternoon sun for their first sight of the newly crowned king. The usually severe Christophe may have finally granted himself a smile of satisfaction as he emerged with the queen at his side to rapturous cheers. Such was the outburst of love and applause to the heavens, Prévost recounts in his official chronicle, that even the soldiers charged with keeping order on the parade ground were moved to tears.[27]

The first royal engagement was to preside over a coronation banquet held in the gardens of the barracks facing Champ de Mars. An army of attendants had set three enormous tables, each seating 200 people. The first was for the royal family, members of the nobility and the kingdom's most honoured guests, including the Royal Navy captains, the Spanish representatives from Santo Domingo and favoured members of the foreign community. The other two tables hosted civil and military officers from every province. As the king and queen invited their guests to sit, a band played the French composition, 'Where can one be better than in the bosom of one's family?'[28]

With 600 glasses charged, a series of toasts celebrated the beginning of Christophe's reign. The first to do so was one of the foreign guests, Captain Douglass of the Royal Navy frigate HMS *Reindeer*. Throughout the coronation ceremony, Christophe joined in with the prayers and hymns but had otherwise maintained a regal silence. Now, after hearing the cheers offered by a British captain, he could finally speak as king. Rising from his seat, he raised his glass and replied with a toast of his own: 'To my brother, King George III— may the Lord Creator preserve him, that he may remain an invincible obstacle to the ambitions of Napoleon, and always a constant friend of Haiti!' To great applause, the names of both the Haitian and British monarchs were drunk three times over while the band played 'God Save the King'.[29]

A military parade followed the feast, leading the royal party back to the palace. Each regiment was accompanied by its band. The whole scene—the music, the ringing of church bells and the 'incessant' volley of celebratory fire (the troops had been given their own feast of wine and roast oxen while the royal banquet was taking place)—'almost stupefied the senses', according to one of the British officers present. Royal heralds marched just ahead of the king, distributing silver coins amidst the wild applause of the crowds.[30]

As the sun finally began to dip, the whole of Cap Henry was illuminated with lamps. In Place d'Armes there was public music and dancing into the night. Inside the palace, members of the nobility performed the new cantatas composed by Chanlatte for the occasion. 'For Henry,' they sang, 'the throne is forever inaugurated ... Receive the spoils of your unique bravery, and may peace and abundance decorate your triumphant path.'[31]

Chanlatte closed with a promise that the heavens themselves would be lit with 'fiery emblems of this new-born state', and as the music faded away an immense firework display lit up the night. The last time the sky had blazed over the city it was at Christophe's own hand, as he set the city alight to deny it to the French. It was the place where he had arrived as a boy, alone and uncertain, and now its people danced into the night to celebrate his ascent to the throne. As he looked to the skies with his queen, their faces catching the lights of the fireworks and the phoenix-shaped lanterns hung from the palace, he could feel truly reborn from the ashes of the past. A new and proud era for Haiti had begun.

12

SANS SOUCI

The five days of celebrations at Cap Henry for the coronation provided ample opportunity to impress the officials attending from the
provinces so they could return home with stories of the glorious
new kingdom they now found themselves subjects of. Before their
return journey they were given the opportunity to visit the Citadelle
fortress, where, according to Julien Prévost, they were rendered
near speechless by the genius of its creation.[1] But to reach this martial guarantor of Haitian independence they had to pass through the
town of Milot, where they saw an equally potent symbol of the
monarchy and its aspirations that Haiti should now take its place
among the cultured nations of the world: the new royal palace of
Sans Souci.

The mansion that Christophe first built here for his family had
been rebuilt in grand neoclassical fashion to form the centre of what
was planned to be his new capital. Milot had originally comprised
of its eponymous plantation and those of Grand Pré and Choiseul,
huddled together where a small river emerged onto the northern
plain between the steep green ridges of the Bonnet-à-l'Evêque and
Grand Gilles mountains. Now enormous groundworks had filled in
its ravines and levelled the area to allow for a large complex of
buildings and ornamental gardens to be laid out. When the officials
arrived in the town, they were met with a sight that was a world
away from the still partially ruined streets of Cap Henry.

The first building in the palace grounds was the enormous
rotunda of the royal chapel, faced with a classical columned porch
and topped with an extravagant dome. Through wrought iron gates
decorated with the king's arms, a path led past the relatively modest

191

palace of the ministers to a grand double staircase that swept up to the royal palace itself. Two bronze lions guarded the ascent and sat on either side of a fountain with a gilt sun bearing the motto, 'I see everything, and everything in the universe is seen by me.' From the top of the stairs, the vast baroque facade of the royal palace dominated everything. More than 50 metres in length, its two storeys were faced with an extravagant twenty-three bays with high rectangular doors and windows and immense pilasters. In the centre of the building was a balconied pavilion topped by a triangular pediment and a curved attic roof that was large enough to act as a third storey. Each end of the palace was framed by further three-storey pavilions with hipped roofs. Finished in yellow plaster with white detailing, the entire palace gleamed in the sun. At the time of the visit, it was almost certainly the grandest building in the Caribbean—and possibly in the Americas.[2]

If the visiting dignitaries were given a tour of the interior, they would have been shown through a series of galleries to the grand salon, audience chamber and throne room, and on to the banqueting hall and a library that held Christophe's large collection of books.[i] Above were the royal family's private apartments. The windows were hung with silk curtains and the floors laid with mahogany boards.[ii] On the walls were splendid mirrors and 'the most beautiful and rarest tapestry, which was amassed at a great expense, and with particular care in the selection'.[3] Christophe commissioned the artist Francisco Velázquez from Santo Domingo to create a giant mural showing scenes from Greek mythology, with the gods and heroes depicted as Africans.[4] The same principle applied in the royal chapel, where there was a large portrait of a black-skinned Virgin Mary, an

---

[i] Some later commentators disputed whether Christophe was literate, but a letter from Milot dated 13 May 1806 to a master carpenter named Lapommeraie, specifically requested the construction of boxes to transport 'my encyclopaedias and other objects'. See Christophe to Lapommeraie, 13 May 1806, Foyle Special Collections Library, King's College, University of London, FCDO2: FOL.F 1924 HEN, *Letterbook 1805–1806*.

[ii] 'I am sending you, Governor, a request made by the engineer in charge, for work to be done on my palace in Milot; would you send me immediately, by two-wheel hand truck, all the items mentioned herein. I am also sending you a three-inch nail that you should use as a model to choose the other pounds of nails mentioned in the said request, to nail down the floors in the said palace. Hurry up.' Henry Christophe to Jean-Pierre Richard, 7 August 1810 (Private collection).

image that is now common throughout Haiti as a representation of the Vodou spirit Ezili Danto. For the audience chamber, a large coat of arms was commissioned in bronze from London, with its shield bearing the crowned phoenix supported by royal lions and encircled by the gold chain of the order of St Henry. The display weighed over 270 kilograms and reputedly cost nearly \$2,600.[5]

The palace's southern facade overlooked ornamental gardens through which ran a stream with its channels diverting into decorative fountains. To the west a long lawn led to the Prince Royal's palace, and at its centre stood a large star apple tree, under which Christophe would receive petitions directly from his subjects once a week.[6] Beyond the gardens were some two dozen other buildings, including barracks for the royal regiments, a mint, a hospital and a printing press. Sans Souci was designed to be a model town embodying Christophe's vision for his kingdom.

No architectural plans have survived from the palace's construction. Recent archaeological digs of the site have placed parts of the structure as being no earlier than 1805 through the discovery of English pearlware of that date in its middens. Excavations have also shown that the Prince Royal's palace stands on the foundations of an earlier building, while the palace of the ministers has a completely different alignment to a building that had previously stood on the site—possibly the mansion first built by Christophe. One midden also revealed extensive examples of indigenous pre-Columbian pottery, a fact that would have pleased Christophe had he known it, given the explicit connections his ascension to the throne had drawn with the island's original Taíno inhabitants.[7]

Only after the extensive remodelling of these buildings was construction of the main palace likely to have begun, to allow its design to sit perfectly within its landscape. Like the Citadelle, Sans Souci's grandeur led many later foreign visitors to pour scorn on the idea that it was designed by Haitians. In 1830 the American visitor Jonathan Brown claimed that the palace was inspired by Frederick the Great's pleasure palace of the same name in Potsdam. Despite the two buildings bearing no physical resemblance, this connection held for more than 160 years, until the Haitian historian Michel-Rolph Trouillot put forward a more compelling explanation for its name, noting that the palace was built on the spot where Christophe had the maroon leader Sans Souci killed in 1803. The act of forgetting this event had begun as early as 1805, when Christophe declined to provide Dessalines with an account of Sans Souci's killing.[8] By so naming the palace in this location, Christophe thus helped ensure the permanent over-writing of the memory of his revolutionary rival, while also pointing the way to Frederick the Great's paternal vision of the enlightened monarch that he aspired to become.

Just as Christophe was the author of this act, so the architects and engineers who built Sans Souci were also Haitian, even when the models that they drew on were those of European neoclassicism. Pre-revolutionary Cap Français had many skilled architects versed in French tastes, including a sizeable number of prosperous men from the free coloured community.[iii] It was from the pool of those who had survived the revolution that Christophe likely turned for his palace. The engineer Faraud who oversaw the raising of the Citadelle would have been in charge of the building project. In 1811 he was raised to the title of baron and named as Intendant of the Royal Buildings as well as Director of the Army Corps of Engineers.[9] The mason André was also probably a senior figure in the construction. He was never ennobled but was later named as an official architect for the palace.[10] Baron Thomas de Béliard was named Intendant of the Royal Palace's Gardens, Waterways and Forests. Béliard would have overseen the enormous earthworks and landscaping needed for the palace grounds, supported by another engineer named Chéri Warloppe. Béliard was close enough to Christophe to have had the king as a witness to his wedding, and more than a century later was still remembered in local folk tales as the only person trusted enough by Christophe to know the secret hiding place of the king's lost gold.[11]

The main inspiration for Sans Souci was most likely the French palace of Malgrange, a building that was never built but whose plans and elevations were engraved in the books on the shelves of every skilled architect. The two bear a striking resemblance to each other, but in recreating an imaginary building the Haitian architects were given free rein to add their own innovations. They

---

[iii] For example, the barracks in Cap Français were a direct copy of Les Invalides in Paris, and the city's gardens were specifically laid out to evoke Versailles.

added a three-storey portico to the palace, capped with an unusual semi-circular pediment and a pavilion with concave walls, which gave them a complex geometrical problem to solve when arched doors and curved windows were added. But Sans Souci's architects were experienced with complex curves, as witnessed by the construction of the circular royal chapel with its 20-metre-wide dome. When a similar building was proposed for French Guadeloupe in 1820, the colonial authorities there dismissed the plans as being too difficult for its builders, but the church in Milot was actually the second similarly domed structure that Christophe's architects had built, having already raised the even more massive cupola of the coronation church in Cap Henry.[12] Such achievements were to be celebrated, which Baron de Vastey did by placing both the palace and the mountaintop Citadelle in a lineage even older than the European traditions they evoked: 'These two structures, erected by descendants of Africans,' he crowed, 'show that we have not lost the architectural taste and genius of our ancestors who covered Ethiopia, Egypt, Carthage, and old Spain with their superb monuments.'[13]

This celebration of Haiti's roots in Africa extended to the military reorganisation that accompanied the formation of the kingdom. Two new units were created under Christophe's direct patronage, the Royal Bonbons and the Royal Dahomets. The former were quartered at Sans Souci to act as the king's personal bodyguards. The Royal Dahomets were designed for a policing role, taking over the job of agricultural inspection from the military. Their name evoked the kingdom of Dahomey in West Africa where some of Christophe's subjects had undoubtedly been born, but the two units were designed to have their ranks filled with 'new' Haitians freshly arrived from Africa.[iv] These soldiers would be untainted by the divisions of the civil war, while the Royal Bonbons were to be made up of men barely out of their teens to allow for the creation of a cohesive unit that would be fiercely loyal to its commander, the king himself.[14]

[iv] In an echo of the erasure of Sans Souci, the French general Pamphile Lacroix suggested in his history of the Haitian Revolution that the name Dahomet was substituted for the more resonant Congo to deny the memory of the Congo maroons under Sylla, who had fought alongside Sans Souci and Petit Noël Prière.

The identity of the men who made up these units has always been shrouded in mystery. The arrival of ships carrying enslaved Africans to Haiti had ended years earlier with Sonthonax's declaration of emancipation in 1793, but several old families in Milot today still claim descent from the Royal Dahomets and proudly recall how their ancestors were brought from Africa to serve under Christophe.[15] Although the exact details may have been lost, that pride is almost certainly derived from the fact that during this period Christophe's navy had started to interdict foreign slaving vessels off Haitian waters, welcoming their liberated captives to a country where slavery had been abolished by force of arms. When the northern navy began its blockade against Pétion's republic, it captured three slave ships bound for Havana in a single year, with two of them carrying 440 and 205 African prisoners respectively. Haitian authorities were proud of their sailors' actions in freeing their 'unfortunate brothers, victims of greed and the odious traffic in human flesh'. In January 1811 Christophe visited the town of Verrettes where he was treated to a dance performance by a number of Hausa children who had recently been liberated from a Portuguese ship off Haitian waters. 'What heart could read of this without emotion?' asked the *Gazette Officielle de l'Etat d'Hayti*, recounting how the sight of the free children reduced their audience to tears. In return the children were said to have embraced Christophe 'as if they saw in him the parents from whom they had been stolen'.[16] These youthful dancers may well have been enlisted into the Royal Bonbons.

Queen Marie-Louise also had her own corps of personal bodyguards, known as the Amazons. The name echoed the famous all-female army of Dahomey as well as being the moniker given to a band of female insurgents operating around Cap Français in the earliest stages of the revolution.[17] Unlike the Royal Bonbons, the Amazons were reportedly drawn from the ranks of the female nobility, and most accounts suggest that they mainly accompanied the queen and princesses when they performed state duties. No description of the king's bodyguards has survived, but the Amazons wore uniforms made up of a blue silk tunic and wide satin trousers with gold or silver garters, and a silver helmet dressed with silk and ostrich feathers. Perhaps as a nod to their mainly ceremonial role, they were armed with a bow and lance. It was apparently the king's pleasure to put the Amazons to the full gallop—and according to one gossipy court observer, sometimes treat their ranks as an extended harem.[18]

Such rumours of the king's licentiousness would become a feature of accounts of the later years of his rule, and their spread was encouraged by Christophe's republican detractors after his death. From his vantage point at Sans Souci, however, Christophe only saw his palace and its people as being the next stage in uplifting his people. Toussaint Louverture had been the chief founder of Haitian liberty and Jean-Jacques Dessalines the guarantor of their independence. Christophe saw his role as the creator of the institutions of a great state. Through his own example, he would be the teacher who would guide the manners and morals of the Haitian people. To this end he formed a royal commission of a dozen of 'the wisest and most enlightened men' to draw up a new legal code for the kingdom, to be known as the Code Henry. It took more than six months of continuous work to compile a legal code deemed 'suitable to our usages, our climate, and our manners'.[19]

A key member of the commission was Baron de Vastey, who had been secretary to the minister of finance André Vernet, but had not been closely associated with Christophe until this point. A number of the commission members had been educated in France (Baron de Dupuy had also worked as a commercial agent in New York), but Vastey describes the drawing up of the new laws as a near miraculous affair, with the guiding light of his monarch leading the way from their state of ignorance to enlightenment: 'We had indeed among ourselves immense resources, but we were ignorant of them; the mine was abundant, but hitherto it had been unexplored. Animated however by the genius of Henry, impelled by necessity, the hardest and most inoperative of all laws, we dared the attempt.'[20]

The resulting nine volumes of law that were published in February 1812 ran to more than 750 pages and covered almost every aspect of life in the kingdom. Almost half of the Code Henry covered civil law, but there were also volumes dedicated to commerce, agriculture, criminal law and punishment, naval prizes and military regulations. At its heart was the principle that from the monarch down, everyone had their carefully prescribed place in society and a useful role to play within it. The first hundred pages of the Civil Code alone covered family law, from the requirement for marriage and the registration of births, to inheritance and obligations regarding the education of children. Family was all. Just as the king was the father of the nation, the opening sentence of the Agricultural Code described landowners as the 'good fathers' of their tenants, with all the family obligations that flowed from such a title.

Where Pétion had been forced to liberalise land ownership in the republic, the Code Henry formalised the plantation system that Christophe had helped Louverture and Dessalines to maintain. As if to draw attention away from this colonial inheritance, Vastey was keen to point out that the old French laws, 'which awakened the recollection of our former oppressors', were struck from the statute. Landowners and tenant farmers were to be bound together in a web of reciprocal obligations, and if those who ran the plantations were to be like fathers, farmers were given the right to have their complaints of poor treatment answered and there were instructions on the duty of care for sick or old workers.[21] Corporal punishment was banned.[v] Farmers were granted the same quarter share of the plantation's income, with special shares reserved for certain skilled labourers such as sugar refiners. Despite this, agricultural workers remained tied to the land. Anyone leaving their place of residence was deemed a vagabond, and marriage was still forbidden between those residing on different plantations. Work began at sunrise, with an hour's rest for breakfast at eight o'clock and a further two hours at noon. In the afternoon, work continued until sunset. On the day of rest, attendance at Sunday prayers was encouraged. Landowners were obliged to send workers for public projects such as the maintenance of the royal highways, to be carried out at the end of the harvest season.[22] To improve food security, landowners were also required to plant new stands of breadfruit and mango trees every year.

---

[v] In what might be one of the earliest laws passed against animal cruelty anywhere in the modern world, Article 87 of the agricultural code also banned the whipping of horses, cattle and other beasts of burden. The penalty for deliberately wounding or killing such animals was one month's imprisonment.

Thus regulated, the population would work in concert to bring prosperity, stability and good morals to the kingdom. The Dessalinean idea of freedom through national self-sufficiency still held sway over the republican concept of individual liberty, but when sections of the Agricultural Code were translated into English five years later, they were praised by abolitionist campaigners as a model system for the relationship between master and worker. The president of the Royal Society Sir Joseph Banks declared it to be the creation of 'the most moral association of men in existence; nothing that white men have been able to arrange is equal to it'. Christophe's vision was the most equitable imaginable:

> To give the labouring poor of the country a vested interest in the crops they raise, instead of leaving their reward to be calculated by the caprice of the interested proprietor, is a law worthy to be written in letters of gold, as it secures comfort and a proper portion of happiness to those whose lot in the hands of white men endures by far the largest portion of misery.[23]

The publication of the Code Henry was the crowning moment of the first year of Haiti's new monarchy. Its publication meant that Christophe could see in 1812 in a bullish mood. The newly regulated sugar and coffee industries had just paid for a new crown to be made for him in London, set with diamonds, emeralds and rubies. Other luxury goods followed, including a Herschel telescope, gold cups and salvers, a diamond collar and several tiaras for the queen and princesses as well as 'sundry diamond and gold pins, broaches, ear-rings, crosses, and watches'. The contents of the order were printed in the English press after it was briefly confiscated by customs agents on the Thames for evasion of duty: the shipping agent had sought to avoid paying export taxes by labelling the consignment as upholstery. Any embarrassment felt in Sans Souci may have been tempered by the description given in *The Gentleman's Magazine* of the sword of state, which said that its eight-foot length 'gives a grand idea of the muscular power of the Emperor'.[24]

The new kingdom's confidence stood in marked contrast to that of its southern neighbour. Two weeks after Christophe's coronation, and fearing that an invasion was imminent, the Port-au-Prince Senate announced that the national treasury was so bare that they could no longer guarantee to feed or pay the army. The silver gourd coin was devalued by punching a hole through its centre, and the city's merchant class was called upon for an emergency loan to the government.[25] A further crisis rocked the republic that August, when General Delva, who had served at Môle Saint-Nicholas with Lamarre and was known to be sympathetic to Rigaud, was imprisoned for conspiring against Pétion.[26] Christophe took advantage of the disarray by issuing a new proclamation 'to the residents of the south and west parts of the kingdom'. In it he declared that having been raised to the throne by the love of his people, he now sought again to reunify 'the scattered fragments of the great Haitian family' and 'to bring back peace, sweet peace, to the bosom of a nation too long torn apart'. An amnesty was offered to all those who would acknowledge him as king. Noble titles were dangled before Pétion's officers as reward for joining him in Haiti's new era. The talk was of unity, but to most listeners the offer to forgive his former enemies and cast their faults into oblivion felt more like a demand for supplication than a genuine attempt to find peace. The royal words fell on deaf ears.[27]

Rigaud died unexpectedly on 18 September in Les Cayes, aged fifty, leading Pétion to hope that this would lead to the swift reunification of the southern peninsula. Rigaud's successor, General Jérôme Maximilien Borgella, offered to reconcile with Pétion, but negotiations between commissioners representing the two parties collapsed in an air of mistrust, in no small part due to Pétion having recently encouraged troops in Jérémie to rebel against the breakaway state (ironically led by a colonel called Henry).[28] Christophe's forgiving mood similarly failed to last, and he encouraged further unrest in the south by shipping more arms to Goman in Grand Anse.[vi]

In January 1812 rumours began to swirl in the republic that another attack on Port-au-Prince was imminent. A Vodou priest called Bosquette from Croix-des-Bouquets, north of the city, was discovered masquerading as a veiled apparition of the Virgin Mary in a fig tree. This false-Virgin attracted many followers, who were

---

[vi] The degree to which Goman was ever truly subservient to Christophe or was just an opportunistic actor has always been unclear, but at least one of his surviving letters contains orders he sent on behalf of the king, signed using his title of the Comte de Jérémie.

terror-struck when he announced that a powerful army would soon appear on the plains and to resist it would be to disobey God. When the tree was set ablaze by the Bishop of Port-au-Prince as a demonstration of faith, Bosquette was captured and unmasked as an agent saboteur for Christophe.[29] Despite this, the story only grew in the febrile atmosphere of Port-au-Prince. When three northern ships appeared on the horizon a few days later, Pétion announced that the tyrant Christophe was preparing to march south, 'to increase the numbers of his slaves'. The army was mustered and orders sent to Jacmel for reinforcements.[30]

The ships were the corvettes *Princess Royal*, *Améthyste* and *Athénaïre*, named for Christophe's two daughters, and the smaller brigantine *Jason*. The capture of Môle Saint-Nicholas and the creation of the secessionist southern state had allowed Christophe's navy to become the master of Haiti's seas. At the end of January he sent the ships to patrol Haiti's southern coastline to test this strength and run supplies to Goman. Admiral Goodall was in England, so in his absence the flotilla was commanded by Vice-Admiral Pierre St Jean, the Comte de la Presqu'île.[vii] News of the consternation that the ships had caused was reported back to Christophe via a Royal Navy ship 'then at Port-aux-Crimes' when it called at Gonaïves a few days later. The royal glee was to prove short-lived. In his proclamation to the south and west, Christophe had made a point of offering a magnanimous hand of peace, but by sending this show of strength to encourage republican defections he fatally exposed the limits of loyalty in his own forces instead.

Unknown to Christophe or his vice-admiral, the quartermaster of the *Améthyste*, Eutrop Bellarmin, was a republican who had found much sympathy for the cause among his crew, most of whom had been pressed into service. When the ship had passed Port-au-Prince and became separated from its sister vessels, the *Améthyste*'s crew mutinied. Two officers joined them and the remainder were locked in the brig. Bellarmin immediately turned the ship into the nearest port at Miragoâne to declare himself for Pétion, unaware that it was under the control of Borgella. Hiding his surprise, Bellarmin declared

---

[vii] Presqu'île is the name of the peninsula that folds like a thumb around Môle Saint-Nicholas to create its formidably defensible bay.

himself for the south and the *Améthyste* was duly renamed *L'Heureuse Réunion* (The Happy Reunion).[31] The ship took on fresh southern troops and quickly embarked under the captaincy of a locally resident Frenchman named Augustin Gaspard to find the *Athénaïre* and *Jason*, in order to persuade them to abandon Christophe.

The task was remarkably easy. After a short parley the crews of the two vessels quickly threw in their lot with Borgella, and the officers who remained loyal to the kingdom were taken prisoner. It was the most disastrous day on the seas for Christophe since the seizure of the *Lord Mulgrave*. Before the ships could return to Miragoâne, a Royal Navy ship appeared on the horizon to complicate matters. Captain Yeo of the frigate *Southampton* demanded to know whose flag *L'Heureuse Réunion* was flying, and was surprised to learn that there was now a third Haitian state claiming its right to a navy. Aware of the complications created by the seizure of the *Lord Mulgrave*, Yeo advised that 'I know of only two contending chiefs of Haiti: Generals Christophe and Pétion' and that only his admiral could rule on Borgella's legitimacy, adding, 'it is very far from my wish to use any violence and I hope that you will proceed to Jamaica for examination quietly, at the same time it is my fixed resolve that you shall go.'[32]

The French captain declined the invitation. With 300 soldiers on board and two more Haitian ships at his back he believed he had the upper hand. After Yeo ordered a warning shot to be fired, *L'Heureuse Réunion* replied with a broadside and moved alongside the *Southampton* to try to board it. The other Haitian captains felt differently, and after a brief exchange of fire they fled to leave the two frigates to pummel it out. The thirty-eight cannons of the *Southampton* were brutally superior, as Gaspard learned when his main and mizzen masts were reduced to splinters above his head. When a further volley looked set to sink his ship completely, he raised the white flag. Yeo allowed the wounded to be landed at Miragoâne, but before setting course for Jamaica he called in at Port-au-Prince to disembark the remainder of the Haitian crew, accidentally muddying the waters when it came to claims over ownership of the vessel.[33]

The mutiny and subsequent intervention by the Royal Navy caused great consternation in Cap Henry, Port-au-Prince and Les Cayes alike. Christophe ordered his secretary of state Julien Prévost to write immediately to Admiral Stirling in Jamaica.[viii] Whereas Christophe never failed to address Pétion's republic in anything less than superior tones, with the British he was more emollient, and Prévost wrote with polite diplomacy. Given 'the law of nations and the accepted customs of civilised powers, and particularly that of the English nation whose probity is well known', he politely requested the return of the ships along with the 'guilty authors of this crime'.[34] It had taken nearly two weeks for a reliable account of what had happened to be confirmed in Cap Henry, but Yeo's brief call at Port-au-Prince had meant that Pétion was able to send his letter to lobby Stirling before Prévost. The mutineers had been bound for his republic, he claimed, and only adverse winds had seen them land in Miragoâne. Thus the British were duty-bound to return the ship to Port-au-Prince. Borgella, who had had no previous dealings with the Royal Navy, sent a letter signed by the half-dozen British merchants based in Les Cayes, who he had taken the precaution of putting under house arrest. 'We are fearful that unless a restitution is made of their frigate and people,' they advised the admiral, 'our properties in this country (which amount at this moment to about half a million dollars) will be confiscated to reimburse their loss.'[35]

Stirling's response was more confident than that of his predecessor over the *Lord Mulgrave*, and in his report to the Admiralty he praised Captain Yeo for his actions in capturing the ship under fire. He dispatched a sloop to Les Cayes under the command of a captain who was well known in the town, and was quickly able to free the British merchants by revealing the bluff with which Borgella had tried to hide the weakness of his hand. London had still never sent instructions on treating Haiti as an independent state, but he was determined to be even-handed to both Christophe and Pétion, and declined to return the ship to either of them. 'I agree most fully with you in reprobating every species of treason,' he wrote to Christophe about the *Améthyste*'s mutineers:

> But as your ship after arrival at Miragoâne had her name changed to *L'Heureuse Réunion*, and was officered and manned by General

---

[viii] Prévost was given the position following the death of the incumbent Joseph Rouanez in December 1811.

Borgella, and fought most desperately the ship belonging to my sovereign, I do not think myself authorized to give her up to any power, and therefore, I shall send a Ship of War immediately to England with a copy of the letter containing your claim, as also the demand of General Borgella and General Pétion on the occasion, and I will write to you as soon as I get an answer.

The king's polite diplomacy had not only failed, but Stirling's letter disappointed him even further by addressing him simply as 'General Christophe'.[36]

Christophe raged at both the loss of his ships and that his own sailors had dared to mutiny against him. He refused to see any fault in the strict discipline of his rule and could do little about the British position, so he blamed the loss of his ships on Pétion and his suspected French paymasters. A nobleman called the Baron de Papalier was singled out as the lead conspirator in the loss of the ships. A native of Les Cayes, who had taken part in the uprising there against Dessalines in 1806, he had been captured at the Battle of Sibert in 1807 and thereafter pledged his loyalty to the northern regime. In his *Essay on the Causes of the Revolution and Civil Wars of Hayti*, Vastey described how Papalier's charm and money allowed him to 'corrupt the sailors of the fleet ... masking his designs beneath the cloak of generosity and patriotism'. He was allegedly aided by two Frenchmen and a former secretary to Toussaint Louverture in Port-au-Prince name Viart, who was denounced as 'a man of colour in complexion but a white Frenchman in principle'. One of the conspirators was none other than Christophe's old friend Joseph Bunel in Philadelphia, who had apparently fallen from favour over a dispute concerning monies owed to a number of American merchants. The second Frenchman, called Montorsier, had been plied with favours by Christophe and allowed to trade directly with Jamaica—a route that it was now alleged allowed him to send letters indirectly to Port-au-Prince. 'Such then is the depravity of the human heart', wrote Vastey. Although he wrote his history to burnish Christophe's reputation, in a rare moment of candour he conceded that the conspiracy was far more extensive than had at first been imagined: 'Since these unfortunate events we have learned that persons whose rank and official situations raised them above suspicion, had taken but too active a share in the conspiracy.' These figures were left unnamed, but Papalier was immediately imprisoned and Montorsier was only granted clemency after providing documents that proved the conspiracy had been a French plot to help drive the two halves of Haiti back into open conflict. Bunel never stepped foot in Haiti again.[37]

Vastey's account of the *Améthyste* affair was not published until 1819. In it he describes the state council debate that followed to discuss what reprisals—if any—should be taken against this southern provocation. He carefully painted Christophe's reluctance to respond militarily, against the more martial opinions of his councillors. Their force of argument won the day. Although a renewed conflict 'was repugnant to his heart ... he saw himself driven to it by an unavoidable fatality'. As the meeting drew to a close Christophe decided that only one avenue was left open to him: to march once more on Port-au-Prince.[38]

In his announcement in Cap Henry of 8 March 1812 of the decision to strike against Pétion, Christophe likened himself to a lion roused from its slumber. No sovereign could ignore the treachery of the miserable scoundrels who had delivered three of his ships to the enemy, he said, and if he had a fault as king it was his 'paternal weakness' in holding back his brave soldiers and giving his enemies time to muster. The time for such regal generosity was over: 'No—I would be guilty towards my people, towards my army and myself, if I delayed any longer in bringing those places still stained by rebellion under obedience.' The people of the south had suffered for too long under Pétion, but now their liberation was nigh:

> Your groans have sounded in my ears; the moment has arrived when I will complete your deliverance. At my appearance [at the gates of Port-au-Prince], rally to your brothers who march under the flag of the legitimate, strong and benevolent authority that has the power and will to consolidate the happiness of all Haitians. You will find forgiveness, safety, protection, respect for your persons and your property.[39]

Lessons had been learned from the failure of the 1807 campaign. This was to be no swift infantry rush, but a slow and methodical approach supported by artillery. The army headed south in two columns: one of 9,000 men under the Duc de Plaisance General

Magny, which was sent via Mirebalais to approach Port-au-Prince from the east, and the second of 6,000 men led by the king taking the coast road from Saint-Marc. The remainder of Christophe's navy would provide logistical support. First contact was made on 27 March near Fort Sibert, just as it had been five years earlier, against republican forces commanded by General Jean-Pierre Boyer. As the royal army swept towards his capital, Pétion was more than 130 kilometres away in the far southwest. Colonel Henry's rebellion in Jérémie had finally proved a success and troops across the southern peninsula had abandoned Borgella en masse. 'After a very hard, bloody, and sanguinary contest, which lasted four days, the links of Rigaud's party were dissolved and Pétion's authority acknowledged in the South', wrote one American who had witnessed the fighting. The leader of the breakaway state had no choice but to bend the knee to Pétion, who travelled to Les Cayes to take his pledge of loyalty in person. That pledge would soon be tested on the walls of Port-au-Prince.[40]

Boyer's forces were spread thinly along the defensive forts lining the Plaine du Cul-de-Sac in front of the capital. There were just 1,350 men under his direct command, and they took almost the entire weight of Christophe's army as it bore down upon them. The republican lines broke and only just managed to retreat to Port-au-Prince, but in the melee they were forced to abandon the garrison at Fort Sibert, leaving it far behind enemy lines. Careful not to leave himself open to a counter-attack from his rear, Christophe drew a complete halt to the advance to invest the fort. After several days of bombardment Sibert duly fell, but the army had lost its momentum. The delay had given time for Pétion to rush up from Les Cayes with 6,000 soldiers to defend the city.[41]

They arrived to find 15,000 northern troops camped along the north and western walls of Port-au-Prince. Christophe's army spent a week digging itself into its positions before unleashing the first artillery bombardment. For an entire month the cannons roared, sometimes landing as many as 200 rounds a day. The damage they caused was extensive; even the presidential palace was riddled with shells. As the weeks went by the city seemed to falter. Money offices were forced to shut which led to a shortage of coinage. Some of Pétion's soldiers were said to have taken up counterfeiting, safe in the knowledge that the sound of their coin stamps was drowned out by Christophe's cannons.[42]

As the siege dragged into May it became clear that however battered it became, Port-au-Prince was unlikely to fall. Worse yet for Christophe, a naval encounter in the bay had ended with the loss of one ship and the capture of another. His supply lines were now vastly overextended, and his army began to run low on both food and ammunition. The defenders on the wall took to taunting his men by throwing bread and plantains at them and crowing that they were free citizens and not the slaves of 'a miserable king'.[43] A new attack was ordered to break the impasse. This time a column of 3,000 men was to completely sweep around the eastern side of the city through the mountains that rose above it, descending near the town of Leogane. They would then cut the city off from the west to starve it of supplies while sending an advance guard to capture Les Cayes, whose loyalty to the republic was still assumed to be soft. The plan might have worked had it not been for the arrival of Borgella's southern troops, who proved their new-found dedication to Pétion by repulsing the force at Morne l'Hôpital above Port-au-Prince.[ix] When the plan was foiled, Christophe left his forces in the field and retired to Saint-Marc to spend time with the queen and take counsel on his next moves.[44]

The fighting around Port-au-Prince had not gone unnoticed by foreign observers. Royal Navy ships offshore kept a cool eye on proceedings. In the middle of May, Admiral Stirling sent a formal offer to mediate between the two sides. Stirling saw that Christophe's forces were exhausted to the point where any retreat might even see his army annihilated should Pétion choose to lead a counter-attack. This was quite unacceptable, as he reported to the Admiralty, because 'it appears to me essential for the interests of this island [Jamaica] that St Domingo should not be under one chief'. Christophe rejected the offer of mediation out of hand anyway; although he was facing defeat, the only terms his pride would allow him to accept remained Pétion's absolute submission.[45]

[ix] The fighting took place around Laboule above modern Port-au-Prince, near the wealthy suburb of Pétionville.

When the end of the siege came it was through political manoeu-
vring rather than the end of a musket. As the situation in the front-
line camps worsened, soldiers began to slowly cross the lines from
the royalist to the republican side. At first this was a trickle, but on
12 June, while the king was still in Saint-Marc, General Magny,
who had fought with Dessalines at Crête-à-Pierrot and heroically
recaptured Gonaïves from Pétion's army in 1807, marched three
regiments of 2,000 men through the gates of Port-au-Prince under
a white flag. Pétion was thrilled to receive such a high value defec-
tor, and duly maintained him in his rank. In his history of the civil
war Vastey refused to accept that Magny had acted under his own
volition, and insisted that conspirators in his ranks had made him
their unwilling prisoner as they sneaked across the battle lines.[46]

Two days later, the captain of HMS *Brazen* called at Saint-Marc
to again offer British mediation—this time to conclude an armistice.
'Should you have any immediate communication to make to General
Pétion,' he wrote to Christophe, 'I beg leave to offer myself as the
channel through which it may be made.'[47] The king, humiliated by
the loss of one of his generals, sent no written reply. He instead
ordered his army to strike the siege and retreat north in the best
order possible. A campaign that had begun with a promise to plant
the royal flag in Port-au-Prince and free his southern subjects had
ended in failure and the bitterness of betrayal.

13

FRENCH PLOTS

Christophe began 1813 in a sour mood. His traditional Independence Day address showed that he was still shaken by the betrayals of the previous year. He urged all Haitians to look among themselves and denounce any potential traitors to the authorities:

> What do they propose to do, these vile agents of the factious? To enslave you, to plunge you back into anarchy, to find in licence and the upheaval of things, a supposed improvement to their fate; but what was the result of their perfidies? Death as the just punishment for their crimes.[1]

His outrage underscored his frustration that both Magny and the *Améthyste* mutineers remained safely beyond his reach. The one death the kingdom had suffered was that of the true loyalist André Vernet, the Prince of Gonaïves, who had passed away in the last week of December 1812 aged seventy. Vernet was buried with full honours in the royal chapel at Milot, and after the funeral Christophe issued an elaborate set of new mourning instructions, ordering black silk dress to be worn at court and for nobles' swords to be tied with black crêpe.[2]

In April Christophe was troubled further when Pétion launched a daring raid into the heart of the kingdom. Fifty men led by the head of his presidential guard, Kayé Larivière, seized the town of Vallière near Grand Rivière. For Larivière the mission was personal: he had grown up on a coffee plantation here and his parents had been killed by Christophe's men.[i] After a daring ride of nearly

---

[i] It was also Kayé Larivière's accusation that Moyse planned to kill every white person in Fort Liberté in 1798 that prompted Hédouville's disastrous attempt to remove him from his post.

100 kilometres, Larivière's men seized Vallière and beheaded the garrison commander. Much of the mission's success hinged on the help it received from the local cultivators, who had risen against Christophe and Dessalines in 1803 following the killing of Sans Souci and had adjusted poorly to the strict rules of the Code Henry that now governed their lives.[3] In the wake of the raid, *Le Télégraphe* newspaper in Port-au-Prince crowed about the republic's growing military confidence, and speculation began to build that a larger expedition north would soon follow.[4] It never did: despite the defections from the north, republican forces were still recovering from the siege of the capital and the failure of another campaign against Goman's maroons. The Senate had again been forced to devalue the gourde and introduce new laws against money counterfeiters. Sanctioning raids like Larivière's remained the limit of Pétion's aspirations against the north.

Christophe could be forgiven for looking inwards to his family for the stability he desired. In May his eldest daughter Améthyste entered her majority when she turned fifteen and became constitutionally able to marry with the permission of her father. In June the new *Gazette Royale d'Hayti* newspaper gave considerable space to a grand celebration in Cap Henry held for the Prince Royal, Victor-Henry, who made his first dedicated public appearance, at the tender age of nine years, reviewing a military parade in his honour. The day was entirely given over to honouring him as the heir presumptive; Christophe did not attend. After a Mass at the cathedral, the nobility lined up to pledge the prince their undying loyalty. In a speech written for him he replied with humility: 'The visit you are making to me today flatters me singularly ... and it is with the greatest sensibility that I receive your tributes and congratulations.' Victor-Henry vowed to dedicate himself to the service of the nation: 'I dare to assure you, Sirs, that [my studies] will not be without fruit, and that they will one day earn me your approval, as well as that of the good people of Haiti.'[5]

Fewer than half a dozen of Christophe's letters to Victor-Henry are known to have survived, but the majority take a keen interest in his son's schooling. He commended his handwriting ('rather good') but expressed disappointment on learning that Victor-Henry had mistreated his servants:

1. King Henry I of Haiti, painted in 1816 by Richard Evans.

2. Memorial to the Chasseurs Volontaires who fought in the siege of Savannah in 1779, showing Henry Christophe as a drummer boy.

3. The slave ship *Marie-Séraphique* at anchor in the bay of Cap Français.

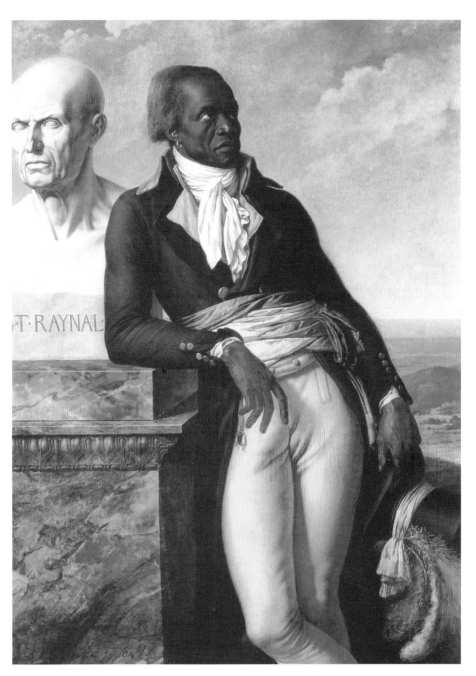

4. Jean-Baptiste Belley.

5. The burning of Cap Français in June 1793, when Christophe fought in defence of the city.

6. Léger-Félicité Sonthonax holding the 1793 emancipation proclamation while pointing to a torn-up copy of the Code Noir.

TOUSSAINT L'OUVERTURE.

7. Engraving of Toussaint Louverture, thought to be taken from a portrait he gave to the French agent Roume.

8. Haitian revolutionary battle.

The Court Martial which sentenced the Author to Death:
General Christophe President.

9. The trial of Captain Marcus Rainsford in 1798. Christophe presides at the centre, with Moyse at his left.

10. A French general and officer, painted in Cap Français in April 1802 by Jan
Anthonie Langendyk, shortly after Christophe's return to the French side.

11. Imagined engraving of Jean-Jacques Dessalines from 1805, shortly after he was crowned Emperor of Haiti.

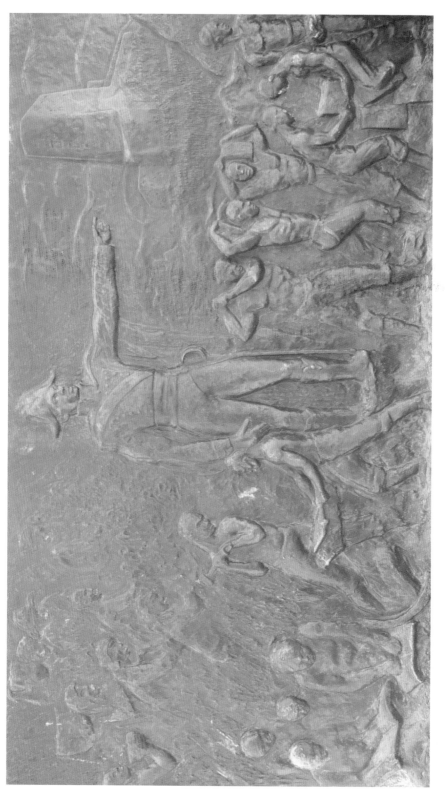

12. Christophe overseeing the construction of the Citadelle in the first years of Haitian independence.

Cristobal comand.te del Exercito recorre la Ysla de
S.to Domingo incendiando, y matando alos in
felices colonos de ella

13. A French propagandist image from 1806 of Christophe burning Spanish towns
during the Santo Domingo campaign.

LE GENERAL ALEXANDRE PÉTION
PRESIDENT D'HAYTI

14. Alexandre Pétion, first President of the Republic of Haiti.

15. Coats of arms of the Kingdom of Haiti: King Henry I, Baron de Vastey, Baron de Béliard, Duc de Marmelade.

16. The Prince Royal Victor-Henry aged 12 painted in 1816 by Richard Evans.

17. William Wilberforce, one of Christophe's most eager correspondents.

R.d Evans pinx.t

C. Turner sculp.

P. Saunders Esq.r

18. Prince Saunders, who introduced smallpox vaccination to the Kingdom of Haiti.

BOYER,

Président de la République d'Haïti.

19. Jean-Pierre Boyer, Pétion's successor as Haitian president.

20. Thomas Clarkson, whose advice and support was actively courted by
Christophe.

21. Ira Aldridge, painted a year after he portrayed Christophe on the London stage in 1825.

NUBIAN JAK COMMUNITY TRUST

MARIE-LOUISE CHRISTOPHE

1778 - 1851

FIRST AND ONLY QUEEN
OF HAITI

LIVED IN THIS HOUSE
WITH HER DAUGHTERS
IN 1824

FANM REBÈL AND THE HAITIAN CHAMBER OF COMMERCE IN GB
TOGETHER WITH COMMUNITY SPONSORS

22. 49 Weymouth Street, Marie-Louise Christophe's final residence in London.

23. The Citadelle Henry today.

24. The ruins of Sans Souci Palace today.

That is not commendable. If you are anxious to merit my esteem and affection, that is not the way to go about it, but rather by means of a more proper conduct, submissiveness to the counsel and advice of those qualified to give them to you, and an affability and kindliness which will make all cherish you.[6]

Victor-Henry's sometimes fractious spirit may have been a reaction against becoming the heir after the death of Ferdinand, a brother he had never known or could ever compete with.

Christophe's attitude towards his son's learning could be stern but it was also countered by a tender nature rarely seen by his subjects. 'I am sending you, my dear son, a sample of some grapes from my garden at Môle Saint-Nicholas, as a mark of affectionate remembrance,' he wrote in August 1813, 'I embrace you with all my heart, and am your loving father, Henry.'[7] A report by an anonymous Royal Navy officer who spent time at Sans Souci the following year also noted that the king was 'a most affectionate father of a family, and that his children in his presence are under no fear or restraint. He has in his palace several little children, the orphans of old officers of his—they are always running about the room, when he has no business, and feeling his pockets for bon-bons.'[8] Such accounts are far from the scenes conjured up by republican writers in Port-au-Prince, who imagined that the crying infant Victor-Henry once so enraged his father that he grabbed him by the leg and tried to throw him from a window, only to be saved by a compassionate bystander.[9]

When there was no southern mobilisation after the Vallière raid, 1813 proved a much-needed year of consolidation for the kingdom. When Haiti marked the tenth anniversary of the declaration of independence in 1814, Christophe's speech bore a remarkably different tone to the bitter rhetoric of the year before. Two days of celebrations were held at Sans Souci, where the king paid homage to the genius of the Haitian people who had broken the chains of French rule: 'Like other nations, our first years were strewed with errors and troubles; like them we have experienced the vicissitudes inseparable from revolutions.' From this trouble the stability of the kingdom had prevailed. There was order and tranquillity in the provinces, a strong code of law and a national treasury free from debts. The manners of the people were more polished and bonds of marriage once more revered: 'The nation is advancing by rapid strides to the highest degree of civilisation … Strong in ourselves, we know no other enemies than those who come with hostile intentions and with arms in their hands.' Christophe also addressed the contingent of foreign merchants who attended the fête and toasted the royal family, reminding them of the warehouses that groaned with coffee and sugar: 'It is for you, gentlemen, by your foreign connections, to encourage your countrymen to undertake with Hayti lucrative commerce, which insures to you great advantages; they will find here, like you, the same profits, the same security for their persons and the properties.'[10]

After the fête, the royal family embarked on a tour of the east. The editor of the *Gazette Royale d'Hayti* painted a picture of a nation at ease with itself: 'The diversions of the chase and fishing may be enjoyed in all seasons; the excellence of the roads, the beautiful habitations by which they are bordered, and a flourishing cultivation, delight the eye and embellish the journey.'[11] The first stop was Bellevue-le-Roi, a renamed French mansion near Limonade, where they celebrated Epiphany by enjoying a performance of the comic opera *Richard Coeur-de-lion*. From here they continued to Fort Royal, where the streets were strewn with flowers and decorated with triumphal arches and they were guests of honour at the wedding of the king's nephew Prince Jean to André Vernet's widow, Eleanor Chancy, an event 'celebrated with pomp, and great rejoicing at court'. After two days of hunting, the royal party continued to Ouanaminthe, where they were entertained by visitors from across the border in Spanish Santo Domingo, who brought guitars and mandolins to play for the king. 'The grave character which distinguishes that nation, even in its amusements, formed a contrast with the sprightliness and bustle of the Haytian songs and dances', noted the royal correspondent. In the spring of 1813 the new governor of Santo Domingo, Don Carlos de Urutia, had entered into a tentative correspondence with Christophe, assuring him of his desire for good neighbourly relations, and the royal border visit in January 1814 may have been part of an attempt to enhance the diplomatic ties between the two men. After three weeks of hunting, pleasure boating, opera performances and a visit to the Bay of Mancenille to enjoy its oysters ('excellent and in great quantity'), the royal family finally returned to Sans Souci.[12]

A month later the palace witnessed a parade of captured republican soldiers by the Prince of Limbe, Paul Romain, after he had
seized Fort Sabourin on the contested border. Hopes for improvements on the foreign as well as the domestic front also received a
boost with news from France. At the end of 1813 reports had
arrived of Napoleon Bonaparte's decisive defeat at the Battle of
Leipzig.[ii] This was now followed by the news that Paris had fallen
and the emperor sent into exile. Christophe praised the victory of
the European coalition that had brought him down but viewed
Bonaparte's surrender with contempt. 'His majesty could never
have divined that he would close his career in a manner so little
worthy of a soldier,' Julien Prévost wrote to Jean-Gabriel Peltier in
London. Bonaparte's fall offered new possibilities for relations with
the newly restored Bourbon regime of Louis XVIII.

The first step was to declare Haiti's ports open for French trade.
'His majesty has never confounded the French people with the governments which oppressed them,' Prévost wrote, describing the
warm welcome that French ships would receive from the kingdom,
'They shall be protected and treated like the subjects of other
friendly powers ... you may give this assurance to the French merchants, and even publish it in your journals.'[13] The *Gazette Royale
d'Hayti* reminded its readers that Haiti's blood sacrifice had contrib-
uted to Bonaparte's downfall and the liberation of Europe. It cau-
tiously welcomed the new French regime, writing that Christophe
would seize the opportunity to establish 'in a solid and lasting manner, links of commerce and friendship, which would be compatible
with the honour, liberty, security and independence of the people
of his Kingdom'. The open hand also came with a warning. The
'absurd and chimerical projects' of France's colonial lobby were
ridiculed and any attempts to reconquer the country would be met
with fire:

> We shall give no quarter, take no prisoners; let them do the same
> to us; it is then that we shall prove to the whole universe what a
> warlike people is capable of, armed for the most just of causes, for

---

[ii] Haitians in the Kingdom and Republic alike would have undoubtedly rejoiced at the news that
the sadistic General Rochambeau, defeated by Dessalines at Vertières, was fatally wounded
during the battle.

213

the defence of its homes, its women, its children, its liberty and its independence.[14]

The appointment of Baron Pierre Victor Malouet as France's new Minister of the Marine[iii] suggested that many in the new regime believed that regaining control of Haiti was neither absurd nor chimerical. It was Malouet who had encouraged Saint-Domingue's planters to defect to the British to preserve slavery in 1793, and he had later written a book detailing the alleged horrors that befell the colony's white population at the hands of black revolutionaries. In a letter to Louis XVIII in June he restated his support for returning Haiti to a state of slavery ('under a gentle regimen'), but underlined that the word itself must never be used publicly. The old planter class were steadfast in offering their support, and lobbied Louis with reminders of the wealth that once flowed from the colony. They were aided in this by the Treaty of Paris that concluded the European wars. A secret clause between England and France effectively ceded London's policy on Haiti to Paris by promising not to obstruct any potential attempt to reclaim its errant colony. Furthermore, France was granted permission to revive its slave trade for five years.[15] For the planters, any future French ships calling at Haiti should be carrying enslaved Africans rather than trading with a free black nation.

In June 1814 Malouet dispatched a diplomatic mission that he hoped would pave the way for Haiti's submission to French rule and return of its people to chains. Three agents were chosen: Jean-Joseph Dauxion Lavaysse, Agoustine Franco de Médina and a third person simply known as Draverman. Lavaysse would travel to Port-au-Prince to meet Pétion. Médina would deal with Christophe, and Draverman was to treat with Borgella in the now defunct breakaway southern state in an attempt to exploit old divisions.[iv] The negotiators were given secret instructions that made France's intentions clear, no matter what they told the Haitians: 'His majesty [Louis XVIII] has resolved to deploy his powers to return the insurgents of Saint-Domingue to their obligations only after having exhausted all

---

[iii] The French equivalent of Colonial Minister.

[iv] Draverman (spelled Draverneau in some contemporary accounts) was chosen as he reportedly had a family connection to Borgella. In the event he fell ill during the Atlantic crossing and returned to France.

measures that his clemency commands.'[16] A client black elite of those who had been free before 1793 would be maintained in the restored colony, but the majority of the population would be returned to slavery. Furthermore, Malouet also erroneously instructed the mission that the king had already ordered a military expedition should their diplomatic efforts fail.

Lavaysse's first letter to Pétion, sent from Jamaica, disowned slavery as the policy of the usurper Bonaparte. It alluded to a general wish of extending the former rights of French subjects and citizens on the island, but he politely addressed the letter to President Pétion and requested permission to visit Port-au-Prince to discuss the matter between them as educated men. An invitation was duly extended. Lavaysse also took it upon himself to write to Christophe, but his letter was far less conciliatory. Writing to *General* Christophe, Lavaysse described himself as the precursor of peace and reconciliation but was quick to urge Christophe to proclaim Louis XVIII as his sovereign. If it was nobility the Haitian leader required, then a title would be granted to him as a servant of the French crown. Beyond this there were only veiled threats. Bonaparte's attempt to reconquer Saint-Domingue had failed as a result of the war in Europe, he wrote, but now the French king had an army of half a million men free to be deployed: 'Compel us not, general, to make soldiers of the negroes we are now importing from Africa; compel us not to have recourse to all possible means of destruction.'[17] Lavaysse closed by appending a copy of his far more respectful address to Pétion ('in proof of the candour in which I act') in the hope of strengthening the French position by further inflaming the division between the two halves of Haiti.

The arrival of Lavaysse's letter at Sans Souci provoked outrage even before it was opened. 'Ten years had elapsed since we had any communication whatever with France', wrote Baron de Vastey, who attended the meeting where it was presented to the king:

A host of contradictory conjectures, as to the object of the French, was instantly afloat. What did they propose? Did they mean to recognise our independence, or to re-enslave us? Did they mean to offer compensation for the injuries they had done us? Had they not injured us sufficiently without wishing to do us further mischief? The pacquets [sic] were yet unopened, and we already viewed them with horror.[18]

Christophe coolly ordered the state council to convene to decide a response. 'Let us begin by doing our duty,' he urged his men, 'If General Pétion and the inhabitants of the south-west do theirs, they will act as we do. If they mean to disgrace and ruin themselves, would you wish us to follow their example?'[19]

A surprise attendee of the council meeting was Montorsier, the Frenchman granted clemency for his alleged role in the *Améthyste* mutiny. Montorsier suggested the French plan was to send Christophe into exile and that the only route to national prosperity was to pledge loyalty to Louis XVIII. He was nearly thrown from the balcony for voicing such perfidy. As the letter was read aloud again the meeting became so febrile that Vastey's pen was barely able to capture the outrage: 'Among the members there were some who had borne the yoke of the French: the marks yet visible on their mutilated limbs attested the length and cruelty of their sufferings, and the barbarity of our tyrants.' As others remembered the loved ones drowned, burned or torn to pieces by the colonist's dogs, they pledged on their swords to defend their country to their dying breath, with cries of 'Long Live the King!' and 'Liberty or Death!'[20] Christophe responded in kind:

> Haytians! The eyes of the whole world are fixed upon us: our conduct then should be such as to confound our detractors, and to justify the opinion formed of us by philanthropists. Let us rally: one wish alone animates us all, that of exterminating our tyrants ... Let us fight gloriously. Let us rather be blotted out of the rank of nations, than resign our liberty and independence ... Should we chance to die previous to the consolidation of your rights; remember our conduct, and should your tyrants endanger your freedom and independence, exhume our bones, they will conduct you anew to victory, and make you triumph over your implacable and everlasting enemies.[21]

This was the atmosphere into which Malouet's envoy Médina stepped. A figure better chosen to further antagonise Christophe could hardly have been imagined. Vastey described him as a 'renegade

Spaniard': he had owned plantations near Santiago in Santo Domingo and served under General Ferrand, making several incursions into Haitian territory including one to Ouanaminthe where several women and children were killed.[22] As a result he was arrested almost the instant he set foot on Haitian soil. A search of his belongings quickly revealed the secret instructions from Malouet.

On 17 November, the eve of the anniversary of the Battle of Vertières, the cathedral in Cap Henry was full for a highly unusual service attended by the king. Médina was paraded before both the king and the crowd and made to stand on a bench. After Mass his secret instructions were read aloud followed by a transcript of the detailed interrogation he had been subjected to. Médina revealed the French plans to revive slavery included mass deportations and a 'purge' of the remaining population of all those above the age of six years. The congregation gasped in horror. Vastey took to the pulpit to rouse them further with his passionate oratory: 'Friends! Let nothing stop the anger you feel upon hearing those words "Slave" and "Master"; the tocsin of liberty has sounded! … Hasten to arms, let your torches be lit, let the carnage begin, and vengeance be taken!' The *Gazette Royale d'Hayti* reported that Médina, believing that he saw a thousand bayonets pointed towards him, collapsed in fear: 'Vinegar and a cordial were required to restore him from his useful terror. What a pity that his two colleagues, Dauxion Lavaysse and Draverman, could not be by his side; what a lovely trio they would have made!'[23] Médina was hauled off to prison, and though his ultimate fate was not recorded, it is widely assumed that he died in captivity soon after.[v]

The performance in the cathedral was designed to echo far beyond its walls. The royal printing presses reprinted Médina's secret instructions in full along with the transcript of his interroga-

---

[v] The Code Henry mandated the death sentence for espionage, but a folk tale collected in the 1930s suggests a more haunting fate. Many years later when a labourer heard mysterious sounds inside the walls of the Citadelle, he found a white man with a long beard who was almost reduced to a skeleton. It was Médina, who was still paying for 'the unpardonable crime of having attempted to deprive the Haitian people of their liberty after they had renounced France forever'. See George E. Simpson and J. B. Cinéas, 'Folk Tales of Haitian Heroes', *The Journal of American Folklore* vol. 54, nos. 213/214 (1941), pp. 176–85.

tion, where he revealed more details of the French plot. These were accompanied by copies of Lavaysse's letters to Pétion, and were distributed widely as proof that only Christophe was capable of protecting the Haitian people against the intrigues from Paris and Port-au-Prince. A slew of other texts followed, in which writers including Vastey, Prévost and Dupuy set out to defend Haitian sovereignty against the slanders of France's colonial lobby. This use of the written word as a form of intellectual national defence had been a work in progress throughout 1814: in his *Notes to Baron Malouet* published earlier in the year, Vastey had already set out a strident rebuttal to the French minister's nostalgia for the slave system in his book on Saint-Domingue. But this short pamphlet only set the scene for the arrival of Vastey's masterwork, *The Colonial System Unveiled*, whose publication in Cap Henry in October proved perfectly timed for the arrival of Malouet's agents.

The Colonial System Unveiled was an extraordinary text that gave not just an account of the horrors enacted by the French in Saint-Domingue but indicted the entire system of European imperialism itself. 'At last it is known, this secret full of horror,' read its epigraph, 'the Colonial System means the domination of Whites, it means the massacre and enslavement of Blacks.'[24] After tracing the destruction of Hispaniola's Taíno people at the hands of Spain, Vastey turned his attention to France's depredations and offered his readers an intimate catalogue of French atrocities. To do this he collected the testimonies of those who had suffered on the plantations and then offered himself as a witness for the hundreds of thousands of dead who never survived Saint-Domingue. European abolitionist tracts of the period typically glossed over slavery's inherent violence through euphemisms such as the 'ill-use' of slaves, but Vastey spared no detail in presenting his readers with accounts of men, women and children maimed, flogged to death, or burned alive. Each account was accompanied by the names of the French settlers, plantation owners and magistrates who had perpetrated the crimes. The charge sheet was unanswerable:

> To France's shame, not a single one of the monsters we have just cited has suffered the penalty that his foul deeds merit … Colonists, those of you who still draw breath, cite me a single one

of your kind whose guilty head was struck down by the sword of the law. I defy you to prove me wrong.

By denying the humanity of Africans, Vastey declared that Europe's colonial project was flawed from the outset and its claim to civilised values was based on pure sophistry. Only Haiti's revolution had fulfilled the potential of the Enlightenment by recognising that all people had been created equal.[25]

Pétion had initially felt confident enough in his position to allow the announcement of the French royal envoy's arrival in Port-au-Prince on 24 October in Le Télégraphe newspaper.[26] Despite the claims of Vastey and others, Pétion showed considerable resilience in defending Haitian sovereignty while maintaining he was open to a variety of approaches to settle relations with France. In his exchange of letters with Lavaysse he suggested a possible compromise whereby Haiti might pay some sort of indemnity to France to buy recognition of its independence, a payment he later described as making 'pecuniary sacrifices to silence your persecutors'. In the eyes of the north, the idea of paying a financial penalty on top of the blood price already borne by the Haitian people was proof of Pétion's treason. Vastey snorted: 'Can you contemplate this prospect without shuddering in horror! Who is the Haytian vile enough to want to pay his portion of this tribute!'[27]

The kingdom's release of the French papers proved damning. Within weeks Pétion was forced to publish his correspondence with Lavaysse in an attempt to demonstrate his good intentions. He defended the sacred rights of hospitality that he had extended to the envoy and stated that any blame for the affair was to be found only in France: 'She has lost for ever her claims upon Hayti, and it is to the French themselves that she is indebted for this loss.'[28] When news of the debacle reached France it proved equally embarrassing. The mission was publicly disavowed and Lavaysse hung out to dry—actions made easy by the unexpected death of Malouet in September. For the Gazette Royale d'Hayti, this was the final proof that French intentions could never be trusted and only fools like Pétion could fall for their honeyed words: 'Their hearts would never change; our slavery and our destruction—that is the only thought that occupies them, even as they caress and flatter us.'[29]

The Malouet affair was a reminder that Haiti's position in the world was still not guaranteed. From his palace high in the Citadelle, Christophe dusted down Dessalines' old plan for national defence and put the nation on high alert in case France sent another armada to its shores. He was determined that they would land in a country that give them no refuge. Kindling was to be gathered in all the towns so that they could be set ablaze at the first sight of French sails. Bridges were to be broken, roads made impassable and even the banks of rivers cut to stymie the invaders. All the livestock would be driven to the interior, where stores of food were ordered to be laid to feed the population as it took shelter around the kingdom's many mountain forts. Christophe declared:

> In the first war of independence, we had to encounter every sort of privation, this time we shall be in want of nothing … You will have for yourselves and families necessaries of every description, which I have collected for the wants of the army and the people. Heretofore we were obliged to traverse the mountains without a place for shelter; our warlike stores, our treasures, and our booty, were all at the mercy of the enemy. Now this is no more the case, we can defend ourselves securely in impregnable citadels.[30]

Christophe also recognised that all of Haiti would need to act together to repel the French: 'No affront which General Pétion can offer to me should prevent me from discharging my duty by giving my fellow citizens the necessary information to prevent their falling into the snares laid by our tyrants', he announced, and in February 1815 he sent four envoys south to Port-au-Prince.[31] All had formerly lived in south, including the Comte de Trou, who had served with Pétion during the revolution as Colonel Toussaint Dupont, and the Baron de Ferrier, a resident of Jacmel who had sat in the Port-au-Prince Senate before throwing in his lot with the north. They arrived in Port-au-Prince wearing gold braid and powdered wigs, hoping that their fine court dress would demonstrate the splendour of the kingdom, but their bright costume was mocked on the street as if they were performers in a carnival parade.[32] Things did not improve when they presented their credentials. 'The people of Haiti can no longer hesitate to reunite and offer a massive resistance [to] the imminent attacks with which our oppressors threaten us', Julien

Prévost wrote in his diplomatic letter to Pétion, a unity that would surely be in concord with 'the wishes of the Haitians in the sector under your command'. Christophe again offered forgiveness to those who would submit to the crown and admission to the kingdom's hereditary nobility for republican leaders who proclaimed their loyalty. Given Pétion's willingness to treat with Lavaysse and apparently eager offer to sell his country back to France, noted Prévost, it was only his king's magnanimity that allowed that such terms could be offered.

Pétion's response was derisive. Christophe's envoys cut such ridiculous figures that the idea of bending the knee could only be scoffed at. In his official reply to the mission, Pétion reminded Prévost of the events of 1802, even mentioning the fate of Christophe's son Ferdinand in a manner that could only have been intended to wound:

> You speak to me, General, of amnesty, pardon, forgetting the past, of paternal authority, of a monarch, of ranks and distinctions, of titles of hereditary nobility. We were far removed from these strange and unseemly ideas, when I asked General Christophe to leave Le Cap in order to escape the gallows, and when I awakened his distrust of the French, whom he understood so little that shortly before he had entrusted his son to General Boudet to take him to France. You do not speak to me of this period in your letter ... He ignores that we are all enlightened on our true interests, that all the means of seduction to deceive us have been used up, that we are and want to be free, and that we do not recognise masters and do not want kings, whoever they may be.

Pétion pointed to Christophe's crimes of aggression against the republic and wondered how a guilty man might offer to pardon the innocent. Should a French army indeed return, he concluded, they would be defeated again by the Haitian people despite the pretensions of an imaginary monarchy and not because of them.[33] Pétion's forthrightness caught the mood in Port-au-Prince: a month later he was re-elected by the Senate to serve another four-year term as president.

The sniping was continued by the Haitian press. With the border between the Kingdom and the Republic now a seemingly permanent condition, each side took to publishing closely written pamphlets and counter-pamphlets expounding their beliefs and hoping to convince the opposing side of the superiority of their position. A steady succession of articles and reprints from the *Gazette Royale d'Hayti* placed in British newspapers further raised the kingdom's international image and touted the progress that Christophe was bringing to the country. Jean-Gabriel Peltier was good at publicity, but as the events of 1814 prompted a renewed effort to win Haiti's acceptance on the international stage, Christophe decided that he had been a poor lobbyist.

Since his appointment Peltier had fallen out with his fellow envoy, Thomas Richardson, over the non-payment of an order of uniforms for the Haitian army, resulting in Richardson unsuccessfully trying to sue him for libel. Money ran through Peltier's fingers like water; in 1812 he briefly declared bankruptcy and was forced to sell his furniture.[34] The French essayist Chateaubriand who saw him in London described him as eaten by vermin, 'a libertine, a rebellious subject, making plenty of money and consuming the same … diplomatic correspondent for Monsieur le Comte de Limonade, drinking as champagne the appointments for which he was paid in sugar'.[35] Admiral Thomas Goodall had also fallen from favour. In 1813 he became embroiled in a divorce scandal after discovering that his lawyer had been sleeping with his Covent Garden actress wife. Goodall was awarded damages, but after an account of the trial was published, including the adulterous love letters and the accusation that Goodall had contracted syphilis in the Caribbean, his reputation was destroyed. He never sailed to Haiti again. Christophe needed new voices to speak on his behalf.

In his parting shot to the French government when his mission was disowned, Lavaysse forthrightly wrote that 'had a Grégoire or a Wilberforce been sent to speak to Christophe in France's interest, their efforts would have had no effect on that madman'.[36] He would have been confounded to learn that it was to these two figures that Christophe now turned for support. The Abbé Henri Grégoire was France's leading abolitionist voice. He had been an early supporter of the rights of Saint-Domingue's free coloured class and later described Haiti as 'a beacon elevated from the Antilles towards which slaves and their masters, oppressed and oppressors, turn their regards'.[37] Prévost wrote to him to tell him Christophe had ordered copies of his writings to be distributed throughout the kingdom, hoping to win Grégoire's support by praising his work: 'Your name is pronounced among Haitians only with the eulogies which are due to the defender of the cause of liberty and unfortunate people ... The happiest day for my sovereign would be the day he could see you and press you to his heart.' Grégoire, a confirmed republican as well as an abolitionist, declined to enter into a correspondence.[38]

Christophe's approaches to William Wilberforce were to prove far more productive. The Yorkshire MP and evangelist who had helped steer the abolition of the slave trade bill through parliament in 1807 was thrilled to receive an approach from the kingdom. In January 1815 he wrote to his fellow abolitionist Zachary Macaulay that he had been excited to receive a surprise package from Haiti: 'I will send you this letter from the Count de Limonade. How strikingly do we see the just and good dispensations of Providence produced by ways, in which at the time we little see the point to which we are tending!'[39] Prévost's letter has not survived, but he would no doubt have written of the high regard in which Wilberforce was held in Haiti, recounting how details of the abolition bill had been reprinted in its newspapers and playing on Christophe's 'English' roots in Grenada, as Peltier had once done. A number of pamphlets were also enclosed, including the papers relating to the Malouet affair, to help convince Wilberforce of the help Haiti needed to protect itself from France.[vi]

It was the second approach from Haiti Wilberforce had received in only a few months. In July 1814, when news of the French restoration was still fresh in Haiti but before his correspondence with Lavaysse was published, Pétion sent one of his secretaries named Garbage to London to lobby for the republic. In a letter to the Prime Minister Lord Liverpool, he asked the British government to stand as an honest broker in negotiating recognition for Haiti's independence from France. It was the first time that Pétion formally put

---

[vi] Prévost's letter weighed nearly 2.5 kilograms. The postmaster tried to charge £37 10s. to deliver it, but eventually let Wilberforce off with 'a pepper-corn of 7s. which I shall gladly pay'. See Robert Isaac and Samuel Wilberforce, *The Life of William Wilberforce*, Vol. 4 (London: John Murray, 1838), pp. 226–7.

the issue of payment of an indemnity on the table. He offered to pay 1 per cent of all customs export receipts to the French crown and a further 5 per cent to the former owners of plantations until the value of their establishments was recovered (the issue of whether that value included its human 'property' was not mentioned). Pétion even tacitly recognised Christophe's control of the north and asked only that if France opened relations with him that they not recognise him as king. Lord Liverpool followed Castlereagh's precedent and ignored the approach, but Garbage sent a copy to Wilberforce, asking for his help. He apparently agreed to the sentiments in the petition, but before matters could go further Garbage passed away in London.[40] Pétion later wrote to Wilberforce directly to praise the abolitionist's work and warn him against dealing with Christophe, but by this time Wilberforce had decided to fully throw his weight behind the Haitian king.[vii]

The attention of an avowedly Anglophile monarch may also have appealed to Wilberforce more than that of the republican Pétion, but Christophe asked for something designed to flatter him even more: his advice. Wilberforce thought himself a pragmatic man and supported the principle of gradual rather than immediate emancipation from slavery, but he recognised a clear opportunity in the Kingdom of Haiti:

> Providence has thrown in our way an opportunity such as has seldom been afforded, of sowing the seeds of civilization, and still more of Christian faith, in this hitherto benighted quarter of the world, where, when they have once taken root, they will gradually diffuse themselves throughout all the coloured inhabitants of the Western hemisphere.[41]

[vii] It is possible (but unclear) that Christophe may also have sent a direct mission to London in early 1814. According to a French émigré planter named Philippe Auguste Laffon de Ladebat, writing from Jamaica, Baron de Vastey himself sailed to England accompanied by the Chevalier Prézeau. De Ladebat recorded that soon after their arrival in England, the unexpected abdication of Bonaparte and restoration of the French crown meant that Jean-Gabriel Peltier immediately sent them back to Haiti. See Baron de Vastey, *The Colonial System Unveiled*, ed. and trans. Chris Bongie (Liverpool University Press, 2014), pp. 74–5. The mission appears nowhere in Vastey's writings or in any other accounts published in the kingdom.

Still, he had doubts about whether a private individual (even a member of parliament such as himself) should enter into what could be construed as a diplomatic correspondence, and decided to forward all future communications to Lord Liverpool, trusting that the prime minister's 'considerable religious principle' would demand attention be paid to the prospects he saw dawning in Haiti.

Wilberforce also began to excitedly share his 'Haytian correspondence' with his friends in high society. Sir Joseph Banks was even more enthused: 'Were I five and twenty as I was when I embarked with Captain Cook, I am very sure I should not lose a day in embarking for Hayti,' wrote the 72-year-old botanist, 'To see a set of human beings emerging from slavery, and making rapid strides towards the perfection of civilization, must I think be the most delightful of food for contemplation.'[42] Banks would later open a direct correspondence with Christophe. Wilberforce also invited England's other great abolitionist, Thomas Clarkson, to write to Christophe and offer his services. After years of Peltier's ineffectual lobbying, the Kingdom of Haiti finally had English friends in high places.

14

THE PRICE OF SUGAR

While waiting for a reply from William Wilberforce, Christophe embarked on a three-week tour of the kingdom's western province in April 1815. In Petite Rivière he held a large military review and visited the site of Dessalines' heroic victory against the French at Crête-à-Pierrot. Over four successive days crowds gathered to catch sight of their king and present him with petitions. According to the *Gazette Royale d'Hayti*, 'He welcomed all with kindness and did justice to those who had some cause for complaint.' Plantations were toured, farmers performed dances to show their love of their sovereign and pensions were disbursed for members of the Order of St Henry. 'Together with the gifts and favours which His Majesty has showered on the people, [he] must have poured a considerable sum of money into this province, and it can be said with truth: wherever His Majesty has passed, he has brought prosperity, peace, and happiness', wrote an anonymous member of the court. Before returning to Sans Souci, Christophe hosted Captain James of the Royal Navy ship HMS *Tanais*, in harbour to take on supplies, whose men were heard to praise the good order of the city garrison.[1]

In London there were the first signs of royal progress of a different kind as Christophe won another English supporter to his cause—someone he had met in person during the revolution. In 1798 he had sentenced the British army officer Marcus Rainsford to death for espionage, only for Toussaint Louverture to have him deported. Rainsford had since been won over to the Haitian cause. He published a book about the revolution describing Haiti as 'a pure emanation of humanity', and by the end of 1814 had started giving public speeches in London in support of King Henry and his court.

For this he was granted the honorary rank of lieutenant-general in the Haitian army. It was in this capacity, on 23 February, that he attended the Prince Regent's levee at Carlton House, in which he was able to present the future George IV with a copy of Christophe's plan for national defence, issued in the aftermath of the Malouet affair.[2] This was exactly the type of lobbying that Christophe had hoped to achieve in London. Julien Prévost wrote to Rainsford, ranking him alongside 'the incomparable Britons' who had campaigned to abolish the slave trade. Rainsford volunteered to come to Haiti to join the army directly, but the offer was politely declined on the basis that Rainsford was more valuable to the kingdom where he was: 'It will be much better to place you in London, with an adequate establishment, to defend our cause.'[3]

Christophe had equally come to understand that his campaign for international legitimacy had to be a mix of soft power as a well as diplomatic lobbying. Just as his royal tours showed him performing the role of king to his people, 1815 saw a new focus on using the kingdom's wealth to cement the idea that Haiti was a power not just to be accepted but also admired. Simply put: if Christophe wanted to be recognised as a king, he had to spend like one.[4] The second half of the year saw a succession of articles in British newspapers commenting on the luxury goods that Christophe was buying in London, wherever possible commissioned from the same craftsmen patronised by the Prince Regent. His jewellers Rundell, Bridge and Rundell created a diamond-hilted sword for Christophe, along with epaulettes studded with precious stones, both of which were put on display to an awed public. A complete bone china dinner service was ordered from the Spode pottery works in Staffordshire. At the centre of each gilt-rimmed plate, a crowned phoenix rose from flames set against a deep blue shield, surmounted by the royal crown.[i] Gold and silver plate was ordered from Milroy's Sadler of Lombard Street, including a gilt bronze ice pail bearing the royal arms. Just as Baron de Vastey's books aimed to demonstrate that Haiti was a true embodiment of Enlightenment values, Christophe's

---

[i] One of the few surviving plates from the Spode service is held by the Victoria & Albert Museum in London.

high spending was designed to show that his kingdom's splendour could match anything in Europe—and it was all paid for by free rather than enslaved labour.

In October 1815 the *Morning Chronicle* dedicated nearly half a column to describe in great detail the 'very superb dresses for the Queen and Princesses of Hayti [which] have just been finished by one of our fashionable Dress-makers'. White satin was chosen for Queen Marie-Louise, embroidered with sunflowers and fringed with gold, and a similarly decorated train that looped up to form a drapery with gold tassels. The outfit was topped off with a rich plume of white feathers and combs. The gown for Princess Améthyste was lilac satin with a gold and silver fringe, silver tissue sleeves and a train with large red roses. Her younger sister Athénaïre's dress was in pink corded satin, decorated with silver roses and lilies-of-the-valley. The price tag was not mentioned, but another bill for royal dresses came to £3,700.[5]

Of all the items bought for Christophe none was more splendid than the series of state carriages put on display to the London public to great acclaim in November, by the coachmakers Crowther and Tapp of Charles Street, Middlesex Hospital. The main eight-horse carriage had a sky-blue body with 'an entirely nouvelle shape' designed to give extra shade from the Caribbean sun. Its panels were painted with the king's coat of arms encircled with an elegant border of flowers and images of military and naval trophies. Rich gilt mouldings framed the whole of the bodywork, and the cornices of the roof were surmounted with golden phoenixes, with a crown at its centre. The interior was lined in velvet embroidered with the emblem of the Order of St Henry and fringed with gold drapery. No one who saw it could fail to be awed by its magnificence. Only mildly less extravagant was the Prince Royal's emerald-green cabriolet with his emblazoned arms, with chased silver fixings and lined with yellow and green morocco leather. The coaches for the princesses had matching lilac panels with the initials 'A. A.' entwined in silver.[6]

In total, 23 carriages were built by Crowther and Tapp for the royal court, plus harnesses for 119 horses and crimson saddles with gold lace and silver-clawed tiger skin saddlecloths. When the carriages were due to be shipped to Haiti, the *Morning Chronicle* sighed to its readers: 'it is to be lamented that more time is not allowed the public, to witness one of the grandest specimens of art and elegance ever combined in one piece of work of the kind that has been sent from this country'. The total cost of the work was estimated to have been £12,000, with Crowther and Tapp hoping to clear a profit of around £10,000 on the commission.[7]

William Crowther had won the order in person. In 1814 he had visited Barbados on business, taking with him several carriages as examples of his work. His ship also called at Cap Henry, and by the time he left he had won the royal commission directly from Prévost. After their London display had won such acclaim, the carriages were packed up to be shipped to Haiti. As well as the ships, the cargo included the dresses for the queen and princesses, more jewellery, cut glass chandeliers, harness and tack for two regiments of cavalry and a marble copy of the Irish-born Italian sculptor Turnerelli's celebrated bust of George III—in total another £6,000-worth of goods. That the king of Haiti spent such sums in Britain was noted with pride in many newspapers, with one commenting that 'it is highly gratifying to observe the constant and increasing superiority our manufacturers are daily obtaining in those ornamental embel-lishments, for which, but a few years ago, enormous sums of money were annually transmitted to other countries'.[8]

The ship arrived at Cap Henry in the middle of January 1816, where the *Gazette Royale d'Hayti* reported on the 'infinite number of goods and luxuries' it was carrying. Also on the ship was 'a black gentleman, Mr Prince Saunders', whose passage had been paid for by Wilberforce. On learning that he was carrying letters of intro-duction from 'illustrious persons in London', Christophe immedi-ately summoned him to Sans Souci for an audience.[9] Saunders' arrival was the first tangible proof that Wilberforce could provide more than just support for the kingdom, and his background allowed him to form a bond with Christophe deeper than anything a white English abolitionist might offer.

Prince Saunders was born in Connecticut in 1775 and had worked as a teacher in Boston's African School, where he formed a close connection with the founder of America's First African Baptist Church, Thomas Paul. Together the two became advocates for black education as well as African American emigration to Africa to escape the racial prejudices of the USA. In 1815 they sailed to London where they made their connection with Wilberforce.[10]

Saunders proved an able high society networker. By omitting the title 'Mr' from his visiting cards he flattered many hosts into thinking they were dealing with a real prince, a notion he was slow to disabuse them of. Before long Saunders was a regular invitee to fashionable parties. In 1816 the noted society hostess the Countess of Cork was said to have been unable to have a party without 'his Highness Prince Saunders'. He proved an equally adept host as well as guest, and in July of that year held a ball attended by more than seventy people including the American ambassador to London (and future president) John Quincy Adams; the two had previously met at a banquet hosted by Prince Frederick, Duke of Sussex.[11]

When Saunders arrived in Cap Henry he brought with him more than just the promise of connections to London society. His luggage contained doses of smallpox lymph along with a pamphlet on its benefits addressed to Christophe from the surgeon James Moore, director of the British National Vaccine Establishment. The king was thrilled and wrote to Moore with thanks:

> The interesting discovery of vaccination is so important to the welfare of mankind, and so honourable to humanity, that I cannot but adopt it in my dominions. On the arrival of Mr. Prince Sanders, I directed that the Haytian Physicians should universally embrace the practice of vaccination ... This benefit will still further increase the gratitude of the Haytians towards the great and magnanimous British nation.[12]

Saunders had reportedly delayed his passage to Haiti so that he could correctly learn how to administer the vaccine, and the *Gazette Royale d'Hayti* soon reported excitedly that the first children at Sans Souci had received their doses, praising Wilberforce for sending such valuable help. Christophe ordered that every parish should start producing the lymph so that a countrywide vaccination programme could be rolled out: 'Fathers and mothers, give thanks to those virtuous philanthropists and for our generous monarch; you will no longer have to fear the deadly scourge of smallpox!' For his role in the new programme, the *Boston Patriot* newspaper in Saunders' hometown dubbed him the 'Jenner of Hayti'.[13]

While Saunders prepared to administer his smallpox lymph, Crowther was getting reacquainted with Cap Henry. He would have been welcomed by the familiar face of Baron de Dupuy, the royal interpreter who served as the main point of contact for anyone arriving to do business in the kingdom, and whose 'ready wit and supple intelligence' was appreciated by the resident foreign merchant community. He would have had plenty to occupy him while he was waiting to be paid—arranging for horses to be put into harness for the two dozen carriages he had brought from London and, not least, overseeing the eight draft horses that would have required special instruction to learn how to pull the king's coach.[14]

We do not know if Crowther won praise for his work in a personal royal audience, but two months after he landed a payment order was issued to him by Baron de Charrier, chief secretary to the Minister of Finance. The invoice would have been personally approved by Christophe, who still retained his need to micromanage the smallest affairs of state. He regularly issued orders for payments to foreign merchants specifying the market rates for sugar and coffee to be paid out. In one instance he instructed an official to refuse the offer of a merchant in Saint-Marc to buy government sugar at 6 gourdes per half hundredweight, instructing him to offer 8 gourdes so that he might allow the merchant to save face by haggling the price down to 7.[15] Payments for all imported goods were made in sugar and coffee, as the export of all gold and silver including specie was forbidden under the kingdom's customs laws.[ii] Crowther was forced into the role of commodity trader to recoup his investment. Ten days after the payment order was issued, however, Crowther signed for the receipt of 147,020 livres of raw sugar priced at 12 gourdes per hundredweight and 152,679 livres of coffee at 22 gourdes per hundredweight. In total the goods were worth roughly £9,255.[16] The receipt states that the payment was made for 'supplies and various objects'. It is impossible to know if this was the sum total for his shipment or a proportion of it, but this was far from the profit he hoped to turn on the trip. Crowther's son later claimed that not only had his father received less than the market rate for the sugar and coffee, but he had also been charged 40 per cent import tax for his goods (customs documents from 1817 set the import duty for carriages and harness at 10 per cent).[17] Either way, Crowther's trip

---

[ii] In the name of national self-sufficiency, the export of copper or scrap iron was also forbidden.

concluded with him being unable to cover all his expenses. He was able to remit goods worth £12,000 back to England, but was then forced to sail home via the United States, after being refused passage on the ship that had brought him after a dispute with its captain. 'He hoped to return to England in a year or two to be able to pay his creditors; in the meantime, however, he did not like to risk a [debtor's] prison', wrote one correspondent two years later. Instead Crowther died en route, and his coach-making firm went bankrupt. His son was forced to spend the next few years defending himself in court against his father's creditors.[18]

As the carriages were being delivered to Sans Souci they would have passed farmers in the fields who had no idea of the drama that was to befall their creator, and all for a slice of the wealth produced by their labour. As the account of the royal tour in the *Gazette Royale d'Hayti* had made clear, plantation agriculture was still at the heart of Christophe's vision for his country. The king had visited several plantations and depots where produce was stored, travelling by horse to better allow him to talk to the farmers and encourage their work: 'He asked whether they were regularly paid the quarter of the revenue due to them; he listened with the greatest interest to those who had some cause for complaint, and told them to approach him with confidence.' So important were the export crops they were growing that in Petite Rivière he ordered Jean Chevreau, a local Royal Dahomet officer, to be awarded the Cross of the Order of St Henry for the 'just and equitable' way in which he directed the farmers under his command in 'the noble labours of agriculture'.[19]

Petite Rivière was in coffee country, and its produce would have been sent down the Artibonite River to be stored in a government warehouse in Saint-Marc to await export. There were sixteen of these warehouses spread across the kingdom, and the survival of a ledger from one of these in Cap Henry gives a rare insight into the state of agricultural production under Christophe's monarchy. Over dozens of pages of closely written column entries, the Schomburg Ledger records deposits of coffee and sugar produced near Cap Henry between February 1814 and October 1816. In February 1816, while Crowther was waiting for payment, 7,370 livres of processed coffee were deposited in the storehouse produced by fifty-six plantations, primarily from the L'Acul du Nord parish a few kilometres west of Cap Henry. Of this, 295 livres were the product of four plantations in Soufrière and L'Acul, of which at least three were run by women. The ledger records the names of the managers as Chiba, Rozalie, Catherine Chirin and Marie. More than a third of the managers in the ledger are identifiably female. The four managers deposited 78, 75, 39 and 103 livres of coffee respectively, which made up half of that month's production and represented the plantation's net profits. The rest was due in state tax and the quarter share given to the farmers who had grown the beans. At the end of the month the storehouse held a total of 79,775.5 livres of coffee. As the year progressed, the harvests grew larger: in May, 153 plantations in the same parish deposited 42,715 livres of coffee, and a further 12,410 in September. This process would have been repeated in storehouses across the country.[20]

Under the Code Henry, prices for the produce had to be published so that buyers could ensure they were receiving a fair price. A state representative issued a certificate to confirm its quality and give advance notice of when payments were due. The recording of the names of the plantation managers was especially important as these were the people who collected the payment; in the case of the managers in L'Acul, this would probably have been issued in nearby Limbe by Joseph Casimir, the town's comptroller. Every month Chiba, Rozalie, Catherine Chirin and Marie would travel to the town to deposit their coffee and receive the payments for the farmers. The quarter share was divided according to their role: farmers received one share, while a *conducteur* who ran the work gangs received three shares. Skilled workers involved in processing were given two shares, with one and a half given to any midwives on the property. Workers deemed to have worked insufficiently hard could have their pay deducted to as little as a quarter share: Christophe regarded idleness as a moral failing.

Such was the strictness with which the Royal Dahomets enforced the plantation system that stories abounded that Christophe's eyes were everywhere watching over the workers, and that his English telescope could observe everyone in the kingdom.[iii] One English

---

[iii] Such was Christophe's reputation for labour enforcement that when travelling in Haiti's northern plain today, it remains a common experience to come across colonial-era irrigation channels and

resident noted that 'there was no idlings [sic] under King Henry's regime, for he permitted none ... When [the king] worked who durst be idle! & who did not know that his eye as well as his arm reached from Cape Henri to St Mark's, from Cape St. Nicholas Môle to Fort Royal.' Managers had to provide a written list of all the workers on their plantation, to be countersigned by the local justice of the peace, who would then be personally liable for any abuses of the resulting payments.[21] The landlord or owner was deliberately excluded from involvement in the quarter payments. In the case of the four plantations in L'Acul du Nord, this was the Comte de Ouanaminthe, an intimate of Christophe who was equerry to the queen, inspector of the royal stud farms and an officer in the Royal Gardes du Corps. His wife was governess to Princess Améthyste and would regularly accompany her charge in one of the carriages made by Crowther—carriages that had possibly been partly paid for by coffee grown on the family land. Just as the ledger shows female plantation managers, the Comtesse may even have been a landowner herself; the Princesse de Limbe, wife of Paul Romain, regularly appears in the ledger as the owner of several coffee plantations.[22]

One expected landowner who appears only infrequently in the Schomburg Ledger was Christophe himself. Some foreign merchants, aware of the close interest that the king took in both agriculture and commodity prices, claimed that it was his aim to personally monopolise all trade in the country. Evidence from the ledger suggests that his personal interest in plantation ownership was relatively modest. The first entry for 'His Majesty' does not come until August 1814, when eight plantations in Milot, Choiseul and Dubreil made deposits of coffee. All were in the immediate vicinity of Sans Souci, with some on the mountain slopes directly visible from the windows of the king's apartments. Given Christophe's love of touring plantations to check on their farmers, it is tempting to speculate on the relationship he may have had with the workers there. The area was certainly productive, and over 51,000 livres of royal coffee were deposited in the warehouse in

---

be told by local farmers that they are the remains of secret tunnels leading back to Sans Souci, built so that Christophe could visit the plantations unannounced.

the first three months of 1815 alone. Three managers are mentioned by name: Vincent, Louise and Délaché, the last of whom is listed in the 1816 royal almanac as being a clerk to Sans Souci's justice of the peace. As such he would have been involved in both receiving the farmers' quarter share and certificating that it had been correctly paid, illustrating that even on the king's estates the letter of the law demanded by the Code Henry was not always strictly adhered to.[23] From mid-1815, Christophe's plantations disappear from the register entirely. Presumably the produce was still sent to Cap Henry but recorded in a ledger that has subsequently been lost. When the state finances were rearranged in April 1817, with the formal creation of a civil list, these Sans Souci coffee plantations were included among the sixteen that were formally listed as property of the crown.[24]

When Prince Saunders published extracts from the Code Henry in London, they were presented as proof of Christophe's aim to 'ameliorate the condition and improve the character of the humblest class, namely, that of the plantation labourers'.[25] There was little talk of royal carriages; rather the reciprocal obligations between proprietor and planter and the moral value of labour.[26] One English observer commented on the banning of idleness and believed that Haiti's labouring poor did well under the new system: 'I believe I can venture to say, that, though one-fourth of the gross produce may have been assigned to them by law, they never had so much: what they had was little enough and yet sufficient to supply their few wants.' As he continued, he revealed his own low expectations of what former slaves demanded from their situation:

> In my rides all over the Plaine du Cap, I found few villages, and those consisted for the most part of ten or a dozen huts. In such places, no person resided who needed more than a few yards of coarse cloth in the year, and perhaps, occasionally, an iron pot to cook their victuals in. These articles and others, if required, were purchased in their weekly, monthly, or yearly journeys to the towns, where the foreign factors had stores.[27]

The writer missed the unresolved tension that hung over agriculture in Haiti, but it was something that the clerk writing in the Schomburg Ledger may have been more attuned to. In February

1816 he noted that there were no deposits made that month of sugar, and that the warehouse had a balance of just 11,608.25 livres. Unlike fast-cropping coffee which could be left to grow with minimum intervention, sugar production was a slow and highly labour-intensive process. The cane had to be pressed for its juice immediately after harvesting, which was then boiled off. The syrup was then placed in clay moulds to dry; the Code Henry stipulated that this process required three months to produce sugar of sufficient quality to export. But while coffee boomed, the ledger shows that sugar production was in decline. In the year up to October 1816, just twenty-six plantations produced sugar to be lodged in the warehouse. Two plantations owned by the queen's brother, Prince Noël (the only royal who appears to have maintained a sugar interest), produced 2,372 livres in December 1815, while two at Breda, where Toussaint Louverture was born, managed to lodge little more than double that in July 1816 under the ownership of the Comte d'Ennery. Even the Gallifet plantation, whose sugar riches had been celebrated in Saint-Domingue, recorded production of just 12,006.5 livres. The Schomburg Ledger records a small but significant year-on-year decline in sugar production. On top of that, only raw brown sugar was recorded in either the ledger or in transactions with foreign merchants: the more highly prized refined white sugar that Saint-Domingue had been famous for was no longer produced anywhere. Writing in the 1840s, the historian Thomas Madiou suggested that sugar exports in the Kingdom of Haiti were barely a quarter of what they had been under French slavery. Christophe knew that people despised working on the sugar plantations: his letters of 1805 to 1806 devoted much time to tracking down farmers who had absconded in the belief that they had won their independence to be free of such labour. The revolution had dealt a mortal blow to the plantation system, and despite years of trying to uphold it by Louverture, Dessalines and now Christophe, it was slowly on its way out—no matter what provisions were made in the Code Henry to turn Haitians into sharecroppers.[28]

Despite the relative decline of sugar production, the booming coffee plantations and the arrival of specially commissioned luxury goods from London appeared enough to convince a casual observer in 1816 that the kingdom was growing ever stronger. Christophe likely believed that he had finally solved the problem of balancing the needs of the state, the landowner and the peasant farmer. The nobility and army were invested in the system in a way that Dessalines had never achieved, and there was a strong police force to enforce the system, however imperfectly. The rewarding of officers like Jean Chevreau was an important part of this. The *Gazette Royale d'Hayti* suggested that such was their dedication to Christophe, the Royal Dahomets clothed and equipped themselves 'voluntarily at their own expense', but the fact that new members of the Order of St Henry were expected to pay for their own medals either in specie, coffee or cotton suggests they were themselves heavily invested in the profits of the plantation system.[29]

The sole public admission that the production of export crops lagged behind expectations came in the *Gazette Royale d'Hayti* of 23 July 1816, which announced that the king had ordered an expansion of sugar, coffee and cotton plantations and was planning another tour 'to learn for himself' what progress was being made to improve national production. The admission was easy to miss, coming as it did straight after a breathless account of the celebrations held for the Prince Royal's birthday. This was the image the kingdom wanted to put across: military parades, lavish banquets and toasts from attendees, whose cries of joy were almost drowned out by cannon salutes and cheers from the public. In the evening, the whole of Sans Souci was illuminated for a ball 'that lasted until two hours after midnight'. As usual, members of the resident foreign community were invited to marvel at the spectacle. 'Let not the reader laugh at the idea of a court-ball at Hayti', wrote one dutifully impressed attendee:

> Let him rather figure to himself the most brilliant '*bal parée*' he has ever seen in the most elegant '*salon*' Paris affords, and he will then have but a faint idea of the magnificence of Sans Souci. Let him people it with all the elegance and fashion, affectation and dandyism that he has ever met with in more civilized countries; let him add titles and uniforms, ribands and stars, ices and refreshments, and all the *et cetera* incidental to wealth and power; let him then call in a magician, and turn all the company black, and he will be able to picture to himself the last court-ball I saw in Haiti.[30]

Even more extravagant celebrations were held the following month in Cap Henry to celebrate the queen's fête, held on 15 August, the date of the Assumption of the Virgin Mary and the city's patron saint. Held over twelve days, the fête was the grandest spectacle held in the country since the coronation: the official account was printed over four successive issues of the *Gazette Royale d'Hayti* before being expanded into a fifty-page book. William Crowther's carriages were the centrepiece of a royal procession the day before the fête from Sans Souci to Cap Henry, along roads that had been specially levelled for the event. If they had impressed audiences when displayed in the gloomy November London, their brilliance must surely have dazzled the crowds who watched them under the bright Caribbean sun. A military escort of artillery, cavalry and infantry preceded the king's carriage, its sky-blue body matching the uniforms of the royal household dragoons. It was followed by the queen's coach, also drawn by eight horses, as were the separate coaches for the Prince Royal and the Princesses Améthyste and Athénaïre. Behind them were coaches for six and four horses apiece, each carrying a female member of court: Princess Jean, the queen's lady-in-waiting, who was married to her nephew, the princesses' governesses the Comtesses d'Ouanaminthe and Terrier-Rouge, the Princesse du Limbe and the wives of the most prominent members of the court including the Barons de Vastey and Dupuy. Bringing up the train 'an infinite number of people of all ranks and sexes followed the procession in carriages and on horseback', eager to be part of the festivities.[31]

On arrival at Haut-du-Cap, Christophe took to horseback and led the procession beneath a garlanded victory arch and along Rue Espagnole, past the ruins of the Couronne inn where he had toiled as a boy. The royal scribe was enraptured:

> The long row of superb carriages all richly harnessed and stretching into the distance, the beauty and splendour of the uniforms of all the troops at arms, the stir of the people and the shouts of joy, joined to the salutes of the cannon, gave this parade a martial air that rendered it truly victorious.[32]

In the evening the city lights blazed and fireworks and music entertained the crowds that had gathered in the main square to join in the celebrations.

Events began the following morning with a salute from Cap Henry's forts and a breakfast where the gathered nobility expressed their loyalty and affection for the mother of the nation. Marie-Louise responded by promising that 'the happiness of the Haitian people will always be the object of my only concern and greatest attention'. With breakfast concluded, heralds then led the king, queen and assembled royal household to the cathedral for Mass. A luncheon feast for 400 guests then followed, held in a specially constructed hall and arranged by the Baronesses Ferrier and Dupuy, who had decorated the interior with wooden panelling, mirrors, paintings and a dizzying number of chandeliers and candelabras.[33] In the evening the royal party attended a performance of the comic opera *Zemire and Azore* in the newly rebuilt theatre, before concluding the day with more fireworks and a grand ball.[iv]

The next day it was the turn of Jean-Pierre Richard, Duc de Marmelade, to host a banquet. Now in his sixties, the city governor was known by visiting Royal Navy officers for his hospitality. In addition to the royal family and nobility, he made sure to invite ten English merchants and three Americans, who were no doubt delighted when Christophe led toasts to George III and US President James Madison, along with assorted other 'brother' monarchs in Europe and 'the immortal Wilberforce'. In turn, the king would have been flattered by the speech given in response by the British merchant Mr White:

> I am English and accustomed to expressing my feelings freely …
> I have observed the customs and laws of the peoples of all the
> countries I have visited, and well, gentlemen, I will tell you the
> truth: I have seen the King of Haiti at the head of his troops, I have
> examined the richness of the uniforms, the conduct and discipline
> of the Haitian army; I have observed the customs and studied the
> laws of this country … In your position today, you must fear
> nobody, you are invincible![34]

[iv] The royal almanac for 1816 lists the theatre director as Chevalier Celestin Petigny, possibly related to the Chasseur Volontaire Petigny who the writer Hérard Dumesle claimed took the young Christophe under his wing on arrival in Saint-Domingue in 1779. Its dancers were Marie Noële, Caroline Lencens, Madame Bienaimé, Madame Charlemagne, Soucy, Josephine and Nizida.

Another military parade followed. Having begged the assembled ladies of the court to put their talents to work by sewing new regimental banners, Christophe mounted his horse to take personal command of the parade, dressed in the red of the Haitian Guards, faced in black velvet with white breeches. Victor-Henry rode behind him in the green and pink of the Prince Royal's Regiment. The celebrations continued for several days, with the queen giving alms to the city's poor and the king granting pardons to a number of criminals. On 20 August there was a trip to Pont Dahomet, accompanied by the queen's elegantly dressed Amazons, who wore 'small hats of the latest fashion, decorated with ostrich feathers, and [were] mounted on superb horses'. The fête culminated in a grand banquet in the queen's honour. The preparations took several days, with an army of cooks, pastry chefs and confectioners preparing the feast, overseen by Baron de Dupuy. Four enormous tables were set in a marquee for 800 guests, but invitations were in such demand that nearly double that number managed to squeeze in. All were served entirely without incident, 'despite the considerable amount of wine that was drunk'. In the evening there was a public performance of *The Barber of Seville* ('Monsieur Heureaux the elder excelled in the role of Bartolo and Monsieur Daguindeau the younger in that of Figaro'), after which a grand ball was held where Christophe reputedly danced with every lady present. When the music ended at dawn, the royal party mounted their carriages and finally retired to Sans Souci.[35]

When the *Gazette Royale d'Hayti* concluded its coverage of the fête, it published a new order issued by the king declaring that a column dedicated to liberty was to be erected in the centre of the parade ground in the Citadelle Henry. The complete Act of Independence was to be cast in bronze, and every Independence Day it would be rededicated in tribute to those who had died to bring Haiti into the world. The names of all the signatories would be included, with the exception of those who had proved themselves traitors to the national cause. There was no explicit mention of Alexandre Pétion, but Christophe knew that just two months earlier the Senate in Port-au-Prince had named him president-for-life and given him the power to nominate his successor. '[Pétion] had one simple thing to do, which would have been to imitate the immortal example of Washington, to make way for someone else', wrote Vastey, snorting that the republican system had been killed by his arbitrary and despotic rule.[36] Perhaps, Christophe might have wondered, the dedicated republican was secretly envious of the authority of a king? And perhaps, flush with the celebrations for his wife's fête, he might also have wondered if the toast given by Mr White also rang true: that he had no one left to fear because his kingdom was invincible.[37]

15

YOUR MAJESTY'S FRIENDS

On the morning of 17 October 1816 a frigate and a brig were spotted on the horizon heading towards Cap Henry. They anchored just outside the range of the city's forts but signalled no intention to enter the harbour. After a day of uncertainty over their aims, the city governor Jean-Pierre Richard dispatched a pilot boat to demand they identify themselves. Only then did the ships reveal their colours, jointly raising the flag of the Haitian republic and the white royalist standard of France. The brig manoeuvred closer to shore and fired a volley from its cannons before both ships set sail and fled west. The following day a merchant ship flying American colours pulled into Cap Henry. It had been intercepted by the mysterious vessels and given a letter to deliver addressed to Monsieur General Christophe at Cap Français.

Two years after the embarrassment of the Malouet mission, Louis XVIII had decided to try for a second time to see if he could reclaim the lost colony of Saint-Domingue. The frigate *Flora* carried his envoy Vicomte François de Fontanges, who the previous week had dined with Alexandre Pétion in Port-au-Prince. At seventy-two, Fontanges was old for such a mission, but he knew the area well. He had commanded the militia in Cap Français in the 1770s and had fought for the colonial forces in the first four years of the Haitian Revolution. Fontanges had almost certainly met Pétion in Saint-Marc in 1790, when the future president briefly found himself under the command of the Frenchman.[1] It is even possible that Fontanges and Christophe had crossed paths at the siege of Savannah in 1779: Fontanges was second-in-command of the Chasseurs Volontaires, although whether he would have made the connection between a twelve-year-old drummer boy and the self-proclaimed king of Haiti is unlikely.[i]

Fontanges had expected the warm welcome he received from Pétion. An unofficial trade had tentatively begun between the two nations, and ships from Bordeaux now regularly appeared in Port-au-Prince's harbour. He was less sure about Christophe, and ordered his ship to stand off Cap Henry in fear of suffering the same fate as the envoy Médina in 1814. His chosen form of address helped guarantee him a poor reception. When Fontanges' letter was delivered by his proxy, 'the [Duc de Marmelade] expressed his extreme surprise and indignation; and told the captain and supercargo that he was astonished that Americans, who had traded for so many years with Hayti ... should have undertaken a commission which was no less dishonourable than misplaced'. Richard returned the letter unopened and demanded the American quit the harbour.[2] In the end the French ship intercepted another vessel near Gonaïves and persuaded its captain to deliver the same package under cover to the commander of the port there.

The letter contained a pronouncement from Louis XVIII expressing that he was 'desirous of extending to Saint-Domingue the blessings he has bestowed on France' and wished to restore the 'legislation of the colony, the internal administration and public order' so that commerce between France and its subjects could prosper. Christophe was requested to enlighten his people as to the 'fatherly disposition of the king'. As if to inflame him further, Fontanges said that Louis had instructed that he should 'repair to Port-au-Prince as a central and intermediate place from whence we can communicate with both the North and the South'.[3]

The *Gazette Royale d'Hayti* carried a detailed account of the letter, but it took Christophe nearly a month to break his uncharacteristic

---

[i] The secretary of the Fontanges mission was another former colonist, Albert de Laujon, who could claim a Christophe connection. In his 1835 memoir, *Souvenirs de trente années de voyages à Saint-Domingue*, he scoffed that 'this monster of nature' had served him as a slave in the Couronne inn in 1791. This was in stark contrast to earlier recollections however: in his 1805 *Précis historique de la dernière expédition de Saint-Domingue*, he wrote about landing in the ruins of Cap Français with Leclerc, and commended the 'intelligent, proud' Christophe for saving the lives of many white people after the 'ferocious' Toussaint Louverture ordered the city to be burned to the ground.

silence. When he did it was in the form of a 5,000-word broadside, most likely drafted with Vastey's help. It recycled many of the themes regularly used to denounce the French, but now there was an increased self-assurance in his voice. The king knew that France was still occupied by the allied European armies that had defeated Napoleon, reducing Louis XVIII to sending a frigate rather than an armada. The royal celebrations held a few months earlier had showed a prospering and confident nation: if Haiti was to deal with France it would be entirely on its own terms:

> Whenever we negotiate, we will withhold our consent from any treaty which does not comprehend the liberty and independence of the whole of the Haytians who inhabit the three provinces of the kingdom, known by the names of the North, the West, and the South, our territory; the cause of the Haytian people being one and indivisible. No overture or communication from the French to the Haytian government, whether oral or written, shall be received, unless made in the form, and according to the usages established in the kingdom for diplomatic communications. Neither the French flag nor individuals of that nation shall be admitted within any of the ports of the kingdom, until the independence of Hayti has been definitively recognised by the French government.[4]

Christophe's confidence was also boosted by the attention he was paid by his new friends in London. Prince Saunders was given a generous stipend as Christophe's new agent and returned to London with a mass of papers and pamphlets that he set about translating into English. The resulting book was called *Haytian Papers: A Collection of the Very Interesting Proclamations, and Other Official Documents; together with Some Account of the Rise, Progress, and Present State of the Kingdom of Hayti*, and its 228 pages offered the British public its first sustained exposure to Haitian voices beyond the short snippets previously reprinted in the newspapers. Saunders explained the importance of refuting the racist narratives put forward by Haiti's enemies:

> Such persons have endeavoured to impress the public with the idea, that those official documents which have occasionally appeared in this country, are not written by black Haytians them-

selves; but that they are either written by Europeans in this country, or by some who, they say, are employed for that purpose in
the public offices at Hayti ... I upon my honour declare, that there
is not a single white European at present employed in writing at
any of the public offices; and that all the public documents are
written by those of the King's Secretaries whose names they bear,
and that they are all black men, or men of colour.[5]

The book made a direct appeal to the English character that had led
to the abolition of the slave trade and could now offer support to a
leader like Christophe, who was showing what a nation freed from
slavery could achieve. In its pages, *Haytian Papers* reminded its readers of how Christophe had stood against Bonaparte by presenting
the combative letters he exchanged with Leclerc in 1802, before
including Prévost's narrative of the king's rise to power written for
his coronation. The various laws establishing the monarchy were
printed to show the sound constitutional basis of his rule, plus
extracts from the Code Henry dealing with agriculture, as proof of
Christophe's aim to 'ameliorate the condition and improve the character of the humblest class, namely, that of the plantation labourers'.[6] The reciprocal obligations between proprietor and planter and
the emphasis put on the moral value of labour was music to those
looking for a model of how Jamaica or Barbados could continue to
prosper if emancipation were to take place.

The frontispiece of *Haytian Papers* included an engraving of
Prince Saunders deep in contemplation, his chin resting lightly on
his fingers. It was drawn by Richard Evans, a young painter who
had been a studio assistant to Sir Thomas Lawrence, the Regency
era's most famed portraitist. When Saunders returned to Cap
Henry in September 1816, he brought Evans with him. William
Wilberforce had asked Christophe to send him his portrait, and
Evans was offered a salary of $5,000 a year to become Christophe's
court painter. Saunders also wooed a sculptor named John Rossi to
work on pieces for Sans Souci. Rossi was minded to accept until he
found himself in the middle of a disagreement over who had the
authority to engage people to travel to Haiti. Saunders, having just
arrived from Cap Henry, appears to have prickled the sensitive
Wilberforce, who was affronted that the Boston man was taking
decisions without his blessing.[7]

A fortnight after arriving in Haiti, Evans was installed at Sans Souci as master of the newly established Academy of Drawing and Painting.[8] Within a year he had painted a full-length portrait in a traditional 'grand manner' style that would become the defining image of Christophe's monarchy. The king is wearing a dark green double-breasted tailcoat lined in red, with the cross of the Order of St Henry pinned to his chest. The frilled cuffs of his white shirt meet yellow gloved hands—the left casually in his coat pocket and the right holding a cane and bicorne with a royal cockade. White breeches and pale brown boots complete the outfit. Christophe is framed by a column and red drapes embroidered with his coat of arms, and his royal crown nestles on a cushion beside him. Behind the king is a vista of cloudy Haitian skies, palm trees and the sweep of a distant coastline that evokes the bay of Cap Henry. The framing suggests the king at ease in his palace, although no such view from Sans Souci existed in reality. Evans may have suggested the pose, but Christophe would have had final approval before the portrait was sent to Wilberforce. He would have recognised the high forehead framed by greying hair, worn long enough at the back to tie into a pigtail, the heavily arched eyebrows, and the hint of moustache stubble. If there was a hint of tiredness in the lines on his forehead, Christophe possibly acknowledged them as evidence of a life that had begun in slavery but had led through war to this moment of triumph. He was forty-nine years old when Evans painted him.[9]

Evans also painted an identically sized portrait of the Prince Royal. Dressed in a dark blue coat cut to match his father's, and an identical Order of St Henry medallion, the twelve-year-old Victor-Henry leans confidently against a palomino horse with a riding crop in his hand, watched by a manservant who emerges from the surrounding foliage. The horse bows its head in the royal presence and waits patiently to be mounted, presumably at the moment when Victor-Henry inherits the crown. The two portraits were dispatched to Wilberforce, who would surely have been flattered even more into thinking that he was correct in playing the philanthropist to the Haitian king. In 1818 they were displayed at the Royal Academy in London, where they surprised one anonymous reviewer who judged them 'uncommonly good pictures, and prove that it is not impossible to attach pomp and dignity even unto a negro: they really look very king-like personages'.[10]

Evans painted several other royal portraits, including one of Christophe mounted on his favourite horse, Boïs-Rouge. Another canvas showed the whole royal family. In it the king was described as wearing a British naval uniform, with Queen Marie-Louise having 'a good-humoured looking personage, as fine as the representation of diamonds and lace in profusion can make her'. Next to the prince and princesses, a black cherub descended 'to crown the brows of the Haytian king with a wreath of laurel'.[11] Sadly, neither of these portraits have survived nor are there any known extant images of the queen, but in 2018 a previously unknown half-length portrait of Victor-Henry with his sisters Améthyste and Athénaïre appeared in a New York auction. In this work the prince wears the same costume as in the Evans portrait, but he appears two or three years older, with one hand thrust confidently into his lapels. Améthyste, whose oval face bears a clear resemblance to her father's, rests a gloved hand on her brother's shoulder, while to her left Athénaïre has the softer and more rounded face of a girl in her late teens. The princesses wear modest muslin day dresses, each carrying a charming hint of the lilac and pink gowns made for them in London. Only pearl necklaces and diamond earrings definitively mark their wealth.[ii]

The painting of the prince and princesses was done by a similar but less refined hand than Evans' and may have been completed by one of his pupils, although Evans only taught in Haiti for one year before returning to England. A possible candidate is an artist named Revinchal, who the royal almanac listed as the King's Painter in 1817 and who succeeded Evans as academy master. Little is otherwise known of the artists who graduated from the school. One may have been Xaviar Gazul, who was born in Port-au-Prince in 1783 and is known to have painted the children of the Duc de Marmelade.[12] One named graduate who appears to have specialised in landscapes rather than portraits was Numa Desroches. His father

---

[ii] The painting was bought for the Musée du Panthéon National Haïtien (MUPANAH) in Port-au-Prince, where it is now on display, next to the Evans portrait of Christophe. Haitian art expert Gérald Alexis has suggested that this may be a copy that was sent to the Czar of Russia. In 1912 the Wilberforce family sold their copy of the Evans portrait (and that of the Prince Royal) to the Haitian diplomat General Alfred Nemours. They now form the centrepiece of the Alfred Nemours Collection of Haitian History at the University of Puerto Rico.

was an officer at the 1807 siege of Port-au-Prince, who was executed for dereliction of duty. When an inventory of his possessions was drawn up, a letter was discovered from his wife announcing the birth of their third son, and stricken with remorse, Christophe apparently ordered the whole family to be taken under his care.[13] Desroches painted several images of Sans Souci showing the palace at the height of the kingdom's power. His style is a world away from that of Evans, with bright expressionistic colours and flattened perspectives that instead point the way to the masters of Haitian painting who emerged in the middle of the twentieth century. While ensuring that his architectural renderings were precise, Desroches also took great pleasure in including cartoonish details, like the lion statues guarding the palace's grand entrance, the stylised star apple tree where the king held his open-air court and the birds flying over the mountain road winding up to the Citadelle.[14]

In less than six months, Prince Saunders had proved himself an invaluable envoy for the kingdom. The correspondence he delivered was as important to Christophe as any painter or vial of smallpox lymph. In February 1816 he brought a letter from Thomas Clarkson, beginning a correspondence between the king and the abolitionist that would run for the next four years. Clarkson was a tirelessly practical campaigner. He was a founding member of the Committee for the Abolition of the Slave Trade, and it was his work in the 1780s interviewing the crews of slave ships in the ports of Bristol and Liverpool, frequently at some risk to himself, that had given impetus to the movement and persuaded Wilberforce to take up the issue in parliament. His brother John had been a leading light in the formation of the free colony of Sierra Leone, and on the eve of the Haitian Revolution Thomas Clarkson even helped Vincent Ogé pay for his return passage to Saint-Domingue after lobbying the French National Assembly for the rights of the colony's free coloured population. Samuel Taylor Coleridge had called him 'the moral Steam-Engine' of abolition, a sentiment that Christophe was quick to agree with.[15] He was effusive in his praise for the abolitionist's work, expressing his

> warm and sincere thanks for all the efforts you have made, and the
> zeal you have shown for the triumph of the cause of the Africans

and of their descendants. The gratitude which I feel toward you
… will never be effaced from my heart, and I shall ever seize all
occasions to give you proof of it.[16]

Christophe explained to Clarkson that his dearest ambition was to
educate his people, which he believed to be the first duty of any
sovereign:

> I am completely devoted to this project. The edifices necessary for
> the institutions of public instruction in the cities and in the coun-
> try are under construction. I am awaiting the professors and
> craftsmen I requested, who will take upon themselves the training
> of our youth. I intend to accord them every encouragement, pro-
> tection, and tolerance in the exercise of their religions, along with
> whatever advantages may be just and reasonable. So if God blesses
> my handiwork, and grants me sufficient time, I hope that the
> inhabitants of Haiti, overcoming the shameful prejudice which has
> too long weighed upon them, will soon astonish the world by their
> knowledge.[17]

The first teacher, Thomas Gulliver, had arrived on the same ship
that carried Saunders and Evans. A school building was provided for
him in Cap Henry, and Christophe was soon writing to Clarkson
that he was eagerly awaiting 'the other masters and professors my
friends are to send me, and [I] intend to station them in various
cities of the kingdom and to staff the Royal College, so as to extend
more widely the benefits of education'. At Wilberforce's recom-
mendation, Gulliver had been sent by the British and Foreign School
Society, whose members were trained in the Lancasterian method
of education, whereby 'one master may conduct a school of 1,000
children with perfect ease'. Gulliver initially had to deal with just
150 pupils (for which he received a salary of 100 gourdes a month),
but Christophe nevertheless professed himself 'astonished at the
effects of this new system, and at the precocious intelligence which
it develops in the pupils'.[18]

By 1818 the royal almanac listed Gulliver as schoolmaster in the
capital alongside English teachers in Sans Souci, Gonaïves and Saint-
Marc, plus Prince Saunders, who had been persuaded to take up a
post in Port-de-Paix.[19] A British visitor to Cap Henry in 1820 visited

the school there and found it 'as perfectly furnished with all the necessary apparatus, as the best schools conducted on this system are prepared in England'.[20] He was equally impressed with the children, all of whom could read, write and do arithmetic, with many of them able to speak English and recite poetry. The star pupil, a boy of sixteen, impressed by translating several written passages between English and French, completing arithmetical problems, and pointing out the major European countries on a map and listing their capitals and geographic features.

In December 1818 the *Gazette Royale d'Hayti* dedicated an entire issue to announcing the creation of a Royal Chamber of Public Instruction to oversee the running of the schools and licensing of teachers. All the nobles who had published books or pamphlets in the kingdom were included on the board, including Julien Prévost and Baron de Vastey. Education was to be provided for any child in good health between the ages of eight and sixteen, with compulsory attendance six days a week and lessons held in English and French. School monitors from the class helped oversee lessons and enforce discipline; pupils had to be cleanly and decently dressed, with any child wearing a headscarf liable to have it confiscated. Corporal punishment was allowed for infractions of the rules, which included arriving after roll call and blaspheming. In the most serious cases, masters were empowered to imprison a child for up to two weeks on bread and water. All schools were subject to regular inspections by supervisors appointed by the Royal Chamber of Public Instruction and had to submit quarterly updates on their pupils' progress. In his report for the last quarter of 1817, Gulliver recorded that he had 189 pupils in eight classes under instruction, with thirteen new attendees and one child made to leave for being too young to attend.[21]

In January 1820 Clarkson sent nineteen-year-old William Wilson, a young teacher 'of correct and moral character', fluent in French, Italian, Spanish and Latin and 'acquainted with the English classical writers both in poetry and prose, and also with ancient and modern history', to be employed on a seven-year contract as tutor to the Prince Royal. At an interview with Christophe at his palace in Cap Henry, the king's 'acute intellect and quick intelligence' impressed the young man. 'His hands were remarkably small, soft and delicate, though he was of lofty stature, broad-chested and strong-limbed', Wilson noted in a later memoir, and he 'spoke the French language with great purity' and understood English, though he preferred not to speak it. Wilson was formally appointed at a salary of $250 per month and given a house in the city run by an ambitious housekeeper named Dédêt, who recommended herself to him as the best coffee maker in the city and proceeded to tell Wilson how he should fit in with the house she intended to run.[iii] He gave three hours of instruction to Victor-Henry each morning and afternoon, and despite at one point spending a month in bed with fever, was soon writing to his father that 'I continue to receive the King's approbation, and am in favour with his son, who makes great progress and now speaks English so well as to procure me a great deal of praise.'[22]

Two female teachers from Philadelphia were engaged as tutors for Princesses Améthyste and Athénaïre. On arrival in Cap Henry they were taken in 'an elegant London-built chariot, drawn by four greys' to Sans Souci, where they were presented to the entire royal family:

> Christophe, with the queen, the prince royal, and the princesses appeared, dressed most handsomely, and with a degree of elegance which we had not expected. The queen was exceedingly obliging and affable; she made kind inquiries respecting our passage and health; she expressed her hope that we should be perfectly happy as long as we should remain with them; and she assured us that she would be always ready to assist us;—and her evident sincerity convinced us that she had a kind and affectionate

---

[iii] Wilson soon came to regard Dédêt with great warmth, but many foreign visitors to Haiti had trouble adjusting to the forthright manner with which Haitians conducted themselves. William Harvey noted this in his *Sketches of Hayti*: 'Servants considered themselves on an equal footing with him whom they served; and if asked why they did not call him master, a title they never used, their usual reply was, "If he is my master, I am his slave; but there are no slaves in this country; we are all free and equal." To render their conduct in this instance still more absurd, they often deemed themselves insulted by those who should omit to address them as *monsieur* or *mademoiselle* ... While waiting at table, they often obtruded their remarks, utterly unconscious of their absurdity, or of the impropriety of their forwardness; and made their observations on the persons and dress of those on whom they waited, with a freedom at times quite provoking.' See William Woodis Harvey, *Sketches of Hayti: From the Expulsion of the French to the Death of Christophe* (London: L. B. Seeley & Son, 1827), pp. 281–2.

heart. Her daughters were equally polite; and appeared quite pleased at the idea of our coming to reside in the palace.

The princesses were instructed in English, French, composition and drawing. 'The princesses differed much in their abilities and dispositions', according to their tutors:

> [Améthyste] sometimes appeared to think the difficulty of acquiring knowledge greater than it was worth. She was disposed to learn, but often yielded to that listlessness so common among natives of tropical climates. [Athénaïre] was lively and amiable; she had great quickness of apprehension; but was rather averse to application, and careless of improvement. Yet the progress of both was considerable; and the queen, and we believe the king also, felt perfectly satisfied with our endeavours.[23]

The kingdom's educational progress was a celebrated in Christophe's 1818 Independence Day address, which took public and private virtue as its central theme:

> Parents who have sent your children to drink at the fountains of instruction and imbibe the precepts of wisdom at the National Schools, you have seconded the fondest wish of our heart, and already feel the happy results of your conduct: continue then to send your children to the public schools where, along with the first rudiments of knowledge they will receive the principles of RELIGION, of VIRTUE and of MORALITY.[24]

Religion and moral instruction were frequent topics of discussion in Christophe's letters to both Clarkson and Wilberforce. One of Clarkson's earliest letters explained the role that the Quakers had played as abolitionists and asked Christophe whether one of their ministers might be allowed to preach the Gospel in the country. The king promised to welcome him with open arms.[25] He was even more encouraging with Wilberforce, who was already privately hoping that his 'Haytian business' would expand the reach of the Christian mission. Christophe wrote a long letter to Wilberforce explaining his desire to remove all the French influences his country had inherited, including its religion. His 1811 constitution had confirmed Catholicism as the state religion and both Christophe and his wife were devout churchgoers, but now he told Wilberforce that the faith was a morally dissolute defender of slavery and expressed a desire to embrace the Anglican religion, so that 'my fellow citizens may possess the virtues of the English for their own happiness'. Asking for an introduction to the British and Foreign Bible Society, the leading missionary society of the day, he also requested that in future Wilberforce write to him only in English.[26]

Wilberforce would have noted that the king's letter was written in French, but despite some scepticism that 'Christophe is not himself governed by religious principles', he believed that the approach was sincere: 'Oh what would I give for a clergyman who should be just such as I could approve!' Finding an appropriate figure to take religious instruction to Haiti proved harder than expected, so in the short term Wilberforce had to rely on his correspondence to lead what he believed was Christophe's education. In one missive that ran to nearly 6,500 words, Wilberforce wrote:

> On this most important subject of religion and morals I will open my mind to your Majesty with frankness; because I remember,— surely I can never forget it,—that you declared yourself my friend, and therefore entitled me to use that best right of friendship, the right to state my sentiments without reserve, assured that justice will be done to the motive which has prompted them, even where doubts may be entertained of their propriety.[27]

At Wilberforce's urging, the president of the British and Foreign Bible Society, Lord Teignmouth, offered to print a Haitian edition of the New Testament with parallel French and English texts. Julien Prévost assured him that the king would 'hasten their distribution in the National Schools and private families for the increase of morality, and the knowledge of the English language'. In the event, when the Bibles finally arrived they were apparently discovered to have been misprinted and deemed useless for the purpose of language instruction.[28] Whether this reflected on the sincerity of Christophe's wish to convert his country, Wilberforce could only surmise, as his first missionaries to the country would not arrive until the middle of 1820.

Christophe's professed desire to convert to Anglicanism was a reminder that he was adept at tailoring his message to suit his audience. At every stage in his correspondence with Clarkson and

Wilberforce he painted an image of a fragile infant country hoping for their paternal guidance. This was a world away from the rhetoric of blood sacrifice frequently deployed in his Independence Day speeches, or his fiery denunciations of Haitian republicans and the French. In one letter to Clarkson, Christophe wrote of his grief at seeing Spanish slave ships within sight of his coasts, lamenting that

> it is not my intention to fit out ships of war against them, because I should never wish to give our enemies any excuse for molesting us. You are aware that they watch our each and every action, and that nothing would make them happier than to find some way of discrediting us in the eyes of the world.

Any mention of the way the *Gazette Royale d'Hayti* regularly celebrated his navy's interdiction of slave ships was studiously avoided.[29]

When dealing with affairs that might damage Haiti's reputation, obfuscation was the chosen tactic. In April 1818 Christophe found himself forced to defend to Clarkson the allegation that in 1816 a British man named Davison had been tortured in a Cap Henry jail after being arrested for espionage—an episode that had been raised in the House of Commons. Davison had been discovered by Baron de Dupuy attempting to leave the city with a letter describing the weakness of the kingdom's navy and suggesting that his fellow merchants could easily do business between Cap Henry and Port-au-Prince without fear of interference.[iv] Davison was clapped into irons and threatened with execution to force him to confess to his source of sensitive information. Prévost passed on Christophe's commendation for Dupuy's actions: 'You did well to put him in solitary confinement. I am ordering the governor to keep him there, in thumbscrews and in irons ... If you continue with your active surveillance, you will catch others. We must get to the bottom of this affair.' To Clarkson, however, he claimed the allegations were the creation of Haiti's enemies:

[iv] For national security reasons, all foreign mail had to be presented to the authorities. Dupuy was charged with checking the letters, but by his own account he commonly allowed correspondence by those he trusted to be posted unchecked; it was only Davison's evasiveness that led Dupuy to discovering the incriminating letter.

Neither Davison nor any of his compatriots complained to me of the type of punishment meted out to him. The only person who brought the matter to my attention at Sans Souci was Mr. Strafford, an English merchant, who came to ask for Davison's release, a request which I immediately granted.[30]

Davison's petition to the House of Commons was dismissed.

This careful navigation by Christophe was needed while his relationship with the British government still remained frustratingly undefined. In February 1817 Thomas Strafford, who had spoken up for Davison, was seized by the Jamaican authorities on his arrival from Cap Henry. He was subsequently convicted of publishing 'several wicked, scandalous, malicious, seditions and inflammatory libels'. He had carried with him a copy of Vastey's recently published *Réflexions sur une lettre de Mazères*, written in reply to a pamphlet by an eponymous French former colonist. It was another stout defence of Haiti's right to have taken up arms against its oppressor, as well as being a sharp dismantling of the theories of racial hierarchies used by colonists to justify their enslavement of Africans. Strafford was accused of being an accomplice of Christophe, and of coming from Haiti 'to disquiet, molest, and destroy tranquillity and the good order of the said Island of Jamaica' by inciting a slave rebellion.[31] The fear of an uprising was a perennial one on the island. In April 1816 there had been a short-lived slave revolt on British Barbados, and just one month before Strafford's arrest, seven enslaved sailors had stolen the ship they were crewing from Jamaica and sailed to Port-au-Prince where they claimed their freedom.[32] Strafford claimed that the copy of Vastey's *Réflexions* had found its way into his luggage by accident. While he was found innocent of any intent to distribute the pamphlet, it was nevertheless judged to be so dangerous that he was fined £500 for its possession.

Ironically, Strafford's indictment led to the authorities producing their own translation of Vastey's pamphlet—the first time one of his complete works had been rendered into English. A proper translation was published in London later in the year with the title *Reflexions on the Blacks and Whites*. Its unapologetic descriptions of the violence inflicted on the enslaved as well as Vastey's energetic claim to his rights as a man were such a shock to the sensibilities of many readers that the translator felt obliged to add a note of explanation:

If in some parts the language of wounded feelings appear too strong, or too acrimonious for English ears, let the reader cast his eye over the latter pages, containing a few specimens of the humanity of the ex-colonists, when power was on their side, and he will there find an apology which no feeling heart can hesitate to admit.[33]

The translator was a botanist named William Hamilton who had moved to Cap Henry in 1817 to study the kingdom's agriculture. He came to the conclusion that transitioning away from crops such as sugar to wheat or potatoes would not only increase the efficiency and self-sufficiency of Haitian farming but, if rolled out across the Caribbean, could successfully undermine the entire economic basis of colonial slavery.[34] Hamilton's puritan edge led him to suggest that if this also reduced Haiti's royal exchequer it would be no bad thing: on learning that a new ballroom was being prepared in the Prince Royal's palace in Cap Henry for a visit by the king, he wrote to Zachary Macaulay that 'I should gladly see more attention to useful, and less to frivolous [expenditure].'[35]

Hamilton's experience in Haiti provided a counterpoint to the rosy image that Christophe showed to his English correspondents. Sending a translation of Christophe's 1818 Independence Day speech, Hamilton added: 'I wish that everything was as stated in this document, but my last letters present a very different picture [emphasis in original].' One issue was that Hamilton had fallen in love with a local woman, but for undisclosed reasons had been prevented from marrying her: 'The objection to my marriage with Josephine is a bad proof of zeal for the cause of morality, when it is well known I might take her as a concubine without difficulty.' Josephine was a 'good and virtuous girl', but he found himself excluded from her society and pleaded for Wilberforce's intervention for his beloved to be allowed to visit England where they might marry. It is not known whether their failure to marry hastened Hamilton's return to England in 1818, but he continued to support the kingdom by translating several works by Vastey, who he judged to be a far more impressive figure than the high-spending Christophe.[36]

Had Hamilton embraced the kingdom by taking Haitian citizenship, his relationship may not have been so easily doomed. A

Scottish doctor in his late twenties named Duncan Stewart also travelled to Haiti at this time with his wife, and found himself so enamoured of Christophe's regime that he became a naturalised Haitian. In quick succession he was named head of the Royal Medical College and then personal physician to the king himself. For this, he was granted the honorary army rank of field marshal and gifted a plantation in Quartier Morin near Cap Henry.[37] Stewart urged Clarkson to ignore those who offered 'inaccurate and contradictory information' about the kingdom, and eagerly sang the praises of his royal patient: 'Perhaps there never was a man, who from the energy and acuteness of his mind and from an intimate knowledge [of] the character of the people he governs, [was] so well calculated to rule a kingdom as the present King of Haiti.'[38]

As a member of the royal household Stewart was able to outfit his hospital to the highest standards of the day, and claimed that there was not a hospital in England better supplied than his own. A visiting Royal Navy officer in 1819 agreed that nothing was wanting for the comfort of his patients, but he raised an eyebrow over the fact that each bed came with a pair of stocks, 'in which the legs of the occupier are immediately put on the least symptom of insubordination'.[39] Both Stewart and Christophe both clearly viewed the sick through a combative lens. Another Royal Navy officer who was present when the king toured the hospital noted:

> there was not an individual that [he] did not know by name, his character, his regimen, disease, end everything about him; and whenever he came to a blackguard (and the Doctor said every one he singled out had been a troublesome patient), he gave him a confounded crack on the head with his cane.[40]

The connections that Christophe forged with Saunders, Wilberforce and Clarkson promised new opportunities for the kingdom where the efforts of Jean-Gabriel Peltier had fallen short. Over the years Peltier had allegedly been paid more than £10,000 for his services, but as he fell from favour and his shipments of Haitian coffee and sugar began to dry up, he resigned his position and blamed 'the Methodists' for trying to usurp him, spitting that they had pulled the rug from under him by promising their blessings to Christophe in return for his money. Now that the Bourbon monarchy had been restored, he tried ingratiating himself with Louis XVIII, but his years of vocal support for Haiti meant that he found few sponsors at the French court. Christophe called him 'criminal' and 'perverted' and cut him off completely. Unable to support his lavish lifestyle, he slid into debt and was forced to close his newspaper and sell off his library. In March 1819 a public appeal was made for funds to 'secure him an asylum from want and misery in his old age'. Peltier put all the blame for his downfall on Christophe and Louis XVIII: 'Each of the two reproaches me for my liaisons with the other, and both have abandoned me to the abyss.'[41]

16

THE KINGDOM REFORMED?

On 3 April 1818, *L'Abeille* newspaper in Port-au-Prince announced that exactly one week after being seized by a fever, Alexandre Pétion had passed away in the small hours of 29 March: 'The mournful sounds of the bells, which had not struck the air during the illness of the father of the country, announced at daylight that he was taken from our love.'[1] It was less than a week since Christophe had given his annual address to mark the anniversary of the creation of the Haitian monarchy. He was fifty years old and at the height of his powers, and of the seven generals who had commanded army divisions under Dessalines and signed Haiti's declaration of independence, he was now the only one left alive.

Pétion's successor as president of the republic was Jean-Pierre Boyer. While awaiting news about what the change in leadership in Port-au-Prince would bring, Christophe took a three-month tour of the kingdom to remind his subjects of the power and splendour of the crown. The royal progress was described in the homeliest of terms, with the king 'in the midst of his people, dispensing his bounty and chatting familiarly with the peasants ... everyone could go and quench his thirst in the wine that flowed at discretion'. In Port-de-Paix Christophe oversaw the mass wedding of several hundred soldiers, paying for the wedding banquet from his own purse. Shortly afterwards, Victor-Henry was encouraged to step further into his role as Prince Royal by overseeing a military review.[2] In Saint-Marc the royal party stopped so that Christophe could spend time considering relations with his southern neighbour. Pride prevented him from addressing Boyer directly, as if to do so would admit his legitimacy. Instead, he decided to exploit what he hoped were divisions he might find in the new regime. Vastey was encouraged to begin a correspondence with the republican secretary of state Joseph Inginac, with whom he had once served under Dessalines, hoping to rekindle their old friendship.

Christophe also met with a foreigner named Shaw from Port-au-Prince, who reported that republican army elements led by an anonymous colonel were ready to throw their lot in with the kingdom and help foster a counter-revolution. Over the previous two years there had been a small number of defections to the kingdom, including a lieutenant-colonel who had been rewarded with the Order of St Henry, so this was music to royal ears.[3] Christophe issued a proclamation to the people of 'the West and South', referring obliquely to Pétion as having been 'the only obstacle to our reunion', and calling on them to join the 'new order of things which shall be just and reasonable, honourable and advantageous for all'. As he had done before, he confirmed that all property rights and army ranks would be respected and promised 'the most splendid rewards and honours' to those who would recognise him as king. To deliver his message he sent three envoys south with a letter to the general and magistrates of Port-au-Prince, commenting that 'if our overtures have not been crowned with all the success we had hoped for, we had the satisfaction at least of believing that this was not owing to any fault of ours'.[4]

As in 1816, his approach did not go down well. 'We are free, independent, and republicans', the generals and magistrates replied curtly:

> We will maintain our rights at the hazard of our lives against all who invade them, wherever they appear, and whoever they may be ... We have already explained ourselves. No communication. No correspondence. We do not wish to have anything in common with General Christophe or with his royalty.[5]

The king departed immediately for Sans Souci. As if to rub salt in the wounds, foreign newspapers later took great pleasure in mocking the royal envoys who 'wore the old French dress', with powdered hair and false pigtails.[6] In Gonaïves, Shaw offered to sail to Jérémie with papers signed by Christophe to encourage a mutiny there, but if the plan was ever enacted it was not recorded by the archive. The split between Haiti's north and south looked as permanent as ever.

The rejection of the royal envoys by the republic was perhaps no surprise to Christophe, but eight weeks later he was shaken by events far closer to home. On 25 August the great stone mass of the Citadelle was shaken when a bolt of lightning struck a temporary powder magazine. The resulting blast was heard at Sans Souci. When Christophe hurried to the scene the garrison was in complete disarray. Several buildings were destroyed in the resulting blaze and the flames were approaching the main magazine where 500,000 pounds of gunpowder were stored, threatening to cause an explosion that would have reduced the fort to a crater. Christophe's energetic intervention helped extinguish the fire and saved the Citadelle, but the bodies of 159 men were left in its ashes. One of these was the Citadelle's governor, Prince Noël, Queen Marie-Louise's brother. 'If the damage that the lightning has done to the Citadelle Henry had been a thousand times greater, I would regard it as nothing had my dear brother been preserved!' Christophe lamented at his funeral.[7]

Noël had been a close confidant of the king. He had fought in the revolution and in 1810 had been mentioned in dispatches for his role in the capture of Môle Saint-Nicholas. He may even have helped in the original construction of the Citadelle, a fact for which he was rewarded with its governorship after Christophe's coronation. Noël's death was the second family member that Christophe and his wife had lost in a year. In July 1817 Marie-Louise's nephew Prince Jean died near Gonaïves after a long illness. His remains were interred in the royal chapel at Sans Souci, where they would soon be joined by those of his uncle.[8] Jean's death was mourned, but Julien Prévost regarded Noël's death as an 'irreparable loss' that particularly afflicted Christophe.

Repairs began on the Citadelle with great urgency. 'Little time will be needed to effect [the work], with the numbers and activity employed about it', noted one foreign resident a few days after the event. But Prévost was conscious of how news of the explosion would be exploited, and wrote to Thomas Clarkson to assure him that 'God be thanked, the Citadel still remains capable of offering a stout resistance ... I am acquainting you with these sad details so that you may reassure our friends; our enemies will not fail to represent this misfortune as infinitely more disastrous than it really was.' Indeed, *L'Abeille* portrayed the explosion as a mortal blow against the monarchy, suggesting that three quarters of the Citadelle had been levelled and the royal treasury scattered, along with the deaths of an 'infinity' of soldiers and prisoners shackled in their cells.[9]

When Prévost wrote to Clarkson the correspondence between the king and his English advisor was reaching its height. 'Sound counsel is worth a thousand men', commented Vastey, in the letter he enclosed when sending Clarkson a copy of his book *Political Reflexions*.[10] In the second half of 1818 Christophe was seeking advice about the current state of French politics in light of news that the Allied occupation of France was soon to end. Clarkson was emphatic in his belief that France's war debts and shrunken navy meant that the likelihood of aggressive moves against Haiti were minimal. This belief was bolstered when he attended the Congress of Aix-la-Chapelle in October, where representatives of the Allied nations who had defeated Napoleon Bonaparte in Europe gathered to draw a final line under the wars first begun by revolutionary France in 1792. Clarkson wrote to Christophe that he had discussed the matter with the Duke of Wellington, who had agreed with him that the French dream of recreating an enslaved Saint-Domingue was a fantasy. Furthermore, Clarkson had met with Czar Alexander I of Russia and taken the liberty of showing him a number of Christophe's letters to impress upon him the progress being made by the kingdom—and how much more it could achieve if the spectre of a French invasion was permanently lifted. The Czar was impressed. 'To see a person rising up in the midst of slavery and founding a free Empire was of itself a surprising thing,' he told Clarkson, but to see Christophe 'founding it on the pillars of education under Christian auspices was more surprising and truly delightful. He hoped he should see the spectacle of a new Empire rivalling the whites in all that was great and good.'[11]

Christophe was thrilled when Clarkson suggested that he write to Alexander directly, which would be arranged courtesy of the Russian ambassador in London. He had toasted his royal 'brother' George III numerous times when dining with English merchants in Cap Henry, but this was the first time he had been invited to open a correspondence with another monarch. A letter was drafted, but Christophe seemed uncharacteristically hesitant before allowing it to be delivered and sought further reassurance from Clarkson, speaking of the 'great emotion' that he had felt in learning that his name was being discussed in the salon of the most powerful man in Europe: 'I am sending you this dispatch unsealed; please read it, my friend, and if you judge that it may be sent on to him, I beg of you to forward it to its destination.'[12] Clarkson approvingly replied that the Russian ambassador would include it in his next diplomatic dispatch to St Petersburg.

'Fame has spread to the most distant countries the report of the noble and generous feelings with which your Imperial and Royal Majesty is inspired towards all nations', Christophe wrote in the opening to his letter to the Czar:

> This universal benevolence has excited my admiration, which has been increased by the accounts I have received from my worthy friend, Mr. Clarkson, of the humane and beneficent disposition of your Imperial and Royal Majesty towards the unfortunate Africans and their descendants, the Haytians; my gratitude and respect for your virtues have inspired me with the desire of addressing this letter to your Imperial and Royal Majesty as a tribute which I feel justly due.

In his letter Christophe recounted the story of the revolution and the moral purpose his throne had endowed him with before linking the struggle for Haitian sovereignty with the battle to save Europe from the ravages of the French army:

> In the bloody contest which your Imperial and Royal Majesty has had to support against the unjust aggression of France, we have not ceased to offer our prayers for the success of your arms, and we cherished the hope that when a general pacification took place in Europe, the people of Hayti would have partaken with the other nations in the blessings of peace, instead of which for sixteen years we have been obliged to be continually on the watch until our independence should be acknowledged by France.[13]

Other points raised by Clarkson in his letters were less favourably received, including his suggestion for a rapprochement with Port-au-Prince. Press reports were circulating that Boyer had approached France for a political settlement, which Clarkson cautioned could end badly for Christophe, should the king maintain an aggressive posture against his rival: 'If France should guarantee his Independence and your Majesty should afterwards see occasion to quarrel with him, he will call in the French to his assistance, and you will then see French armies finding a safe and easy passage through his territories into yours.'[14] He also suggested repeatedly that the size of the Haitian army be reduced. Christophe rejected this out of hand but did concede that one idea of Clarkson's contained merit—that part of the army be reorganised into a militia force, allowing troops to be released for cultivation: 'This measure has an unusual appeal for me. Even before the reception of your letter, I had already sent a certain number of soldiers—older men and the physically unfit— into agriculture.' Christophe could only hope that guarantees against France would allow him to do more.[15]

Christophe had already started to think of agricultural reform, but his initial actions had been very limited. Between April and July 1817 Christophe issued several edicts to reorganise state land. Considerable tracts of fertile plantation land had remained uncultivated, and these 'ci-devant properties of the ci-devant colonials', as Vastey put it, were put up for sale.[16] As part of the process their colonial names were abandoned and new names recorded on the deed of sale. One plantation at Grand Pré was renamed *La Victoire* and the coffee plantations that formed part of the once notorious Gallifet estates became *Belle Avenue*. As Christophe told Clarkson:

> I am trying, insofar as I can, to augment the number of property owners by granting equally to all Haitians, whatever may be their rank or station in life, the right to purchase land, plantations, and houses. I have given special consideration to the heads of families and to the most laborious and deserving tillers of the soil.[17]

In fact, many of the properties were initially gifted directly to the crown. An 1817 civil list listed all the properties now under royal control. The king personally owned ten palaces, including Sans Souci and one for each city in the kingdom, along with the same number of chateaux (mostly old French houses associated with sugar estates) and a further sixteen coffee plantations, six cotton plantations, four horse studs and six cattle farms. The civil list also granted him an annual endowment of one million gourdes for the maintenance of crown properties. The rest of the royal family were equally rewarded. Queen Marie-Louise was granted 120,000 gourdes per year to maintain her thirteen chateaux and four horse studs.[i] Prince Victor-Henry had sixteen chateaux and 200,000 gourdes, while his sisters were given 60,000 gourdes and a similar number of houses and plantations.[18] With a stroke of the pen, the royal family became the biggest private landowner in the country.

For those without recourse to the royal treasury land could be purchased on credit, with the price of the plantation held against future taxes and the revenue sharing of produce mandated by the Code Henry. It appeared to work. In January 1818 the *Gazette Royale d'Hayti* published a list of 4 sugar plantations, 154 coffee plantations and 21 cotton plantations that had successfully been bid on after being offered for sale, inviting their new owners to claim their deeds from the land commission in Sans Souci. Of these properties just thirteen were acquired by existing members of the nobility, of which two were sugar plantations, suggesting that only those close to power had the wherewithal to run such labour-intensive agriculture. A small handful of the properties went to army or civil officers, but the vast majority went to private citizens.[19] It was a result that delighted Christophe, who wrote to Clarkson that while the reforms were aimed at all Haitians irrespective of their rank or station in life, special consideration had been given to 'the heads of families and to the most laborious and deserving tillers of the soil. This measure has already had the most fortunate effects on our agriculture and has fulfilled all my expectations.'[20]

The need to broaden land ownership perhaps spoke to a slowly dawning recognition of the tensions that had lain at the heart of Haiti's agricultural economy since independence. Tenant farmers

---

[i] One of these, the queen's palace of Délices de la Reine on the former Duplaa plantation, less than 5 kilometres east of Cap-Haïtien's airport, is one of the most fascinating historic sites in northern Haiti. The chimney of the French sugar-processing plant still stands, but the flooded basin of its brick watermill is what draws visitors. It is home to Lovana, a Vodou spirit who takes the form of a fish with a silver earring and grants boons to those who see her. Crowds gather at the site, now called Habitation Lovana, for her fête, held annually on 27 September.

remained tied to their plantations by the Code Henry. For some, their labour was ever more tightly governed. As coffee production continued to grow in importance, new strict rules were introduced for its cultivation, even down to the banning of certain types of companion planting of food crops alongside the coffee bushes.[21] Many workers responded by simply absconding. The kingdom was large and sparsely populated in places, and despite the best efforts of the Royal Dahomets and rural magistrates there was plenty of space for people to disappear into the landscape and cultivate their own plots unmolested by the authorities.

'In the latter part of Christophe's reign, their number was said rather to have increased, than diminished', wrote an English travel-ler who was hosted by a maroon after becoming lost on the road. The maroon told his guest that he had fought against the French, but fell silent when asked how many others there were like him in the vicinity: 'They fixed their residence, erecting temporary huts and cultivating the adjacent ground, till the fear of discovery, or the desire of change, induced them to remove to other spots equally remote and secluded.' The maroon was reportedly a generous host, providing the traveller with a breakfast of home-grown plantains and cassava, grooming his horse and accompanying him on the trail back to Cap Henry before retreating to his hidden farm. Despite this the writer could only see the maroon's 'abandonment' of character as a disappointing contrast to the plantation farmers, who 'were not wanting in that degree of subordination which characterizes a well-governed people'.[22] The rejection of state-organised labour in favour of the total independence represented by the subsistence plot was a concept that baffled him.

Prince Saunders came up with his own plan for increasing the num-ber of property-owning farmers. In December 1818 he gave a speech in Philadelphia to the American Convention for Promoting the Abolition of Slavery and Improving the Condition of the African Race, in which he called for African Americans to escape the fear of bondage by emigrating to the free soil of Haiti. 'God in the mysterious opera-tion of His providence has seen fit to permit the most astonishing changes to transpire upon that naturally beautiful and (as to soil and productions) astonishingly luxuriant island', he told his audience. But Saunders was aware that an American audience would not necessarily be sympathetic to the idea of being ruled by a king, and (without revealing his own sympathies) dedicated a significant portion of his speech to his hope that the two halves of Haiti would soon be reconciled with each other: 'If the two rival Governments of Hayti were consolidated into one well-balanced pacific power, there are many hundreds of the free people in New England and Middle States who would be glad to repair there immediately to settle.'[23]

Saunders had not proposed his plan to Christophe, but risked his displeasure by referring even-handedly to both the king and the president. By July the following year Christophe seems to have received a hint of Saunders' tone and warned Clarkson that he had left Haiti under a cloud: 'I feel that I owe you this word of warning in case he should try to take advantage of you, using my name. We dealt with him most generously during his stay with us.'[24] Clarkson had in fact already written to the king to suggest that the Philadelphia abolitionists should join with him to make Haiti 'a safe asylum for such free people of colour as may choose to immigrate there'. The numbers of potential emigrants were so large, he believed, that he even floated a bizarre plan whereby the USA would be persuaded to purchase Santo Domingo and then cede the land to Christophe for the new arrivals to settle on. 'Many of them also would be very valuable to you because they are skilled in different trades; and if only two-thirds of them were to be put upon farms, cultivation would be going on to a considerable extent, while you would not be obliged to disband your present military', he concluded.[25]

Saunders' departure from his position as a teacher in Christophe's employ to pursue his plans for African American emigration showed the difficulties of attracting foreigners to the kingdom's schools. Thomas Gulliver thrived in Cap Henry, but Mr Sweet in Gonaïves lasted little over a year before dying at his desk ('an excellent riddance by all accounts of those that knew him ... he was a most detestable canting hypocrite', remarked one observer) and Saunders' replacement in Port-de-Paix was found drunk at midday by Christophe himself during his royal tour. Despite this, the education programme was judged to be a great success. One Briton travelling in the north some years after Christophe's death and the subsequent closure of his schools remarked on the high levels of education he frequently encountered, including a basic proficiency in English, which he put down to the 'agreeable' institutions of the king.[26]

Other innovations were less successful. In October 1818 William Wilberforce concluded one of his epic letters to Christophe on morality by noting that having discovered that Haitian farmers tilled by hand, he had 'therefore taken the liberty of sending two iron ploughs, which I am assured are of the best construction', in the hope that they would assist in the gathering of the 'rich and glorious harvest from the seed which you are now sowing'.[27] When two 'honest rustics' from Suffolk duly arrived in Cap Henry, Christophe wrote to Clarkson that they had set about cultivating potatoes and wheat. 'Inevitably,' Christophe lamented, 'since they know not a word of French, they have been having some difficulty in instructing the young men who were sent to learn from them. I believe then that we shall bring in only these two, until we begin to see the results of the experiment.'[28] One of the trial plots yielded a respectable crop but the other (perhaps on land exhausted by years of sugar cultivation) was less fertile. Furthermore, the second plot was far from the city, and its farmer, who had optimistically brought his family with him, was left widowed and childless after they were struck down with fever. He spent the rest of his time in Haiti suffering from 'constant trouble and vexation'. Christophe did eventually agree to expand the use of the plough, but he had perhaps been too polite to tell Wilberforce that Haitians were already aware of its potential benefits: when he ennobled the Comte de Trou and made him Inspector General of Agriculture in 1811, Christophe granted him the motto 'Culture of Plenty', with a coat of arms showing a plough supported by two oxen.[29]

Another anticlimax was the attempt by English missionaries to proselytise in Haiti, despite the warm welcome promised by Christophe. Two Methodist missionaries, William Harvey and Elliot Jones, arrived in Cap Henry in February 1820 bearing letters of introduction from Wilberforce and Clarkson. They were initially well received and believed that they had found fertile ground for the Gospel. 'There was not so much as the semblance of religion to be seen, except that mass was performed once on the Sabbath day, at which the King and court attended ... the troops were taught one religious rite,' wrote Harvey, 'Every morning at break of day, and again at sunset, they sung a hymn to the Virgin Mary.'[30] Jones was soon taken ill and left for America, but Christophe assured Clarkson that he had ordered 'that [Harvey] be accorded all necessary facilities and protection for the accomplishment of his mission'.[31] This was a lie. Harvey successfully held one prayer meeting but was perplexed when no one arrived for the follow-up, and even more so when the Baron de Dupuy refused to see him or answer his letters when he sought a proper place for a chapel. He privately hired a room and successfully held prayer meetings for three Sundays in a row until his congregation vanished: 'The boys soon required, by an order from the king, not to attend our chapel, but to attend Mass at the church, and there is great reason to believe the Archbishop threatened to punish the few that attended if they continued to do so.'[32] Over the following months Harvey grew increasingly despondent and asked for permission to sail back to England. After he returned he wrote a well-observed description of life in the kingdom from his time there (it was Harvey who had spent the night in the maroon's hut while travelling from Cap Henry). He attempted to be even-handed about what he had experienced, praising the education system in particular, but he blamed the Haitians' 'vague and incorrect notions of Christianity' on their love of Vodou (which he called Obeah, as it was known in Jamaica) and their African traditions, that allowed for the apparently lax morals that offended his prudish Methodist soul.[ii]

The cleric who had thwarted Harvey's preaching was the kingdom's new archbishop, Jean de Dieu Gonzales, a Spaniard from Cuba who had become Christophe's personal chaplain and was later ennobled as the Duc de Gonzales. The Breton archbishop Corneille Brelle had fallen from grace with the king he had crowned only seven years earlier. The rift appeared to have started in late 1816, when Christophe wrote a strident complaint to Brelle accusing him of embezzlement. Since the earliest days of independence, European

---

[ii] It may have helped Harvey to reflect that he was at least allowed to leave the kingdom on his own terms. John Brown and James Catts, the Methodist missionaries sent to Port-au-Prince, were not so lucky. They initially made a small number of conversions, but when one of their congregation, who was mentally ill, murdered his mother, their meeting house was attacked and the missionaries left unable to move around the city without a military escort. In response, Boyer drolly suggested that they withdraw from the island for their safety and that their school be taken over by the government.

visitors had noted that Brelle was an eager attendee of banquets and quick with a song, but now it was said that he rarely carried out clerical visits, and when he did it was 'ostensibly for the purpose of baptizing children, and marrying; but in reality, for the collection of his fees'. Fees levied on the masses might have been one thing, but when he demanded 500 gourdes from the family of the recently dead Comte de Trou for his funeral (whose coat of arms had so proudly displayed its plough), Christophe was outraged: 'If the cost of a funeral does not come down, especially for the funeral of dignitaries, it would be better for the family ... that the deceased dignitaries be interred without the benefits of a church service because those services, which they can well do without, will reduce them to beggars,' the king complained, 'It's enough to make one a Huguenot, or even an atheist.'[33] When rumours spread that Brelle was sympathetic to Louis XVIII's approach towards Haiti, he was stripped of his ecclesiastical title and placed under house arrest in Cap Henry for preaching subversive doctrines. He was subsequently kept under a regime of ever dwindling rations until he died from scurvy in July 1819.[34]

Even Christophe's supporters sometimes had cause to comment on his punishment of notables like Brelle, not least on the sometimes apparently arbitrary nature with which he could mete them out. Several observers noted that even a figure as powerful as the governor of Cap Henry, Jean-Pierre Richard, was not immune to censure. For offending the king by correctly performing a duty, but varying in several places from Christophe's instructions without authorisation, he was imprisoned in the Citadelle for several months. Here he was compelled to 'associate with the workmen, and even to assist in their labour' before being restored to his rank and office. The punishment was so extraordinary that it was still retold as a folk tale in the region more than a century later by peasant farmers, who, keenly aware of Christophe's reputation as a hard taskmaster, rewrote the 'crime' as being one of excessive laziness.[35]

Other old acquaintances met an even harsher fate. In 1802 the merchant Vilton, godfather to Christophe's daughters, had tried to persuade him to surrender to General Leclerc. He had remained in Haiti after independence, maintaining sufficient rank to have been a signatory to the pledge of allegiance given to Christophe after the

Lavaysse affair in 1814. But after being accused of having an affair with a Countess X and put under official surveillance after gifting her 'brandy, almonds and prunes', he was put to death.[iii] What happened to the adulterous countess was not recorded, but a visiting Royal Navy officer in 1819 noted that for the same 'breach of chastity' the Comtesse de Rosiers, the white wife of the royal playwright, Juste Chanlatte, 'was obliged to ride through the streets of Sans Souci in a state of perfect nudity, at noon-day, on the back of a donkey, with her face toward the tail'.[36]

Despite the often capricious nature of these punishments, nobles could soon find themselves back in the king's good books once their sentence had been served. In August 1819 Richard was rewarded for his service to the kingdom by having his title of Duc de Marmelade made hereditary—a privilege that he appears to have previously been excluded from, despite the original 1811 edict that such titles could be inherited. In an extravagant display of royal largesse, sixty-five new counts, barons and chevaliers were created that month, with two counts raised to dukedoms and the Ducs de Fort Royal and l'Artibonite elevated to the rank of princes of the realm, to fill the spaces left by the deaths of Christophe's brother-in-law and nephew.[37] The new nobles were mostly serving army officers. It was the biggest shake-up of the ruling order since the formation of the monarchy and was promoted by another royal tour of the kingdom. This time, however, Christophe remained at Sans Souci and sent the Prince Royal in his stead.

In March 1819 Victor-Henry had turned fifteen and was now of legal age to inherit the throne, and the tour appeared designed to cement him as heir in the minds of the people. The itinerary included two weeks in the Artibonite Valley, the region closest to the disputed border with the republic, and Victor-Henry personally handed out many of the decorations to the newest members of the nobility and took their oaths of loyalty. 'Behold the well-beloved son of our good father, behold the dearest hope of Hayti,' wrote the editor of the *Gazette Royale d'Hayti* in his description of the tour, 'He is already of an age to second [the king] and to partake of his fatigues

---

[iii] Writing in 1824, Hérard Dumesle gossiped that Vilton's crime had been to confess that he had fallen in love with Queen Marie-Louise.

and labours.' As if to pave the way for his future ascension to the throne, Victor-Henry visited the fort at Crête-à-Pierrot to honour the bloody siege endured by Dessalines, fought two years before he had been born, and paid the debts that were owed by several prisoners being held there so that they might be freed.[38] In the nearby town of Petite Rivière he may also have overseen the choosing of a new site for a royal palace in his honour called Belle-Rivière, known locally today as the 'Palais de 365 Portes' for its large number of doors and floor-to-ceiling windows.[39]

The expansion of the nobility went hand in hand with an equally significant extension of the land reform programme. Despite having opened the sale of land to the wider public, Christophe announced himself 'grieved to find that a great many soldiers, because of lack of means, have not yet been able to share in the benefits arising from the sale of public land'. Wishing to aid these champions, 'to whom the nation owes a debt of gratitude, and to help them to find at the end of their days, amidst their infirmities, an honoured security which they may pass on to their descendants', a royal edict announced a series of grants giving land directly to all soldiers who did not own any. The size of the land grants was dependent on rank: privates were given 1 carreaux apiece (approximately 1.3 hectares), with corporals receiving double this, all the way to lieutenants and captains being given 8 and 10 carreaux each. Colonels of each regiment were rewarded with 20 carreaux. Of 1,853 recorded land grants issued by the crown that year, the overwhelming majority were single carreaux plots given to enlisted men.[40] In a letter describing the reforms, Christophe gave all the credit to Clarkson, insisting that 'I did not depart from the plan which you proposed to me', and that land reform and a reduction in the size of his standing army would now proceed hand in hand:

> I shall begin little by little to familiarize the troops with the transition from the soldier's life to that of the farmer by giving them leave, a group at a time, to go and cultivate their land for brief periods; then, when I can do so with complete security, I shall go even further and carry out in its entirety your plan of maintaining only a militia.[41]

Even a small 1-carreaux plot could be enormously productive under the mixed cropping agriculture practised in Haiti, and it would not have escaped Christophe's detail-oriented mind that the grants made to enlisted men were of a similar size to the hidden farms cultivated by the kingdom's maroons. In the same way that the granting of new noble titles tied more army officers to the crown, the land reform project may have been designed in part to buy the loyalty of individual soldiers and reduce the chances of desertion. In a letter to an unnamed English correspondent in September 1819, Prévost said that grants had been given to 8,000 soldiers. Crucially, all of them were in the immediate environs of the Citadelle. In a further suggestion that Christophe's attentions were focused inward, he also announced that the king was no longer supporting the continuing insurrection in Grand Anse, pointedly referring to the rebel leader there as Goman instead of using his title of Comte de Jérémie.[42]

Prévost wrote that although Goman's men were 'badly armed and without ammunition for nine months past', their continued resistance against the government in Port-au-Prince was a sign of the republic's enduring weakness. He did not know that Boyer had launched a major new campaign in the region that had succeeded in capturing Goman's stronghold and taking his wife prisoner. In February 1820 Boyer triumphantly announced the complete pacification of the Grand Anse. The insurgents had been misled 'by the treacherous agents of Christophe', crowed *L'Abeille* newspaper, but twelve years since Goman had taken up arms against Pétion, the republic was finally a single unified state.[43] Christophe may have indicated to Clarkson that he wished one day to shrink the size of his army, but with an increasingly confident Boyer on his southern border it appeared that strengthening the loyalty of his soldiers to the crown would have to take precedence.

17

THE FATAL STROKE

January 1820 began with the royal performance of a new play called *The King's Hunting Party* by Juste Chanlatte. The play opened in a forest glade, where young women and soldiers of the Royal Dahomets danced around a pyramid dedicated to Haitian independence, singing the praises of 'Papa Henry'. A village teacher, probably played by Chanlatte himself, then narrated the story of the love between a knight and a shepherd's daughter, who are united through their fidelity to their king. Their perfect love match and the peasant girl's acceptance at court demonstrated in flowery terms the reciprocal obligations and benefits holding together the Haitian monarchy's semi-feudal system.[1]

Christophe may have felt that he had earned such flattery. In his Independence Day speech that year, he praised the recent reforms that granted land to the 'brave men' who defended the nation and announced that the opening of six new schools in the provinces would soon be followed by the establishment of colleges and universities. The continuing limbo over Haiti's status on the international stage was being addressed, thanks to its influential friends in England and beyond. 'Such liaisons, communications and mutual and uninterrupted correspondences,' he declared, were 'equivalent to the formal recognition of our independence.' His speech also made particular reference to his 'beloved son' Victor-Henry having entered his legal majority, and to the reception he had received on his tour of the Artibonite: 'The testimonies of love and affection which he received from our fellow citizens are the most precious reward which can touch the heart of a father and sovereign.'[2]

A portrait made of the king around this time paints a more complicated picture than this sunny optimism. In the painting Christophe's
face appears rounder and heavier. His eyes are hooded and heavily
bagged and there is more than a hint of white in his grey hair. The
simple green coat of the 1816 Evans portrait has been replaced by a
scarlet uniform with a profusion of gold embroidery and braided
epaulettes. On his head is a similarly decorated bicorne, topped with
red and black ostrich plumes. The painting was a near-identical copy
of a portrait of George III by Sir William Beechey, but the addition of
the extra costume swagger suggests a need to overcompensate on the
sitter's part. Christophe looks tired and possibly ill.[i]

The portrait was almost certainly by Johann Gottfried and
Wilhelm Eiffe, brothers from Hamburg who were hired to paint the
royal family and the rooms at Sans Souci.[3] Since 1815 there had
been a small but growing commercial intercourse between the kingdom and Germany. Just as the English press had trumpeted the
luxury goods bought for Christophe in London, so there were
reports of 'rich damask tablecloths' and 'services for the table, bril-
liants, pearls, &c, which have been paid for in ready money' for the
royal household ordered from Bremen, Bielefeld and other
Hanseatic cities.[4] In 1815 Hamburg newspapers had even reported
the arrival of a Haitian envoy named General Lapaix to explore
commercial opportunities and possibly even open a diplomatic
office. The *Gazette Royale d'Hayti* refuted the story, saying that he
was merely a private citizen travelling back to Haiti with his wife,
reminding its readers that the king would never send an official
mission without the precondition of Haitian independence.[5]
Nevertheless, when Lapaix arrived in Cap Henry he was accompanied by a gardener for Sans Souci and several musicians, and it was
reported that he sought further Germans to work for Christophe,
including a wood turner, a wool spinner, a dance tutor and those
with military experience.

One soldier who travelled there was Lieutenant Grünthal, a
Hessian Jew who served as Christophe's drillmaster for four years.

---

[i] This painting first surfaced in 2014 when it was sold at auction in Berlin from a private Austrian
collection. Tragically it was lost in transit in 2020 by an American shipping company, and its
whereabouts are currently unknown.

A young Hanoverian vet named Otto Philipp Braun found himself overseeing the construction of new stables at Sans Souci on a salary of 1,200 Spanish dollars a year, rounding up wild horses for the king's stud and dealing with the incessant attentions of Prince Victor-Henry, whom he described as 'a horse lover extraordinaire'.[6] Other Germans met unhappier fates. Braun wrote home about the 'poor fate' of the architect and family friend Ludwig Neuber, who was employed as a military engineer. He was accused of attempting to steal military plans and imprisoned on starvation rations before being executed. Even Johann Gottfried Eiffe reportedly died from 'very severe treatment' at Haitian hands.[7]

The Haitian court also attempted to forge links with influential Germans. Baron de Vastey exchanged letters with the Prussian academic Friedrich Wilhelm Gubitz, discussing social reform and education. Gubitz was also a talented artist and had been given a copy of the Code Henry by the Prussian consul in Bremen, along with a Haitian proposal that he might provide illustrations to accompany a translated copy.[8] Julien Prévost cultivated the journalist Johann Baptist Pfeilschifter, seeking common ground by invoking the spectre of French aggression: 'The Germans have been, like us, the victims of oppression; they have been raised, like us, to the rank of their former dignity. These conditions are too similar for them not to inspire mutual respect between the two peoples.' He even wrote to a Viennese art collector, offering to buy for Christophe the art collections of Emperors Maximillian II and Rudolf II of Habsburg from Prague.[9]

For all this, close relations with Britain remained the kingdom's key goal. At the turn of 1820 a significant step forward appeared to have been taken when Admiral Sir Home Riggs Popham, the commander of the Jamaica Station, visited Cap Henry. Home Popham was just five years older than Christophe, and his appointment as commander of the Caribbean fleet was the last in a long career in which he had won acclaim for devising the navy's signal code, used by Nelson at the Battle of Trafalgar, and then ignominy after leading a disastrous unauthorised attack on Buenos Aires in 1806. In 1818 he had sent a ship to Port-au-Prince to monitor events following Pétion's death, and perhaps influenced by the views of English merchants there wrote soon after to Viscount Melville, the First Lord of the Admiralty, that he believed Christophe to be 'an arbitrary savage, aiming at absolute Monarchy, cruel in the extreme, [and] universally hated'.[10] Nevertheless, in May 1819 Melville directed Home Popham to make a fact-finding mission to the kingdom and to call on Christophe directly.

The delegation was received by a guard of honour and taken by carriage to a house allocated for their stay that was 'uncommonly clean, well furnished, and provided with a library and plenty of servants', according to an account written by an anonymous lieutenant who accompanied the admiral.[11] After Cap Henry's English merchants had paid their respects, Jean-Pierre Richard hosted a reception for the party where, in the words of the *Gazette Royale d'Hayti*, 'the most free and the greatest cordiality reigned between the English and Haytian officers', with patriotic toasts raised to both Christophe and George III and to 'a perpetual union' between the two countries, after a banquet so splendid that 'the greatest gourmand would have smiled at the succession of courses and the good things that constituted them'.[12] The following day the visitors toured the schools, hospital and several sites relating to the 'desperate battles' against the French during the revolution. 'The Haytians feel an honest pride pointing out these places, rendered sacred by their heroic achievements', noted the lieutenant.

Christophe arrived at the palace in Cap Henry on the third day accompanied by Victor-Henry. Everything about the meeting was designed to impress. 'The entrance to the palace is both handsome and convenient', wrote the lieutenant:

> In the hall are the prints of distinguished British statesmen, soldiers, and sailors, together with several military and naval victories.[ii] We were conducted, through two lines of officers, to a large and splendidly furnished room, rendered delightfully cool by artificial means ... The more one sees of this interesting country, the more one admires the man, whose strong mind, indefatigable conduct, and great natural abilities, have brought his subjects

---

[ii] When the officer visited the Haitian archbishop the following day, he expressed his pleasure at finding a series of prints depicting the life of Cardinal Wolsey decorating his walls, and a collection of Wilberforce's sermons in his library.

(previously sunk in the most degrading slavery and ignorance) to so high a state of order, and even refinement.[13]

Christophe was judged even more impressive in person: 'His hair is perfectly grey, his countenance very intelligent, and his whole person well proportioned; his manners are particularly pleasing, without the slightest appearance of affectation or arrogance.' In contrast, Victor-Henry was 'one of the fattest fellows I ever saw' who looked ten years older than his age of fifteen, but who was nevertheless a 'good-natured boisterous lad' who wore his court dress handsomely, down to the large plume of ostrich feathers in his hat. The king thanked Home Popham for a visit he had long wished for and paid him the compliment of saying that his signal code had been adopted by the Haitian navy. The meeting lasted for four hours and concluded with Christophe in high spirits, 'speaking in a witty refrain, and [laughing] heartily at the malevolence of the French, who make a ridiculous practice of inventing the most ridiculous stories about him'. As their king retired to Sans Souci, the Haitian side reported with great pleasure that the admiral had been 'very well pleased with the particular attention he received from His Majesty'.[14]

The Haitian charm offensive worked wonders on Home Popham. He sent a long report to Melville on what he had been able to learn about the size of the Haitian army and labour force, the state of agriculture and the freedoms allowed to its people: important intelligence gathering for an imperial power that had abolished the slave trade but had yet to commit to abandoning slavery itself. In his covering letter, Home Popham fell short of recommending recognition of Haiti, but became the first British official to refer to Christophe as 'king'. He also noted the 'lively' commerce being carried on between Haiti and the Danish colony of Saint Thomas, suggesting a commercial agreement between Britain and Haiti so that British vessels could undercut this trade. Thomas Clarkson would have been surprised to learn that the admiral had even discussed his peculiar proposal for African American emigration to Santo Domingo—an idea that Baron de Dupuy immediately dropped for fear of causing offence. 'You may rely upon it Admiral,' he was quoted as telling Home Popham, 'that the king will never enter into any arrangement with America or Spain that is likely to militate against the interests of England.' Christophe went even further, committing himself to a declaration that fugitives from Jamaica escaping enslavement would no longer be given asylum in the kingdom. Believing that he had struck up a rapport with a man he had months earlier decried as a savage, Home Popham concluded that 'if there is anything of reason which you wish to be accomplished at Hayti, I can at this moment get it done'.[15]

Christophe wrote glowingly to Clarkson of the 'personal audience' that he had given Home Popham, 'in a manner befitting his rank', and correctly surmised that a full report of the visit would make its way back to the British government. The letter mentioned another visit two months after Home Popham's, when HMS *Tartar* called at Cap Henry. Its commander was George Collier, who led the Royal Navy's West Africa Squadron, charged with enforcing the British ban on the slave trade. Christophe was particularly fascinated by the fate of the enslaved Africans on the ships indicted by Collier's fleet. They were disembarked in Freetown, where Christophe clearly saw parallels with the state he had built from the ashes of Saint-Domingue, noting that 'He gave us very gratifying information concerning the progress toward civilization which our African brothers in Sierra Leone are making, to my own great satisfaction. Through him we learned then that our friends are forging ahead, and we continue to hope that all their efforts will be crowned with success.'[16]

Christophe decided that the time was finally right to make his own approach to France, rather than wait for whatever the government there might try to agree with Boyer. At the end of 1819 he wrote to Clarkson to ask him to make overtures to Paris in the hope of opening negotiations for a potential peace treaty, and instructed Prévost to accredit him with full diplomatic credentials affixed with his royal seal. Clarkson was given carte blanche to proceed as he saw fit. 'There is no need for us to indicate to a friend as informed and wise as yourself the essentials upon which we must insist in the projected treaty. You know as well as we do the points on which we can never yield, because you are fully aware of the best interests of Haiti,' wrote the king, before underlining the terms in case Clarkson was unsure, 'Haiti be recognised as a free sovereign and independent nation; that her commerce be free; and that the demands of the ex-colonists be abandoned.'[17]

Clarkson's instructions from Prévost contained rather more detail. Haiti offered France the status of most favoured trading nation and its neutrality in the event of any future war in Europe. To counter questions that Christophe's rule only extended across the north, this 'momentary division' of the country was judged as merely 'a family matter of no concern to a foreign government'. The 1804 Act of Independence declared the nation to be indivisible, and this was enough to give Christophe the right to sign a treaty in the name of all Haitians.[18] To help with any expenses that Clarkson might incur, the London firm of Reid, Irving and Company was instructed to forward him the sum of £6,000 and to charter a ship to sail every three months to Cap Henry to carry his dispatches.[19]

In March 1820, before Christophe could learn of Clarkson's progress, he received a second visit from Home Popham. This time, Prince Victor-Henry was given a more prominent ceremonial role and conducted a parade of nine regiments of foot and dismounted cavalry for the British, who judged their drills to be precise and 'the whole thing admirably done'.[20] After a royal reception Christophe hosted a breakfast where the guests were served on 'the most superb English china', with light wines, claret and preserved fruits. One anonymous navy officer noted his surprise that though the service appeared in all manners French, the food was 'more substantial though at the same time more mysterious [than the] products of Parisian cookery'.[iii] The following day, the British were taken inland by carriage so that the king could show off his palace at Sans Souci. 'We wandered with black maids of honour over lawns smiling with the richest and softest beauty', wrote the officer in a memoir published thirty years later:

> We were served by footmen in the royal livery of blue and black, with thin shoes and silk stockings ... I still remember the grizzled head of Christophe as he rose to speak; and, being over-come with some thought, passed his hand before his forehead, and sat down while the breeze was sighing audibly in the thick foliage outside an adjoining open window.[21]

[iii] Recent analysis at Sans Souci of animal bones found alongside locally produced cooking vessels suggests that the palace diet was rich in Afro-Caribbean stews featuring cow, pig, goat, chicken, fish and conch—not unlike much Haitian cuisine today.

The *Gazette Royale d'Hayti* again pronounced it a successful visit, but struck a mournful tone that the recent death of George III had made inappropriate the grand balls and other amusements which would otherwise have been held for the visitors: 'The circumstance necessarily deprived us of an opportunity of manifesting more striking proofs of the pleasure which we felt at the presence of the officers of a nation which has given many instances of its good will towards the Haitians.'[22]

After departing Cap Henry Home Popham sailed directly to Port-au-Prince to offer his services as a peace broker between the north and south. It was his first meeting with Boyer, with whom he had recently been in dispute over the case of the *Flying Fish*, a Jamaican vessel whose enslaved sailors had fled to Port-au-Prince and whose extradition the Haitian authorities refused. Perhaps because of this, Home Popham found himself disinclined to enjoy good relations with the president, despite the lavish reception he received. He presented himself as a guarantor of Christophe's sincere and peaceful intentions, but had been so won over by the hospitality shown to him on his two visits that he went as far as referring to him in his letter as 'the king'. This was a victory for Christophe, but it hardly presented Home Popham as a neutral observer, a point that was underlined when he warned Boyer against taking any aggressive action towards the kingdom.

Boyer's reply was unsurprisingly bullish. It was three months since he had declared his final victory over Goman, and he confidently predicted that Christophe would be the next to fall: 'In less than a year his reign of terror will be ended and the Haitians of the Artibonite and the North will be once more united with their brothers in the West and South. Christophe is reduced to complete impotence.' Boyer even suggested that the royal army was not so impressive as it had appeared on the parade ground to the British: 'When he came as far as Saint-Marc last year he did not dare to cross our frontier—his troops would have deserted him and joined ranks with ours.'[23] After Home Popham sailed from Port-au-Prince, the local press suggested that he was actually in league with Christophe, and that he had signed a treaty to bring 40,000 Africans captured from slave ships by the Royal Navy to the kingdom to serve in his army, with up to $45 paid for every person landed in the north.[24]

Amid all this came Clarkson's reply to Christophe's proposals to approach France. After consulting with Wilberforce and James Stephen (a fellow abolitionist, who had written a biography of Toussaint Louverture), he concluded that now was not the time for an official approach to Paris. It was his official appointment that proved the stumbling block: were the French cabinet to receive him as an ambassador, they would be acknowledging Haitian independence before negotiations even began. Christophe's proposals might even be seen as a sign of Haitian weakness given his uncompromising response to the Lavaysse and Fontanges missions in 1814 and 1816:

> This sudden change from austere inflexibility to a voluntary yielding on your part, so as even to send an Envoy to that very Court whose messengers you have twice refused to receive, would make you be considered by the French Government as an humble supplicant for peace, a situation of which they would directly take advantage, either by means of some well-concerted plan of intrigue, or by an open invasion or blockade of your Dominions.[iv]

Clarkson caused Christophe even more dismay by telling him that the French government would demand more than just free trade in return for recognition. However unjust the ex-colonists' claims, the king should be prepared to be flexible on the subject of an indemnity: 'Unless you can offer something more to France ... all hope of a treaty is at an end.' Christophe would be better served by consolidating his rule and pursuing unofficial contacts. With these objections stated, Clarkson drew £300 from his Haitian funds and set out for Paris to gather information as a private individual, while carrying his diplomatic papers with him 'in case of an unexpected turn'.[25]

One of Clarkson's contacts in Paris was the abolitionist Baron de Turkheim, a well-connected French deputy from Alsace. Through

---

[iv] Fontanges wasn't the only envoy rejected for failing to address Christophe by his royal title. In 1817 and 1818 the US government sent two commercial agents to do business at 'Cape François, in the island of St Domingo'. Both refused to recognise Christophe as king and were subsequently ordered to take their leave of the island. This only confirmed the conclusion of one American merchant that Christophe 'treats Englishmen with respect, but the Americans with every mark of scorn'. *Morning Post*, 27 June 1814.

him Clarkson made discreet enquiries about the disposition of the French cabinet regarding Haiti. The report he sent back to Christophe at the end of July was a mixed bag. On the likelihood of the French launching another military adventure against Haiti, the chances were nil, he wrote to the king, adding that their final defeat in Saint-Domingue had been so spectacular that it had coined a new proverb among the army: to be as hopeless and disastrous as the Leclerc Expedition. The only caveat was related to a possible conflict between the two rival Haitian powers. While Home Popham had proved more than sympathetic towards Christophe, France viewed him as an expansionist warmonger. In the event of hostilities between the two powers, Clarkson advised that France might seek to gain advantage by sending troops to aid Boyer and overthrow the northern regime.

On the chances of French recognition of Haiti, Clarkson was explicit:

> [The Minister of the Marine and Colonies] has no objection to make a treaty with your Majesty and General Boyer on very favourable terms, provided you would acknowledge the King of France as your nominal sovereign; nor would he refuse, I believe, even to acknowledge the Independence of Hayti, but then he would make you pay very dearly for it.

Louis XVIII would only make a treaty with General Christophe, and even then, recognition would be dependent on the payment of an indemnity and an exclusive trading deal lasting up to fifty years. Clarkson apologised for bearing such news, recognising that 'the conditions are too degrading and too burdensome to be submitted to', and that even were Christophe prepared to make a 'pecuniary sacrifice' he would be better to wait until the political winds in France had changed so as to find better terms. 'Would you prefer making no treaty at all and abide by the consequences?' he asked.

Clarkson recommended a number of steps that Christophe could take to bolster his position. Firstly, the Kingdom of Haiti should continue its programme of land and army reform, and do everything it could to increase its population by encouraging African American emigration. Everything should be done to avoid conflict with Boyer or give the appearance of interfering with the affairs of neighbouring slave islands, for fear of attracting unwanted foreign attention. In France itself, Clarkson suggested a continuation of visits like the one he had just taken, so that Christophe's friends could cultivate relationships with liberal French politicians. Such efforts should go hand in hand with the production of new works by Baron de Vastey that could be sent to 'the most illustrious potentates of Europe' and printed in the widely read *Revue Encyclopédique*, to spread the word about the king's 'wise, liberal, just and virtuous government'.[26] It was a policy that might take years to bear fruit, but Clarkson was convinced it was the only way forward. Regrettably, Christophe's response to the advice was never recorded.

On 15 August 1820 two very different cataclysms struck north and south Haiti. An enormous fire swept through Port-au-Prince, destroying more than 250 buildings before it was put under control. The blaze was blamed on provocateurs sent by Christophe in revenge for the conquest of Grand Anse.[27] A few days later stories began to circulate that Christophe had been struck down by illness and paralysed. Few believed it, but for once the rumours were true. As Port-au-Prince burned, Christophe and the royal court were travelling to the palace of Bellevue-le-Roi in Limonade to celebrate Queen Marie-Louise's fête. At a Mass held in the town church, Christophe's eyes suddenly turned glassy and he slumped into his seat with his hands twitching so violently that he struck the queen's lapdog with his cane. As those around him became aware of his condition, Christophe reportedly cried out the name of the former Archbishop Brelle, asking if others could see the ghostly figure that had appeared before him. Before anyone could answer he lost consciousness and collapsed onto the floor. As the murmuring in the congregation turned to cries for help, the royal children formed a protective cordon around their father and waited anxiously for the arrival of the king's doctor Duncan Stewart.[28]

A second doctor in Christophe's service, the Englishman Jabez Sheen Birt, left one of the few first-person accounts of all that followed:

> [Doctor Stewart] had the King removed into the open air, and put into his carriage, where he bled him largely, which restored him somewhat. He was then taken to the chateau of Bellevue, where

it was necessary to bleed him largely again, when his perception returned. Being sent for from the Cape, I arrived at Bellevue about 9 o'clock at night; the antechamber was full of officers, but all was quiet round about. The King could not raise his head from the pillow, and all the physicians of his household were called about his person.

Christophe remained at the palace for ten days before he was judged well enough to be returned to Sans Souci. His life was out of immediate danger, but his stroke had left him partially paralysed on his right side. According to some reports his speech was also impaired. Vastey remained constantly at his side as he received the most senior members of the court. Worried that the king's illness would give Boyer the perfect excuse to launch a surprise attack, the Prince of Limbe, Paul Romain, ordered commanders on the southern border to quietly strengthen their defences. Amid all this, Birt recorded that the country remained 'most orderly and quiet'.[29]

Under the care of Stewart and Birt, Christophe's health steadily improved over the following weeks. He regained enough ability in his right leg to walk around his apartment and was able to sit comfortably in a chair talking to his inner circle. At the beginning of October the English tutor William Wilson wrote to his father: 'The King, I regret to say, has for more than two months been indisposed; but he is now convalescent and attends as before to the affairs of his government, in which he is assisted by the Prince, my pupil.'[30] According to Stewart, writing some months later, Christophe spent much of his convalescence in self-reflection, as if the sudden weakness of his body made him question the way he ruled:

> I used often to converse with him for hours. He seemed sensible that be had used his people harshly and that he ought to have been more liberal to his soldiers, but he had a very correct knowledge of the character of the people he governed and how necessary occasional severities were.

Stewart had loyally sung his master's praises only a year earlier. Since then, Christophe's faults had been exposed more clearly and Stewart described how he had become licentious and prostituted the wives of the nobility. Many of his policies showed 'much good sense and liberality', but they were 'sadly stained by acts of oppressive cruelty and dreadful injustice towards his people'.[31] Any regrets brought on by illness did not soften Christophe completely however. On 22 September he ordered Baron Joseph de la Tortue, vice-president of the court of auditors, to be sentenced to hard labour at the Citadelle to work off a debt he owed to the government.[32]

For foreigners in the kingdom, Christophe's illness put life on hold. Wilson found himself at a loose end while Victory-Henry had no time for lessons due to helping his father. Prince Saunders, only recently returned to Cap Henry, worked on his proposals to bring African Americans to Haiti and waited for his chance to present them at court. While the Austrian biologist Karl Ritter waited for an audience, he obtained permission to travel to Fort Royal to collect specimens and returned with several live crocodiles that he presented to Jean-Pierre Richard, the governor of Cap Henry, who displayed them in his garden.[33] They appeared completely unaware of the currents of disquiet that were washing through the country as Haitians discussed the news of the king's illness and his chances of making a complete recovery.

Christophe's stroke helped spark a series of events in Saint-Marc that would soon have a catastrophic effect. It was the northern city closest to the border with the republic and was the place that Boyer had pointed to when he taunted Home Popham over the uncertain loyalties of some royal regiments. In 1812 a sizeable number of troops from Saint-Marc had defected in the closing days of Christophe's failed siege of Port-au-Prince. In September 1820 the same 8th Regiment was again disquieted. They had only just completed a period of heavy labour on the kingdom's public works and were dismayed to be so quickly sent back into the field when the order came to reinforce the defences along the frontier. When directed to reprimand his soldiers for their attitude, a junior officer named Paulin refused, choosing to defend his men instead. A fellow officer, Jean-Claude, quietly complained up the ranks about this disloyalty, and they were both sent to Sans Souci to answer the charge in front of the king. At the subsequent tribunal, Paulin was sent to the Citadelle, where he defiantly stated that he would rather have been shot than be mistreated.[34]

When Jean-Claude returned to his post he was followed closely by Romain, who brought with him several companies of the Prince

Royal's 4th Regiment and the 14th Regiment from Gonaïves, which he placed on manoeuvres a short march away in Petite Rivière. The troops in Saint-Marc were dismayed when they learned how their defender Paulin has been treated, and the decision was made to mutiny. On the evening of the first day of October, seven weeks after Christophe's stroke, the plan was put into action by Constant Paul, a lieutenant-colonel who nursed secret republican sympathies. Constant Paul persuaded the artillery quartermaster to quietly hand over the keys to the town arsenal. Ammunition was quickly distributed, and when Jean-Claude learned what was happening he was shot and then beheaded to cries of 'Long live the Republic!' An officer named Thoby tore the uniform from Jean-Claude's back and promoted himself to general on the spot. By morning the entire garrison had declared itself in opposition to Christophe. Seven of the mutinous officers were sent on a rapid march south to Port-au-Prince, carrying Jean-Claude's head in a sack as proof of their actions.[35]

Romain ordered his forces to surround Saint-Marc and rushed word to Christophe. The king assumed that the mutiny was the signal that Boyer was waiting for to declare war and ordered the northern army to ready itself for action. His most loyal troops, quartered in Fort Royal, Grand Rivière and Limbe, immediately headed south. From this point on, events unravelled at great speed.

Conspiracies are hard to prove, but at some point during Christophe's convalescence Richard took time off from admiring his new pet crocodiles and began to make discrete enquiries of other nobles who might be sympathetic to regime change. He approached those he knew had little love left for the king, possibly those like him who had already endured a spell in the Citadelle's labour camps. None of them were republicans, but they worried that Christophe's illness might end up favouring Boyer, to the detriment of their own situation. Knowing that power ultimately came from the end of a bayonet, Richard relaxed the harsh discipline he normally maintained over the regiments that he commanded in Cap Henry and further bought their loyalty by allowing them to frequent the city's brothels. When Richard was subsequently presented with an order signed by the Prince Royal to send his own troops to Saint-Marc, he refused to march.[36]

When the royal heralds had created Richard's coat of arms as the Duc de Marmelade, they awarded him a pair of hyenas—animals

notorious for bringing down already wounded prey. Perhaps pro-
phetically, each wore a crown. As rumours flooded into Cap Henry
about the uprising in Saint-Marc, Richard seized his moment to grab
power before any possible republican wave had the chance to roll
north. On 6 October he rallied his troops. 'I heard a great uproar
in the Place d'Armes and adjoining streets such as I had not heard
before in that most orderly and quiet city. I could distinguish cries
of *A bas le tyran*, down with the tyrant etc', wrote Wilson. He was
prevented from investigating by his housekeeper, who ordered that
Wilson surrender his money and valuables to her for safe-keeping
and say nothing if soldiers came to question him.[37] The main square
was now abuzz, thronging with soldiers at arms, cavalry horses
stamping their feet and infantry drums beating out orders. Above
the noise, Richard could just be heard haranguing the troops: 'We
have broken the chains of slavery!' he shouted, 'I ask you to follow
our example and help us defend the sacred rights of the people!'[38]

The scene was much clearer the next day—and for Christophe,
even more alarming. Richard had been joined by Placide Lebrun
(the Comte de Gros-Morne) who commanded the royal artillery
regiment, Charles Pierre (the Duc de Terrier-Rouge) and the
Minister of Justice, General Monpoint (Baron Monpoint), who was
also one of Christophe's equerries. At Richard's right hand was the
Chevalier Nord Alexis of the Royal Dragoons, who was married to
an illegitimate daughter of Christophe's named Blésine Georges.[v]
As well as the 1st and 2nd Regiments and the Royal Dragoons, a
further thousand armed citizens had gathered, carrying muskets
taken from a German merchant in the city. When Wilson gathered
the courage to step outside his door, he was immediately confronted
with the spectacle of an officer from Sans Souci having his horse's
bridle grabbed and being told to return to the palace, 'to tell
General Christophe there was no longer a king'. In the afternoon,
the army decamped to Haut-du-Cap on the outskirts of Cap Henry,
whose bridge was the only river crossing between the city and Sans
Souci. Here, Richard chose to wait to see how Christophe would

---

[v] Nothing more is known of Blésine Georges or her relationship with Christophe, but the son she
had with Nord Alexis, named for his father, became President of Haiti in December 1902, aged
eighty-two.

respond. The following day Birt was invited by General Monpoint to see the army camp, though he was refused permission to send a letter across the lines to Doctor Stewart, who was still in attendance to the king. Birt offered his services as a doctor to the rebels in case of fighting and fell in with Christophe's artillery instructor, a Swedish officer named Johan de Frese, who had done the same.[39]

The news of the insurrection had reached Christophe just after midnight the night before. Baron Dessalines, one of Marie-Louise's cousins, had fled Cap Henry before he could be seized by Richard's men. Noel Joachim, the Duc de Fort Royal, was ordered to take to the field to stop the revolt spreading further. On Sunday, 8 October, as Birt was touring the lines, Joachim brought his troops up to the riverbank. 'While this manoeuvre was taking place, the Governor's party, were heard to cry out: "*Vive la Liberté!*"' Birt reported. 'Immediately the Duke of Fort Royal, taking off his hat, waved it, and cried: "*Vive le Roi!*"'

> The Duke gave command to open the rank, that the cannon might commence playing. He was not obeyed. He immediately galloped upon the men, sword in hand, to enforce his commands, when he saw the cavalry of the Governor's party close at hand, so that he was obliged to wheel his horse and fly.

The royalist troops fell to arguing among themselves about whether they should fire on their brother soldiers before deciding to surrender. Joachim escaped, but Baron Dessalines was cut down by a sabre wielded by one of Nord Alexis' dragoons. The remainder of the ranks then joined the rebels.[40]

The position in Sans Souci was little better. A messenger from Richard had promised soldiers in the palace regiment a month's salary to desert their positions. Many failed to answer the call to arms when Christophe mustered them on the Sunday morning. Worse yet, when he donned his uniform to address the remaining troops, the lingering paralysis on his right side meant that he was unable to mount his horse and he was forced to review them from a chair. The night before he had been in fine voice, and had discussed physiology with Duncan Stewart and what riches the English Duke of Bedford had accrued by sheep farming. Now the shock of events almost completely robbed him of his voice. Jacques Simon, the Duc de Saint Louis, had to denounce the mutineers on his behalf. In this reduced state, the king was forced to ensure the loyalty of his remaining troops by having his daughters, Améthyste and Athénaïre, dole out to them 4 gourdes apiece.[41] At this stage he still assumed that Joachim's regiment had prevailed, and ordered his men to proceed to Cap Henry and simply hold their position. With that, Christophe retired to the royal apartments and took to his bed.

A few hours later he had to be woken to be given news of the disaster at Haut-du-Cap. 'Aha! Is it so?' he asked. All his attendants were dismissed with the exception of Baron de Dupuy and Duncan Stewart. A pistol had already been loaded; Christophe had a pair with the heads of royal lions engraved on the handles. Stewart was asked to repeat some of the previous night's discussion about physiology, with particular attention given to the workings of the circulatory system.[42] Henry Christophe had helped lead the revolution against France. He had outlasted Toussaint Louverture, Jean-Jacques Dessalines and Alexandre Pétion. He had forged a kingdom by force of personality, but his vision of a proud and modern nation claiming its rightful place on the world stage had failed to carry his people with him. In the 1811 address that announced the accession of King Henry I to the throne, the state council declared that a distinguished monarch such as Christophe must be ready 'to brave every danger, to perish for the safety of his people, and rather to bury himself under the ruins of his throne than crouch beneath an ignominious yoke'.[43] Christophe ordered Dupuy and Stewart from his chamber and shot himself in the heart.

18

AFTERMATH AND EXILE

Following the death of André Vernet at the end of 1812, a detailed set of instructions was issued to govern the mourning of members of the royal household. But there was to be no black crêpe for King Henry I, no silenced drums or six months of public remembrance.

During his final hour Christophe had gathered his family around him to tell them that the rebels would not let him live. 'All is lost, but the bandits will not lay their hands on me', he said. He asked Victor-Henry if he had his love, to which his son could only reply 'Yes father', and made him promise not to let his body be stripped by his enemies. They knew what he intended. After the fatal shot rang out and before the shock of his death could set in, Améthyste and Athénaïre wrapped Christophe's body in a sheet with the help of Baron de Dupuy and the king's secretary Chevalier Prézeau. Marie-Louise, who had faithfully accompanied her husband through the revolution and the war of independence, and who for nearly ten years had been publicly honoured as mother of the nation, directed the party to carry her husband to the Citadelle. No one attempted to stop them.

Victor-Henry stayed behind at Sans Souci to attempt to rally what troops he could. Duncan Stewart was dispatched to Cap Henry with a letter for General Richard to ask for a parley, but even as Baron de Vastey tried to proclaim 'Vive Henry II!' he was met with cries of 'Vive la liberté!' The household guards rose up as one while the people of Milot gathered at the gates of Sans Souci. At first they held back as if cowed by the power of the king's reputation, but as the news of Christophe's death was confirmed they flooded in to run with abandon through the palace grounds and into the throne room, the grand salons and the royal apartments. Portraits of Christophe were slashed and the enormous mirrors that lined the halls were broken into a thousand pieces.[1]

After a difficult two-hour climb the royal party reached the gates of the Citadelle. As well as Christophe's body they carried with them Victor-Henry's first and final order as presumptive king, freeing all the prisoners held in the fortress, including Paulin of the 8th Regiment in Saint-Marc whose disobedience had helped light the fuse for the uprising. No soldiers volunteered to help with Christophe's burial. Despite their exhaustion, the queen and princesses were left to dig a grave with their own hands and, with the help of Dupuy and Prézeau, to lower the wrapped corpse into the ground as gently as they could. A prayer was said, and then, to fulfil the promise that Victor-Henry had given his father not to let him become a trophy for the mutineers, the grave was covered in lime. Christophe had built the largest and most advanced fortress in the Americas, armed with hundreds of pieces of cannon captured from the defeated colonial powers. It was meant to stand as Haiti's final guarantee of independence and a symbol of the great dynasty he thought he had founded. Now, all that remained of his aspirations were buried with him in a shabby, urgently dug grave. The Kingdom of Haiti was dead. Marie-Louise and her daughters, still stunned, left the Citadelle to return to the palace for one last time. The following morning they were taken into custody. As Victor-Henry gave up his rapier, he declared to his captors that he was nothing but a simple citizen.[2]

The news of Christophe's death was greeted with a mix of jubilation and nervousness in Cap Henry. Richard hurried to the Citadelle to secure the royal treasury, but many troops had already seized strongboxes of money for themselves, which they proceeded to spend with abandon in the city's taverns. Order broke down completely as officers struggled to control their troops. Outside the city, plantation workers made the most of their unexpected liberation from the strictures of the Code Henry. 'All on the plain was a state of confusion', wrote Doctor Birt:

> They had pillaged all the King's castles [sic], and were driving off his oxen to kill. There were many slaughtered by the roadside, and anyone who passed took what he pleased; yet much was left

to putrefy. Most people that I saw were still apprehensive of disturbance, and all were afraid of being pillaged.

It took three days for order to be fully restored.

On Thursday, 12 October Birt was able to travel to Sans Souci with Stewart, who showed him the spot where Christophe had taken his life. Only the king's bloody shirt hanging on the door offered proof of the event; the bed in which he had killed himself had already been stolen.[3] 'The looting and destruction was so complete that there was not even a chair left when I went there the morning after [Christophe's death],' commented the Swedish artillery officer De Frese, 'The library, which was my favourite place, was gone. On the terrace in front of the palace, there were several broken pianofortes and a couple of excellent pedal harps. Nobody has ever seen a destruction of that kind carried out so fast.'[4] By the time an American named Captain Condry visited a few months later there was barely anything left; the few soldiers left on guard were stripping out the mahogany floorboards and wainscoting and ceilings, 'selling them for whatever they would fetch'. Condry managed to acquire a portrait of Queen Marie-Louise ('said to be an accurate representation, taken by the Court Painter') which he carried with him back to Newburyport in Massachusetts.[5]

Standing amid the wreckage of the kingdom, the foreigners who had been in Christophe's service now began to hastily revise their public opinions about their former employer. William Wilson wrote to Thomas Clarkson to tell him that his 'long cherished opinion' of the king was distorted. Christophe's preoccupation with foreign recognition had been to the detriment of the care of his people:

> Before the white man in his dominions he was affable, mild, generous, and magnificent, just to a fault, and almost anxious to conciliate. In his foreign correspondence he breathed nothing but a spirit of philanthropy ... All this appears but too plainly to have been a mask—a mask with which he successfully covered the deformity of his heart and his actions.

For Wilson, the Haitian people had required a strong hand to guide them to nationhood, but Christophe had abused his position of trust: 'If he made good laws, he was the first to violate them.'[6]

Clarkson heard similar views from Stewart. Christophe's sensible policies were stained by his acts of oppressive cruelty: 'Even if the hand of God had not laid him in a sick bed, the vengeance of his people would not long have been delayed.' Knowing that Clarkson had been sent a tidy sum of money by Christophe, Stewart concluded his letter with a plea for an astonishing £20,000 that he claimed he was owed as back wages, plus an equal sum he said the king had privately promised him.[7]

The letters showed the bubble that the foreigners had lived in, where it was hard to know truth from rumour. Some of their letters claimed knowledge of events that had taken place long before they had arrived in the country. The artillery officer De Frese was particularly stinging in his unpublished memoir, but he was heavily influenced by lurid descriptions of Christophe drawn directly from pamphlets and newspapers published in Port-au-Prince. Of the accounts provided by former supporters of the crown, the most dramatic was by the king's own playwright, Juste Chanlatte, written four weeks after Christophe's death. In it he described his former patron as a slave to his passions, far crueller even than Nebuchadnezzar and having the 'grimace of a tiger' that displayed 'a double row of long pointed cannibal teeth'.[8] Chanlatte may have written this while remembering the very public naked humiliation of his wife. Despite writing for the king, he had remained far from the royal inner circle, and William Wilson later described him as being little more than a pauper, who 'frequently came to borrow of me five, three or even two dollars'.[9] Chanlatte's description was clearly designed to win the favour of whoever came after Christophe.

General Richard had plenty to do to ensure that would be him. One key problem was what to do with Victor-Henry and the core group of Christophe loyalists in his custody. The solution he decided upon was brutal. On the evening of 18 October they were brought into the yard of the city jail in front of a large crowd. 'Had I been able to foresee what would happen, I would certainly have stayed home', wrote De Frese, who had been out patrolling on horseback to enforce the nightly curfew. Victor-Henry was brought before Richard, who told him that even though he was a blameless child, the 'tranquillity of the state' demanded his execution. Victor-Henry accused him of inhumanity, but his protests fell on deaf ears. De

Frese described how 'Richard waved his hand, and four bayonets felled the brave young man from behind. A regimental carpenter was ready and cut off his head just as he fell.' Christophe's illegitimate son Eugène, the Duc de Môle, only gave his executioners 'a glance full of disdain' before he too was run through. Noël Joachim, who had led the kingdom's final stand at Haut-du-Cap, died with 'Long live the king!' on his lips. Five more were to die, including Baron de Vastey, who begged for his life and offered to emigrate if he was spared. His head was cleaved by the carpenter's axe. The final victim was an unnamed twelve-year-old boy, described only as one of Christophe's illegitimate children. The bodies were dumped on waste ground and when foreign merchants came to see them the following afternoon, Vastey's body still twitched with faint signs of life. The executioners disdained how clean the killings were.[10]

Even as Vastey lay suffering, the leaders of the revolt made their first statement as the self-proclaimed rulers of the former kingdom. A new constitution was announced, with the country to be governed by a ruling senate. Richard wrote to 'Citizen President Boyer' to proclaim the revolution and dissuade the republic from sending any troops north. Boyer had been quick to act after learning of the mutiny in Saint-Marc. He publicly claimed credit for the plot and expressed his satisfaction that his brothers-in-arms who had laboured in blindness under a cruel yoke would soon return to the fatherland.[11] Republican troops had quickly occupied Saint-Marc, but Boyer's understanding of what had taken place remained blurry. When he learned of Christophe's suicide, he claimed that Richard's troops were already lined up under the banners of the republic and that only the staunchly royalist Romain was left to resist the wishes of the Haitian people.[12] Romain had in fact quickly retreated north, discarding his noble rank and ordering the roads to Cap Henry to be fortified in anticipation of an advance from Port-au-Prince. In his letter to Boyer, Richard explained that the northern generals were responsible for the Saint-Marc uprising. After a brief outbreak of violence in the north, peace had now been restored. Richard praised Boyer and pledged him his loyalty but made it clear that the north intended to remain a self-governing part of Haiti. He demanded that republican troops return to their barracks in Port-au-Prince lest they be mistaken for an invading force, 'which would undoubtedly lead to brawls in which Haitian blood would be pointlessly shed'. Should such an eventuality arise, he wrote that Boyer alone would bear the responsibility.[13]

It was a hopelessly optimistic declaration. Romain marched south again with his troops to deliver the letter but found that Boyer had already rushed his army to take control of Gonaïves, which had fallen without a fight. His advance guard had been led by General Etienne Magny, the former Duc de Plaisance, whose defection in 1812 had prompted the collapse of the siege of Port-au-Prince. As the news filtered north, the generals realised that their best hope of retaining any power was to pledge their full allegiance to Boyer. On 21 October the military command in Cap Henry announced 'with the greatest joy' that 'there is only one government and one constitution in Haiti today'. All Haitians were reunited as brothers, and with a cry of 'Long live the Republic of Haiti! Long live independence!' they invited President Boyer to lead his army into the city to exchange kisses of peace and brotherhood. Romain was the first to append his signature to the proclamation, followed by Richard. Dupuy, who had been with Christophe until his last, signed, as did Julien Prévost, who had so energetically driven the kingdom's attempts to woo Britain as the Duc de Limonade. There were nearly 100 signatories in total, comprising every significant former member of the Kingdom of Haiti's nobility. The rebel state had lasted barely a fortnight.[14]

On the morning of 26 October the republican army marched through the gates of the hastily rechristened Cap-Haïtien with President Boyer at its head. Birt commented on their fresh appearance—evidence of how peaceful their advance north had been. At a celebration Mass, Boyer announced that this was the happiest day of his life:

> Children of the same family, you are all united under the shade of the sacred tree of liberty: the constitution of the state is recognized throughout Haiti. From the north to the south, from the east to the west, the Republic is now made only of citizens dedicated to its prosperity and independence.

The 'brave patriots' who had taken a stand against the royal tyranny were praised; the only regrets Boyer admitted to were the deaths of

Victor-Henry and Christophe's inner circle, claiming that he had sent an aide-de-camp north with orders that they be spared.[15]

Two days after Boyer's arrival city residents were shocked to find two French warships approaching the harbour. Old fears that Boyer was working in concert with France were not calmed when the president hosted their officers overnight. Haiti was not the ships' intended destination: they had been sailing from Puerto Rico when they learned of Christophe's death and had come seeking the release of six sailors and a cabin boy they claimed were being held captive. Boyer's secretary of state Joseph Inginac attended the meeting and recorded that trading relations were also discussed, with one of the French captains being smart enough to raise Pétion's old idea of paying an indemnity to France for recognition. This intelligence would have been quickly relayed back to Paris.[16]

Boyer stayed in the north for three weeks. In each town he visited he ordered a tree of liberty to be planted to celebrate Christophe's demise. Despite this reunification was no straightforward task. 'Practically every day plots are discovered or punished,' wrote De Frese, 'instigated by the blacks who are most dissatisfied with a mulatto as their ruler, and gens de couleur fill most and the highest offices.'[17] Richard was returned to his old role as city commander, but reporting to General Magny. The majority of the northern generals were replaced by Boyer loyalists, and at least once Boyer had to rush back to Cap-Haïtien when Richard's garrison threatened to mutiny after being left unpaid. Dupuy and Prévost were allowed to return to civilian life. Boyer visited Sans Souci and the Citadelle, and although his reactions were not recorded, he moved afterwards to stop any more of the wealth that had been looted from the royal treasury leaving the country and announced a general amnesty for the return of 'the diamonds, the jewels and the silverware that belong to the state'. One American newspaper winked at its readers over the looting, when it reported that the king's crown had been bought by a speculator 'who, we dare say, will have wit enough to "pop the bauble into a crucible"'.[18] Other goods ordered by Christophe now never made it to Sans Souci but were diverted at source: one box of brass army buttons made in Britain and stamped with Christophe's phoenix was sent instead to Oregon, where they were eventually used as trade goods for Native American tribes.[19]

A few more profitable items were offered for sale in England and the US, but the fate of the vast majority of items looted from Sans Souci remains a mystery.[i]

The only royal jewellery known to survive the uprising was that carried on the persons of Marie-Louise and her daughters. Contrary to the fate suffered by Victor-Henry they were treated well by the revolutionaries, and when Boyer returned to Port-au-Prince in December they were made to accompany him. Boyer appears to have treated them with genuine compassion, writing privately to his mistress Joute Lachenais that 'you will feel, I am sure, that in my position I had to act as I do, to give an example of goodness and generosity'.[20] Nevertheless, there was no question that he would allow them to stay in the north, and they were provided with a house in Port-au-Prince until the old kingdom had been fully brought under republican control.

The final pacification took many months. Both Saint-Marc and Gonaïves saw short-lived mutinies against Boyer's rule, and at the end of February 1821 Richard was arrested for attempting to raise the banner of revolt for a second time. A military commission quickly found him guilty of treason and on 3 March he was condemned to death. 'Those who nourish the guilty hope of rekindling the flames of discord that they may be able to regain their ridiculous privileges of noblesse, may feel that their execution is vain and their wishes impotent', crowed the Port-au-Prince press.[21] In April, Romain was arrested and charged with helping to organise the mutiny in Gonaïves. This time Boyer allowed the sentence to be commuted to a prison term. In August 1822 Romain was found dead in suspicious circumstances, after allegedly trying to grab the rifle of a prison guard.[22]

It was in this fevered environment that Boyer received his first letter from Thomas Clarkson. News of Christophe's death had

---

[i] In *Island Possessed*, the American dancer and anthropologist Katherine Dunham hinted at one item still being used in local Vodou ceremonies in the 1950s: 'At Nan Campêche, near the Citadel of Christophe, a dinner plate from the table service of Napoleon I, Sèvres blue and crested with golden bees, was a prize altar piece. Christophe was supposed to have eaten sacrificial food from this plate, and rumor had it that at Nan Campêche his suicide was predicted.' See Katherine Dunham, *Island Possessed* (University of Chicago Press, 1994), p. 114.

reached England in early December. The king was so well known a figure that on 29 January the Royal Coburg Theatre debuted a new play called *The Death of Christophe—King of Hayti*, based on the most lurid details of his demise that had found their way into the London press. Clarkson had received a clearer image of Richard's uprising from the English teachers he had helped send to the kingdom, while William Wilberforce blamed himself for Christophe's apparent descent into despotism. Noting that 'all kings are apt to be too fond of arms and reviews—of course except the King of Great Britain,' he regretted that

> [he] did not more press Christian principles upon poor Christophe, and instruct him in the knowledge of a Saviour; yet I was afraid of losing my influence with him by going too far. I sent him books, and said what I thought I could, but I have been uneasy since. I know not that a day has passed that I have not prayed for him.[23]

Clarkson's reaction was far more practical, seeking to salvage what he could of his Haitian interests with Boyer. He apologised for never previously having opened a correspondence with the president, but expressed his hope that 'the Revolution which has taken place in Hayti may terminate in the Independence and happiness of its people'. After offering a commentary on the current French thinking regarding Haiti, he closed by asking that Marie-Louise and her daughters were comfortable and happy, since 'Many people in England are interested in their fate.'[24] Boyer responded coolly to Clarkson's approach. While he wrote that he would always be interested to read the abolitionist's observations, he declined to enter further into any exchange of letters.

The approach from England did at least allow Boyer to draw the firmest of lines under the fate of the former royal family. The president claimed that Marie-Louise had asked that she, Améthyste and Athénaïre be allowed to visit England, 'for the sake of their health'. It was a request that Boyer told Clarkson he was happy to accept: 'They will have the privilege of delivering this letter to you. As you seem to take a great interest in their welfare, I have no doubt you will do what you can to be of service to them.'[25] On the last day of July the three woman and their maid Zephyrine boarded a ship bound for London. In a letter to Boyer written before they left 'this

303

homeland where we were born and which we will never cease to cherish', Marie-Louise thanked the president for the kindness he had shown her family over the previous months. Before departing she gave General Magny power of attorney to manage the property she had been allowed to keep in Cap-Haïtien and named Améthyste and Athénaïre as her legal heirs.[26] As the ship pulled out of Port-au-Prince's harbour she had no idea that they were sailing into permanent exile.

The Christophes arrived in London in September and took rooms at Osborne's Hotel, Adelphi. They were accompanied by Captain Robert Sutherland Jr, the son of the late Port-au-Prince-based English merchant who had helped bankroll the Pétion government. The arrival of the royal party attracted the attention of a London press that both pitied their situation and marvelled at rumours of their fabulous wealth. Reports had been published of the millions allegedly found at the Citadelle after Christophe's death, and some observers were undoubtedly disappointed when Marie-Louise was granted control of the money that her husband had lodged with his London solicitors to fund his London ventures, and the sum was revealed to be a rather more modest £9,000.[27] 'Neither mother nor daughters will be dependent on anyone except for counsel and kindness in this land of strangers. They will be amply provided for from their own resources', wrote the abolitionist Zachary Macaulay to his wife in late September:

> I saw the ex-Queen of Hayti yesterday and her two daughters. She and they are in deep mourning, which, with their coal-black countenances, give them a somewhat sombre aspect. The mother is, I should think, about fifty-five years of age, pleasing and modest. The daughters are, I should think, twenty-four and eighteen, pretty good-looking ... I have no doubt whatever that the young women are perfectly modest and virtuous.[28]

A month later the Haitian women received an invitation to lodge with Thomas Clarkson and his wife Dorothy at Playford Hall in Suffolk. It was a timely move. Not long after they arrived in London the Royal Coburg Theatre revived *The Death of Christophe*. The play's producers may even have hoped to capitalise on the newsworthiness of the arrival of the widowed former queen and

princesses.[ii] But the pantomime recounting of the kingdom's collapse could only have wounded them and Suffolk offered a far
more welcoming retreat. They arrived at Playford one year to the
week after Christophe had died.

Clarkson was overjoyed to welcome Marie-Louise and her
daughters into his home. 'A more delightful family never entered
a person's house,' he told Macaulay, 'Their dispositions are so
amiable, their tempers under such complete subjugation, and their
minds so enlightened, that it is a pleasure to live with such people.'[29] Clarkson was less impressed with Captain Sutherland, who
was acting as the family's financial proxy, and whom he distrusted
for the profligate way he suggested they spend their money. It was
only with some persuasion (and the intervention of his wife) that
Clarkson accepted Sutherland's offer to reimburse him for the
costs of hosting the women. Thus settled, the former queen and
princesses made tentative steps out into local society, keenly
aware of the novelty status they carried with them. As Clarkson
wrote to Macaulay:

> I am persuaded that there is nothing which the Christophes desire
> so much as to be respectable. There is nothing to do but to show
> them all possible kindness as opportunities occur, and not to
> appear to wish to influence them ... I have observed that very few
> persons can bear to be reminded of any circumstances in their
> history which may be thought degrading.[30]

The winter of 1821 was particularly wet and must have been difficult for the Caribbean women. Years earlier Marie-Louise had written to her friend Marie Bunel in Philadelphia and sent her gifts of
guava and mango jam as reminders of home. Now they were taken
on bracing country walks, wearing clogs to guard against the wet,
to be shown the greenhouses of the Clarkson's friends and what
might grow under a thin English sun. As Athénaïre spoke English,
she was often the voice for her mother and sisters. One guest won

---

[ii] Others certainly attempted to profit from their presence in London. For nearly thirty years,
one or more swindlers calling themselves 'Prince Christophe' regularly tried to claim financial
support in London as a result of the loss of 'their' kingdom. In 1848 the last of them died in the
workhouse, after serving a prison sentence for fraud.

favour by proudly showing off her collection of shells from Haiti ('many of which they recognised as natives of their country'), but the women's grief proved inescapable. Ann Alexander, who had shared her clogs with the sisters, wrote that she once found Athénaïre in tears and that she admitted to her, 'I think of the dead every night.'[31] The Clarksons proved loyal protectors of their new friends. In April 1822 they hosted a dinner attended by Wilberforce and William Wordsworth and his wife. The poet joked that Playford Hall was now a 'royal residence' and laughingly performed a parody verse on the subject of the 'sable princess'. It did not go down well with the Clarksons, who cut the Wordsworths as a result.[32] In later years Clarkson even criticised Wilberforce for ungraciously keeping his distance from Marie-Louise and her daughters, noting 'a sort of shrink at admitting them into high society', after it took him nearly seven months to pay them a visit.[iii]

By the second half of 1822 the three women began to realise that their sojourn from Haiti might be permanent. Letters to Boyer inviting him to send the female members of his family to visit England went unanswered. After another spell in London the family moved to Hastings on the south coast. Marie-Louise had begun to suffer from rheumatism, which was no doubt aggravated by the English climate. For a further two years they moved between residences, settling for a while in Blackheath and Hastings before returning to London; but they could find no peace in England. On 13 September 1824 they wrote to Dorothy Clarkson that 'it is with sincere regret that we now find ourselves obliged thus to take our affectionate leave of you'. An advertisement was placed in the *Morning Post* for an auction, at 30 Weymouth Street in Marylebone, of 'the property of Madame Christophe, leaving England'.[33] When the sale was complete, Marie-Louise, Améthyste, Athénaïre and

---

[iii] Clarkson perhaps unfairly failed to note that the Christophes' residence with him coincided with the death of Wilberforce's beloved daughter Barbara, after which he and his wife withdrew from social commitments. It was a pain that Marie-Louise would have clearly understood: her daughters wrote to Wilberforce on her behalf that 'our mother desires to be remembered to you and she begs of us to assure you that your kindness to us will be a lasting source of consolation to her'. Améthyste and Athénaïre Christophe to William Wilberforce, 6 November 1821, Bodleian Library, MS Wilberforce c.45.

Zephyrine boarded a steam-packet to Ostend.[iv] Over the next few years newspapers tracked the Christophes as they travelled around Europe. They were spotted in Vienna, at the Carlsbad spas and in Dresden, where one of the former princesses was rumoured to have become engaged to a Prussian officer. In Florence the writer Alexandre Dumas saw them at the opera in a room with a host of other exiled royals that included Napoleon Bonaparte's younger brother Louis, who had reigned briefly as the King of Holland. What he and Marie-Louise talked about can only be imagined.[34]

The family eventually settled in Pisa. In 1840 the abolitionist Robert Inglis and his wife, who had known them in Blackheath, diverted their grand tour after hearing rumours of 'the ex-empress of Haiti' living in the city. They found a rheumatic Marie-Louise living in a rented palazzo with the faithful Zephyrine still in attendance. The intervening years had not been kind: Améthyste had passed away in 1831 from a long-term respiratory condition, while her sister Athénaïre had died in 1839 after a fall near Lake Maggiore in Piedmont. A tearful Marie-Louise told her guests that 'she would never have left [England] but for the health-sake of her daughters; but that now she had only to lie down & die, that she was daily endeavouring to prepare for it'.[35] Marie-Louise wrote again to Boyer, imploring him to send her a passport so that she might return home:

> I feel the need to find myself once more with people with whom
> I have ties of blood and who do not look on me as a stranger …
> You will understand that a woman like myself, bent under the
> weight of years and misfortunes, desires only to see her country
> once again and will remain entirely apart from politics.[36]

She never received a reply, but when she drew up her will she still refused to list her Italian address as anything but temporary, stating emphatically that she was a resident of Cap-Haïtien, 'which domicile she never intends to abandon'.[37] She lived for another ten years before succumbing to pneumonia on 11 March 1851 aged seventy-three, and was buried in the Convent of the Reverend Capuchins at Chiesa San Donnino in Pisa, next to her daughters.

[iv] In February 2022 a blue plaque was unveiled at this address (now 49 Weymouth Street, Marylebone) to commemorate their final residence in England.

The former queen outlived the president who had exiled her by eight months. Boyer had also died far from his Haitian birthplace. In 1843 a popular rebellion had forced him from office and pushed him of the country, first to Jamaica and then France. In an echo of the pillage of Sans Souci, the presidential palace was looted when he fled, with its furniture broken and portraits slashed.[38] Boyer had ruled Haiti for twenty-five years, but his legacy failed to match the promise offered by his reunification of the country in October 1820. He had marched his army into Santo Domingo in 1822 to fulfil Dessalines' dream of bringing the entire island of Hispaniola under the control of one flag, and three years later he even managed to finally win recognition of Haiti's independence from France. But the manner in which it came proved ruinous for the country.

In July 1825 a flotilla of French warships approached Port-au-Prince. They carried a royal ordinance from King Charles X that promised to recognise 'the full and complete independence' of Haiti, which the document referred to as 'the French part of Saint-Domingue'. There were two conditions: the first was that France would become Haiti's favoured trading nation, with reduced tariffs on its goods; the second commanded the Haitian government to deposit 150 million francs in the French treasury in compensation for the losses incurred by its former colonists. Failure to agree would be considered a declaration of war. Haitian commissioners rejected this gunboat diplomacy out of hand, but the French envoy secured a private personal meeting with Boyer. The president recognised Pétion's old proposal of paying an indemnity for recognition and accepted the proposal on the spot.

Haiti could not afford to pay even the first of the five instalments to France, which amounted to ten times the country's annual budget. Boyer was forced to take out an enormous loan from French banks at a high rate of interest, plus a 20 per cent fee for the privilege of arranging the money. Even though the indemnity was eventually negotiated down to 60 million francs, its repayment consumed nearly a third of the national income, and it was not until 1883 that the debt was paid off.[39] When it was, the controlling levers of the economy were almost entirely in French hands, including the national bank. Payments on subsidiary debts associated with the indemnity lasted until 1947, when the Haitian government issued certificates to celebrate Haiti's financial independence, 143 years after claiming its freedom in 1804. With no small degree of irony, the certificates were decorated with an image of the Citadelle Henry, the fortress that Christophe had always intended to be the last line of defence against foreign control of the country.

Boyer imagined that Haiti could manage the debt through its agricultural exports. Coffee was booming, but after the destruction of the Kingdom of Haiti the last vestiges of large-scale sugar production disappeared from the country. Freed from the strictures of royal rule the farmers had abandoned the plantations to cultivate their own plots and find prosperity through self-sufficiency. For them, the personal freedom promised by the Haitian Revolution had finally arrived. In 1826, a year after agreeing to the indemnity, Boyer tried to revive state-controlled agriculture, once again tying the rural poor to plantations, outlawing farmer's cooperatives and mandating labour on state projects such as road building. The new Code Rurale was the Code Henry in all but name, down to the quarter share of profits it promised to the farmers, but without Christophe's overbearing control it proved entirely unenforceable. Peasants simply moved into areas further away from state control, set up their own markets and denied Port-au-Prince its tax revenues.[40]

In May 1842 northern Haiti was struck by a tremendous earthquake that flattened Cap-Haïtien and killed thousands. Boyer was notably slow to send relief to the region. The palace of Sans Souci, long stripped bare of its rich decoration, was almost completely toppled and the walls of the Citadelle were rent by huge cracks which can still be seen today. The most visible remaining symbols of Christophe's rule were laid low. They were reduced even further five years later when the Port-au-Prince writer Thomas Madiou published the first book of his epic seven-volume *Histoire d'Haïti*. Much of the work was based on documents that have now been lost, as well as the recollections of ageing veterans of the revolution and civil war who Madiou was able to interview. It was followed soon by Beaubrun Ardouin's equally grand *Etudes sur l'histoire d'Haïti*. Together they helped lay the foundational narrative of modern Haitian history. Both writers were firm republicans who downplayed Christophe's role in the foundation of the country in favour of that of Alexandre Pétion. Ardouin in particular was prone to exaggerate the worst sins of Christophe's rule, while one of Madiou's key interviewees was Joseph Inginac, who was secretary of state for both Pétion and Boyer.

None of the leading players from the north had survived to be interviewed, while most of the royal archives were lost during the anarchy that followed Christophe's death. The ability of the Kingdom of Haiti to best shape how it would be remembered died when Vastey was bayoneted to death alongside Victor-Henry. Christophe's own secretary of state, and the kingdom's other major writer, Julien Prévost, died in 1827 without ever picking up his pen again. He lived just long enough to see the publication of *Voyage dans le nord d'Hayti* by Hérard Dumesle from Les Cayes, which was a scabrous travelogue that picked over the ruins of Christophe's kingdom and set the tone for how the triumphant republic would shape the story of its victory. The Haitian historian Henock Trouillot later lamented that Christophe and his supporters' fault was that 'they disappeared too soon … before the future historians of his most relentless adversaries'.[41]

In present day downtown Port-au-Prince, five statues survey the open area of Champ de Mars in front of the site of the Presidential Palace that was felled in Haiti's 2010 earthquake. The Nèg Mawon, or Unknown Slave, kneels with an arched back and broken shackles, blowing on a conch shell to rouse the masses to revolt. Behind him stands a patrician Toussaint Louverture. A short distance away Jean-Jacques Dessalines sits atop a horse on a grassy mound: the most commanding position in the square granted to the man who ushered Haiti into independence. The statue of Alexandre Pétion stands to the south, surrounded by marble reliefs of peasant men and women showing their gratitude to the man whose land reform policy began the final dissolution of the colonial plantation system. Henry Christophe's statue stands at a safe distance from his great rival opposite the Musée du Panthéon National Haïtien, which houses his portrait painted by Richard Evans and that of his children, which was returned to the country in 2021. Like Dessalines, he too is mounted, but his plinth is shaped like the great prow of the Citadelle. A massive bronze plaque on one side shows Christophe directing the fort's construction; its opposite side has him holding a flaming torch, preparing to destroy his city rather than allow the armada sent by Napoleon Bonaparte to land safely. He is both the defender of liberty and the man who forced his free people to labour defending it. The paradoxes of his rule deserve to be better remembered.

NOTES

INTRODUCTION

1. *John Bull*, 13 November 1825.
2. Bernth Lindfors, *Ira Aldridge: The Early Years, 1807–1833* (Rochester, NY: University of Rochester Press, 2007), pp. 73–5.
3. *Public & Daily Advertiser*, 16 May 1825.
4. Lindfors, *Ira Aldridge*, p. 50.
5. Ibid. p. 81.
6. David Worrall, *Harlequin Empire: Race, Ethnicity and the Drama of the Popular Enlightenment* (London and New York: Routledge, 2007), p. 136.
7. Laurent Dubois, *Haiti: The Aftershocks of History* (New York: Henry Holt & Co., 2012), p. 102.
8. *The Death of Christophe—King of Haiti*, Act 1, Scene 3: Harvard Theatre Collection, Houghton Library, Harvard University.
9. Ibid., Act 3, Scene 1.
10. Lindfors, *Ira Aldridge*, p. 91.
11. Quoted in Robert Isaac and Samuel Wilberforce, *The Life of William Wilberforce*, Vol. 4 (London: John Murray, 1838), p. 354.

1. BEGINNINGS

1. *Blackwood's Magazine* vol. 1 (1818), p. 130.
2. For more on Vastey's complicated early biography, see Marlene Daut's *Baron de Vastey and the Origins of Black Atlantic Humanism* (New York: Palgrave Macmillan, 2017), pp. 29–32.
3. Baron de Vastey, *Political Remarks on some French Works and Newspapers, concerning Hayti* (London, 1818), p. 9.
4. The original source appears to be the Scottish pamphleteer Pierre McCallum's *Travels in Trinidad During the Months of February, March, and April, 1803* (London: Longman, Hurst, Rees, and Orme, 1805). McCallum claimed special knowledge from having worked as an advisor to Toussaint Louverture, though no evidence exists that he ever visited Saint-Domingue.
5. For example, Peltier to Castlereagh, *Trois mémoires*, October 1807, The National Archives, London, TNA WO 1/79, f188.

6. Baron de Vastey, *An Essay on the Causes of the Revolution and Civil Wars of Hayti* (Exeter, 1823), p. 112. Like many writers, Vastey may also have struggled with deadlines. Writing in 1819 to Thomas Clarkson after the book's publication, he commented: 'I was able to devote only two months to the composition of this work and furthermore I was ill most of the time, so you will no doubt find it full of imperfections.' Vastey to Thomas Clarkson, 29 November 1819, in Earl Leslie Griggs and Clifford H. Prator, *Henri Christophe and Thomas Clarkson: A Correspondence* (New York: Greenwood Press, 1968), pp. 178–82.

7. [Edward Burk], *The Hurricane: A Poem, by an Eyewitness. Also, Historical Notices of St. Domingo, from the seizure of Toussaint l'Ouverture to the Death of Christophe* (Bath, 1844), p. 57.

8. Cathcart to Maitland, 26 November 1799, TNA WO 1/74.

9. Corbet report, 28 January 1803, TNA CO 137/110 f339–344.

10. Beverley A. Steele, *Grenada: A History of its People* (Oxford: Macmillan Caribbean, 2003), p. 35.

11. Kit Candlin, *The Last Caribbean Frontier, 1795–1815* (Basingstoke and New York: Palgrave Macmillan, 2012), p. 9.

12. William Woodis Harvey, *Sketches of Hayti: From the Expulsion of the French to the Death of Christophe* (London: L. B. Seeley & Son, 1827), p. 48.

13. Ottobah Cugoano, *Narrative of the Enslavement of Ottobah Cugoano, a Native of Africa* (London, 1825), pp. 124–5.

14. Ibid., p. 126.

15. William Wilson, 'Unpublished Memoir', Musée du Panthéon National Haïtien (MUPANAH) collection, Port-au-Prince.

16. Baron de Vastey, *The Colonial System Unveiled*, ed. and trans. Chris Bongie (Liverpool University Press, 2014), p. 98.

17. Ibid., p. 94.

18. Nicole Phillip, *Producers, Reproducers, and Rebels: Grenadian Slave Women, 1783–1833*, unpublished paper, Grenada Country Conference, January 2002, http://www.open.uwi.edu/sites/default/files/bnccde/grenada/conference/papers/phillip.html (accessed 30 April 2022).

19. Steele, *Grenada: A History of its People*, p. 73.

20. Joseph Saint-Rémy, *Pétion et Haïti, étude monographique et historique*, Vol. 4 (Paris, 1857), p. 150.

2. FROM SAVANNAH TO SAINT-DOMINGUE

1. Vastey, *An Essay on the Causes of the Revolution*, p. 113.

2. Anon., *Vue du cap Français et du Nvr La Marie Séraphique de Nantes, capitaine Gaugy, le jour de l'ouverture de sa vente, troisième voyage d'Angole, 1772–1773* (watercolour, 1775–1800), Musée

d'histoire de Nantes, http://www.chateaunantes.fr/fr/collections?ref=14528 (accessed 30 April 2022).

3. *Affiches Américaines*, 6 April 1779.

4. John Garrigus, 'Catalyst or Catastrophe? Saint-Domingue's Free Men of Color and the Savannah Expedition, 1779–1782', *Review/Revista Interamericana* vol. 22, nos. 1/2 (1992), pp. 109–25.

5. Stewart R. King, *Blue Coat or Powdered Wig: Free People of Color in Pre-Revolutionary Saint Domingue* (Athens, GA: University of Georgia Press, 2010), p. 67.

6. Hérard Dumesle, *Voyage dans le nord d'Hayti, ou, Révélations des lieux et des monuments historiques* (Cayes: Imprimerie du Gouvernement, 1824), p. 229.

7. *Affiches Américaines*, 31 July 1781 and 30 July 1783.

8. King, *Blue Coat or Powdered Wig*, p. 56.

9. George P. Clark, 'The Role of the Haitian Volunteers at Savannah in 1779: An Attempt at an Objective View', *Phylon* vol. 41, no. 4 (1980), pp. 356–8.

10. Thomas Madiou, *Histoire d'Haïti*, Vol. 1: *1492–1799* (Port-au-Prince: J. Courtois, 1847), p. 26.

11. For a full account of the action, see David Wilson's *The Southern Strategy: Britain's Conquest of South Carolina and Georgia, 1775–1780* (Columbia: University of South Carolina Press, 2008), pp. 150–1.

12. Ibid., pp. 162–70.

13. Médéric-Louis-Élie Moreau de Saint-Méry, *Description topographique, physique, civile, politique et historique de la partie française de l'isle Saint-Domingue*, Vol. 1 (Philadelphia, 1797), pp. 300–1; David Geggus, 'The Major Port Towns of Saint-Domingue in the Later Eighteenth Century', in Franklin W. Knight and Peggy K. Liss (eds.), *Atlantic Port Cities: Economy, Culture, and Society in the Atlantic World, 1650–1850* (Knoxville: University of Tennessee Press, 1991), p. 99.

14. David Geggus, 'The Slaves and Free People of Color of Cap Français', in Jorge Cañizares-Esguerra et al. (eds.), *The Black Urban Atlantic in the Age of the Slave Trade* (Philadelphia: University of Pennsylvania Press, 2016), pp. 101–21.

15. Moreau de Saint-Méry, *Description topographique*, Vol. 1, p. 487; Vastey, *The Colonial System Unveiled*, pp. 133–4.

16. There are several first-hand accounts of Christophe's ability to understand English. See, for example, Vashon to Rowley, 16 March 1811, TNA WO 1/76 f183–188.

17. Dumesle, *Voyage dans le nord d'Hayti*, p. 229.

18. Special thanks to Tabitha McIntosh for sharing her exhaustive spreadsheet of the different claims to Henry Christophe's origins.

19. *Affiches Américaines*, 25 April 1789. Thanks to John Garrigus for providing me with a copy of the 1787–8 cadastral survey of Cap Français.

20. For example, 'The king is in his person what in England you would call a fine portly looking man, about 5 feet 10 inches … he is quite black', as noted by a Royal Navy officer who met Christophe in 1814 and 1818. *Blackwood's Magazine* vol. 1 (1818), p. 130.

21. 'Observations d'un François sur la traite des noirs et sur l'état actuel de Saint-Domingue', in Fredéric Schoell, *Recueil de pièces officielles: Destinées à détromper les François sur les événemens qui se sont passés depuis quelques années*, Vol. 7 (Paris: Librairie Grecque-Latine-Allemande, 1815), p. 287. The attribution to Lavaysse is inscribed on a copy held by the Bibliothèque nationale de France.

22. L. J. Clausson, *Précis historique de la révolution de Saint-Domingue* (Paris: Pillet Aîné, 1819), p. 122.

23. Cathcart to Maitland, 26 November 1799, TNA WO 1/74 f57.

24. Cited in Deborah Jenson, *Beyond the Slave Narrative: Politics, Sex, and Manuscripts in the Haitian Revolution* (Liverpool University Press, 2011), p. 202.

25. *Affiches Américaines*, 27 February 1781, 1 November 1788 and 27 January 1790.

26. *Quarterly Review* vol. 21, no. 62 (1819), p. 454.

27. Ian Thomson, *Bonjour Blanc: A Journey Through Haiti* (London: Vintage, 2012), p. 341.

28. Moreau de Saint-Méry, *Description topographique*, Vol. 1, p. 544; King, *Blue Coat or Powdered Wig*, p. 163.

29. Moreau de Saint-Méry, *Description topographique*, Vol. 1, p. 433.

30. Geggus, 'The Slaves and Free People of Color of Cap Français', pp. 101–21.

3. THE COLONY ABLAZE

1. Discussion of this 'military leadership group' is a central thesis of Stewart King's *Blue Coat or Powdered Wig*.

2. Jean-Louis Donnadieu, 'Derrière le portrait, l'homme: Jean-Baptiste Belley, dit "Timbaze", dit "Mars" (1746?–1805)', *Bulletin de la Société d'Histoire de la Guadeloupe*, no. 170 (2015), pp. 29–54, doi:10.7202/1029391ar. Donnadieu suggests that Belley may have been born in Leogane in the southern part of the colony, but later used the story of his African birth to further the cause of emancipation.

3. Archives Nationales d'Outre Mer, Aix-en-Provence, ANOM, 85 MIOM 34.

4. Doris Garraway, 'Race, Reproduction and Family Romance in Moreau de Saint-Méry's "Description … de la partie francaise de l'isle Saint Domingue"', *Eighteenth-Century Studies* vol. 38, no. 2 (2005), pp. 227–46, Project MUSE, doi:10.1353/ecs.2005.0008.

5. Laurent Dubois, *Avengers of the New World: The Story of the Haitian Revolution* (Cambridge, MA: Harvard University Press, 2004), pp. 62, 70.

6. David Powers, 'The French Musical Theater: Maintaining Control in Caribbean Colonies in the Eighteenth Century', *Black Music Research Journal* vol. 18, nos. 1/2 (1998), pp. 229–40.

7. Sudhir Hazareesingh, *Black Spartacus: The Epic Life of Toussaint Louverture* (London: Allen Lane, 2020), p. 38.

8. Moreau de Saint-Méry, *Description topographique*, Vol. 1, p. 342.

9. Trans-Atlantic Slave Trade Database, www.slavevoyages.org (accessed 20 April 2021).

10. Dubois, *Avengers of the New World*, pp. 45–7.

11. Vastey, *The Colonial System Unveiled*, pp. 108, 112, 124.

12. Dubois, *Avengers of the New World*, p. 56.

13. Trevor Burnard and John Garrigus, *The Plantation Machine: Atlantic Capitalism in French Saint-Domingue and British Jamaica* (Philadelphia: University of Pennsylvania Press, 2016), pp. 104–7.

14. Dubois, *Avengers of the New World*, p. 75.

15. John Garrigus, 'Opportunist or Patriot? Julien Raimond (1744–1801) and the Haitian Revolution', *Slavery & Abolition* vol. 28, no. 1 (2007), pp. 1–21; John Garrigus, 'Vincent Ogé "Jeune" (1757–91): Social Class and Free Colored Mobilization on the Eve of the Haitian Revolution', *The Americas* vol. 68, no. 1 (2011), pp. 33–62.

16. Jeremy Popkin, 'Jean-Jacques Dessalines, Norbert Thoret, and the Violent Aftermath of the Haitian Declaration of Independence', in Julia Gaffield (ed.), *The Haitian Declaration of Independence: Creation, Context, and Legacy* (Charlottesville: University of Virginia Press, 2016), pp. 115–35.

17. Carolyn Fick, *The Making of Haiti: The Saint-Domingue Revolution from Below* (Knoxville: University of Tennessee Press, 1990), p. 83.

18. Ibid., pp. 105–6.

19. Ibid., pp. 92–3. For a fuller discussion of Toussaint Louverture's likely participation at Bois-Caïman, see Hazareesingh, *Black Spartacus*, pp. 48–50.

20. Fick, *The Making of Haiti*, p. 93.

21. Nathaniel Cutting to Thomas Jefferson, 28 December 1791, Founders Online, https://founders.archives.gov/documents/Jefferson/01-22-020428 (accessed 30 April 2022).

22. Saint-Rémy, *Pétion et Haïti, étude monographique et historique*, Vol. 4, p. 151; Wilson, 'Unpublished Memoir'.

23. Stewart R. King, 'The Maréchaussée of Saint-Domingue: Balancing the Ancien Régime and Modernity', *Journal of Colonialism and Colonial History*, vol. 5, no. 2 (2004), Project MUSE, doi:10.1353/cch.2004.0052.

24. Dubois, *Avengers of the New World*, p. 118.

25. Marlene Daut, *'Genocidal Imaginings' in the Era of the Haitian Revolution*, 25 January 2016, https://ageofrevolutions.com/2016/01/25/genocidal-imaginings-in-the-era-of-the-haitian-revolution/ (accessed 30 April 2022).

26. Nathaniel Cutting to Thomas Jefferson, 1 March 1792, Founders Online, https://founders.archives.gov/documents/Jefferson/01–23–02–0165 (accessed 30 April 2022).

27. Dubois, *Avengers of the New World*, p. 130.

28. Robert Louis Stein, *Léger Félicité Sonthonax: The Lost Sentinel of the Republic* (Rutherford, NJ: Fairleigh Dickinson University Press, 1985), p. 69.

29. Ibid., p. 72.

30. Dubois, *Avengers of the New World*, p. 156.

31. Saint-Rémy, *Pétion et Haïti*, Vol. 4, p. 151.

32. Civil commissioner orders, 20 June 1793. Archives Nationales France (ANF), D XXV 7. My thanks to Jeremy Popkin for sharing this reference with me.

33. Dubois, *Avengers of the New World*, p. 157.

34. Berard Verzel, *Plan de la ville du Cap Français sur lequel sont marqués en teinte noire les ravages du premier incendie, et en rouge les islets, parties d'islets, édifices, etc. qui existent encore le 21 juin 1793*, Bibliothèque nationale de France (BnF), GED-913 (Res) ark:/12148/btv1b55005281x (accessed 30 April 2022).

35. Stein, *Léger Félicité Sonthonax*, pp. 75–6.

4. DEFENDING THE REVOLUTION

1. *Almanach Royal d'Hayti pour l'année bissextile 1814, Onzième de l'indépendance, et la troisième du règne de sa majesté* (Cap Henry: P. Roux, 1814), p. 5.

2. 'Last Will and Testament of Marie-Louise Christophe', 8 July 1851, TNA PROB 11/ 2135/332.

3. ANOM, 85 MIOM 34.

4. Jacques Coidavy, 'Etat de service militaire, 24 Prairial An 6', ANOM, COL E 86.

5. ANOM, 85 MIOM 34.

6. King, *Blue Coat or Powdered Wig*, p. 118.

7. Jenson, *Beyond the Slave Narrative*, pp. 380–2.

8. Dubois, *Avengers of the New World*, pp. 169–70.

9. Hazareesingh, *Black Spartacus*, pp. 41, 58.

10. Saint-Rémy, *Pétion et Haïti*, Vol. 4, p. 151.

11. Claude Moïse (ed.)., *Dictionnaire Historique de la Révolution Haïtienne, 1789–1804* (Montréal: CIDIHCA, 2014), p. 195.

12. Coidavy, 'Etat de service militaire, 24 Prairial An 6'. Fort Belair no longer exists, but in Christophe's time it stood on the hill overlooking Barrière Bouteille, the traditional gates of the city.

13. Dubois, *Avengers of the New World*, p. 168.

14. *Almanach Royal d'Hayti pour l'année bissextile 1814*, p. 5.

15. Dubois, *Avengers of the New World*, p. 179.

16. Philippe Girard, *Toussaint Louverture: A Revolutionary Life* (New York: Basic Books, 2016),

p. 72. A new biography of Dessalines by Julia Gaffield, provisionally titled *Jean-Jacques Dessalines and the Haitian Revolution* is due to be published in 2024 by Yale University Press.

17. Madiou, *Histoire d'Haïti*, Vol. 1, p. 208.

18. Toussaint to Laveaux, 25 January 1795, cited in Joseph Boromé, *Toussaint Louverture: A Finding List of His Letters and Documents in Archives and Collections (Public and Private) of Europe and America*, Schomburg Center for Research in Black Culture, Sc MG 714, Box 2, New York Public Library. My thanks to Sudhir Hazareesingh for sharing his copy of this document with me.

19. David Geggus, *Slavery, War, and Revolution: The British Occupation of Saint Domingue, 1793–1798* (Oxford: Clarendon Press, 1982), pp. 121, 154.

20. J. R. McNeill, *Mosquito Empires: Ecology and War in the Greater Caribbean, 1620–1914* (Cambridge University Press, 2010), p. 248.

21. Hazareesingh, *Black Spartacus*, pp. 82–3.

22. Marcus Rainsford, *An Historical Account of the Black Empire of Haiti*, ed. Paul Youngquist and Grégory Pierrot (Durham, NC: Duke University Press, 2013), pp. 134–5.

23. Hazareesingh, *Black Spartacus*, p. 86; Dubois, *Avengers of the New World*, p. 160.

24. Dubois, *Avengers of the New World*, p. 164.

25. Ibid., p. 188.

26. Hazareesingh, *Black Spartacus*, p. 133.

27. Madiou, *Histoire d'Haïti*, Vol. 1, p. 236; Stein, *Léger Félicité Sonthonax*, p. 127.

28. Hazareesingh, *Black Spartacus*, p. 99.

29. Henry Perroud, *Précis des derniers troubles qui ont eu lieu dans la partie du Nord de Saint-Domingue* (Cap Français: P. Roux, 1796), p. 4.

30. Vastey, *An Essay on the Causes of the Revolution*, p. 26.

31. Hubert Cole, *Christophe: King of Haiti* (New York: Viking Press, 1967), p. 49.

32. Jeremy Popkin, *You Are All Free: The Haitian Revolution and the Abolition of Slavery* (Cambridge University Press, 2010), p. 282.

33. Hazareesingh, *Black Spartacus*, pp. 113–14; Dubois, *Avengers of the New World*, p. 204.

34. Citizen Barbault-Royer, 'Sur les députations de Saint-Domingue au corps legislatif', 15 Pluviôse, Year 5 (3 February 1796), British Library (BL) f.716.7.8.

35. Madiou, *Histoire d'Haïti*, Vol. 1, pp. 280–1.

36. General Desfourneaux to the Minster of the Marine, quoted in *Kentish Weekly Post*, 14 July 1797.

5. TOUSSAINT LOUVERTURE SUPREME

1. Rainsford, *An Historical Account of the Black Empire of Haiti*, pp. 143–4.

2. See, for example, *Morning Herald*, 19 March 1817.

3. Geggus, *Slavery, War, and Revolution*, p. 376.

4. Hazareesingh, *Black Spartacus*, pp. 194–5.

5. Vergniaud Leconte's *Henri Christophe dans l'histoire d'Haïti* (Paris: Berger-Levrault, 1931) suggests the house was on the corner of Rue Hazard, but the *Gazette Officielle de Saint-Domingue* of 6 July 1803 places it just off Place d'Armes, behind the main church.

6. *Almanach Royal d'Hayti pour l'année bissextile 1814*, p. 5.

7. Stein, *Léger Félicité Sonthonax*, pp. 146–8.

8. Philippe Girard and Jean-Louis Donnadieu, 'Toussaint before Louverture: New Archival Findings on the Early Life of Toussaint', *The William and Mary Quarterly* vol. 70, no. 1 (2013), pp. 41–78.

9. Pamphile de Lacroix, *Mémoires pour servir à l'histoire de la révolution de Saint-Domingue*, Vol. 2 (Paris: Pillet Aîné, 1819), p. 47; Hazareesingh, *Black Spartacus*, p. 290.

10. Toussaint Louverture to Henry Christophe, 28 Pluviôse, Year 7 (16 February 1798); quoted in Boromé, *Toussaint Louverture: A Finding List*.

11. Thomas Cathcart to General Maitland, 26 November 1799, TNA WO 1/74.

12. Jacques Périès, *Revolution de St. Domingue, par M. Peries, Tresorier on 1799, 1800, 1801*, BL Add MS 38074.

13. Michel Etienne Descourtilz, *Voyages d'un naturaliste, et ses observations* (Paris: Dufart, 1809), vol. 3, p. 248; vol. 2, p. 82.

14. Dubois, *Avengers of the New World*, p. 221; Hazareesingh, *Black Spartacus*, p. 141.

15. Dubois, *Avengers of the New World*, p. 217.

16. Madiou, *Histoire d'Haïti*, Vol. 1, p. 321.

17. Hazareesingh, *Black Spartacus*, pp. 150, 188.

18. Beaubrun Ardouin, *Etudes sur l'histoire d'Haïti*, Vol. 4 (Paris: Dezobry & E. Magdeleine, 1853), p. 106.

19. Vastey, *An Essay on the Causes of the Revolution*, p. 23.

20. Ibid.

21. Madiou, *Histoire d'Haïti*, Vol. 1, p. 346.

22. Toussaint Louverture to Henry Christophe, 5 Thermidor, Year 8 (24 July 1799); quoted in Boromé, *Toussaint Louverture: A Finding List*.

23. Madiou, *Histoire d'Haïti*, Vol. 1, p. 359.

24. 'Letters of Toussaint Louverture and of Edward Stevens, 1798–1800', *The American Historical Review* vol. 16, no. 1 (October 1910), pp. 64–7.

25. Thomas Cathcart to General Maitland, 26 November 1799, TNA WO 1/74.

26. Ibid.

27. Moïse, *Dictionnaire Historique de la Révolution Haïtienne*, pp. 45–6.

28. Thomas Madiou, *Histoire d'Haïti*, Vol. 2: *1799–1803* (Port-au-Prince: J. Courtois, 1847), p. 15.

29. Ibid., p. 15.

30. 'Letters of Toussaint Louverture and of Edward Stevens, 1798–1800', pp. 64–7.

31. Madiou, *Histoire d'Haïti*, Vol. 2, p. 18.

32. Ibid., pp. 20–1.

33. Ibid., p. 23.

34. Noël Colombel, *Réflexions sur quelques faits relatifs à notre existence politique* (Paris: F. Scherff, 1818), pp. 12–13.

35. 'I see all these children plunged into pain/ Assaulted beneath their roofs, by Christophe slain!/ I see Christophe, alas, hurl them pell-mell/ Into a shaft serving as a new tomb as well!' Alcibiade Pommayrac, *Le siège de Jacmel*. My thanks to Nathan Dize for providing a new translation of the poem.

36. Joseph Saint-Rémy, *Pétion et Haïti, étude monographique et historique*, Vol. 2 (Paris, 1854), pp. 223–6.

37. Madiou, *Histoire d'Haïti*, Vol. 2, p. 26.

38. Dubois, *Avengers of the New World*, p. 236; Saint-Rémy, *Pétion et Haïti*, Vol. 2, pp. 223–6.

39. Dumesle, *Voyage dans le nord d'Hayti*, p. 243. According to Dumesle, Vilton was godfather to both Christophe's daughters.

40. Périès, *Revolution de St. Domingue, par M. Peries*.

41. Toussaint Louverture to Henry Christophe, 23 Floréal, Year 9 (13 May 1800) and 18 January 1801; quoted in Boromé, *Toussaint Louverture: A Finding List*.

42. Lacroix, *Mémoires pour servir à l'histoire de la révolution de Saint-Domingue*, Vol. 2, p. 45; Ardouin, *Etudes sur l'histoire d'Haïti*, Vol. 4, p. 331.

43. Hazareesingh, *Black Spartacus*, p. 277.

44. Johnhenry Gonzalez, *Maroon Nation: A History of Revolutionary Haiti* (New Haven, CT: Yale University Press, 2019), pp. 116–18.

45. Philippe Girard (ed. and trans.), *The Memoir of General Toussaint Louverture* (New York: Oxford University Press, 2014), p. 97.

46. Hazareesingh, *Black Spartacus*, p. 240.

47. Laurent Dubois, Julia Gaffield and Michael Acacia (eds.), *Documents constitutionnels d'Haïti, 1790–1860* (Berlin: De Gruyter, 2013), p. 53.

48. Dubois, *Avengers of the New World*, pp. 243–5.

49. Lacroix, *Mémoires pour servir à l'histoire de la révolution de Saint-Domingue*, Vol. 2, pp. 29–30.

50. Roume to the Minister of Navy, New York, 3 Vendémiaire, Year 10 (25 September 1801), ANOM, CC9 B2.

51. Vastey, *An Essay on the Causes of the Revolution*, p. 26.

52. Tobias Lear to James Madison, 22 October 1801, Founders Online, https://founders.archives.gov/documents/Madison/02–91–02–0184 (accessed 25 April 2022).

53. 'Récit des évènements qui se sont passés dans la partie Nord de Saint-Domingue depuis le 29 Vendémiaire jusqu'au 13 Brumaire an X', *Le Moniteur Universel*, 16 Pluviôse, Year 10 (5 February 1802).

54. Tobias Lear to James Madison, 27 October 1801, Founders Online, https://founders.archives.gov/documents/Madison/02–02–02–0309 (accessed 25 April 2022).

55. 'Récit des évènements qui se sont passés dans la partie Nord de Saint-Domingue depuis le 29 Vendémiaire jusqu'au 13 Brumaire an X'; W. Whitfield to Lord Nugent, 5 December 1801, TNA CO 137/106.

56. Lacroix, *Mémoires pour servir à l'histoire de la révolution de Saint-Domingue*, Vol. 2, p. 48.

57. Madiou, *Histoire d'Haïti*, Vol. 2, p. 119.

58. Dubois, *Avengers of the New World*, pp. 248–9.

59. Madiou, *Histoire d'Haïti*, Vol. 2, p. 123.

6. INVASION

1. Philippe Girard, *The Slaves Who Defeated Napoleon: Toussaint Louverture and the Haitian War of Independence, 1801–1804* (Tuscaloosa: University of Alabama Press, 2011), p. 48.

2. 'Notes pour servir aux instructions a donner au capitaine général Leclerc', in Paul Roussier, *Lettres du général Leclerc, commandant en chef de l'armée de Saint Domingue en 1802* (Paris: Société de l'Histoire des Colonies Françaises, 1937), p. 269.

3. Dubois, *Avengers of the New World*, pp. 254–5.

4. Philippe Girard, 'Napoleon Bonaparte and the Emancipation Issue in Saint-Domingue, 1799–1803', *French Historical Studies* vol. 32, no. 4 (2009), p. 601. For a discussion around the sensitivity of the plan for Saint-Domingue order, see Dubois, *Avengers of the New World*, pp. 259–60.

5. Louverture proclamation, 19 Frimaire, Year 10 (20 December 1801), in Hazareesingh, *Black Spartacus*, pp. 296–7.

6. Lacroix, *Mémoires pour servir à l'histoire de la révolution de Saint-Domingue*, Vol. 2, p. 63.

7. Madiou, *Histoire d'Haïti*, Vol. 2, p. 143.

8. 'Extrait du registre des délibérations de l'administration municipale du Cap. Séance du 16 pluviose an 10', in *Le Moniteur universel* no. 212, 2 Floréal, Year 10 (22 April 1802), p. 855.

9. 'Proclamation of the First Consul to the Inhabitants of Saint-Domingue', 17 Brumaire, Year 10 (8 November 1801), in Prince Saunders, *Haytian Papers: A Collection of the Very Interesting Proclamations, and Other Official Documents; together with Some Account of the Rise, Progress, and Present State of the Kingdom of Hayti* (London: W. Reed, 1816), pp. 1–3.

10. Leclerc to Christophe, 13 Pluviôse, Year 10 (2 February 1802), in Saunders, *Haytian Papers*, pp. 4–5.

11. Christophe to Leclerc, 13 Pluviôse, Year 10 (2 February 1802), in Saunders, *Haytian Papers*, pp. 6–8.

12. Christophe to Louverture, 13 Pluviôse, Year 10 (2 February 1802), MUPANAH Papers.

13. 'Extrait du registre des délibérations', p. 856.

14. Tobias Lear to James Madison, 12 February 1802, Founders Online, https://founders.archives.gov/documents/Madison/02–91–02–0288 (accessed 25 April 2022).

15. Rumours have persisted that Louverture was in Cap Français directing negotiations, but there is no mention of him in the official municipal report written the day after Cap Français burned, and Louverture's own correspondence places him in Hinche.

16. Girard, *The Memoir of General Toussaint Louverture*, p. 65.

17. Christophe to Louverture, 18 Pluviôse, Year 10 (7 February 1802), MUPANAH Papers.

18. Girard, *The Memoir of General Toussaint Louverture*, p. 67.

19. Lacroix, *Mémoires pour servir à l'histoire de la révolution de Saint-Domingue*, Vol. 2, p. 137.

20. Madiou, *Histoire d'Haïti*, Vol. 2, p. 222.

21. Baron Henry Bro de Comères (ed.), *Mémoires du Général Bro (1796–1844)* (Paris: Plon, 1914), p. 13; Dugua to Berthier, 5 Germinal, Year 10 (24 March 1802), in Pierre Caron, *Correspondance intime du Général Jean Hardy, de 1797 à 1802* (Paris: Plon, 1901), p. 275.

22. Madiou, *Histoire d'Haïti*, Vol. 2, p. 184.

23. Dubois, *Avengers of the New World*, p. 269.

24. The Artibonite River has meandered considerably in two centuries and no longer flows directly past the foot of the escarpment. For a historical survey of the fort, see 'La Crête-à-Pierrot, site de hauts faits d'armes', *Bulletin de l'ISPAN* no. 22 (March 2011), pp. 1–12.

25. Lacroix, *Mémoires pour servir à l'histoire de la révolution de Saint-Domingue*, Vol. 2, p. 159.

26. Descourtilz, *Voyages d'un naturaliste, et ses observations*, vol. 3, p. 359; George E. Simpson and J. B. Cinéas, 'Folk Tales of Haitian Heroes', *The Journal of American Folklore* vol. 54, nos. 213/214 (1941), pp. 176–85.

27. Christophe to Louverture, 23 Ventôse, Year 10 (14 March 1802); Boston Public Library (BPL), MS Haiti 67–7; Madiou, *Histoire d'Haïti*, Vol. 2, p. 227.

28. Tobias Lear to James Madison, 29 March 1802, Founders Online, http://founders.archives.gov/documents/Madison/02–91–02–032 (accessed 25 April 2022).

29. Antoine Metral, *Histoire de l'expédition des Français a Saint-Domingue* (Paris, 1825), p. 77; Christophe to Louverture, 19 March 1802, quoted in Girard, *The Slaves Who Defeated Napoleon*, p. 132.

30. Caron, *Correspondance intime*, p. 280.

31. Madiou, *Histoire d'Haïti*, Vol. 2, p. 242; Henry Christophe, *Plan général de défense du Royaume*, 20 November 1814, p. 6; Hardy to Rochambeau, 18 Germinal, Year 10 (8 April 1802), University of Florida Library (UFL) Rochambeau Papers 207.

32. Romain to Louverture, 15 Germinal, Year 10 (5 April 1802), UFL Rochambeau Papers 198.

33. Louverture to Boudet, 21 Germinal, Year 10 (11 April 1802), quoted in Hazareesingh, *Black Spartacus*, p. 312.

34. Henry Christophe, *Manifeste du Roi* (Cap Henry: P. Roux, 1814), p. 44. The letters were printed in English two years later by Prince Saunders in his semi-official *Haytian Papers*.

35. Vilton to Christophe, 28 Germinal, Year 10 (16 April 1802), in Saunders, *Haytian Papers*, p. 31. For Louverture in Gonaïves, see Huin to Rochambeau, 25 Germinal, Year 10 (15 April 1802), UFL Rochambeau Papers 237.

36. Leclerc to Christophe, 29 Germinal, Year 10 (17 April 1802), in Saunders, *Haytian Papers*, p. 9.

37. Christophe to Vilton, 30 Germinal, Year 10 (20 April 1802), in Saunders, *Haytian Papers*, p. 36.

38. Hardy to Christophe, 30 Germinal, Year 10 (20 April 1802), in Saunders, *Haytian Papers*, p. 22.

39. Christophe to Hardy, 2 Floréal, Year 10 (22 April 1802), in Saunders, *Haytian Papers*, pp. 26–30.

40. Christophe to Leclerc, 2 Floréal, Year 10 (22 April 1802), in Saunders, *Haytian Papers*, p. 10.

41. Leclerc to Christophe, 4 Floréal, Year 10 (24 April 1802), in Saunders, *Haytian Papers*, p. 14.

42. Christophe to Louverture, 4 Floréal, Year 10 (24 April 1802), MUPANAH Papers 55.

43. Christophe to Louverture, 5 Floréal, Year 10 (25 April 1802), in Saunders, *Haytian Papers*, p. 17.

44. Leclerc to the Governor of Cuba (draft) and Leclerc proclamation (draft), 5 Floréal, Year 10 (25 April 1802), UFL Rochambeau Papers 273 and 277.

45. Lacroix, *Mémoires pour servir à l'histoire de la révolution de Saint-Domingue*, Vol. 2, p. 180. Thomas Madiou suggests a lower figure of 800 troops under Christophe's command.

46. Leclerc to Christophe, 8 Floréal, Year 10 (28 April 1802), in Saunders, *Haytian Papers*, p. 19.

47. Dugua to Décres, 17 Prairial, Year 10 (6 June 1802), ANF CC9B19, quoted in Claude Bonaparte Auguste, *L'Expédition Leclerc, 1801–1803* (Port-au-Prince, H. Deschamps, 1985), p. 179.

48. For the Christophe family in Petite Anse, see, for example, Jacques Alexandre François Allix, 'Souvenirs militaires et politiques de M. le Lieutenant-Général Allix', *Journal des sciences militaires des armées de terre et der mer*, Vol. 16 (1829), p. 64. The location today is close to the site of the Cap-Haïtien airport.

49. Louverture to Christophe, 8 Floréal, Year 10 (28 April 1802), in Hazareesingh, *Black Spartacus*, p. 314.

50. J de. Norvins, *Souvenirs d'un historien de Napoléon*, Vol. 2 (Paris: E. Plon Nourrit et Cie, 1896), pp. 394–5.

51. Ibid., p. 397.

52. Leclerc to Napoleon Bonaparte, 17 Prairial, Year 10 (6 June 1802), in Roussier, *Lettres du général Leclerc*, pp. 11–12.

53. McNeill, *Mosquito Empires*, p. 255.

54. General Hardy to his wife, 16 Floréal, Year 10 (6 May 1802); Caron, *Correspondance intime*, pp. 286–7.

55. Philippe Girard, 'Jean-Jacques Dessalines et l'arrestation de Toussaint Louverture', *Journal of Haitian Studies* vol. 17, no. 1 (2011), pp. 123–38.

56. Lacroix, *Mémoires pour servir à l'histoire de la révolution de Saint-Domingue*, Vol. 2, p. 203.

7. WAR OF INDEPENDENCE

1. 'Report from Cap Français, 5 Messidor, Year 10' (23 June 1802), in *Le Moniteur Universel*, no. 308, 8 Thermidor, Year 10 (27 July 1802), p. 1262. Other observers were convinced that Dessalines alone had acted against Louverture: see, for example, 'Journal of Proceeding at Cap François, Between April and Nov. 1802, given by a French Officer of rank to a Officer of a British Man of War then lying at Cap François. Nov. 21, 1802', *Saunder's News-Letter and Daily Advertiser*, 5 February 1803.

2. Leclerc to Bonaparte, 6 Messidor, Year 10 (24 June 1802), in Auguste, *L'Expédition Leclerc*, p. 187.

3. Lacroix, *Mémoires pour servir à l'histoire de la révolution de Saint-Domingue*, Vol. 2, p. 220; Fressinet to Leclerc, 7 July 1802, in Auguste, *L'Expédition Leclerc*, p. 189.

4. Chataigner to Thouvenot, 27 Messidor, Year 10 (16 July 1802), in Joseph Saint-Rémy, *Pétion et Haïti, étude monographique et historique*, Vol. 3 (Paris, 1855).

5. Lacroix, *Mémoires pour servir à l'histoire de la révolution de Saint-Domingue*, Vol. 2 (Paris, 1854), pp. 227–8.

6. Madiou, *Histoire d'Haïti*, Vol. 2, p. 269.

7. 'Revolt of the Blacks in St Domingo, communicated by a Gentleman on the Spot', 28 January 1803, TNA CO 137/110.

8. 'Extrait d'une lettre du Cap du 18 vendémiaire an 11', CARAN, AF/IV/1213, dossier 6, quoted in Jean-Pierre Le Glaunec, *The Cry of Vertières: Liberation, Memory, and the Beginning of Haiti* (Montreal: McGill-Queen's University Press, 2020), p. 66.

9. For officers of colour in Leclerc's army, see Matthieu Brevet, *Les expéditions coloniales vers Saint-Domingue et les Antilles*, PhD thesis, Université Lumière Lyon 2, Lyon (2007), p. 123.

10. Metral, *Histoire de l'expédition des Français a Saint-Domingue*, pp. 109–10.

11. Thouvenot to Dugua, 2 October 1802, quoted in Le Glaunec, *The Cry of Vertières*, p. 144.

12. Lacroix, *Mémoires pour servir à l'histoire de la révolution de Saint-Domingue*, Vol. 2, p. 232.

13. Leclerc to Bonaparte, 29 Fructidor, Year 10 (16 September 1802), in Roussier, *Lettres du général Leclerc*, p. 229.

14. Jenson, *Beyond the Slave Narrative*, pp. 202–7.

15. Lacroix, *Mémoires pour servir à l'histoire de la révolution de Saint-Domingue*, Vol. 2, p. 226.

16. Leclerc to Bonaparte, 15 Vendémiaire, Year 11 (7 October 1802), in Roussier, *Lettres du général Leclerc*, p. 256.

17. Allix, 'Souvenirs militaires et politiques', pp. 64–5.

18. Madiou, *Histoire d'Haïti*, Vol. 2, p. 345. In Madiou's account, Christophe was stationed at St Michel rather than Petite Anse, but the two are immediately next to each other.

19. Ibid., p. 346.

20. Ibid.

21. 'Jakub Filip Kierzkowski: Recollections from Saint Domingue', in Jonathan North and Marek Tadeusz Łałowski, *War of Lost Hope: Polish Accounts of the Napoleonic Expedition to Saint Domingue, 1801 to 1804* (Jonathan North, 2017), pp. 34–5; Jan Pachonski and Reuel K. Wilson, *Poland's Caribbean Tragedy: A Study of Polish Legions in the Haitian War of Independence, 1802–1803* (New York: Columbia University Press, 1986), p. 99.

22. Saint-Rémy, *Pétion et Haïti*, Vol. 3, p. 116.

23. Girard, *The Slaves Who Defeated Napoleon*, p. 249.

24. Madiou, *Histoire d'Haïti*, Vol. 2, p. 399

25. Ibid., p. 400.

26. Ibid., p. 403; Vertus Saint-Louis, 'Sans-Souci et Darfour: Deux figures de l'Afrique dans l'histoire d'Haiti', in Bérard Cénatus et al. (eds.), *Haïti de la dictature à la démocratie?* (Montreal: Mémoire d'encrier, 2016), p. 93.

27. Christophe to Dessalines, 6 September 1805, Foyle Special Collections Library, King's College, University of London, FCDO2 FOL.F 1924 HEN (hereafter *Letterbook 1805–1806*).

28. Labelinaye to Rochambeau, 8 Pluviôse, Year 11 (28 January 1802), UFL Rochambeau Papers 1570.

29. *Affiches Américaines*, 18 Pluviôse, Year 11 (7 February 1803); Madiou, *Histoire d'Haïti*, Vol. 2, p. 404.

30. Madiou, *Histoire d'Haïti*, Vol. 2, p. 404.

31. Ibid.

32. Christophe, *Manifeste du Roi*, p. 11; Dubois, *Avengers of the New World*, pp. 292–3.

33. Pachonski and Wilson, *Poland's Caribbean Tragedy*, p. 124. The capture and interrogation of Montfort, one of Christophe's aides, revealed to the French that the rebels had been resupplied by a British ship.

34. Madiou, *Histoire d'Haïti*, Vol. 2, pp. 432–3; Girarmd, *The Slaves Who Defeated Napoleon*, p. 243.

35. For more on the semi-mythical figure of Catherine Flon and the oral histories surrounding the creation of the Haitian flag, see Nicole Willson, 'Unmaking the Tricolore: Catherine Flon, Material Testimony and Occluded Narratives of Female-Led Resistance in Haiti and the Haitian Dyaspora', *Slavery & Abolition*, vol. 41, no. 1 (2020), pp. 131–48.

36. Dessalines to Jefferson, 23 June 1803, in Thomas Jefferson, *The Papers of Thomas Jefferson*, Vol. 40: *4 March to 10 July 1803*, ed. Barbara B. Oberg (Princeton University Press, 2018), pp. 597–8; Hazareesingh, *Black Spartacus*, p. 3.

37. Cathcart to Nugent, 30 August 1803, National Library of Jamaica, Kingston (NLJ), MS 72 Box 2.

38. Walker to Admiral Duckworth, 9 September 1803, quoted in Thomas Southey, *Chronological History of the West Indies*, Vol. 3 (London: Longman, Rees, Orme, Brown, and Green, 1827), pp. 259–60.

39. Thomas Madiou, *Histoire d'Haïti*, Vol. 3: 1803–1807 (Port-au-Prince: J. Courtois, 1848), pp. 56–7.

40. *Gazette Officielle de Saint-Domingue*, 1 Prairial, Year 11 (21 May 1803); 17 Messidor, Year 11 (6 July 1803).

41. Le Glaunec, *The Cry of Vertières*, p. 43. Christophe's patrols also sought to prevent others supplying the city: several maroon bands were known to trade with the French, swapping food for ammunition.

42. Jean-Jacques Dessalines, *Journal de la campagne du nord*, 2 December 1803, in *Revue de la Société Haïtienne d'Histoire, de Géographie et de Géologie*, nos. 253–6 (2014), pp. 101–7

43. Girard, *The Slaves Who Defeated Napoleon*, pp. 309–10; Dessalines, *Journal de la campagne du nord*.

44. Southey, *Chronological History of the West Indies*, Vol. 3, pp. 252–3; 'Memoir of Ludwik Mateusz Dembowski' (1803) in North and Łałowski, *War of Lost Hope*, p. 48.

8. CITADEL OF FREEDOM

1. Gaffield, *The Haitian Declaration of Independence*, p. 246.

2. David Geggus, 'The Naming of Haiti', *New West Indian Guide/Nieuwe West-Indische Gids* vol. 71, nos. 1/2 (1997), pp. 43–68.

3. Quoted in David Geggus, *Haitian Revolutionary Studies* (Bloomington and Indianapolis: Indiana University Press, 2002), p. 208.

4. Louis Félix Boisrond-Tonnerre, *Mémoires pour servir à l'histoire d'Haïti* (Port-au-Prince: Imprimerie Centrale, 1804).

5. Quoted in Laurent Dubois and John Garrigus, *Slave Revolution in the Caribbean, 1789–1804: A Brief History with Documents* (New York: Bedford/St Martin's, 2006), pp. 188–91.

6. Julia Gaffield, *Haitian Connections in the Atlantic World: Recognition after Revolution* (Chapel Hill: University of North Carolina Press, 2015), p. 85; Madiou, *Histoire d'Haïti*, Vol. 3, p. 124.

7. Gonzalez, *Maroon Nation*, p. 93.

8. Dessalines' Order, 14 January 1804, is reprinted in Southey, *Chronological History of the West Indies*, Vol. 3, p. 292; Dessalines' Order, 20 January 1804, is translated by Julia Gaffield at https://haitidoi.com/2013/08/09/post-independence-labor-and-migration-restrictions/ (accessed 8 June 2021).

9. Cathcart to Christophe, 16 January 1804; Christophe to Cathcart, 11 February 1804: NLJ MS 72 Box 3 612.

10. Condy Raguet, 'Memoirs of Hayti … In a Series of Letters', *The Port Folio 2*, no. 1 (1809), Letter III, pp. 34–5.

11. Ibid., Letter IV, pp. 111–12.

12. Ibid., Letter IV, pp. 111–12, 114.

13. Ibid., Letter V, pp. 189–90.

14. *Blackwood's Magazine*, vol. 10 (1821), p. 549. The queen gave her account to an anonymous Royal Navy lieutenant who visited Sans Souci in 1819.

15. *Almanach Royal d'Hayti pour l'année bissextile 1814*, p. 5.

16. George Servant, 'Ferdinand Christophe, fils du roi d'Haïti, en France', *Revue de l'histoire des colonies françaises* no. 23 (1913), pp. 228–32; Deborah Jenson, 'From the Kidnapping(s) of the Louvertures to the Alleged Kidnapping of Aristide: Legacies of Slavery in the Post/Colonial World', *Yale French Studies* no. 107 (2005), pp. 162–86.

17. *Gazette Royal d'Hayti*, 10 October 1817. In the same year, Vastey also wrote of Ferdinand's 'melancholy death' in his *Political Remarks*, p. 14.

18. Gaffield, *Haitian Connections in the Atlantic World*, pp. 83–4.

19. Perkins to Duckworth, 17 March 1804, TNA ADM 1/254.

20. 'Report from Captain Micks, lately arrived at Charleston from Cape-François', *Evening Post (New York)*, 6 April 1804.

21. Raguet, 'Memoirs of Hayti' (1809), Letter VI, p. 418.

22. Ibid., Letter VIII, p. 492.

23. Ibid., Letter VIII, pp. 493–6. When Whitby gave his report on the affair in Jamaica, Admiral Duckworth reportedly reprimanded him thus: 'What! You young son of a b——, threaten to blow a town down, and not do it: G—d——you—You're a disgrace to his majesty's service—I'll report you to the lords of the admiralty, and you shall be tried and hanged, by G—.'

24. Madiou, *Histoire d'Haïti*, Vol. 3, p. 124; Raguet, 'Memoirs of Hayti' (1809), Letter VIII, pp. 493–6.

25. Madiou, *Histoire d'Haïti*, Vol. 3, p. 135.

26. Ibid., p. 137.

27. Ibid.

28. Dessalines' Proclamation, 28 April 1804, is reprinted in Southey, *Chronological History of the West Indies*, Vol. 3, pp. 295–8.

29. Quoted in Carlos Célius, 'Neo-Classicism and the Haitian Revolution', in David Geggus and Norman Fiering (eds.), *The World of the Haitian Revolution* (Bloomington and Indianopolis: Indiana University Press, 2009), p. 381.

30. Beaubrun Ardouin, *Etudes sur l'histoire d'Haïti*, Vol. 6 (Paris: Dezobry & E. Magdeleine, 1856), p. 109.

31. Peltier, *Trois mémoires remis à Lord Castlereagh*, October 1807, TNA WO 1/79.

32. Corneille Brelle would later prosper under Christophe's patronage. For Justamont in Cap-Haïtien, see *Gazette Politique et Commerciale d'Haïti*, 29 November 1804; as surgeon-general under Christophe, see Saint-Rémy, *Pétion et Haïti*, Vol. 4, p. 249.

33. R. P. Cabon, 'Les Religieuses du Cap à Saint-Domingue (suite et fin)', *Revue d'histoire de l'Amérique française* vol. 3, no. 3 (1949), pp. 402–22.

34. Raguet, 'Memoirs of Hayti' (1809), Letter VI, p. 327; Letter VIII, p. 212.

35. Girard, *The Slaves Who Defeated Napoleon*, p. 321.

36. 'Constitution impériale d'Haiti: Dispositions générales, article 28, 20 May 1805', in Louis-Joseph Janvier, *Les constitutions d'Haïti, 1801–1855* (Paris: C. Marpon et E. Flammarion, 1886), pp. 30–42.

37. For a complete list of the forts ordered by Dessalines, see 'Les Fortifications de Marchand-Dessalines', *Bulletin de l'ISPAN* no. 3 (August 2009).

38. Raguet, 'Memoirs of Hayti' (1809), Letter VI, pp. 415–16.

39. 'La Citadelle Henry: un monument qui le mît debout', *Bulletin de l'ISPAN* no. 28 (September 2011).

40. Christophe to Barré, 6 September 1805 (*Letterbook 1805–1806*).

41. Gauvin Bailey, *The Palace of Sans-Souci in Milot, Haiti, ca. 1806–1820: The Untold Story of the Potsdam of the Rainforest* (Berlin: Deutscher Kunstverlag, 2017), p. 59.

42. *Gazette Politique et Commerciale d'Haïti*, 15 November 1804.

43. Madiou, *Histoire d'Haïti*, Vol. 3, p. 185.

44. Condy Raguet, 'Memoirs of Hayti …In a Series of Letters', *The Port Folio 5*, no. 1 (1811), Letter XX, p. 409.

45. Madiou, *Histoire d'Haïti*, Vol. 3, pp. 169–70.

46. 'Coronation of Jacques I', *Caledonian Mercury*, 7 January 1805; Madiou, *Histoire d'Haïti*, Vol. 3, p. 174.

47. Dessalines to Bonaparte, 9 October 1804, Archives départementales de la Gironde, Bordeaux, Collection Marcel Chatillon 61 J 25.

48. Fernando Picó, *One Frenchman, Four Revolutions: General Ferrand and the Peoples of the Caribbean* (Princeton, NJ: Markus Wiener, 2011), pp. 38–40; Ardouin, *Etudes sur l'histoire d'Haïti*, Vol. 6, pp. 121–2.

49. Madiou, *Histoire d'Haïti*, Vol. 3, pp. 186–7.

50. Nugent to Camden, 12 October 1804, NLJ MS 72 Box 3 560; Nugent to Camden, 15 December 1804, NLJ MS 72 Box 3 511.

51. Christophe to Dessalines, 26 January 1805 (*Letterbook 1805–1806*).

52. Christophe to Raymond, 14 February 1805; Christophe to Romain, 14 February 1805; Christophe to Administrator at Cap-Haïtien, 16 February 1805; Christophe to Commandant de la place, Fort Liberté, 21 February 1805 (*Letterbook 1805–1806*).

53. Christophe to Dessalines, 13 February 1805 (*Letterbook 1805–1806*).

54. General Bazelais, 'Journal de campagne tenu pendant l'Expédition de Santo-Domingo, par le général de division H. Christophe', *Gazette Politique et Commerciale d'Haïti*, 13 June 1805.

55. Christophe to Taváres, 16 March 1805 (*Letterbook 1805–1806*). Haitian accounts Frenchify his name to 'Tabarre', 'Thabares', or similar.

56. Christophe to Dessalines, 13 March 1805 (*Letterbook 1805–1806*).

57. Ferrand to commander at Samaná, quoted in Picó, *One Frenchman, Four Revolutions*, p. 43.

58. Madiou, *Histoire d'Haïti*, Vol. 3, pp. 200–1.

59. Christophe to Dessalines, 24 March 1805 (*Letterbook 1805–1806*).

60. According to the official campaign diary by General Bazelais, the Haitians estimated that 4,000 French soldiers had been landed.

61. Bazelais, 'Journal de campagne tenu pendant l'Expédition de Santo-Domingo'.

62. Christophe to Commandant Achille, 2 April 1805; Christophe to Colonel Antoine, 2 April 1805; Christophe to Colonel Tiphaine, 27 March 1805 (*Letterbook 1805–1806*).

63. Henry Christophe, 'Journal de campagne tenu pendant l'Expédition de Santo-Domingo, par le général de division H. Christophe', *Gazette Politique et Commerciale d'Haïti*, 20 June 1805.

64. Circular to military commanders, 19 April 1805; Christophe to Gaston, 5 May 1805; Christophe to Joachim, 6 June 1805 (*Letterbook 1805–1806*.

65. Christophe to Admininstrator, 24 April 1805; Christophe to Joachim, 25 June 1805; Christophe to Tiphaine, 11 July 1805; all *Letterbook 1805–1806*).

66. 'La formidable artillerie de la Citadelle Henry', *Bulletin de l'ISPAN* no. 14 (July 2010).

67. Christophe to Dessalines, 16 June 1805 (*Letterbook 1805–1806*).

68. Constitution impériale d'Haïti, 20 May 1805.

69. Christophe to Dessalines, 15 June 1805 (*Letterbook 1805–1806*); Madiou, *Histoire d'Haïti*, Vol. 3, pp. 228–9.

70. Ardouin, *Etudes sur l'histoire d'Haïti*, Vol. 6, p. 103. Ardouin, whose writings are ardently anti-Christophe, concedes that Clerveaux may equally have died of natural causes.

71. 'Décret relatif à diverses promotions dans l'armée', 28 July 1805.

72. Christophe to Pourcely, 20 May 1805; Christophe to Dessalines, 22 May 1805 (*Letterbook 1805–1806*).

9. THE EMPIRE OF HAITI

1. Raguet, 'Memoirs of Hayti' (1811), Letter XVIII, p. 247; Christophe to Dessalines, 11 January 1806 (*Letterbook 1805–1806*).

2. Christophe to Guillemot, 24 July 1805 (*Letterbook 1805–1806*).

3. Gonzalez, *Maroon Nation*, p. 94.

4. Christophe to Capoix, 11 November 1805 (*Letterbook 1805–1806*). The area is now part of the Parque Nacional Monte Cristi in the Dominican Republic.

5. Gonzalez, *Maroon Nation*, p. 142; Christophe to Romain and Capoix, 21 November 1805 (*Letterbook 1805–1806*).

6. Christophe to Commissiare de l'etat civil du Limbe, 8 August 1806 (*Letterbook 1805–1806*).

7. Gonzalez, *Maroon Nation*, pp. 112, 140.

8. Ibid., pp. 114–18.

9. Jean-Claude Nouët, Claude Nicollier and Yves Nicollier (eds.), *La vie aventureuse de Norbert Thoret dit 'L'Americain'* (Paris: Editions du Port-au-Prince, 2013), pp. 59–63; Christophe to Dessalines, 9 April 1806 (*Letterbook 1805–1806*).

10. Christophe to Capoix, 15 December 1805 and 21 December 1805 (*Letterbook 1805–1806*); Gonzalez, *Maroon Nation*, p. 125.

11. Madiou, *Histoire d'Haïti*, Vol. 3, pp. 214, 229.

12. François Dalencour, *Biographie du général François Cappoix* (Port-au-Prince, 1957), pp. 161–4; Madiou, *Histoire d'Haïti*, Vol. 3, p. 317. Most accounts of Capoix's death have derived from the works of Thomas Madiou or Beaubrun Ardouin, but both give an incorrect date for his killing, of 8 and 19 October respectively.

13. Gonzalez, *Maroon Nation*, p. 92; Chelsea Stieber, *Haiti's Paper War: Post-Independence Writing, Civil War, and the Making of the Republic, 1804–1954* (New York University Press, 2020), p. 50.

14. Madiou, *Histoire d'Haïti*, Vol. 3, pp. 307–8, 309–10.

15. Christophe to Dessalines, 16 October 1806 (*Letterbook 1805–1806*).

16. Stieber, *Haiti's Paper War*, pp. 52–3.

17. Madiou, *Histoire d'Haïti*, Vol. 3, p. 316.

18. Ibid., pp. 324–5; Joan Dayan, *Haiti, History, and the Gods* (Berkeley: University of California Press, 1998), pp. 42–3.

19. Madiou, *Histoire d'Haïti*, Vol. 3, p. 335.

20. Ibid., pp. 333–4.

21. Stieber, *Haiti's Paper War*, pp. 54–5.

22. Christophe to Vernet, 19 October 1806 (*Letterbook 1805–1806*).

23. Madiou, *Histoire d'Haïti*, Vol. 3, pp. 295–6. It remains unclear how Geffrard died: varying accounts have him dying of an unexpected illness, from a stomach abscess caused by a fall from his horse, or of being poisoned on Dessalines' orders.

24. Christophe to Romain, 17 October 1806 (*Letterbook 1805–1806*).

25. Christophe to Vernet, 19 October 1806; Christophe to Romain, Brave and Dartiguenave, 19 October 1806; Christophe to Besse, 19 October 1806; Christophe to Toussaint, commandant at Saint-Marc, 19 October 1806 (*Letterbook 1805–1806*).

26. Christophe to Pétion, 19 October 1806 (*Letterbook 1805–1806*).

27. Christophe to Mme Dessalines, 21 October 1806 (*Letterbook 1805–1806*).

29. Pétion to Mme Dessalines, 19 October 1806, quoted in Madiou, *Histoire d'Haïti*, Vol. 3, pp. 326–7.

29. Christophe to Vernet, 22 October 1806 (*Letterbook 1805–1806*).

30. 'Adhésion des officiers du Nord à l'acte intitulé: *Résistance à l'oppression*, et à la nomination de Christophe', 23 October 1806, in A. Linstant-Pradine, *Recueil général des lois et actes du gouvernement d'Haïti*, Vol. 1: *1804–1808* (Paris: A. Durand, 1886), pp. 163–5.

31. Christophe to Pétion, 23 October 1806; Christophe to Gérin, 23 October 1806. Both quoted in Linstant-Pradine, *Recueil général des lois et actes*, Vol. 1, pp. 164–5; 163–4 respectively.

32. Madiou, *Histoire d'Haïti*, Vol. 3, pp. 346–8.

33. 'Adresse au peuple et à l'Armée d'Haïti', *Gazette Politique et Commerciale d'Haïti*, 20 November 1806.

34. *Gazette Politique et Commerciale d'Haïti*, 6 November 1806.

35. Madiou, *Histoire d'Haïti*, Vol. 3, p. 358.

36. Ibid., p. 360.

37. Ibid., pp. 360–3.

38. Ibid., pp. 366–70, 371.

39. Ibid., pp. 366–72, 373.

10. CIVIL WAR

1. Vastey, *An Essay on the Causes of the Revolution*, pp. 82–3.

2. Madiou, *Histoire d'Haïti*, Vol. 3, p. 375.

3. Ibid., p. 376.

4. Ibid., p. 378.

5. Ibid., p. 382.

6. Léon-François Hoffmann, 'An American Trader in Revolutionary Haiti: Simeon Johnson's Journal of 1807', *The Princeton University Library Chronicle* vol. 49, no. 2 (1988), pp. 182–99.

7. Madiou, *Histoire d'Haïti*, Vol. 3, p. 400.

8. Christophe Proclamation, 19 February 1807 (Cap-Haïtien, P. Roux, 1807).

9. Madiou, *Histoire d'Haïti*, Vol. 3, pp. 405–9.

10. Linstant-Pradine, *Recueil général des lois et actes*, Vol. 1, pp. 358–61.

11. Vastey, *An Essay on the Causes of the Revolution*, p. 72.

12. Madiou, *Histoire d'Haïti*, Vol. 3, pp. 420, 425; Gonzalez, *Maroon Nation*, pp. 125–6.

13. Madiou, *Histoire d'Haïti*, Vol. 3, pp. 436; Thomas Madiou, *Histoire d'Haïti*, Vol. 4: *1807–1811* (Port-au-Prince: H. Deschamps, 1987), pp. 9–14, 213–14.

14. Madiou, *Histoire d'Haïti*, Vol. 4, pp. 18–28, 65–9; Vol. 3, pp. 436–7.

15. Juste Chanlatte, 'Quelques réflexions sur le prétendu Sénat du Port-au-Prince', *Gazette Officielle de l'Etat d'Hayti*, 2 July 1807 (serialised over five issues). Chanlatte's pen was so valued that after the killing of Dessalines, Pétion tried unsuccessfully to woo him to his side.

16. Rouanez to Peltier, 1 April 1807, TNA WO 1/79. Pétion had also recognised Peltier's skills and asked him to serve at his side in Port-au-Prince.

17. Christophe to Richardson, 13 July 1807, TNA WO 1/79.

18. *Public Ledger & Daily Advertiser*, 1 May 1816.

19. Peltier to Castlereagh, 5 October 1807; Richardson to Castlereagh, 15 October 1807: TNA WO 1/79.

20. Peltier to Castlereagh, 28 October 1807; Peltier to Castlereagh, *Trois mémoires*, October 1807: TNA WO 1/79. For a full discussion of the treaty proposal, see Gaffield, *Haitian Connections in the Atlantic World*, pp. 170–4.

21. On the basis of his order for buttons, Sutherland 'could not mark the number [of soldiers] more than twenty thousand'. Sutherland to Shee, 12 October 1806, TNA WO 1/75.

22. Dacres to Admiralty, 16 August 1807, TNA CO 137/120.

23. 'A Biographical Sketch of Thomas Goodall, Esq', *The European Magazine*, vol. 53 (May 1808), pp. 323–8; Letter of marque, 24 April 1806, TNA ADM 7/649.

24. *Hampshire Telegraph*, 9 November 1807.

25. 'Account by Captain Goodall', *Dublin Evening Post*, 28 April 1808. Henry Christophe, 'Order of the Day', 11 February 1807, reprinted in the *Oxford University and City Herald*, 23 April 1808. Henry Christophe to Thomas Goodall, 6 February 1808, reprinted in *The European Magazine*, vol. 53 (May 1808), p. 326.

26. One of Goodall's crew, in a poetic memoir of his service in Haiti, noted the significance of one of these hymns to the Haitians in particular: 'Rule Britannia, next they played/ Of Slav'ry now no more afraid.' See Thomas Herring, *Reminiscences of Haiti, in the years 1807–8–9, during the government of the celebrated negro-chief Christophe, afterward Henry the First, King of Haiti, and that of his no-less celebrated and formidable Rival, Pétion, President of Port-au-Prince* (Portsmouth, 1833).

27. *Morning Advertiser*, 16 April 1808.

28. Burk, *The Hurricane*, p. 57.

29. *Morning Chronicle*, 25 April 1808 and 17 May 1808.

30. *The European Magazine*, vol. 53 (May 1808), pp. 323–8. It is not known whether the hemp was ever cultivated, but just over a century later the area around Fort Liberté become one of the biggest suppliers of sisal for ropemaking to the US Navy.

31. Christophe to Goodall, 4 October 1808, NLJ MS 36a.

32. Cole, *Christophe: King of Haiti*, p. 168.

33. Ibid., p. 172.

34. Ibid., p. 169.

35. Ibid., p. 175.

36. *Gazette Officielle de l'Etat d'Hayti*, 23 November 1809.

37. Christophe, 'Address to the Merchants of the United States', 2 July 1809, reprinted in *The Republican Watch-Tower* (New York), 28 July 1809.

38. Christophe to Joseph Bunel, 25 November 1809, in Madiou, *Histoire d'Haïti*, Vol. 4, pp. 245–6; John Graham to James Madison, 11 September 1809, Founders Online, https://founders.archives.gov/documents/Madison/03–01–02–0410 (accessed 25 April 2022).

39. Christophe to Someruelos, 1 November 1808, in Ada Ferrer, *Freedom's Mirror: Cuba and Haiti in the Age of Revolution* (Cambridge University Press, 2014), p. 256.

40. Anne Eller, '"All would be equal in the effort": Santo Domingo's "Italian Revolution," Independence, and Haiti, 1809–1822', *Journal of Early American History* vol. 1, no. 2 (2011), pp. 105–41; *Caledonian Mercury*, 8 April 1809.

41. Taváres to Christophe, 30 December 1808, in *Caledonian Mercury*, 8 April 1809.

42. Junta to Someruelos, 18 February 1809, in Ferrer, *Freedom's Mirror*, pp. 258–9.

43. Christophe, 1 January 1809, quoted in *Caledonian Mercury*, 8 April 1809.

44. Known today as the Coidavid Battery, this immense structure remains the Citadelle's most recognisable feature. For the different stages of construction, see Jean-Hérold Pérard, *La Citadelle restaurée: Le livre qui invite à (re)visiter la Citadelle Laferrière* (Port-au-Prince, 2010), pp. 86–7.

45. *Gazette Officielle de l'Etat d'Hayti*, 12 October 1809; Cole, *Christophe: King of Haiti*, p. 174; Burk, *The Hurricane*, p. 57. I discuss the construction of Sans Souci in more detail in Chapter 12 of this volume.

46. Madiou, *Histoire d'Haïti*, Vol. 4, pp. 150–5; 'Report made by Brigadier General Almanjor, acting as Chief Officer of the Staff of the Army, respecting the actions of the said Army, against the Insurgents at Port-au-Prince', 25 November 1808, *Public Ledger & Daily Advertiser*, 8 April 1809.

47. Madiou, *Histoire d'Haïti*, Vol. 4, p. 227.

48. Ibid., pp. 228–33. In his account, Madiou misspells Sourde as 'Sonde'.

49. Ibid., pp. 235–6.

50. Ibid.

51. Ibid.

52. Peltier to Lord Liverpool, 24 June 1810, British Library, London, BL Add MS 38245.

53. Captain Woolridge to Admiral Rowley, 14 May 1810, TNA WO 1/75.

54. Madiou, *Histoire d'Haïti*, Vol. 4, pp. 276–9.

55. Vastey, *An Essay on the Causes of the Revolution*, pp. 82–3.

56. Madiou, *Histoire d'Haïti*, Vol. 4, pp. 286–7.

57. Christophe, 'Proclamation to the land and naval armaments of the State of Hayti', 8 October 1810, in Saunders, *Haytian Papers*, pp. 99–107.

58. Madiou, *Histoire d'Haïti*, Vol. 4, pp. 311–17.

59. The three envoys were Baubert, a member of the old free coloured party; Bortrand Lemoine, who had taken part in the 1806 constitutional assembly; and Louis Dessalines, a nephew of the former emperor. See ibid., p. 323.

60. Ibid., p. 325.

11. BIRTH OF A KINGDOM

1. After Christophe's death, the town's name reverted to Fort Liberté, which it holds today.

2. Saunders, *Haytian Papers*, pp. 116–17.

3. See, for example, *Gazette Officielle de l'Etat d'Hayti*, 12 October 1809. The title was also applied to Christophe's wife.

4. *Gazette Officielle de l'Etat d'Hayti*, 3 January 1811; Lloyds List, 14 April 1811.

5. Sutherland to Scott, 18 December 1810, TNA WO 1/76 f33–34; Rowley to Montresor, 19 January 1811, TNA WO 1/76 f65–67.

6. Rouanez to Rowley, 16 March 1811, TNA WO 1/76 f215–217.

7. Pétion to the Senate, 10 March 1811. Quoted in A. Linstant-Pradine, *Recueil général des lois et actes du gouvernement d'Haïti*, Vol. 2: *1809–1817* (Paris: A. Durand, 1860), p. 79.

8. Saunders, *Haytian Papers*, p. 124.

9. Ibid., p. 120–1.

10. Ibid. p. 123.

11. Ibid., p. 124.

12. Ibid., pp. 142–3.

13. Ibid., p. 147.

14. Ibid., pp. 146–50.

15. Julien Prévost, *Relation des glorieux événemens qui ont porté Leurs Majestés Royales sur le trône d'Hayti* (Cap Henry: P. Roux, 1811), p. xvi.

16. Edit du Roi, 'Portant Création des Princes, Ducs, Comtes, Barons et Chevaliers du Royaume', 8 April 1811, in Prévost, *Relation des glorieux événemens*, p. 68.

17. Beaubrun Ardouin, *Etudes sur l'histoire d'Haïti*, Vol. 7 (Paris: Chez l'auteur, 1856), p. 410. It is not known if the Pontiff replied.

18. Clive Cheesman (ed.), *The Armorial of Haiti: Symbols of Nobility in the Reign of Henry Christophe* (London: The College of Arms, 2007), p. 18.

19. 'Ordonnance du roi, qui détermine le Grand Costume de la Noblesse', 12 April 1811, in Prévost, *Relation des glorieux événemens*, pp. 113–14.

20. Prévost, *Relation des glorieux événemens*, pp. 117–18.

21. Ibid., pp. 128–31.

22. *Cobbett's Weekly Register*, 21 September 1811. The correspondent was an unnamed Royal Navy officer who attended the coronation.

23. *Hampshire Telegraph*, 9 November 1807. The coach's decoration had also included an African man holding a Phrygian cap, but this republican symbolism would surely have been removed for the coronation.

24. Prévost, *Relation des glorieux événemens*, p. 113.

25. See Louis-Philippe de Ségur, *Procès verbal de la cérémonie du sacre et du couronnement de*

LL. MM. l'empereur Napoléon et l'impératrice Joséphine (Paris: Imprimerie Impériale, 1805), pp. 164–81.

26. With thanks to Llewelyn Morgan for the translation from the original Latin.

27. Prévost, *Relation des glorieux événemens*, p. 155.

28. Composed by André Grétry in 1769, it was adopted by the Bourbons as a loyalist air after the restoration of the French monarchy.

29. Prévost, *Relation des glorieux événemens*, p. 157; *Cobbett's Weekly Register*, 21 September 1811.

30. *Cobbett's Weekly Register*, 21 September 1811.

31. Prévost, *Relation des glorieux événemens*, p. 159. Translation by Nathan Dize.

12. SANS SOUCI

1. Prévost, *Relation des glorieux événemens*, p. 192.

2. Bailey, *The Palace of Sans-Souci*, pp. 19, 87. The White House, built for US President John Adams fewer than ten years earlier, had a modest eleven bays compared to Sans Souci's twenty-three.

3. Saunders, *Haytian Papers*, p. 83.

4. Sybille Fischer, *Modernity Disavowed: Haiti and the Cultures of Slavery in the Age of Revolution* (Durham, NC: Duke University Press, 2004), p. 257; Danilo de los Santos, *Memoria de la Pintura Dominicana: Raíces e impulso nacional*, Vol. 1 (Santo Domingo: Grupo León Jimenes, 2003), p. 131; Leconte, Henri Christophe dans l'histoire d'Haïti, p. 340.

5. After Christophe's death the arms were stolen and taken to Boston where they were briefly put on public display, along with 'a portrait, in oil, of his Majesty Christophe dressed in full uniform'. Their whereabouts today are unknown. *Columbian Centinel*, 21 November 1821.

6. Saunders, *Haytian Papers*, p. 83.

7. J. Cameron Monroe, 'New Light from Haiti's Royal Past: Recent Archaeological Excavations in the Palace of Sans-Souci, Milot', *Journal of Haitian Studies*, vol. 23, no. 2 (2017), pp. 5–31.

8. Jonathan Brown, *The History and Present Condition of St. Domingo*, Vol. 2 (Philadelphia: William Marshall & Co., 1837), p. 216; Michel-Rolph Trouillot, Silencing the Past: Power and the Production of History (Boston, MA: Beacon Press, 1995), pp. 44, 59–61; Christophe to Dessalines, 6 September 1805 (Letterbook 1805–1806).

9. Bailey, *The Palace of Sans-Souci*, pp. 41–5, Cheesman, The Armorial of Haiti, p. 140.

10. *Almanach Royal d'Hayti pour l'année bissextile 1815, Douzième de l'indépendance, et la quatrième du règne de sa majesté* (Cap Henry: P. Roux, 1815), p. 10.

11. Cheesman, *The Armorial of Haiti*, p. 140; Simpson and Cinéas, 'Folk Tales of Haitian Heroes', pp. 176–85. Christophe's first biographer, Vergniaud Leconte, named Chéri Warloppe as the principal architect of Sans Souci, but the kingdom's almanacs consistently list him as a mechanic (dealing with waterways) rather than under the category of royal architect.

12. Bailey, *The Palace of Sans-Souci*, pp. 117, 145.

13. Vastey, *An Essay on the Causes of the Revolution*, p. 137.

14. Henock Trouillot, *Le gouvernement du roi Henri Christophe* (Port-au-Prince: Imprimerie Centrale, 1972), p. 35.

15. Personal fieldwork in Milot by the author.

16. Ferrer, *Freedom's Mirror*, pp. 260–2; Gazette Royal d'Hayti, 10 October 1817; Gazette Officielle de l'Etat d'Hayti, 3 January 1811.

17. Crystal Nicole Eddins, *African Diaspora Collective Action: Rituals, Runaways, and the Haitian Revolution*, PhD thesis, Michigan State University (2017), pp. 112–13.

18. H. Trouillot, Le gouvernement du roi Henri Christophe, pp. 61–2; Gaspard Théodore Mollien, *Haïti ou Saint-Domingue*, Vol. 2 (Paris: L'Harmattan, 2006), p. 166. Mollien quotes the memoir of Charles-Pierre, Comte du Terrier-Rouge under Christophe, the location of which is unknown.

19. 'Discours adressé au Roi par le Conseil Privé, en presentant à la santion de Sa Majesté les Lois qui composent le Code Henry', *Code Henry* (Cap Henry: P. Roux, 1812), p. i.

20. Vastey, *An Essay on the Causes of the Revolution*, p. 115.

21. 'Loi concernant la Culture', *Code Henry*, pp. 1–2.

22. Code Henry clauses.

23. Quoted in Daut, *Baron de Vastey*, pp. 82–3.

24. Lancaster Gazette, 21 December 1811; *The Gentleman's Magazine* vol. 81 (1811), p. 478.

25. Linstant-Pradine, *Recueil général des lois et actes*, Vol. 1, pp. 100–5.

26. Thomas Madiou, *Histoire d'Haïti*, Vol. 5: 1811–1818 (Port-au-Prince: H. Deschamps, 1988), pp. 12–30.

27. Henry Christophe, 'Aux Habitans du Sud et de partie de l'Ouest du Royaume', 4 September 1811 (Cap Henry: P. Roux, 1811).

28. Madiou, *Histoire d'Haïti*, Vol. 5, pp. 32, 39, 42.

29. Ibid., p. 112. Madiou himself casts doubt on the story, noting that Christophe actually suppressed Vodou during his rule; but having just spent several pages denouncing the religion for being anti-Christian, he found the story of the cross-dressing priestly spy too good to pass up.

30. Ibid., pp. 56–7.

31. Ibid., pp. 58–9.

32. Yeo to Stirling, 5 February 1812, TNA ADM 1/263.

33. Ibid.

34. Prévost to Stirling, 13 February 1812, TNA WO 1/77. Prévost appears to have been unaware that only the *Améthyste/Heureuse Réunion* had been taken to Jamaica, and requested that the British return all three ships that had mutinied.

35. Pétion to Stirling, 4 February 1812, TNA WO 1/77; Hugh McLeod et al. to Stirling, 10 February 1812, TNA WO 1/77.

36. Stirling to Croker, 14 February 1812, TNA WO 1/77; Stirling to Pétion, 20 February 1812, TNA WO 1/77; Stirling to Christophe, 20 February 1812, TNA WO 1/77.

37. Vastey, *An Essay on the Causes of the Revolution*, pp. 122–7. Although Bunel remained in the USA, his wife Marie had returned alone to settle in Cap Henry in late 1810, and was still recorded as a resident there in 1812.

38. Ibid., pp. 128–9.

39. Henry Christophe, 'Proclamation', 8 March 1812, quoted in Madiou, *Histoire d'Haïti*, Vol. 5, pp. 66–8.

40. Madiou, *Histoire d'Haïti*, Vol. 5, pp. 98–9; 'Extract of a letter from an American gentleman in Port-au-Prince', *New York Herald*, 27 May 1812.

41. Madiou, *Histoire d'Haïti*, Vol. 5, pp. 118–21.

42. 'Extract of a letter from an American gentleman in Port-au-Prince'; Linstant-Pradine, *Recueil général des lois et actes*, Vol. 2, p. 128; Madiou, *Histoire d'Haïti*, Vol. 5, p. 133.

43. Madiou, *Histoire d'Haïti*, Vol. 5, p. 133.

44. Ibid., pp. 141–3.

45. Stirling to Croker, 17 May 1812, TNA WO 1/77.

46. Madiou, *Histoire d'Haïti*, Vol. 5, pp. 148–9; Vastey, *An Essay on the Causes of the Revolution*, p. 134.

47. Davies to Christophe, 14 June 1812, TNA WO 1/77.

13. FRENCH PLOTS

1. Madiou, *Histoire d'Haïti*, Vol. 5, p. 220.

2. Henry Christophe, *Règlement pour les deuils de cour* (Cap Henry: P. Roux, 20 January 1813).

3. Madiou, *Histoire d'Haïti*, Vol. 5, pp. 214–16; S. Rouzier, *Dictionnaire géographique et adminis-tratif universel d'Haïti*, Vol. 4 (Port-au-Prince: Charles Blot, 1892), pp. 235–6.

4. Stirling to Croker, 23 May 1813, TNA ADM 1/264.

5. *Gazette Royale d'Hayti*, 26 July 1813.

6. Christophe to Victor-Henry, 17 October 1813, in Griggs and Prator, *Henri Christophe and Thomas Clarkson*, p. 88.

7. Christophe to Victor-Henry, 19 August 1813, in Griggs and Prator, *Henri Christophe and Thomas Clarkson*, p. 87.

8. 'Letter concerning Hayti', *Blackwood's Magazine*, vol. 4 (1818), p. 132.

9. Quoted in Daut, *Baron de Vastey*, p. 53.

10. *Gazette Royale d'Hayti*, 5 January 1815. The entire issue containing Christophe's speech was also reprinted in translation in the British press. See, for example, *The Leicester Chronicle*, 8 October 1814.

11. *Gazette Royale d'Hayti*, 26 January 1815, quoted in *The Leicester Chronicle*, 8 October 1814.

12. Ibid.; Madiou, *Histoire d'Haïti*, Vol. 5, pp. 221–2.

13. Prévost to Peltier, 19 June 1814, quoted in James Barskett, *History of the Island of St. Domingo, from its First Discovery by Columbus to the Present Period* (New York: Mahlon Day, 1824), pp. 251–3.

14. *Gazette Royale d'Hayti*, 16 August 1814.

15. Friedemann Pestel, 'The Impossible Ancien Régime Colonial: Postcolonial Haiti and the Perils of the French Restoration', *Journal of Modern European History* vol. 15, no. 2 (2017), pp. 261–79.

16. Quoted in Stieber, *Haiti's Paper War:*, p. 74.

17. Lavaysse to Christophe, 1 October 1814, quoted in Vastey, *An Essay on the Causes of the Revolution*, appendix F, document 2.

18. Vastey, *An Essay on the Causes of the Revolution*, p. 141.

19. Ibid., p. 142.

20. Ibid.

21. 'Address of the General Council of the Nation to the King, on the arrival of the French emissaries, Dauxion Lavaysse, Médina, and Dravermann, with his Majesty's reply', quoted in Vastey, *An Essay on the Causes of the Revolution*, appendix F, document 4.

22. Vastey, *An Essay on the Causes of the Revolution*, p. 139; Stieber, *Haiti's Paper War*, p. 74.

23. *Gazette Royale d'Hayti*, 19 November 1814, quoted in Vastey, *The Colonial System Unveiled*, pp. 55.

24. Quoted in Daut, *Baron de Vastey*, p. 4.

25. Vastey, *The Colonial System Unveiled*, p. 123. To counter the contradictions of European Enlightenment thinking, the leading Vastey scholar, Marlene Daut, has suggested the term 'Black Atlantic Humanism' to better describe his writing.

26. *Le Télégraphe*, 6 November 1814 and 20 November 1814.

27. Quoted in Vastey, *The Colonial System Unveiled*, p. 61.

28. Vastey, *An Essay on the Causes of the Revolution*, appendix B, document 9.

29. *Gazette Royale d'Hayti*, 17 April 1815.

30. Henry Christophe, *Plan générale de défense du Royaume*, 20 November 1814; Vastey, *An Essay on the Causes of the Revolution*, p. 187.

31. Vastey, *An Essay on the Causes of the Revolution*, p. 149.

32. Beaubrun Ardouin, *Etudes sur l'histoire d'Haïti*, Vol. 8 (Paris: Chez l'auteur, 1858), p. 140.

33. Pétion to Prévost, 10 February 1815, in Linstant-Pradine, *Recueil général des lois et actes*, Vol. 2, pp. 308–15.

34. Quoted in Simon Burrows, *French Exile Journalism and European Politics, 1792–1814* (London: Royal Historical Society, 2000), pp. 33–4.

35. Ibid., p. 33.

36. Lavaysse to the Minster of Marine, 28 February 1815, quoted in Vastey, *The Colonial System Unveiled*, p. 55.

37. Alyssa Sepinwall, *The Abbe Gregoire and the French Revolution: The Making of Modern Universalism* (Berkeley: University of California Press, 2005), p. 286.

38. Ibid., p. 288.

39. R. I. and S. Wilberforce, *The Life of William Wilberforce*, Vol. 4, pp. 227–8.

40. Madiou, *Histoire d'Haïti*, Vol. 5, pp. 315–16; Pétion to Wilberforce, 12 December 1815, NLJ MS 692.

41. R. I. and S. Wilberforce, *The Life of William Wilberforce*, Vol. 4, p. 335.

42. Quoted in ibid., p. 354.

14. THE PRICE OF SUGAR

1. *Gazette Royale d'Hayti*, 15 April 1815. The Haitian account of the tour rendered the name of the ship *Tanais* as '*Athénaïs*', perhaps to suggest a subtle British tribute to Christophe's youngest daughter. My thanks to Jacqueline Reiter for helping uncover its real name.

2. *Morning Chronicle*, 25 February 1815; Limonade to Rainsford, 19 July 1815, quoted in *Morning Herald*, 19 March 1817.

3. Prévost to Rainsford, 19 July 1815, quoted in *Morning Herald*, 19 March 1817.

4. Tabitha McIntosh and Grégory Pierrot, 'Capturing the Likeness of Henry I of Haiti (1805–1822)', *Atlantic Studies* vol. 14, no. 2 (2016), pp. 127–51, doi:10.1080/14788810.2016.1203214.

5. *Morning Chronicle*, 31 October 1815; B. Sutherland to Thomas Clarkson, 22 November 1821, in Griggs and Prator, *Henri Christophe and Thomas Clarkson*, p. 261.

6. *Morning Chronicle*, 1 November 1815.

7. *Morning Chronicle*, 1 November 1815; *Evening Mail*, 4 February 1818.

8. *Bury & Norwich Post*, 15 November 1815; *Sussex Advertiser*, 13 November 1815; *Dublin Evening Post*, 16 November 1815.

9. *Gazette Royale d'Hayti*, 15 April 1815.

10. Arthur O. White, 'Prince Saunders: An Instance of Social Mobility Among Antebellum New England Blacks', *The Journal of Negro History* vol. 60, no. 4 (1975), pp. 526–35.

11. Joseph Farington, *The Farington Diary*, vol. 8 (London: Hutchinson & Co., 1928), p. 88; Charles Robert Leslie, *Autobiographical Recollections* (London: John Murray, 1860), p. 163; John Quincy Adams, *Memoirs of John Quincy Adams, comprising portions of his diary from 1795 to 1848*, Vol. 3, ed. Charles Francis Adams (Philadelphia: J. Lippincott & Co., 1874), pp. 370, 385.

12. Christophe to Moore, 5 February 1816, reprinted in *Hampshire Chronicle*, 8 October 1816.

13. *Gazette Royale d'Hayti*, 6 February 1816; *Boston Patriot*, 8 July 1816.

14. Wilson, 'Unpublished Memoir'; Harvey, *Sketches of Hayti*, p. 338.

15. Christophe to Comte de la Taste, 11 December 1817, NLJ MS36–11.

16. Baron de Charrier to William Crowther, 18 March 1816; BPL, MS Haiti 71–32. In a letter

to Thomas Clarkson in 1821, William Wilson estimated that 300 gourdes was worth around 60 guineas.

17. *Morning Chronicle*, 27 February 1821; Henry Christophe, *Ordonnance du Roi, Concernant les Douanes et Tarif des Droits d'Entrée et de Sortie pour le Commerce étrange*, 20 March 1817.

18. *Evening Mail*, 4 February 1818; *Morning Chronicle*, 27 February 1821.

19. *Gazette Royale d'Hayti*, 15 April 1815.

20. Schomburg Ledger, Schomburg Center, Kurt Fisher Haitian collection (additions) Sc MG 683 (b.2f.2).

21. William Wilson to Thomas Clarkson, 16 September 1827, BL MSS 41,266; 'Loi concernant la Culture', *Code Henry*, paragraphs 60–71.

22. Schomburg Ledger; *Almanach Royal d'Hayti pour l'année bissextile 1816, Treizième de l'indépendance, et la cinquième du règne de sa majesté* (Cap Henry: P. Roux, 1816).

23. Schomburg Ledger; *Almanach Royal d'Hayti pour l'année bissextile 1816*.

24. Schomburg Ledger; Madiou, *Histoire d'Haïti*, Vol. 5, pp. 343–4.

25. Saunders, *Haytian Papers*, pp. i–vi.

26. Quoted in White, 'Prince Saunders', pp. 526–35.

27. William Wilson to Thomas Clarkson, 16 September 1827, BL MSS 41, 266.

28. Madiou, *Histoire d'Haïti*, Vol. 5, p. 319.

29. Saunders, *Haytian Papers*, p. 203; Madiou, *Histoire d'Haïti*, Vol. 5, p. 349.

30. *Gazette Royale d'Hayti*, 23 July 1816; 'Madame Christophe', *The New Monthly Magazine and Literary Journal*, vol. 1 (1828), p. 483.

31. *Gazette Royale d'Hayti*, 21 August 1816.

32. Baron de Vastey, *Relation de la Fête de S. M. la Reine d'Hayti, des Actes de Gouvernement qui ont eu lieu durant cet Événement, et de tout ce qui s'est passé à l'occasion de cette Fête* (Cap Henry: P. Roux, 1816), p. 9.

33. *Gazette Royale d'Hayti*, 22 August 1816.

34. Ibid.

35. *Gazette Royale d'Hayti*, 24 and 26 August 1816.

36. Vastey, *An Essay on the Causes of the Revolution*, p. 206.

37. *Gazette Royale d'Hayti*, 26 August 1816; Madiou, *Histoire d'Haïti*, Vol. 5, pp. 363–4.

15. YOUR MAJESTY'S FRIENDS

1. L. Cérisier Fils, *Biographie de Pétion* (Port-au-Prince: T. Bouchereau, 1842), pp. 10–11.

2. Vastey, *An Essay on the Causes of the Revolution*, p. 232.

3. Ibid., appendix F, no. 9.

4. 'Declaration of the King', 20 November 1816, quoted in Vastey, *An Essay on the Causes of the Revolution*, appendix F, no. 1.

5. Saunders, *Haytian Papers*, p. iii.

6. Ibid., pp. i–vi.

7. R. I. and S. Wilberforce, *The Life of William Wilberforce*, Vol. 4, p. 356; Farington, *The Farington Diary*, Vol. 8, pp. 80, 88.

8. *Almanach Royal d'Hayti pour l'année bissextile 1817, Quatorzième de l'indépendance, et la sixième du règne de sa majesté* (Cap Henry: P. Roux, 1817); Madiou, *Histoire d'Haïti*, Vol. 5, p. 348. According to Madiou, Evans' letter of appointment from Christophe stipulated that he was to be paid 400 gourdes a month, or 25,000 francs per year.

9. Rosalie Smith McCrea, 'Portrait Mythology? Representing the "Black Jacobin": Henri Christophe in the British Grand Manner', *The British Art Journal* vol. 6, no. 2 (2005), pp. 66–70.

10. *New Monthly Magazine*, 1 July 1818.

11. *Yorkshire Gazette*, 25 August 1821; McIntosh and Pierrot, 'Capturing the likeness of Henry I of Haiti'.

12. This painting was sold for $4,200 by Christie's Auction House in New York on 27 January 1993. Its current whereabouts are unknown.

13. Edgar La Selve, *Le pays des nègres: Voyage à Haïti* (Paris: Hachette et Cie, 1881), pp. 22, 44. La Selve records seeing paintings of Cap Henry by Numa Desroches showing buildings that were later destroyed in Haiti's 1842 earthquake.

14. The painting is owned by Bibliothèque de l'Ecole des frères de Saint Louis de Gonzague in Port-au-Prince. Following a crowdfunding drive in 2018 by the Toussaint Louverture Cultural Foundation, it was restored by the conservator Franck Louissaint in his studio at Université Quisqueya. A second copy of the painting was sold to an American collector named Harry Bull in 1936, when it was described as one of three views of Sans Souci. It was subsequently owned by the New York art dealer André Wauters, and was displayed at the United Nations and the Brooklyn Museum in 1978. It was sold in 1986 and its current whereabouts are unknown. My thanks to Barnaby Wauters for sharing his father's papers about the painting with me.

15. Griggs and Prator, *Henri Christophe and Thomas Clarkson*, p. 63.

16. Christophe to Clarkson, 5 February 1816, in Griggs and Prator, *Henri Christophe and Thomas Clarkson*, pp. 91–3.

17. Ibid.

18. Griggs and Prator, *Henri Christophe and Thomas Clarkson*, pp. 97–8; Madiou, *Histoire d'Haïti*, Vol. 5, p. 348.

19. *Almanach Royal d'Hayti pour l'année bissextile 1818, Quinzième de l'indépendance, et la troisième du règne de sa majesté* (Sans Souci: Imprimerie Royale, 1818).

20. Harvey, *Sketches of Hayti*, p. 203.

21. *Gazette Royal d'Hayti*, 28 December 1819; Henry Christophe, 'Ordonnance', 1 January 1819,

in Griggs and Prator, *Henri Christophe and Thomas Clarkson*, pp. 261–7; Thomas Gulliver, 'Quarterly Report of the State of the School at Cap Henry, for the Period commencing 1st Octob. 1817 & ending 1st Jan. 1817', Zachary Macaulay Papers, Huntington Library, San Marino, MY303, Box 5, Folder 27.

22. Clarkson to Christophe, 25 January 1820; William Wilson to his father, 1 October 1820: both in Griggs and Prator, *Henri Christophe and Thomas Clarkson*, pp. 186, 209. See also Wilson, 'Unpublished Memoir'.

23. The teachers' memoir is reprinted in Harvey, *Sketches of Hayti*, pp. 226–32. Sadly, their names were not recorded, nor are they listed in any of the royal almanacs.

24. Translation of Christophe's Independence Day address by William Hamilton sent to Zachary Macaulay, 4 January 1818, Zachary Macaulay Papers, MY303, Box 5, Folder 27.

25. Clarkson to Christophe, 4 May 1816; Christophe to Clarkson 18 November 1816: both in Griggs and Prator, *Henri Christophe and Thomas Clarkson*, pp. 94–6, 103.

26. Christophe to Wilberforce, 18 November 1816, in Robert Isaac and Samuel Wilberforce (eds.), *The Correspondence of William Wilberforce*, Vol. 1 (Philadelphia: H. Perkins, 1841), pp. 262–6.

27. R. I. and S. Wilberforce, *The Life of William Wilberforce*, Vol. 4, p. 355; Wilberforce to Christophe, 8 October 1818, in R. I. and S. Wilberforce, *The Correspondence of William Wilberforce*, Vol. 1, pp. 262–6.

28. Limonade to Teignmouth, 18 November 1816 and 2 April 1817, British and Foreign Bible Society Collection, Cambridge University Library, BSAX/1.

29. Christophe to Clarkson, 26 April 1818, in Griggs and Prator, *Henri Christophe and Thomas Clarkson*, pp. 105–6.

30. Christophe to Clarkson, 20 March 1819, in Griggs and Prator, *Henri Christophe and Thomas Clarkson*, p. 128.

31. Daut, *Baron de Vastey*, p. 63.

32. Ada Ferrer, 'Haiti, Free Soil, and Antislavery in the Revolutionary Atlantic', *The American Historical Review*, vol. 117, no. 1 (2012), pp. 40–66.

33. Daut, *Baron de Vastey*, p. 70.

34. Ibid., pp. 77–8.

35. William Hamilton to Zachary Macaulay, 4 January 1818, Zachary Macaulay Papers, MY303.

36. When Hamilton sent his translation of Christophe's 1818 Independence Day address to Zachary Macaulay, he commented that 'the illness of Baron de Vastey has deprived the Proclamation of this year of half its beauties—it is I am sorry to say a tame and spineless performance. I have done my best to enliven it in translation, but my ability was far from proportional to my wish. However Baron Dupuy is well satisfied with it and had directed me to furnish 2 copies of it for publication in America.' Zachary Macaulay Papers, MY303, Box 5, Folder 27.

37. *Almanach Royal d'Hayti pour l'année bissextile 1820, Dix-septième de l'indépendance, et la neuvième du règne de sa majesté* (Sans Souci: Imprimerie Royale, 1820); Madiou, *Histoire d'Haïti*, Vol. 5, p. 348.

38. Duncan Stewart to Thomas Clarkson, 4 December 1819, in Griggs and Prator, *Henri Christophe and Thomas Clarkson*, pp. 183–5.

39. 'Iphigenia, Port Royal, June 6, 1819', *Blackwood's Magazine* vol. 10 (1821), p. 549.

40. 'Letter concerning Hayti', p. 134.

41. Madiou, *Histoire d'Haïti*, Vol. 5, pp. 418–19; Hélène Maspero-Clerc, *Un journaliste contre-révolutionnaire: Jean-Gabriel Peltier (1760–1825)* (Paris: Société des études Robespierristes, 1973), p. 244; *Morning Post*, 18 March 1819; Jean-Gabriel Peltier to William Croker, 19 March 1819, John Wilson Croker Papers, David M. Rubenstein Rare Book & Manuscript Library, Duke University, Durham, NC, RL.00271.

16. THE KINGDOM REFORMED?

1. *L'Abeille*, 3 April 1818.

2. Vastey, *An Essay on the Causes of the Revolution*, p. 247; *Newburyport Herald*, 24 July 1818; Madiou, *Histoire d'Haïti*, Vol. 5, p. 503.

3. Madiou, *Histoire d'Haïti*, Vol. 5, pp. 504–5; *Gazette Royale d'Hayti*, 24 May 1816. This issue also names several other figures in the republic allegedly killed for their royalist sympathies.

4. 'The King to the Haytians of the West and South', 9 June 1818, in Vastey, *An Essay on the Causes of the Revolution*, appendix G, no. 1.

5. 'Reply of the Magistrates of the Republic', 1 July 1818, in Vastey, *An Essay on the Causes of the Revolution*, appendix G, no. 3.

6. *Lancaster Gazette*, 11 July 1818.

7. *Gazette Royale d'Hayti*, 1 October 1818.

8. *Gazette Royale d'Hayti*, 30 July 1817. To add to the confusion that would later cloud discussions over Christophe's place of birth, the *Gentleman's Magazine* of December 1817 erroneously reported that Prince Jean was 'embalmed and sent to St. Lucie, the place of his birth, to be interred with full military honours'.

9. Limonade to Clarkson, 14 September 1818, in Griggs and Prator, *Henri Christophe and Thomas Clarkson*, p. 118; *L'Abeille*, 1 October 1818.

10. Vastey to Clarkson, 24 March 1819, in Griggs and Prator, *Henri Christophe and Thomas Clarkson*, p. 136.

11. Clarkson to Christophe, 30 October 1818, in Griggs and Prator, *Henri Christophe and Thomas Clarkson*, pp. 121–2.

12. Christophe to Clarkson, 20 March 1819, in Griggs and Prator, *Henri Christophe and Thomas Clarkson*, p. 131.

13. Christophe to the Czar Alexander, 20 March 1819, in Griggs and Prator, *Henri Christophe and Thomas Clarkson*, pp. 132–5.

14. Clarkson to Christophe, 30 October 1818, in Griggs and Prator, *Henri Christophe and Thomas Clarkson*, p. 123.

15. Christophe to the Czar Alexander, 20 March 1819, in Griggs and Prator, *Henri Christophe and Thomas Clarkson*, p. 129.

16. Vastey, *An Essay on the Causes of the Revolution*, p. 247.

17. Christophe to Clarkson, 26 April 1818, in Griggs and Prator, *Henri Christophe and Thomas Clarkson*, p. 105.

18. Madiou, *Histoire d'Haïti*, Vol. 5, pp. 432–5.

19. *Gazette Royale d'Hayti*, 25 January 1818. Names of new owners were compared against the 1817 *Almanach Royal d'Hayti*, which lists army personnel down to the rank of lieutenant.

20. Christophe to Clarkson, 26 April 1818, in Griggs and Prator, *Henri Christophe and Thomas Clarkson*, pp. 104–9.

21. Madiou, *Histoire d'Haïti*, Vol. 5, pp. 430–2; Julian Prévost, *Instructions pour les établissemens et la culture des habitations caféyères de la Couronne* (Sans Souci: Imprimerie Royale, 24 March 1818).

22. Harvey, *Sketches of Hayti*, pp. 267–8, 279.

23. Alice Moore Dunbar-Nelson (ed.), *Masterpieces of Negro Eloquence: The Best Speeches Delivered by the Negro from the Days of Slavery to the Present Time* (New York: Bookery Publishing Company, 1914), pp. 14–19.

24. Christophe to Clarkson, 29 June 1819, in Griggs and Prator, *Henri Christophe and Thomas Clarkson*, pp. 149–2.

25. Clarkson to Christophe, 29 July 1819, in Griggs and Prator, *Henri Christophe and Thomas Clarkson*, p. 150.

26. 'Letter concerning Hayti', p. 133; Charles Mackenzie, *Notes on Haiti: Made During a Residence in that Republic*, Vol. 1 (London, 1830), p. 158. Mackenzie's book was illustrated by a graduate of Christophe's Royal Academy of Painting and Drawing.

27. Wilberforce to Christophe, 8 October 1818, in R. I. and S. Wilberforce, *The Correspondence of William Wilberforce*, Vol. 1, p. 285.

28. Christophe to Clarkson, 14 April 1820, in Griggs and Prator, *Henri Christophe and Thomas Clarkson*, pp. 97–8; Madiou, *Histoire d'Haïti*, Vol. 5, p. 348.

29. Harvey, *Sketches of Hayti*, pp. 250–1; Cheesman, *The Armorial of Haiti*, p. 74.

30. D. Fraser, *A Memoir of the late Rev. Elliot Jones, Missionary to Hayti* (London: Blanshard, 1823), p. 132.

31. Harvey to Taylor, 20 July 1820, Methodist Missionary Society Archives, SOAS, University of London, Box 115

32. Ibid.

33. Harvey, *Sketches of Hayti*, p. 308; Christophe to Brelle, 1 October 1816, Schomburg Center, Kurt Fisher Haitian collection SCM 08–48, Folder 22.

34. Madiou, *Histoire d'Haïti*, Vol. 5, pp. 353–4.

35. Harvey, *Sketches of Hayti*, pp. 150–1; Simpson and Cinéas, 'Folk Tales of Haitian Heroes', p. 183.

36. Mackenzie, *Notes on Haiti*, Vol. 2, p. 214; 'Iphigenia, Port Royal, June 6, 1819', p. 549.

37. *Gazette Royale d'Hayti*, 30 August 1819.

38. *Gazette Royale d'Hayti*, 10 September 1819.

39. The exact dates of the palace are unknown, but the architect and former head of ISPAN, Daniel Elie, who oversaw its restoration, suggests that construction began in 1819–20 (personal communication).

40. *Edict of the King providing for concessions of land to the soldiers, subalterns and officers of the army who have not yet received a portion of the public domain*, 14 July 1819, reprinted in Griggs and Prator, *Henri Christophe and Thomas Clarkson*, pp. 268–71; Gonzalez, *Maroon Nation*, p. 177.

41. Christophe to Clarkson, 28 July 1819, in Griggs and Prator, *Henri Christophe and Thomas Clarkson*, pp. 150–1.

42. Prévost to unknown correspondent, 2 September 1819, reprinted in *Morning Chronicle*, 4 January 1820.

43. *L'Abeille*, 1 May 1820.

17. THE FATAL STROKE

1. Juste Chanlatte, *La Partie de chasse du roi* (Sans Souci: Imprimérie Royale, 1820); Nathan Dize, *The Drama of History: Representation and Revolutionaries in Haitian Theater, 1818–1907*, MA thesis, University of Maryland (2014).

2. Thomas Madiou, *Histoire d'Haïti*, Vol. 6, *1819–1826* (Port-au-Prince: H. Deschamps, 1988), p. 65.

3. Tabitha McIntosh and Grégory Pierrot, *In the Court of the Mohrenkönig: Germans in Henry's Kingdom of Haiti*, unpublished paper, Haitian Studies Association 29th Annual Conference, New Orleans, Louisiana, 3 November 2017.

4. *Bury and Norwich Post*, Wednesday, 22 January 1817.

5. *Gazette Royale d'Hayti*, 25 January 1816.

6. Otto Philippe Braun to his parents, 18 May 1820, quoted in Hans Braun, *Grundlagen zu einer Geschichte der Familie Braun mit Beiträgen zur hessischen Familien und Orts Beschreibung* (Berlin: A. Hoffmann, 1914), p. 234.

7. Friedmann Pestel, 'An Atlantic Restoration: Political legitimation, Material Cultures and Mobility between Germanic and Haiti Countries, 1804–1825', *Annales historiques de la Révolution française* vol. 3, no. 397 (2019), pp. 77–97; Mackenzie, *Notes on Haiti*, Vol. 2, p. 209.

8. Cary Hector, 'Quelques perspectives des rapports "paradiplomatiques" entre la Prusse de Friedrich Wilhelm III. et le Royaume d'Henry Christophe (1811–1820)', *Revue de la Société Haïtienne d'histoire, de Géographie et de Géologie*, nos. 245–8 (2012), pp. 182–202.

9. Pestel, 'An Atlantic Restoration', pp. 77–97.

10. Hugh Popham, *A Damned Cunning Fellow: The Eventful Life of Rear-Admiral Sir Home Popham, KCB, KCH, KM, FRS, 1762–1820* (Tywardreath, Cornwall: Old Ferry Press, 1991), p. 230.

11. 'Iphigenia, Port Royal, June 6, 1819', p. 549.

12. *Boston Daily Advertiser*, 19 July 1819. The original copy of the *Gazette Royale d'Hayti* whose report the newspaper translated has been lost. See 'Iphigenia, Port Royal, June 6, 1819', p. 549.

13. 'Iphigenia, Port Royal, June 6, 1819', p. 549.

14. Ibid., pp. 550–1; *Boston Daily Advertiser*, 19 July 1819.

15. 'Information on the subject of Northern Hayti collected by Sir H. R. Popham (1819)', and Home Popham to Lord Melville, 29 July 1819, Bodleian Library, Correspondence of Henry Dundas and Robert Saunders Dundas MSS. W.Ind.s.7–8 f321; Madiou, *Histoire d'Haïti*, Vol. 6, pp. 38–9.

16. Clarkson to Christophe, 29 July 1819, in Griggs and Prator, *Henri Christophe and Thomas Clarkson*, p. 150.

17. Christophe to Clarkson, 20 November 1819, in Griggs and Prator, *Henri Christophe and Thomas Clarkson*, pp. 168–70.

18. Limonade to Clarkson, 20 November 1819, in Griggs and Prator, *Henri Christophe and Thomas Clarkson*, p. 175.

19. Christophe to Clarkson, 20 November 1819, in Griggs and Prator, *Henri Christophe and Thomas Clarkson*, p. 167.

20. 'Breakfast with the Black Prince', *Household Words* vol. 24 (1854), pp. 345–51.

21. Ibid.

22. *Aberdeen Journal*, 9 August 1820. The extract from the *Gazette Royal d'Hayti* of 30 May 1820 is the last known published issue of the newspaper.

23. Ardouin, *Etudes sur l'histoire d'Haïti*, Vol. 8, p. 428.

24. Madiou, *Histoire d'Haïti*, Vol. 6, p. 90; *Arkansas Gazette*, 2 December 1820.

25. Clarkson to Christophe, 28 April 1820, in Griggs and Prator, *Henri Christophe and Thomas Clarkson*, p. 196–9.

26. Clarkson to Christophe, 10 July 1820, in Griggs and Prator, *Henri Christophe and Thomas Clarkson*, pp. 200–7.

27. Madiou, *Histoire d'Haïti*, Vol. 6, pp. 104–5.

28. Ibid., pp. 111–12. Although Madiou interviewed several members of the royal regime for his book, he does not reveal whether the source of Christophe's words witnessed the scene at first hand.

29. 'The Last Days of Christophe', *Littell's Living Age* vol. 48 (January–March 1856), pp. 799–804.

30. William Wilson to his father, 1 October 1820, in Griggs and Prator, *Henri Christophe and Thomas Clarkson*, p. 209.

31. Duncan Stewart to Thomas Clarkson, 8 December 1820, in Griggs and Prator, *Henri Christophe and Thomas Clarkson*, p. 209.

32. Limonade to Baron Dupuy, 22 September 1820, in Mackenzie, *Notes on Haiti*, Vol. 2, p. 215.

33. Karl Ritter, *Naturhistorische Reise zur westindischen Insel Haiti* (Stuttgart: Hallberger, 1836), p. 98.

34. Madiou, *Histoire d'Haïti*, Vol. 6, pp. 114–16. Madiou gives Paulin the rank of colonel, but the 1820 royal almanac gives his rank as lieutenant. In his 1864 memoir, General Guy Joseph Bonnet, Pétion's envoy to Christophe in October 1806, adds the juicy but unsourced allegation that Paulin was further outraged by Christophe having slept with his sister.

35. Madiou, *Histoire d'Haïti*, Vol. 6, p. 118.

36. Ibid., p. 121.

37. Wilson, 'Unpublished Memoir'.

38. Johan Albrekt Abraham de Freese, 'Anteckningar under mitt vistande på Haiti' [Memorandum drafted during my stay in Haiti], dated 'Cap Haïtien, Januari 21, 1821', shelfmark X 415 a, Uppsala University Library, Sweden. My thanks to Fredrik Thomasson for sharing his unpublished translation.

39. 'The Last Days of Christophe', pp. 799–804; Madiou, *Histoire d'Haïti*, Vol. 6, p. 121; Wilson, 'Unpublished Memoir'.

40. 'The Last Days of Christophe', pp. 799–804.

41. Madiou, *Histoire d'Haïti*, Vol. 6, p. 125; 'The Last Days of Christophe', pp. 799–804.

42. 'The Last Days of Christophe', pp. 799–804.

43. Saunders, *Haytian Papers*, p. 152.

18. AFTERMATH AND EXILE

1. Madiou, *Histoire d'Haïti*, Vol. 6, p. 127. Madiou wrote that his account was taken from an interview with Chevalier François Sévère of the Royal Household Guards, who was on duty when Christophe killed himself.

2. Ibid., p. 127; De Freese, 'Anteckningar under mitt vistande på Haiti'.

3. 'The Last Days of Christophe', pp. 801–2.

4. De Freese, 'Anteckningar under mitt vistande på Haiti'.

5. *Rhode-Island American and General Advertiser*, 8 June 1821; *Newburyport Herald*, 2 June 1821. The portrait was reportedly offered to the Museum of the Linnaean Society of Newburyport, Massachusetts, before promptly disappearing from the historical record.

6. William Wilson to Thomas Clarkson, 5 December 1820, in Griggs and Prator, *Henri Christophe and Thomas Clarkson*, pp. 217–18.

7. Duncan Stewart to Thomas Clarkson, 8 December 1820, in Griggs and Prator, *Henri Christophe and Thomas Clarkson*, pp. 222–3.

8. Juste Chanlatte on Henry Christophe, 28 October 1820; BPL, MS Haiti 72–8. Extracts from this were published in the American press, for instance in the *Baltimore Patriot & Mercantile Advertiser*, 9 February 1821.

9. William Wilson to Thomas Clarkson, 16 September 1827, BL Clarkson Papers MSS 41, 266.

10. Fredrik Thomasson, 'Sweden and Haiti, 1791–1825: Revolutionary Reporting, Trade, and the Fall of Henry Christophe', *Journal of Haitian Studies* vol. 24, no. 2 (2018), pp. 4–35.

11. Jean-Pierre Boyer, *Circulaire du Président d'Haïti, aux commandants d'arrondissement, annonçant la prise d'armes de la garnison de Saint-Marc contre Christophe*, 5 October 1820, in A. Linstant-Pradine, *Recueil général des lois et acts du gouvernement d'Haïti*, Vol. 3: *1818–1823* (Paris: A. Durand, 1860), pp. 334–5.

12. Jean-Pierre Boyer, *Circulaire aux commandants d'arrondissement, à l'occasion de la mort de Christophe et de la défection de ses troupes* 12 October 1820, in Linstant-Pradine, *Recueil général des lois et acts*, Vol. 3, pp. 332–3.

13. Madiou, *Histoire d'Haïti*, Vol. 6, pp. 137–9.

14. Ibid., p. 142.

15. Ibid., p. 143.

16. Ibid., pp. 147–8.

17. De Freese, 'Anteckningar under mitt vistande på Haiti'.

18. Jean-Pierre Boyer, *Proclamation qui ordonne le dêpot au trésor public des diamants et joyaux de la couronne de Christophe*, 1 November 1820, in Linstant-Pradine, *Recueil général des lois et acts*, Vol. 3, pp. 352–3; *Columbian Centinel*, 24 January 1821.

19. Emory Strong, 'The Enigma of the Phoenix Button', *Historical Archaeology* no. 9 (1975), pp. 74–80.

20. Boyer to Joute Lachenais, 20 October 1820, reprinted in Pierre-Eugene de Lespinasse, *Gens d'autrefois ... vieux souvenirs...* (Paris: Editions de la Revue Mondiale, 1926), p. 19.

21. *Morning Chronicle*, 2 May 1821.

22. Beaubrun Ardouin, *Etudes sur l'histoire d'Haïti*, Vol. 9 (Paris: Dezobry & E. Magdeleine, 1860), pp. 34, 174.

23. R. I. and S. Wilberforce, *The Life of William Wilberforce*, Vol. 5, p. 83.

24. Thomas Clarkson to President Boyer, 25 May 1821, in Griggs and Prator, *Henri Christophe and Thomas Clarkson*, pp. 224–5.

25. Boyer to Thomas Clarkson, 30 July 1821, in Griggs and Prator, *Henri Christophe and Thomas Clarkson*, pp. 229–30.

26. Madiou, *Histoire d'Haïti*, Vol. 6, pp. 225–6; *Testament de Marie-Louise Christophe*, 18 July 1821 (Collection of Gaetan Mentor).

27. *Morning Post*, 19 September 1821; *Morning Chronicle*, 17 October 1821.

28. Margaret Knutsford, *The Life and Letters of Zachary Macaulay* (London: Edward Arnold, 1900), p. 368.

29. Thomas Clarkson to Zachary Macaulay, 19 November 1821, in Griggs and Prator, *Henri Christophe and Thomas Clarkson*, pp. 237–40.

30. Thomas Clarkson to Zachary Macaulay, 31 January 1822, in Griggs and Prator, *Henri Christophe and Thomas Clarkson*, p. 245.

31. 'Copy of a letter of Ann Alexander's to Higham Lodge with a report of the visit of the ex-Empress of Haiti and daughters', 23 October 1821, Suffolk Archives HD827/1/1/4/7/2. My particular thanks to Dr Nicole Willson for sharing this letter with me.

32. Ellen Gibson Wilson, *Thomas Clarkson: A Biography* (London: Macmillan, 1989), p. 153.

33. The Christophes to Dorothy Clarkson, 13 September 1824, in Griggs and Prator, *Henri Christophe and Thomas Clarkson*, p. 254; *Morning Post*, 24 September 1824.

34. Alexandre Dumas, *Impressions de voyage: Une année à Florence* (Paris: Dumont, 1841), p. 182.

35. Journal of Robert Inglis, 20 October 1840, Canterbury Cathedral Archives, Inglis/Harrison Papers CCA-U210/4/10.

36. Marie-Louise Christophe to President Boyer, 7 November 1839, reprinted in Lespinasse, *Gens d'autrefois*, pp. 54–5.

37. 'Last Will and Testament of Marie-Louise Christophe', 8 July 1851, TNA PROB 11/2135/332. The will was composed on 6 July 1841.

38. Dubois, *Haiti*, p. 123.

39. Ibid., pp. 97–104.

40. Ibid., pp. 105–6.

41. H. Trouillot, *Le gouvernement du roi Henri Christophe*, p. 9.

BIBLIOGRAPHY

Newspapers

Affiches Américaines (Cap Français, 1779–91; 1802–3)
Gazette Officielle de l'Etat d'Hayti (Cap-Haïtien, 1807–11)
Gazette Officielle de Saint-Domingue (Cap Français, 1802–3)
Gazette Politique et Commerciale d'Haïti (Cap-Haïtien, 1804–06)
Gazette Royale d'Hayti (Cap Henry and Sans Souci, 1813–20)
L'Abeille (Port-au-Prince, 1817–20)
Le Télégraphe (Port-au-Prince, 1814–20)

Archives

Archives départementales de la Gironde, Bordeaux, Collection Marcel Chatillon
Archives Nationales d'Outre Mer (ANOM), Aix-en-Provence, France
Archives Nationales France (ANF)
Bibliothèque nationale de France (BnF)
Boston Public Library (BPL)
British Library (BL)
British and Foreign Bible Society Collection, Cambridge University Library
Canterbury Cathedral Archives, Inglis/Harrison Papers
Centre d'accueil et de recherche des Archives nationales (CARAN), Paris
Foyle Special Collections Library, King's College London
Harvard Theatre Collection, Houghton Library, Harvard University
Institut de Sauvegarde du Patrimoine National (ISPAN), Port-au-Prince
John Wilson Croker Papers, David M. Rubenstein Rare Book & Manuscript Library, Duke University, Durham, NC
Methodist Missionary Society Archives, School of Oriental and African Studies (SOAS), University of London
Musée du Panthéon National Haïtien (MUPANAH), Port-au-Prince

BIBLIOGRAPHY

University of Florida Library (UFL) Rochambeau Papers

National Library of Jamaica, Kingston

Schomburg Center for Research in Black Culture, New York Public Library

The National Archives, London (TNA)

Wilberforce and Melville Papers, Bodleian Library, Oxford

Zachary Macaulay Papers, Huntington Library, San Marino, CA

Books and Research Papers

Adams, John Quincy. *Memoirs of John Quincy Adams, comprising portions of his diary from 1795 to 1848*, Vol. 3, ed. Charles Francis Adams (Philadelphia: J. Lippincott & Co., 1874).

Allix, Jacques Alexandre François. 'Souvenirs militaires et politiques de M. le Lieutenant-Général Allix', *Journal des sciences militaires des armées de terre et der mer*, Vol. 16 (1829), pp. 52–71.

Almanach Royal d'Hayti pour l'année bissextile 1814, Onzième de l'indépendance, et la troisième du règne de sa majesté (Cap Henry: P. Roux, 1814).

Almanach Royal d'Hayti pour l'année bissextile 1815, Douzième de l'indépendance, et la quatrième du règne de sa majesté (Cap Henry: P. Roux, 1815).

Almanach Royal d'Hayti pour l'année bissextile 1816, Treizième de l'indépendance, et la cinquième du règne de sa Majesté (Cap Henry: P. Roux, 1816).

Almanach Royal d'Hayti pour l'année bissextile 1817, Quatorzième de l'indépendance, et la sixième du règne de sa majesté, présenté au roi (Cap Henry: P. Roux, 1817).

Almanach Royal d'Hayti pour l'année bissextile 1818, Quinzième de l'indépendance, et la troisième du règne de sa majesté (Sans Souci: Imprimerie Royale, 1818).

Almanach Royal d'Hayti pour l'année bissextile 1820, Dix-septième de l'indépendance, et la neuvième du règne de sa majesté (Sans Souci: Imprimerie Royale, 1820).

Ardouin, Beaubrun. *Etudes sur l'histoire d'Haïti*, Vol. 4 (Paris: Dezobry & E. Magdeleine, 1853).

———— *Etudes sur l'histoire d'Haïti*, Vol. 6 (Paris: Dezobry & E. Magdeleine, 1856).

———— *Etudes sur l'histoire d'Haïti*, Vol. 7 (Paris: Chez l'auteur, 1856).

———— *Etudes sur l'histoire d'Haïti*, Vol. 8 (Paris: Chez l'auteur, 1858).

———— *Etudes sur l'histoire d'Haïti*, Vol. 9 (Paris: Dezobry & E. Magdeleine, 1860).

Auguste, Claude Bonaparte. *L'Expédition Leclerc, 1801–1803* (Port-au-Prince: H. Deschamps, 1985).

Bailey, Gauvin. *The Palace of Sans-Souci in Milot, Haiti, ca. 1806–1820: The Untold Story of the Potsdam of the Rainforest* (Berlin: Deutscher Kunstverlag, 2017).

Barskett, James. *History of the Island of St. Domingo, from its First Discovery by Columbus to the Present Period* (New York: Mahlon Day, 1824).

Bazelais, General. 'Journal de campagne tenu pendant l'Expédition de Santo-Domingo, par le général de division H. Christophe', *Gazette Politique et Commerciale d'Haïti*, 13 June 1805.

Boisrond-Tonnerre, Louis Félix. *Mémoires pour servir à l'histoire d'Haïti* (Port-au-Prince, Imprimerie Centrale, 1804).

Boyer, Jean-Pierre, *Circulaire aux commandants d'arrondissement, à l'occasion de la mort de Christophe et de la défection de ses troupes* 12 October 1820, in A. Linstant-Pradine, *Recueil général des lois et actes du gouvernement d'Haïti*, Vol. 3: *1818–1823* (Paris: A. Durand, 1860), pp. 332–3.

———— *Circulaire du Président d'Haïti, aux commandants d'arrondissement, annonçant la prise d'armes de la garnison de Saint-Marc contre Christophe*, 5 October 1820, in Linstant-Pradine, *Recueil général des lois et actes*, Vol. 3, pp. 334–5.

———— *Proclamation qui ordonne le dépot au trésor public des diamants et joyaux de la couronne de Christophe*, 1 November 1820, in Linstant-Pradine, *Recueil général des lois et actes*, Vol. 3, pp. 352–3.

Braun, Hans. *Grundlagen zu einer Geschichte der Familie Braun mit Beiträgen zur hessischen Familien und Orts Beschreibung* (Berlin: A. Hoffmann, 1914).

Brevet, Matthieu. *Les expéditions coloniales vers Saint-Domingue et les Antilles*. PhD thesis, Université Lumière Lyon 2, Lyon (2007).

Bro de Comères, Baron Henry (ed.). *Mémoires du Général Bro (1796–1844)* (Paris: Plon, 1914).

Brown, Jonathan. *The History and Present Condition of St. Domingo*, Vol. 2 (Philadelphia: William Marshall & Co., 1837).

[Burk, Edward]. *The Hurricane: A Poem, by an Eyewitness. Also, Historical Notices of St. Domingo, from the seizure of Toussaint l'Ouverture to the Death of Christophe* (Bath, 1844).

Burnard, Trevor, and John Garrigus. *The Plantation Machine: Atlantic Capitalism in French Saint-Domingue and British Jamaica* (Philadelphia: University of Pennsylvania Press, 2016).

Burrows, Simon. *French Exile Journalism and European Politics, 1792–1814* (London: Royal Historical Society, 2000).

Cabon, R. P. 'Les Religieuses du Cap à Saint-Domingue (suite et fin)', *Revue d'histoire de l'Amérique française* vol. 3, no. 3 (1949), pp. 402–22.

Candlin, Kit. *The Last Caribbean Frontier, 1795–1815* (Basingstoke and New York: Palgrave Macmillan, 2012).

Cañizares-Esguerra, Jorge, et al. (eds.). *The Black Urban Atlantic in the Age of the Slave Trade* (Philadelphia: University of Pennsylvania Press, 2013).

Caron, Pierre. *Correspondance intime du Général Jean Hardy, de 1797 à 1802* (Paris: Plon, 1901).

Célius, Carlos. 'Neo-Classicism and the Haitian Revolution', in David Geggus and Norman Fiering (eds.), *The World of the Haitian Revolution* (Bloomington and Indianapolis: Indiana University Press, 2009), pp. 352–92.

Cénatus, Bérard, et al. (eds.). *Haïti: De la dictature à la démocratie?* (Montreal: Mémoire d'encrier, 2016).

Cérisier, L., Fils. *Biographie de Pétion* (Port-au-Prince: T. Bouchereau, 1842).

Chanlatte, Juste. *La Partie de chasse du roi* (Sans Souci: Imprimérie Royale, 1820).

———— 'Quelques réflexions sur le prétendu Sénat du Port-au-Prince', *Gazette Officielle de l'Etat d'Hayti*, 2 July 1807.

Cheesman, Clive (ed.). *The Armorial of Haiti: Symbols of Nobility in the Reign of Henry Christophe* (London: The College of Arms, 2007).

Christophe, Henry. 'Aux Habitans du Sud et de partie de l'Ouest du Royaume', 4 September 1811 (Cap Henry: P. Roux, 1811).

———— 'Journal de campagne tenu pendant l'Expédition de Santo-Domingo, par le général de division H. Christophe', *Gazette Politique et Commerciale d'Haïti*, 20 June 1805.

———— *Manifeste du Roi* (Cap Henry: P. Roux, 1814).

———— *Ordonnance du Roi, Concernant les Douanes et Tarif des Droits d'Entrée et de Sortie pour le Commerce étranger* (Cap Henry: P. Roux, 20 March 1817).

———— *Plan générale de défense du Royaume* (Cap Henry: P. Roux, 20 November 1814).

———— *Règlement pour les deuils de cour* (Cap Henry: P. Roux, 20 January 1813).

Clark, George P. 'The Role of the Haitian Volunteers at Savannah in 1779: An Attempt at an Objective View', *Phylon* vol. 41, no. 4 (1980), pp. 356–66.

Clausson, L. J. *Précis historique de la révolution de Saint-Domingue* (Paris: Pillet Aîné, 1819).

Code Henry (Cap Henry: P. Roux, 1812).

Cole, Hubert. *Christophe: King of Haiti* (New York: Viking Press, 1967).

Colombel, Noël. *Réflexions sur quelques faits relatifs à notre existence politique* (Paris: F. Scherff, 1818).

Cugoano, Ottobah. *Narrative of the Enslavement of Ottobah Cugoano, a Native of Africa* (London, 1825).

Dalencour, François. *Biographie du général François Cappoix* (Port-au-Prince, 1957).

Daut, Marlene. *Baron de Vastey and the Origins of Black Atlantic Humanism* (New York: Palgrave Macmillan, 2017).

Dayan, Joan. *Haiti, History, and the Gods* (Berkeley: University of California Press, 1998).

Descourtilz, Michel Etienne. *Voyages d'un naturaliste, et ses observations*, 3 vols. (Paris: Dufart, 1809).

Dessalines, Jean-Jacques. *Journal de la campagne du nord*, 2 December 1803, in *Revue de la Société Haïtienne d'Histoire, de Géographie et de Géologie*, nos. 253–6 (2014), pp. 101–7.

Dize, Nathan. *The Drama of History: Representation and Revolutionaries in Haitian Theater, 1818–1907*. MA thesis, University of Maryland (2014).

Donnadieu, Jean-Louis. 'Derrière le portrait, l'homme: Jean-Baptiste Belley, dit "Timbaze", dit "Mars" (1746?–1805)', *Bulletin de la Société d'Histoire de la Guadeloupe*, no. 170 (2015), pp. 29–54.

Dubois, Laurent. *Avengers of the New World: The Story of the Haitian Revolution* (Cambridge, MA: Harvard University Press, 2004).

——— *Haiti: The Aftershocks of History* (New York: Henry Holt & Co., 2012).

Dubois, Laurent, Julia Gaffield and Michael Acacia (eds.). *Documents constitutionnels d'Haïti, 1790–1860* (Berlin: De Gruyter, 2013).

Dubois, Laurent, and John Garrigus. *Slave Revolution in the Caribbean, 1789–1804: A Brief History with Documents* (New York: Bedford/St Martin's, 2006).

Dumas, Alexandre. *Impressions de voyage: Une année à Florence* (Paris: Dumont, 1841).

Dumesle, Hérard. *Voyage dans le nord d'Hayti, ou, Révélations des lieux et des monuments historiques* (Cayes: Imprimerie du Gouvernement, 1824).

Dunbar-Nelson, Alice Moore (ed.). *Masterpieces of Negro Eloquence: The Best Speeches Delivered by the Negro from the Days of Slavery to the Present Time* (New York: Bookery Publishing Company, 1914).

Dunham, Katherine. *Island Possessed* (University of Chicago Press, 1994).

Eddins, Crystal Nicole. *African Diaspora Collective Action: Rituals, Runaways, and the Haitian Revolution*. PhD thesis, Michigan State University (2017).

Eller, Anne. '"All would be equal in the effort": Santo Domingo's "Italian Revolution," Independence, and Haiti, 1809–1822', *Journal of Early American History* vol. 1, no. 2 (2011), pp. 105–41.

Farington, Joseph. *The Farington Diary*, Vol. 8 (London: Hutchinson & Co., 1928).

Ferrer, Ada. *Freedom's Mirror: Cuba and Haiti in the Age of Revolution* (Cambridge University Press, 2014).

——— 'Haiti, Free Soil, and Antislavery in the Revolutionary Atlantic', *The American Historical Review*, vol. 117, no. 1 (2012), pp. 40–66.

Fick, Carolyn. *The Making of Haiti: The Saint-Domingue Revolution from Below* (Knoxville: University of Tennessee Press, 1990).

Fischer, Sybille. *Modernity Disavowed: Haiti and the Cultures of Slavery in the Age of Revolution* (Durham, NC: Duke University Press, 2004).

Fraser, D. *Memoir of the late Rev. Elliot Jones, Missionary to Hayti* (London: Blanshard, 1823).

Gaffield, Julia. *Haitian Connections in the Atlantic World: Recognition after Revolution* (Chapel Hill: University of North Carolina Press, 2015).

Gaffield, Julia (ed.). *The Haitian Declaration of Independence: Creation, Context, and Legacy* (Charlottesville: University of Virginia Press, 2016).

Garraway, Doris. 'Race, Reproduction and Family Romance in Moreau de Saint-Méry's "Description ... de la partie francaise de l'isle Saint Domingue"', *Eighteenth-Century Studies* vol. 38, no. 2 (2005), pp. 227–46, Project MUSE, doi:10.1353/ecs.2005.0008

Garrigus, John. 'Catalyst or Catastrophe? Saint-Domingue's Free Men of Color and the Savannah Expedition, 1779–1782', *Review/Revista Interamericana* vol. 22, nos. 1/2 (1992), pp. 109–25.

——— 'Opportunist or Patriot? Julien Raimond (1744–1801) and the Haitian Revolution', *Slavery & Abolition* vol. 28, no. 1 (2007), pp. 1–21.

——— 'Vincent Ogé "Jeune" (1757–91): Social Class and Free Colored

Mobilization on the Eve of the Haitian Revolution', *The Americas* vol. 68, no. 1 (2011), pp. 33–62.

Geggus, David. *Haitian Revolutionary Studies* (Bloomington and Indianopolis: Indiana University Press, 2002).

———— *Slavery, War, and Revolution: The British Occupation of Saint Domingue, 1793–1798* (Oxford: Clarendon Press, 1982).

———— 'The Major Port Towns of Saint-Domingue in the Later Eighteenth Century', in Franklin W. Knight and Peggy K. Liss (eds.), *Atlantic Port Cities: Economy, Culture, and Society in the Atlantic World, 1650–1850* (Knoxville: University of Tennessee Press, 1991), pp. 87–116.

———— 'The Naming of Haiti', *New West Indian Guide / Nieuwe West-Indische Gids* vol. 71, nos. 1/2 (1997), pp. 43–68.

———— 'The Slaves and Free People of Color of Cap Français', in Jorge Cañizares-Esguerra et al. (eds.), *The Black Urban Atlantic in the Age of the Slave Trade* (Philadelphia: University of Pennsylvania Press, 2016), pp. 101–21.

Girard, Philippe. 'Jean-Jacques Dessalines et l'arrestation de Toussaint Louverture', *Journal of Haitian Studies* vol. 17, no. 1 (2011), pp. 123–38.

———— 'Napoleon Bonaparte and the Emancipation Issue in Saint-Domingue, 1799–1803', *French Historical Studies* vol. 32, no. 4 (2009), pp. 587–618.

———— *The Slaves Who Defeated Napoleon: Toussaint Louverture and the Haitian War of Independence, 1801–1804* (Tuscaloosa: University of Alabama Press, 2011).

———— *Toussaint Louverture: A Revolutionary Life* (New York: Basic Books, 2016).

Girard, Philippe (ed. and trans.). *The Memoir of General Toussaint Louverture* (New York: Oxford University Press, 2014).

Girard, Philippe, and Jean-Louis Donnadieu. 'Toussaint before Louverture: New Archival Findings on the Early Life of Toussaint', *The William and Mary Quarterly* vol. 70, no. 1 (2013), pp. 41–78.

Gonzalez, Johnhenry. *Maroon Nation: A History of Revolutionary Haiti* (New Haven, CT: Yale University Press, 2019).

Griggs, Earl Leslie, and Clifford H. Prator. *Henri Christophe and Thomas Clarkson: A Correspondence* (New York: Greenwood Press, 1968).

Harvey, William Woodis. *Sketches of Hayti: From the Expulsion of the French to the Death of Christophe* (London: L. B. Seeley & Son, 1827).

Hazareesingh, Sudhir. *Black Spartacus: The Epic Life of Toussaint Louverture* (London: Allen Lane, 2020).

Hector, Cary. 'Quelques perspectives des rapports "paradiplomatiques" entre la Prusse de Friedrich Wilhelm III. et le Royaume d'Henry Christophe (1811–1820)', *Revue de la Société Haïtienne d'histoire, de Géographie et de Géologie* nos. 245–8 (2012), pp. 182–202.

Herring, Thomas. *Reminiscences of Haiti, in the years 1807–8–9, during the government of the celebrated negro-chief Christophe, afterward Henry the First, King of Haiti, and that of his no-less celebrated and formidable Rival, Pétion, President of Port-au-Prince* (Portsmouth, 1833).

Hoffmann, Léon-François. 'An American Trader in Revolutionary Haiti: Simeon Johnson's Journal of 1807', *The Princeton University Library Chronicle* vol. 49, no. 2 (1988), pp. 182–99.

'Iphigenia, Port Royal, June 6, 1819', *Blackwood's Magazine* vol. 10 (1821), p. 549.

Janvier, Louis-Joseph. *Les constitutions d'Haïti, 1801–1885* (Paris: C. Marpon and E. Flammarion, 1886).

Jefferson, Thomas. *The Papers of Thomas Jefferson*, Vol. 40: *4 March to 10 July 1803*, ed. Barbara B. Oberg (Princeton University Press, 2018).

Jenson, Deborah. *Beyond the Slave Narrative: Politics, Sex, and Manuscripts in the Haitian Revolution* (Liverpool University Press, 2011).

——— 'From the Kidnapping(s) of the Louvertures to the Alleged Kidnapping of Aristide: Legacies of Slavery in the Post/Colonial World', *Yale French Studies* no. 107 (2005), pp. 162–86.

King, Stewart R. *Blue Coat or Powdered Wig: Free People of Color in Pre-Revolutionary Saint Domingue* (Athens, GA: University of Georgia Press, 2010).

——— 'The Maréchaussée of Saint-Domingue: Balancing the Ancien Régime and Modernity', *Journal of Colonialism and Colonial History* vol. 5, no. 2 (2004), Project MUSE, doi:10.1353/cch.2004.0052

Knight, Franklin W., and Peggy K. Liss (eds.). *Atlantic Port Cities: Economy, Culture, and Society in the Atlantic World, 1650–1850* (Knoxville: University of Tennessee Press, 1991).

Knutsford, Margaret. *The Life and Letters of Zachary Macaulay* (London: Edward Arnold, 1900).

'La Crête-à-Pierrot, site de hauts faits d'armes', *Bulletin de l'ISPAN* no. 22 (March 2011), pp. 1–12.

La Selve, Edgar. *Le pays des nègres: Voyage à Haïti* (Paris: Hachette et Cie, 1881).

Lacroix, Pamphile de. *Mémoires pour servir à l'histoire de la révolution de Saint-Domingue*, Vol. 2 (Paris: Pillet Aîné, 1819).

'The Last Days of Christophe', *Littell's Living Age* vol. 48 (January–March 1856), pp. 799–804.

Leconte, Vergniaud. *Henri Christophe dans l'histoire d'Haïti* (Paris: Berger-Levrault, 1931).

Le Glaunec, Jean-Pierre. *The Cry of Vertières: Liberation, Memory, and the Beginning of Haiti* (Montreal: McGill-Queen's University Press, 2020).

Leslie, Charles Robert. *Autobiographical Recollections* (London: John Murray, 1860).

Lespinasse, Pierre-Eugene de. *Gens d'autrefois … vieux souvenirs …* (Paris: Editions de la Revue Mondiale, 1926).

'Letter concerning Hayti', *Blackwood's Magazine*, vol. 4 (1818), p. 132.

Lindfors, Bernth. *Ira Aldridge: The Early Years, 1807–1833* (Rochester, NY: University of Rochester Press, 2007).

Linstant-Pradine, A. *Recueil général des lois et actes du gouvernement d'Haïti*, Vol. 1: *1804–1808* (Paris: A. Durand, 1886).

————— *Recueil général des lois et actes du gouvernement d'Haïti*, Vol. 2: *1809–1817* (Paris: A. Durand, 1860).

————— *Recueil général des lois et actes du gouvernement d'Haïti*, Vol. 3: *1818–1823* (Paris: A. Durand, 1860.

Louverture, Toussaint. 'Letters of Toussaint Louverture and of Edward Stevens, 1798–1800', *The American Historical Review* vol. 16, no. 1 (October 1910), pp. 64–101.

Mackenzie, Charles. *Notes on Haiti: Made During a Residence in that Republic*, 2 vols. (London, 1830).

'Madame Christophe', *The New Monthly Magazine and Literary Journal*, vol. 1 (1828), p. 483.

Madiou, Thomas. *Histoire d'Haïti*, Vol. 1: *1492–1799* (Port-au-Prince: J. Courtois, 1847).

————— *Histoire d'Haïti*, Vol. 2: *1799–1803* (Port-au-Prince: J. Courtois, 1847).

————— *Histoire d'Haïti*, Vol. 3: *1803–1807* (Port-au-Prince; J. Courtois, 1848).

————— *Histoire d'Haïti*, Vol. 4: *1807–1811* (Port-au-Prince: H. Deschamps, 1987).

———— *Histoire d'Haïti*, Vol. 5: *1811–1818* (Port-au-Prince: H. Deschamps, 1988).

———— *Histoire d'Haïti*, Vol. 6: *1819–1826* (Port-au-Prince: H. Deschamps, 1988).

Maspero-Clerc, Hélène. *Un journaliste contre-révolutionnaire: Jean-Gabriel Peltier (1760–1825)* (Paris: Société des études Robespierristes, 1973).

McCallum, Pierre. *Travels in Trinidad During the Months of February, March, and April, 1803* (London: Longman, Hurst, Rees, and Orme, 1805).

McCrea, Rosalie Smith. 'Portrait Mythology? Representing the "Black Jacobin": Henri Christophe in the British Grand Manner', *The British Art Journal* vol. 6, no. 2 (2005), pp. 66–70.

McIntosh, Tabitha, and Grégory Pierrot. 'Capturing the Likeness of Henry I of Haiti (1805–1822)', *Atlantic Studies* vol. 14, no. 2 (2016), pp. 127–51, doi:10.1080/14788810.2016.1203214

———— *In the Court of the Mohrenkönig: Germans in Henry's Kingdom of Haiti.* Unpublished paper, Haitian Studies Association 29th Annual Conference, New Orleans, Louisiana, 3 November 2017.

McNeill, J. R. *Mosquito Empires: Ecology and War in the Greater Caribbean, 1620–1914* (Cambridge University Press, 2010).

Metral, Antoine. *Histoire de l'expédition des Français a Saint-Domingue* (Paris, 1825).

Moïse, Claude (ed.). *Dictionnaire Historique de la Révolution Haïtienne, 1789–1804* (Montréal: CIDIHCA, 2014).

Mollien, Gaspard Théodore. *Haïti ou Saint-Domingue*, Vol. 2 (Paris: L'Harmattan, 2006).

Monroe, J. Cameron, 'New Light from Haiti's Royal Past: Recent Archaeological Excavations in the Palace of Sans-Souci, Milot', *Journal of Haitian Studies*, vol. 23. no. 2 (2017), pp. 5–31.

Moreau de Saint-Méry, Médéric-Louis-Élie. *Description topographique, physique, civile, politique et historique de la partie française de l'isle Saint-Domingue*, Vol. 1 (Philadelphia, 1797).

North, Jonathan, and Marek Tadeusz Łałowski. *War of Lost Hope: Polish Accounts of the Napoleonic Expedition to Saint Domingue, 1801 to 1804* (Jonathan North, 2017).

Norvins, J de. *Souvenirs d'un historien de Napoléon*, Vol. 2 (Paris: E. Plon Nourrit et Cie, 1896).

Nouët, Jean-Claude, Claude Nicollier and Yves Nicollier (eds.). *La vie aventureuse de Norbert Thoret dit 'L'Americain'* (Paris: Editions du Port-au-Prince, 2013).

Pachonski, Jan, and Reuel K. Wilson. *Poland's Caribbean Tragedy: A Study of Polish Legions in the Haitian War of Independence, 1802–1803* (New York: Columbia University Press, 1986).

Pérard, Jean-Hérold. *La Citadelle restaurée: Le livre qui invite à (re)visiter la Citadelle Laferrière* (Port-au-Prince, 2010).

Perroud, Henry. *Précis des derniers troubles qui ont eu lieu dans la partie du Nord de Saint-Domingue* (Cap Français: P. Roux, 1796).

Pestel, Friedemann. 'An Atlantic Restoration: Political Legitimation, Material Cultures and Mobility between Germanic and Haiti Countries, 1804–1825', *Annales historiques de la Révolution française* vol. 3, no. 397 (2019), pp. 77–97.

———— 'The Impossible Ancien Régime Colonial: Postcolonial Haiti and the Perils of the French Restoration', *Journal of Modern European History* vol. 15, no. 2 (2017), pp. 261–79.

Phillip, Nicole. *Producers, Reproducers, and Rebels: Grenadian Slave Women, 1783–1833*, unpublished paper, Grenada Country Conference, January 2002, http://www.open.uwi.edu/sites/default/files/bnccde/grenada/conference/papers/phillip.html (accessed 30 April 2022).

Picó, Fernando. *One Frenchman, Four Revolutions: General Ferrand and the Peoples of the Caribbean* (Princeton, NJ: Markus Wiener, 2011).

Popham, Hugh. *A Damned Cunning Fellow: The Eventful Life of Rear-Admiral Sir Home Popham, KCB, KCH, KM, FRS, 1762–1820* (Tywardreath, Cornwall: Old Ferry Press, 1991).

Popkin, Jeremy D. 'Jean-Jacques Dessalines, Norbert Thoret, and the Violent Aftermath of the Haitian Declaration of Independence', in Julia Gaffield (ed.), *The Haitian Declaration of Independence: Creation, Context, and Legacy* (Charlottesville: University of Virginia Press, 2016), pp. 115–35.

———— *You Are All Free: The Haitian Revolution and the Abolition of Slavery* (Cambridge University Press, 2010).

Powers, David. 'The French Musical Theater: Maintaining Control in Caribbean Colonies in the Eighteenth Century', *Black Music Research Journal* vol. 18, nos. 1/2 (1998), pp. 229–40.

Prévost, Julien. *Instructions pour les établissemens et la culture des habitations caféyères de la Couronne* (Sans Souci: Imprimerie Royale, 24 March 1818).

———— *Relation des glorieux événemens qui ont porté Leurs Majestés Royales sur le trône d'Hayti* (Cap Henry: P. Roux, 1811).

Raguet, Condy. 'Memoirs of Hayti … In a Series of Letters', *The Port Folio* (1809–11).

Rainsford, Marcus. *An Historical Account of the Black Empire of Haiti*, ed. Paul Youngquist and Grégory Pierrot (Durham, NC: Duke University Press, 2013).

Ritter, Karl. *Naturhistorische Reise zur westindischen Insel Haiti* (Stuttgart: Hallberger, 1836).

Roussier, Paul. *Lettres du général Leclerc, commandant en chef de l'armée de Saint Domingue en 1802* (Paris: Société de l'Histoire des Colonies Françaises, 1937).

Rouzier, S. *Dictionnaire géographique et administratif universel d'Haïti*, Vol. 4 (Port-au-Prince: Charles Blot, 1892).

Saint-Rémy, Joseph. *Pétion et Haïti, étude monographique et historique*, Vol. 2 (Paris, 1854),

———— *Pétion et Haïti, étude monographique et historique*, Vol. 3 (Paris, 1855).

———— *Pétion et Haïti, étude monographique et historique*, Vol. 4 (Paris, 1857).

Santos, Danilo de los. *Memoria de la Pintura Dominicana: Raíces e impulso nacional*, Vol. 1 (Santo Domingo: Grupo León Jimenes, 2003).

Saunders, Prince. *Haytian Papers: A Collection of the Very Interesting Proclamations, and Other Official Documents; together with Some Account of the Rise, Progress, and Present State of the Kingdom of Hayti* (London: W. Reed, 1816).

Schoell, Frédéric. *Recueil de pièces officielles: Destinées à détromper les François sur les événemens qui se sont passés depuis quelques années*, Vol. 7 (Paris: Librairie Grecque-Latine-Allemande, 1815).

Ségur, Louis-Philippe de. *Procès verbal de la cérémonie du sacre et du couronnement de LL. MM. l'empereur Napoléon et l'impératrice Joséphine* (Paris: Imprimerie Impériale, 1805).

Sepinwall, Alyssa. *The Abbe Gregoire and the French Revolution: The Making of Modern Universalism* (Berkeley: University of California Press, 2005).

Servant, George. 'Ferdinand Christophe, fils du roi d'Haïti, en France', *Revue de l'histoire des colonies françaises* no. 23 (1913), pp. 228–32.

Simpson, George E., and J. B. Cinéas. 'Folk Tales of Haitian Heroes', *The Journal of American Folklore* vol. 54, nos. 213/214 (1941), pp. 176–85.

Southey, Thomas. *Chronological History of the West Indies*, Vol. 3 (London: Longman, Rees, Orme, Brown, and Green, 1827).

Steele, Beverley A. *Grenada: A History of its People* (Oxford: Macmillan Caribbean, 2003).

Stein, Robert Louis. *Léger Félicité Sonthonax: The Lost Sentinel of the Republic* (Rutherford, NJ: Fairleigh Dickinson University Press, 1985).

Stieber, Chelsea. *Haiti's Paper War: Post-Independence Writing, Civil War, and the Making of the Republic, 1804–1954* (New York University Press, 2020).

Strong, Emory. 'The Enigma of the Phoenix Button', *Historical Archaeology* no. 9 (1975), pp. 74–80.

Thomasson, Fredrik. 'Sweden and Haiti, 1791–1825: Revolutionary Reporting, Trade, and the Fall of Henry Christophe', *Journal of Haitian Studies* vol. 24, no. 2 (2018), pp. 4–35.

Thomson, Ian. *Bonjour Blanc: A Journey Through Haiti* (London: Vintage, 2012).

Trouillot, Henock. *Le gouvernement du roi Henri Christophe* (Port-au-Prince: Imprimerie Centrale, 1972).

Trouillot, Michel-Rolph. *Silencing the Past: Power and the Production of History* (Boston, MA: Beacon Press, 1995).

Vastey, Baron de. *An Essay on the Causes of the Revolution and Civil Wars of Hayti* (Exeter, 1823).

———— *Political Remarks on some French Works and Newspapers, concerning Hayti* (London, 1818).

———— *Relation de la Fête de S. M. la Reine d'Hayti, des Actes de Gouvernement qui ont eu lieu durant cet Événement, et de tout ce qui s'est passé à l'occasion de cette Fête* (Cap Henry: P. Roux, 1816).

———— *The Colonial System Unveiled*, ed. and trans. Chris Bongie (Liverpool University Press, 2014).

White, Arthur O. 'Prince Saunders: An Instance of Social Mobility Among Antebellum New England Blacks', *The Journal of Negro History* vol. 60, no. 4 (1975), pp. 526–35.

Wilberforce, Robert Isaac, and Samuel Wilberforce. *The Life of William Wilberforce*, Vol. 4 (London: John Murray, 1838).

———— *The Life of William Wilberforce*, Vol. 5 (London: John Murray, 1839).

Wilberforce, Robert Isaac, and Samuel Wilberforce (eds.). *The Correspondence of William Wilberforce*, Vol. 1 (Philadelphia: H. Perkins, 1841).

Willson, Nicole. 'Unmaking the Tricolore: Catherine Flon, Material

Testimony and Occluded Narratives of Female-Led Resistance in Haiti and the Haitian Dyaspora', *Slavery & Abolition* vol. 41, no. 1 (2020), pp. 131–48.

Wilson, David K. *The Southern Strategy: Britain's Conquest of South Carolina and Georgia, 1775–1780* (Columbia: University of South Carolina Press, 2008).

Wilson, Ellen Gibson. *Thomas Clarkson: A Biography* (London: Macmillan, 1989).

Worrall, David. *Harlequin Empire: Race, Ethnicity and the Drama of the Popular Enlightenment* (London and New York: Routledge, 2007).

INDEX

Account of the Glorious Events Which Brought Their Royal Majesties to the Throne of Haiti, An (Prévost), 182
Act of Independence (1804), 283
Adams, John Quincy, 231
Affiches Américaines (newspaper), 27, 33–4
African Theatre (New York), 2
Agoustine Franco de Médina, 214–17
Aldridge, Ira, 1, 2–3, 4, 5–6, 7
  Oroonoko play (Behn), 2, 3
Alexis, Nord, 291
Allix, Jacques Alexandre François, 114
Amazons, 196–7
Ambroise, Magloire, 162
American Revolution (1775), 19–21, 23
  See also Chasseurs Volontaires
Améthyste (ship), 201, 205, 216
Anglicanism, 254–5
Angola, 26
Arcahaie, 74–5, 78, 119–20, 157, 159
Arnaud, Monsieur, 132
Artibonite River, 233
Artibonite Valley, 60, 64, 116, 273
Athénaïre (ship), 201

Badeche (Christophe's owner), 33, 34

Balles, Trois, 88
Banks, Joseph, 7, 199, 225
Barbados, 256
Barber of Seville, The (play), 241
Barré, Henry, 133
Battle of Leipzig, 213
Battle of Sibert, 204
Battle of Trafalgar, 143
Battle of Vertières, 123, 146, 217
Bauvais, Louis Jacques, 80
Beechey, William, 278
Behn, Aphra, 2
Bélair, Charles, 113
Béliard, Baron de, 183
Belle Avenue, 266
Bellevue-le-Roi, 212
Belley, Jean-Baptiste, 39, 53–4, 58–9
Biassou, George, 47, 51, 60, 63
Birot, 80–1, 82
Birt, Jabez Sheen, 287–8, 296–7
Bois-Caïman uprising (Aug 1791), 46–52
Boisrond-Tonnerre, Louis Félix, 120, 125, 135, 136, 150, 154
Boïs-Rouge, 248
Bonaparte, Napoleon, 3, 8, 83–4, 87, 88, 95, 106, 169, 181, 187, 213, 215, 246, 310
  as Emperor of France, 135
  military expedition, preparation for, 91–2

slavery restoration plan, 92

Bonnet, Guy Joseph, 153–4, 155

Bonnet-à-l'Evêque, 191

Borgella, Jérôme Maximilien, 200

Boston Patriot (newspaper), 231

Boudet, Jean, 98, 113

Boyer, Jean-Pierre, 3–4, 6, 28, 206, 261–2, 284
  Cap-Haïtien arrival, 300–1
  letter from Clarkson, 302–3
  Santo Domingo attack, 308

Braun, Otto Philipp, 279

Breda plantation, 47, 48

Breda, Toussaint, 40–1

Brelle, Corneille, 187–8, 271–2

Brest port, 91

British, 182, 223–4, 256, 282
  Christophe's engagement with, 163–7, 172
  Dessalines relationship with, 120–3
  France war against, 20
  Grenada takeover, 16
  rule in Grenada, 20
  and siege of Savannah, 29

British and Foreign Bible Society, 254

British army, 63, 64, 71
  Maitland and withdrawal treaty, 74
  Port-au-Prince, capture of, 60
  Saint-Marc, fall of, 60

British National Vaccine Establishment, 231

Brown, Jonathan, 193

Buenos Aires, 279

Bunel, Joseph, 83, 168, 169, 171, 204

Bunel, Marie, 305

Burke, Edmund, 64

Caciques, 181

Cap Français (Saint-Domingue)
  Christophe's arrival, 30
  Christophe's early life at, 32–4
  description, 30–1
  as destination for transatlantic slaving voyages, 26
  establishment, 25
  plantations, 31, 32
  population, 30, 31
  slave market, 25–6
  sugar and coffee plantations, 31
  treasury, 75, 76
  See also Couronne inn; Saint-Domingue colony (Cap Français)

Cap Henry, 250–1
  army, 199–201, 205–10
  Christophe's coronation, 177–83
  Code Henry, 12, 196–9, 210, 233–7, 267, 296
  coronation ceremony day, 186–90
  French papers, 217–22
  government warehouse, 233–6
  herald and coronation, 183–5
  royal palace, 191–5
  ships, 196, 201–5
  vaccination programme, 231–2

Cap Henry jail, 255

Cap-Haïtien massacre, 130–2

Cap-Haïtien, 127, 129–32, 154, 157, 165, 174

Capoix, François, 122, 144, 146, 151, 162

Caribbean empire, 25

Caribbean, 183, 192, 257
  piracy, 24
  slaves shipped to, 17, 18

Casimir, Jean, 144

Casimir, Joseph, 234

Castlereagh, Lord, 163–4, 168

Cathcart, Hugh, 14–15, 35, 75–6, 79–80, 120

central Africa, 181

Champ de Mars, 184, 186, 189, 310

Chanlatte, Juste, 135, 150, 162–3, 273, 298

Charles Henri, Jean-Baptiste, the Comte d'Estaing, 20–1
  commanding French and American forces, 29–30
  on free coloured militia, 27
  his fleet, 24, 25, 28–9
  negotiation for British surrender, 29

Charles X (King), 308

Charlton, 167–8

Charrier, Baron de, 232

Chasseurs Volontaires, 23–4, 26–30, 32, 37, 52

Chavannes, Jean-Baptiste, 45, 63

Chevreau, Jean, 233, 238

Chiba, 234

Chirin, Catherine, 234

Choiseul, 191

Christ, Jesus, 189

Christophe, Anne-Athénaïre, 83, 94, 129, 184, 186, 248, 307
  tutors for, 252

Christophe, Françoise-Améthyste, 75, 94, 129, 184, 186, 209–10, 248, 307
  tutors for, 252

Christophe, François-Ferdinand, 61, 75, 94, 113–14, 128–9

Christophe, Henry
  actions after Dessalines' death, 152–7
  Affiches Américaines advertisement, 33–34
  against Vodou dances, 146
  Allix and, 114
  his ambition, 8
  Arcahaie campaign, 74
  arrival in Cap Henry, 280–1
  attack on French Santo Domingo, 136–8
  authoritarian rule, imposition of, 9
  banquet hosting, 127–8
  Belley and, 39
  bondage period, 16, 19
  and Britain's abolitionist movement members, 7–8
  and British engagement, 163–7, 172
  burial of, 296
  Cap Français arrival, 30
  Cathcart's letter to, 126–7
  Catholic faith, 40–1
  as chief elector of Petite Anse, 71
  as colonel, 70
  coronation ceremony day, 186–90
  coronation, 177–83
  Couronne inn link, 33, 34–6, 37, 41
  death of, 4, 5, 6, 293
  declaration of independence, 125
  Dessalines's death, 150–1
  drummer role, 23, 28
  during Haut-du-Cap attack, 114–16
  during Laveaux's arrest, 69

during mass uprising (Aug 1791), 48–51
during uprising against Louverture, 89, 90
early life at Cap Français, 32–4
Ferdinand to Paris, 113–14
fight for general emancipation, 52–5
fled to Marmelade, 118
free coloured militia member-ship, understanding, 46
French citizens, treatment of, 129–30
full-scale invasion of the south, 79–80
Gérin and Pétion pledging loyalty to, 150
Gérin and Wagnac's letter to, 148
Haitian independence, second anniversary of, 143
Hardy and, 102–3
as head of the Haitian army, 140
headquarters issue, 117
herald and, 183–5
Independence Day speech (1809), 170
issued edicts to reorganise state land, 266
Jacmel port, seige of, 80–3
joined d'Estaing fleet, 24, 25, 26
as king, 134
and Leclerc's Haut-du-Cap meeting, 104
letter to Admiral Rowley in Jamaica, 167
letter to Leclerc, 103
letter to Romain, 151
letter to Vilton, 101–2

letters to Pétion, 151–2, 153, 155–6
letters to Vernet, 151, 152
London waxworks, 4, 7
Louverture letter to, 75
as maréchaussée (rural police), 49
marriage, 57–8
move against Louverture, 109–10
nation-building, 8–9
new constitutional council, 161
as new head of state, 149, 150, 154
opera visit, 40
ordered to march south, 157
his origins stories, 13–16, 18–19, 21
at Petite Guinée district (Cap Français), 36–7
popularity, 4
promoted to Brigadier General, 85
promoted to major, 63–4
raid against Limbe, 116
Rainsford and, 73–4
response to Hédouville's issue, 77
rivalry between Pétion and, 82–3
sale of slaves, witnessed, 26
Savannah campaign participa-tion(1779), 23–4, 26–30
Shaw and, 262
and Spain diplomatic relation-ship, 169–70
supervisory role, 77
taken off from Grenada story, 20–1
his troops drill, 65

Vilton's letter to, 101
wealth of, 74–6
Christophe, Marie-Louise, 57–8,
   61, 83, 94, 96, 105, 113, 128,
   134, 297, 303–4
   Amazons, 196–7
   army, 199–201
   Christophe's coronation, 177–
      83
   Code Henry, 196–9
   coronation ceremony day, 186–
      90
   death of, 307
   herald and coronation, 183–5
   royal palace, 191–5
Christophe, Victor-Henry, 128
Citadelle Henry fortress, 6, 9, 138,
   139, 170–1, 191
   construction of, 133–4, 170
   structure of, 12
civil war (Empire Of Haiti),
   159–74
   British role in, 163–7
   Fort St Joseph, siege of, 160,
      161
   Pétion and Gérin as outlaws, 161
   Pétion vs. Christophe's forces,
      159
   Pétion's campaign from
      Mirebalais, 171–2
   Pétion's escape, 159–60
   Pétion's military expedition to
      Saint-Marc, 171
Clarkson, Dorothy, 306
Clarkson, Thomas, 7, 44, 45, 225,
   249–50, 251, 258, 263–4,
   302–3
   Christophe on religion, 253–4
   Christophe's letter to, 255

Clerveaux, Augustin, 112–13,
   114–15, 122, 140, 177–8
Club Massiac, 44, 45, 59
Code Henry, 12, 196–9, 210,
   267, 296
   coffee plantations, 233–7
Code Noir (1672), 42
Code Rurale, 309
Coidavid, Jacques, 58, 61
Coidavid, Marie-Louise. See
   Christophe, Marie-Louise
Coidavid, Noël, 39, 41, 58
Coleridge, Samuel Taylor, 249
Collier, George, 282
Colonial Assembly, 47, 50
Colonial System Unveiled, The
   (Vastey), 13, 18, 42, 218
Columbus, Christopher, 24, 123
Come Creator Spirit (hymn), 188
Comte de Jérémie. See Grand Anse
Condry, 297
Congress of Aix-la-Chapelle, 264
Cook (Captain), 225
Corbet, Edward, 15
Council of State, 178–9
Count de Limonade, 223
Couronne inn (Cap Français), 33,
   34–6, 37, 41, 54
Crête-à-Pierrot, 208
Croix-des-Bouquets, 200
Crowther, William, 229–30, 239
   vaccination programme, 231–2
Cuban hunting dogs, 119
Cugoano, Ottobah, 16–17
Culture of Plenty, 270
Cutting, Nathaniel, 48, 51
Czar Alexander I, 264–5

Daedalus, HMS, 167
Dahomey, 196

Dartiguenave, 155, 156
Datty, Etienne, 67–8
Davison, 255–6
de Grasse, Admiral, 41
de Rouvray, Madame, 50, 51
The Death of Christophe—King of Hayti (play), 1, 2, 3–7, 303, 304–5
Declaration of the Rights of Man and of the Citizen, 45
Dédêt (housekeeper), 252
Délaché, 236
Delva, 200
Descourtilz, Michel Etienne, 76
Desirée, HMS, 130
Desroches, Numa, 248–9
Desrouleaux, Louis, 36, 64
Dessalines, Jean-Jacques, 62, 63, 68, 75, 77, 79, 85, 90, 97, 98–9, 106, 107, 111–12, 113, 117, 145, 220, 238, 293
    army, 199–208
    and British relationship, 120–3
    Christophe's coronation, 177–83
    Code Henry, 196–9
    conference at Pétion's head-quarters (Arcahaie), 119–20
    coronation ceremony day, 186–90
    declaration of independence, 123, 125–6
    as Emperor Jacques I, 135
    fall of Port-au-Prince, 122
    governor-general title, adaptation of, 126
    Haitian independence, second anniversary of, 143
    herald and coronation, 183–5
    Inspector of Agriculture, 86
    land reforms, 147–8
    letter to Bonaparte, 135
    letter to Jefferson, 120
    marched on Dondon, 118
    move against Louverture, 109–10
    murder of, 149–52
    national defence plan, 132–4
    naturalising Haiti's French citizens, 130
    response to French threat, 129–31, 136–9
    royal palace, 191–5
    ships, 196, 201–5
    wedding of, 88
    See also Santo Domingo; Jacmel port, seige of
Dessalines, Madame, 127–8, 134
d'Estaing. *See* Charles Henri, Jean-Baptiste, the Comte d'Estaing
Dondon, 117
Douglass, 189
Draverman, 214, 217
Dufay, Louis, 58–9
Duke of Sussex, 231
Dumas, Alexandre, 307
Dumesle, Hérard, 27, 32–3, 34
Dupont, Toussaint, 220
Dupuy, Alexis, 182, 218, 239
Dutty, Boukman, 47, 48, 50

Eiffe, Johann Gottfried, 279
Eiffe, Wilhelm, 278
Empire Of Haiti, 143–57
    identity cards, 145
    labour and movement, restric-tions on, 145–6
    labour system, 144–5
    land reforms, 147–8

new constitution, 156–7
population, 144
state-building, 143
Enlightenment racial theory, 40
Ennery plantation, 97, 105, 106, 107
Enrique, 181
Essay on the Causes of the Revolution and Civil Wars of Hayti, An (Vastey), 11, 69–70, 78, 88, 204
Estates General, 43–4, 49
Etudes sur l'histoire d'Haïti (Ardouin), 309
Evans portrait (1816), 278
Evans, Richard, 7–8, 246–8, 310

Fernando VII, 169
Ferrand, Jean-Louis, 136, 137–8
Ferrier, Baron de, 220
Ferrier, Félix, 126
Flon, Catherine, 120
Flora (frigate), 243
forced labour, 9, 18, 31
Fort Belair, 61, 69, 119
Fort Crête-à-Pierrot, siege of, 98–100
Fort Dauphin. *See* Fort Liberté
Fort La Ferrière, 132, 133
Fort Liberté, 76–7, 96, 121, 125, 177
Fort Sabourin, 213
Fort Sibert, 206
Fort Sourde, 171
Fort St Joseph, 160, 161, 162
Fort Trois Pavillons, 140–1
France
    abandoned Fort Liberté, 121
    control over Grenada, 15
    Haiti's indemnity payment to, 3–4
    imperial ambitions over Hispaniola, 25
    joined the war against the British, 20
    London's peace deal, 91
    official abolition of slavery, 86
    Ouanaminthe raid, 146
    response to mass uprising (Aug 1791), 50–2
    war declaration (1792), 50
    withdrawal from Saint-Domingue, 123, 129
François de Fontanges, 243
Franklin Square (Savannah, Georgia), 23
Frederick (Prince), 231
free coloured community, 39–40, 44, 50, 68
French Catholicism, 47
French constitution (1799), 103
French National Assembly, 51
French republicans, 60
French Revolution, 59

Galbaud, François-Thomas, 52–4
Gallifet plantation, 41, 42, 46, 50
Gaspard, Augustin, 202
Gazette Officielle de l'Etat d'Hayti, 162, 170–1, 182, 196
Gazette Officielle de Saint-Domingue, 121
Gazette Politique et Commerciale d'Haïti (newspaper), 134, 154–5
Gazette Royale d'Hayti (newspaper), 12, 210, 212, 213, 217–22, 239, 267, 278
    announcement, 251
    on Christophe, 227
    Crowther's winning, 230

on slave ships, 255
vaccination programme, 231
Gazul, Xaviar, 248
Geffrard, Nicholas, 151
Gentleman's Magazine, The, 199
George III, 230, 240, 278, 284
Gérin, Etienne Elie, 147–50, 153, 161, 171, 172
Goman, 172, 173, 178, 200, 210
Gonaïves, 120, 125, 154, 160, 244, 262–3, 300
Gonzales, Jean de Dieu, 271
Goodall, Thomas, 165, 166–7, 168, 171, 186, 201, 222
Gottfried, Johann, 278
Grand Anse, 162, 173, 178, 181, 200, 275
Grand Chamberlain, 187
Grand Gilles mountains, 191
Grand Pré, 191, 266
Grande Rivière, 45, 62, 63, 71, 96, 99, 117, 171
Grégoire, Abbé Henri, 222
Grenada, 14, 19
  arrivals of French slave ships in, 17, 18
  during American Revolution (1775), 19–21
  economy and trade, 15–16
  location, 15
  as refuge to 'maroons', 17–18
  sectarian division within colonists, 19–20
  slavery in, 16
  sugar plantation, slaves condition in, 17
  treatment of slaves, 17, 19
Guadeloupe, 112–13
Gubitz, Friedrich Wilhelm, 279
Gulliver, Thomas, 250–1, 269

Haiti
  attack on French Santo Domingo, 136–8
  birth of, 125–6
  national defence plan, 132–4
  new imperial constitution, 140, 143
Haitian Vodou, 47–8
Hamilton, William, 257–8
Hardy, Jean, 97, 99–100, 101, 102–3
Harvey, William, 16, 270
Hausa children, 196
Haut-du-Cap, 51, 53–4, 114, 115, 239, 291
Haytian Papers, 245–6
Hazlitt, William, 1
Hédouville, Gabriel, 74, 76–7
Henry I (King of Haiti). *See* Christophe, Henry
Héricourt unrest, 78
Hispaniola, 24–5, 308
Histoire d'Haïti (Madiou), 309
Historical Account of the Black Empire of Hayti, An (Rainsford), 73
Hopewell (ship), 165
Hospice des Orphelins, 129
Hyperion, HMS, 178

Indigenous Army, 120
Inginac, Joseph, 151, 262, 301
Inglis, Robert, 307

Jacmel port, seige of, 80–3
Jacmel River, 83
Jamaica, 14, 60, 74, 123, 163, 165, 167, 172, 178, 202–3, 204, 220, 256, 308
James (Captain), 227
Jean (Prince), 212

Jean Rabel, 166, 167
Jean, Pierre St, 201
Jefferson, Thomas, 48, 120
Jérémie, 60, 63, 129, 173, 206
Joachim, Noel, 133, 292, 299
Johnson, Simeon, 160
Jones, Elliot, 270–1
Josephine, 257
Joshua, 188
Juge, Jean-Baptiste, 185
Juste Chanlatte, the Comte des
    Rosiers, 182–3

Kalinago people, 15
King's Hunting Party, The (play), 277
kingdom of Dahomey, 195
Kingdom of Haiti
    fall of, 5
    royal almanacs, 14
Kingdom of Kongo, 181

L'Abeille (newspaper), 261, 275
L'Acul du Nord, 233, 234–5
L'Ambigu (newspaper), 163
l'Artibonite, Duc de, 187
L'Haïtienne (ship), 168
La Fossette cemetery, 131–2
La Pique, HMS, 126–7
La Tortue island, 166
Lachenais, Joute, 302
Lacroix, Pamphile de, 98
Lafayette, Marquis de, 44
Lagroue, Baron de, 187
Lake Maggiore, 307
Lamarre, 162, 167, 173, 200
Langendyk, Jan Anthonie, 111–12
Lapaix, 278
Larivière, Kayé, 209–10
Lavaysse, Dauxion, 34, 35

Lavaysse, Jean-Joseph Dauxion,
    214–19
Laveaux, Etienne, 61, 62, 63, 64,
    68, 70–1
Lawrence, Thomas, 246
Laxavon, 118
Le Télégraphe (newspaper), 210, 219
Lear, Tobias, 88, 89, 94, 95, 99
Lebrun, Placide, 291
Leclerc, Charles Victoire
    Emmanuel, 91, 92, 92, 94, 96,
        98, 100, 101, 102, 104–5, 110,
        112, 113, 272–3
    death of, 114, 116
    Haut-du-Cap attack, 114–15
    letters to Bonaparte, 109, 113–
        14
    See also Santo Domingo
Leogane, 80, 162, 207
Les Cayes, 147, 148, 200, 206–7
Libertine, The (play), 3
Limbe, 88, 105, 122
Liverpool, Lord, 223–5
London, 180–1, 182, 186, 192–3,
    213, 214, 222, 227–32
Lord Duncan (ship), 165
Lord Mulgrave (ship), 167–8
Louis XVI, 43
Louis XVIII, 213–14, 215, 216,
    243–5, 259, 286
Louverture, Isaac, 92, 113
Louverture, Paul, 104, 118
Louverture, Placide, 92, 113
Louverture, Toussaint, 8, 47, 48,
    59–60, 61–2, 70, 73–90, 92, 95,
    100, 293
    balance of power, opportunity
        for, 70–1
    Bonaparte's letter to, 86

Christophe's letter to, 99, 103–4

Christophe's unit under, 63

conspiracy and uprising against, 88–90

constitutional assembly formation, 86–8

death of, 109

guerrilla tactics adaptation, 65

Hédouville's power reduction attempt, 76–8

Hispaniola island unification plan, 84–5

letter to Bonaparte, 109

letter to Christophe, 78–9, 85

letter to Laveaux, 64–5, 67

marched into Les Cayes, 84

maroon's trust issues, 66

martial law in plantations, 85–6

meeting with Brunet, 107

meeting with Leclerc, 105–6

Môle Saint-Nicholas uprising, 78–9

Port-de-Paix uprising (1796), 67–8

response to Laveaux's arrest, 69

Rigaud against, 77–8

secret correspondence with Boudet, 100

Sonthonax views on, 70

treaty between Maitland and (Arcahaie), 74–5, 78

views on colony's function, 68

See also Fort Crête-à-Pierrot, siege of; Jacmel port, seige of

Macandal, François, 43, 47

Macaulay, Zachary, 223, 257, 304

Macaya, 66

Madiou, Thomas, 82, 150–1, 237, 309

Madison, James, 240

Magny, Etienne, 205–6, 208, 209, 300, 304

Maitland, 74, 80

Malouet, Baron Pierre Victor, 214–15, 217

Malouet, Pierre Victor, 60

Mandinka people, 18

Marcadieu, Charlotin, 149

Marchand, 136–7, 143

maréchaussée (rural police), 49

Marie-Séraphique (slave ship), 25–26

Marriage of Figaro, The (play), 40

Maximillian II (Emperor), 279

McCulloch, John, 165–6

Melville, Viscount, 279–80, 281–2

Mentor, Etienne, 154

Mills, Jean-Baptiste, 58

Milot, 12, 117, 118, 132, 133, 134, 153, 170, 191–6, 209, 235

See also Sans Souci palace (Milot, Haiti)

Milscent, Jules Solime, 83

Mirebalais, 71, 171

Môle Saint-Nicholas, 60, 68, 74, 78–9, 120, 140, 143, 167, 173–4, 175, 200, 201, 211, 263

Monpoint, 292

Montesquieu, 180

Montorsier, 204–5, 215–16

Moore, James, 231

Morne l'Hôpital, 207

Morning Chronicle (newspaper), 229

Moyse, 62, 63, 65, 73–4, 75, 76–7, 79, 83, 85

conspiracy against Louverture, 89–90

as Inspector of Agriculture, 86
Mr White, 240–1

*Narrative of the Enslavement of
Ottobah Cugoano, a Native of
Africa* (Cugoano), 17
National Convention (Paris), 58–9
Native American tribes, 301
Negro's Curse, The (play), 3
Neuber, Ludwig, 279
Noël (Prince), 185, 237
Normand-le-Mézy plantation, 122
Notes to Baron Malouet, 218
Nugent, George, 120

*Observations of a Frenchman on the
Slave Trade and the State of
Saint-Domingue*, 34
Ogé, Vincent, 44–5, 62–3, 249
Olivier, Vincent, 27
Oroonoko (Behn), 2, 3
Ouanaminthe, 118
Ozama River, 137

Papa Henry, 277
Papalier, Baron de, 204–5
Papillon, Jean-François, 47, 60, 63, 71
Paquot, Monsieur, 34
Paris, Treaty of, 214
Paul, Thomas, 230–1
Pauline Leclerc, 112–13
Peltier, Jean-Gabriel, 14, 163, 182, 213, 223–5, 258–9
Pétion, Alexandre, 49, 82, 92, 98, 106, 114–15, 147, 148–50, 152, 154, 155, 156–7, 162, 171, 198, 200, 206, 220–1, 261, 293
army, 199–200

campaign from Mirebalais, 171–2
Christophe's coronation, 177–83
coronation ceremony day, 186–90
herald and coronation, 183–5
Lavaysse's letter, 214–19
letter to Rigaud, 172
military expedition to Saint-Marc, 171
mission's success, 209–12
royal palace, 191–5
ships, 196, 201–5
as outlaws, 161
See also civil war (Empire Of Haiti)
Petit-Cormier plantation, 62
Petite Anse, 58, 70, 71, 75, 84, 105, 114, 115
Petite Guinée (Cap Français), 36–7, 61
Petite Rivière, 233, 274, 290
Petit-Goâve, seizure of, 78
Philadelphia, 268
Pierre-Michel, 61, 63, 69, 70, 71, 78
pirates, 19, 25
Pius VII (Pope), 182
Plaine du Cul-de-Sac, 206
Plymouth, 178
Poles, 115, 116
Political Reflexions (Clarkson), 264
Polverel, Etienne, 51, 52–3, 54, 55, 70
Pommayrac, Alcibiade, 83
Pont Dahomet, 241
Popham, Home Riggs, 279–80, 281–2
Port de France, 122

Port Margot, 88

Port Royal, 167, 178

Port-au-Prince, 50, 52, 64, 80, 96–7, 100, 119, 154, 157, 160, 161, 169, 174, 178, 182, 200–2, 204–8, 211, 218–21, 241–4, 261, 308
  fall of, 122
  ship, 256
  treasury, 172

Port-de-Paix, 96, 111, 115, 162, 167

Potsdam, 193

Praxelles, 58

Prévost, Julien, 119, 151, 182, 186–91, 202–3, 213, 218, 220–1, 255, 300, 310
  Crowther won, 230
  letter to Rainsford, 228
  on board, 251

Prézeau, Chevalier, 295

Prière, Petit Noël, 66, 114, 115–16, 118

Prince des Gonaïves. *See* Vernet, André

Prince du Limbe. *See* Romain, Paul

Princess Royal (ship), 201

Princesse de Limbe, 235

Puerto Rico, 169

Quartier Morin, 258

Raguet, Condy, 127–8

Raimond, Julien, 44–5, 86–7

Rainsford, Marcus, 73–4, 227, 228

Ramírez, Juan Sánchez, 169, 170

Ravine-à-Couleuvres, 97

Reflexions on the Blacks and Whites (Vastey), 256

Réflexions sur une lettre de Mazères (Vastey), 256

Regent (Prince), 227

Resistance à l'Oppression, 148–9

Revinchal (artist), 248

Revue Encyclopédique, 287

Richard, Jean-Pierre, 127, 181, 240, 272, 273, 280

Richardson, Thomas, 163–4, 165, 222

Rigaud, André, 52, 61, 63, 70, 77–8, 82, 83, 92, 147, 172–3, 174, 177–8, 200, 206

Ritter, Karl, 289

Rochambeau, Donatien Marie Joseph de, 111, 118, 119, 120, 123

Romain, Paul, 100, 116, 140, 146, 178–9, 185, 213, 288, 302

Rossi, John, 246

Rouanez, Joseph, 163, 178, 182, 187–8

Roume, Philippe-Rose, 77, 84, 85, 88

Rouvray, Marquis de, 34, 49–50

Rowley, 167–8, 178

Royal Academy, 7

Royal Bonbons, 195–6

Royal Chamber of Public Instruction, 251

Royal Coburg Theatre (London), 1–2, 3, 4, 5, 6, 9, 303, 304
  See also *The Death of Christophe—King of Hayti* (play)

Royal College, 250

Royal Dahomets, 195–6, 234–5, 238, 268, 277

Royal Medical College, 258

Royal Navy, 16, 20, 120, 121, 163, 164, 172, 143, 178
Rozalie, 234
Rudolf II (Emperor), 279

Sabbath day, 270
Saint-Domingue colony (Cap Français), 39–56, 214–15, 237
   Bois-Caïman uprising/mass uprising (Aug 1791), 46–51
   British army arrival, 60
   brutality in, 42–3
   Catholic faith, 40–1
   ceremony at Bois-Caïman, 47–8
   colonial assemblies, 45
   debate over colonial representation, 43–5
   declaration of independence, 123, 125
   economic crisis and reconstruction, 66–7
   elections, 70–1
   enslaved people population, 32
   fight for general emancipation, 52–5
   food shortage and disease, 64
   fourth anniversary, 57
   free coloured militia membership, 46
   free coloured militia, 27
   introduction of sugar to, 25
   as largest slave society, 25–6
   Louverture's new constitution, 86–8
   martial law in plantations, 85–6
   mass uprising, aftermath (Aug 1791), 51–2
   Place Clugny market ('Black's Market'), 32
   Port-de-Paix uprising (1796), 67–8
   privilege for slaves, 41–2
   public executions, 45–6
   racial discrimination census, 40
   racial discrimination, abolition of, 51
   secret meeting (mass uprising), 46–7
   slave revolt, 45–56
   slavery, abolition of, 59
   slaves birth and mortality rates, 42
   sugar plantations, abandoned, 75
   sugar plantations, burning of, 46
   support network necessity, 39–40
   under Louverture's rule, 85
   worth, 31–2
   See also Cap Français (Saint-Domingue)
Saint-Marc, 60, 64, 88, 98, 121, 151, 160–1, 171, 208, 289–90, 299
Saint-Méry, Moreau de, 32, 35, 40, 47
Saint-Michel, 63
Saint-Raphaël, 63
Saint-Rémy, Joseph, 21, 49
Sans Souci (maroon leader), 66, 106, 110–11, 117, 118, 194
Sans Souci palace (Milot, Haiti), 191–7, 211, 227, 262
   coffee plantations, 233–8
   Desroches painting, 248–9
   Gulliver as schoolmaster, 250–1

Lavaysse's letter, 214–16
structure of, 11–12, 170–1
vaccination programme, 231
Santo Domingo, 182, 192, 217, 269
    arrest of Louverture, 107
    battle at Fort Crête-à-Pierrot, 97–8
    Christophe and his forces' withdrawal, 97
    Christophe responses during, 94–5
    Christophe's letter to Louverture, 94
    Christophe's preparation, 92, 94
    Fort Crête-à-Pierrot, siege of, 98–100
    Fort Liberté, capture of, 94
    French citizens, treatment of, 129–31
    French fleet, 92–3
    French fleet's L'Acul landing, 94–5
    French invasion of, 91–107
    Leclerc and troops Cap Français arrival, 96
    Leclerc's letter to Christophe, 93–4
    Louverture and Christophe as outlaws, 96–7
    Louverture's retreat order, 95–6
    peace deal and surrender, 104–7
    proclamation, 91, 92
    and yellow fever, 106–7, 112
Saunders (Prince), 230–1, 236, 245–6, 249–50, 258, 268–9, 289

Savannah River, 28
Savannah, siege of (1779), 23, 28–30
Schomburg Ledger records, 233, 235–7
Senegambia, 18
Seven Years War, 16, 20
Sierra Leone, 18, 249
Simon, Jacques, 292–3
Sketches of Hayti (Harvey), 16
slave ships, 17, 24, 41, 64, 255
slavery
    abolition of, 58–9, 85
    restoration of, 92, 112–13
smallpox lymph, 231–2
Société des Amis des Noirs, 44, 50
Solomon, 188
Someruelos (Governor of Havana), 169, 170
Sonthonax, Léger-Félicité, 51, 52–3, 54, 55, 59, 61–2, 66, 70
    declaration of emancipation, 196
    elections, 70–1
    storming of the Bastille (Paris), fourth anniversary, 57
Soufrière, 234
Southampton, 202
Spain, 24, 62, 169
    authorities, 50
    battle with France, 63
    Christophe's diplomatic relationship with, 169–70
    interest in Hispaniola, 24
    prisoners, 138, 139, 145
St George, 19, 20
St Mark, 235
St Petersburg, 265
Stephen, James, 285

Stevens, Edward, 79, 81
Stewart, Duncan, 258, 287–9, 292
Stirling, Admiral, 207
Strafford, Thomas, 256
Sutherland, Robert, 164–5
Sutherland, Robert, Jr, 304

Taíno people, 24, 181
Tanais, HMS, 227
Taváres, José Campos, 137, 169–70
Teignmouth, Lord, 254
Télémaque, César, 94, 156–7
Tenant farmers, 267–8
Tiburon, 120
Times, The (newspaper), 1
Tortue, Baron Joseph de la, 289
Tortuga island, 24
Toussaint Louverture, François-Dominique, 180, 197–8, 227, 237
Treaty of Basel (Jun 1795), 63
Trouillot, Henock, 310
Trouillot, Michel-Rolph, 193–4
Troy, David, 171
Turkheim, Baron de, 285–6
Tybee Island, 28

United States (USA), 81, 125, 180, 230
    trade embargo on Haiti, 168–9

vagrancy, 85–6
Vallière, 209–11
Vanguard, HMS, 121
Vashon, 178
Vastey, Baron de, 11, 27, 29, 42, 69–70, 78, 88, 159, 181, 195, 197, 228–9, 239–42, 256
    background, 12
    on Christophe's place of birth, 14–15, 18–19
    on Christophe's siege of Savannah participation, 23
    Lavaysse's letter, 215–19
    letters exchange between Gubitz and, 279
    on board, 251
    role, 12–13
Velázquez, Francisco, 192
Vernet, André, 150, 157, 171, 178–9, 185, 197, 209, 212, 295
Viart, 204
Victor-Henry (Prince Royal), 177, 186, 210–11, 241, 248, 252, 273–4, 295–6
    Christophe's coronation, 177–83
    coronation ceremony day, 186–90
    Evans painting, 246–8
    herald and coronation, 183–5
Villatte, Jean-Louis, 61, 68–9
Vincent, Charles, 71, 87–8, 91–2, 134
Voyage dans le nord d'Hayti (Dumesle), 32–3

Wagnac, 148
War of Knives, 78, 147
West Africa Squadron, 282
West Africa, 195
Wilberforce, William, 7, 11, 162, 223–4, 258, 270
    Christophe on religion, 253–4
    Evans painting, 246–8
    recommendation, 250
    vaccination programme, 231–2

Wilson, William, 18, 49, 251–2, 288, 297
Windward Islands, 15
Wordsworth, William, 4

Yayou, 149, 156, 162
yellow fever, 106–7, 112
Yeo, 202
Young Roscius (ship), 165–6